NEWS CULTURE

Third Edition

ISSUES in CULTURAL and MEDIA STUDIES

Series Editor: Stuart Allan

Published titles

News Culture, 3rd edition
Stuart Allan

Media, Risk and Science
Stuart Allan

Television and Sexuality
Jane Arthurs

Understanding Alternative Media
Olga Bailey, Bart Cammaerts and Nico Carpentier

Television, Globalization and Cultural Identities
Chris Barker

Science, Technology and Culture
David Bell

Cultures of Popular Music
Andy Bennett

Masculinities and Culture
John Beynon

Cinema and Cultural Modernity
Gill Branston

Television, Audiences and Everyday Life
Matt Briggs

Understanding Popular Science
Peter Broks

Violence and the Media
Cynthia Carter and C. Kay Weaver

Critical Readings: Media and Gender
Edited by Cynthia Carter and Linda Steiner

Ethnic Minorities and the Media
Edited by Simon Cottle

Global Crisis Reporting
Simon Cottle

Mediatized Conflict
Simon Cottle

Moral Panics and the Media
Chas Critcher

Critical Readings: Moral Panics and the Media
Edited by Chas Critcher

Culture on Display
Bella Dicks

Game Cultures
Jon Dovey and Helen W. Kennedy

Media Convergence
Tim Dwyer

Perspectives on Global Cultures
Ramaswami Harindranath

Media, Politics and the Network Society
Robert Hassan

Museums, Media and Cultural Theory
Michelle Henning

Domestic Cultures
Joanne Hollows

Media Talk
Ian Hutchby

Citizens or Consumers: What the Media Tell Us about Political Participation
Justin Lewis, Sanna Inthorn and Karin Wahl-Jorgensen

Media Technology: Critical Perpectives
Joost van Loon

Media Discourses
Donald Matheson

Modernity and Postmodern Culture, 2nd edition
Jim McGuigan

Rethinking Cultural Policy
Jim McGuigan

Critical Readings: Media and Audiences
Edited by Virginia Nightingale and Karen Ross

Media and Audiences
Karen Ross and Virginia Nightingale

Sport, Culture and the Media, 2nd edition
David Rowe

Critical Readings: Sport, Culture and the Media
Edited by David Rowe

Cities and Urban Cultures
Deborah Stevenson

Cultural Citizenship
Nick Stevenson

Compassion, Morality and the Media
Keith Tester

Critical Readings: Violence and the Media
Edited by C. Kay Weaver and Cynthia Carter

Identity and Culture: Narratives of Difference and Belonging
Chris Weedon

NEWS CULTURE

Third Edition

Stuart Allan

Open University Press

Open University Press
McGraw-Hill Education
McGraw-Hill House
Shoppenhangers Road
Maidenhead
Berkshire
England
SL6 2QL

email: enquiries@openup.co.uk
world wide web: www.openup.co.uk

and Two Penn Plaza, New York, NY 10121-2289, USA

First published 1999
Reprinted 2000, 2001, 2002, 2003
Second edition 2004
Reprinted 2005, 2007, 2008
First published in this third edition 2010
Reprinted 2011

A catalogue record of this book is available from the British Library

ISBN-13: 978-0-33-523565-0 (pb)
ISBN-10: 0-33-523565-4 (pb)

Library of Congress Cataloging-in-Publication Data
CIP data applied for

Typeset by RefineCatch Limited, Bungay, Suffolk
Printed in Great Britain by Bell & Bain Ltd, Glasgow

The McGraw·Hill Companies

For my parents, Beverly and Robert Allan,
with love and respect

CONTENTS

SERIES EDITOR'S FOREWORD

The Issues in Cultural and Media Studies series aims to facilitate a diverse range of critical investigations into pressing questions considered to be central to current thinking and research. In light of the remarkable speed at which the conceptual agendas of cultural and media studies are changing, the authors are committed to contributing to what is an ongoing process of re-evaluation and critique. Each of the books is intended to provide a lively, innovative and comprehensive introduction to a specific topical issue from a fresh perspective. The reader is offered a thorough grounding in the most salient debates indicative of the book's subject, as well as important insights into how new modes of enquiry may be established for future explorations. Taken as a whole, then, the series is designed to cover the core components of cultural and media studies courses in an imaginatively distinctive and engaging manner.

Stuart Allan

INTRODUCTION: THE CULTURE OF NEWS

> Have you noticed that life, real honest-to-goodness life, with murders and catastrophes and fabulous inheritances, happens almost exclusively in the newspapers?
>
> (Jean Anouilh, dramatist)

> I believe that no mass journalism in history has lived up to its responsibilities as well as have American network television news organizations. But we need to find some innovations without lowering our standards. There is only a limited professional satisfaction in informing people who have gone to sleep.
>
> (Harry Reasoner, broadcast journalist)

Excited declarations that we live in a 'news-saturated society' are being made so frequently these days that they almost risk sounding clichéd. Still, if we accept that 'news' of some description has been in circulation since the earliest days of human communities, then assessing its relative degree of 'saturation' for people's lives over the years proves a rather challenging task. What would appear to be above dispute, however, is that the sheer range of different forms of news discourse has never been greater than it is today.

Interesting in this regard are the views of Alan Rusbridger (2008), editor of the *Guardian* in London. In describing the 'new world order' of journalism, he recalled the words of *Washington Post* columnist David Broder written nearly three decades ago. Broder was offering a definition of the newspaper, an intriguing question to pose in its own right, long before current claims about the 'death of the newspaper' had begun to circulate in the brave new world of the internet. He stated:

> I would like to see us say over and over until the point has been made . . . that the newspaper that drops on your doorstep is a partial, hasty, incomplete, inevitably somewhat flawed and inaccurate rendering of some of the things we heard about in the past 24 hours . . . distorted despite our best efforts to eliminate gross bias by the very process of compression that makes it possible for you . . . to read it in about an hour. If we labeled the paper accurately then we would immediately add: But it's the best we could do under the circumstances, and we will be back tomorrow with a corrected updated version . . .
>
> (Broder, cited in Rusbridger 2008: 248)

For Rusbridger, who first read this description when he was a young reporter in Washington, its insight retains its value today. 'The greater the speed required of us in the digital world – and speed does matter, but never at the expense of accuracy or fairness or anything which would imperil trust – the more we should be honest about the tentative nature of what is possible', he observes. This type of self-reflexivity does not belie a lack of conviction, of course. Rather, it appears to signal Rusbridger's commitment to reassessing what the 'conceptual shifts' occurring in the news industry will mean for the future of journalism and the value of the record it creates. Precisely how this process will unfold is anything but clear, but is certain to prove 'enormously difficult to manage' in his view, and involve 'quite painful re-engineering of traditional workforces and re-allocation of resources' (2008: 249). The option of standing still, to wait and see what will happen, is not sustainable; the 'revolutionary experiment' is already underway and gathering speed. And in 'a 24/7 world – which is what we're all moving to – it has to begin with a searching examination of what journalism is', he believes, as challenging as this may prove to be.

Looking back over the course of the last one hundred years or so, it is possible to place current developments in the news culture of countries such as Britain and the United States within a larger context. In the first decades of the century, for instance, the newspaper press ruled the day – 'press barons', such as Northcliffe, Rothermere and Beaverbrook in Britain or Hearst and Pulitzer in the US, were able to exert considerable control over the public agenda. Competition over the definition of the most pressing news stories of the day also came from the cinema. Newsreels were a regular feature in cinemas by the time of the First World War, informing captivated audiences about a world far beyond their personal experience. *Time*, the first weekly news magazine in the US, began publication in 1923, with its main competitor *Newsweek* appearing ten years later. Broadcast news similarly began in the 1920s with the BBC in

Britain and fledgling commercial stations in the US, although radio journalism would not fully develop until the Second World War. Television newscasts had assumed a form that we would recognize today by the mid-1950s, and had displaced newspapers as the most popular source of news by the 1960s. During the 1970s, journalists began using ENG videotape cameras to record their stories, and were able to relay them from virtually any point in the world via portable communications satellite link-ups by the late 1980s. Website enthusiasts – the word 'blogger' not in general use – shared their eye-witness accounts, photographs and camcorder video clips on 11 September 2001. The 2003 US-led invasion of Iraq saw journalists scoop their rivals by filing stories from the field using satellite telephones and notebook computers. Citizen journalists, using mobile or cell phones equipped with cameras, helped to document the tragedies of the South Asian tsunami, the London bombings and Hurricane Katrina. In 2008, the journalistic potential of social networking – not least Twitter – came to the fore during the terror attacks in Mumbai, India. Needless to say, each of these developments, among a myriad of others, has had profound implications for how journalists go about their work and, just as importantly, how their audiences relate to the world around them.

In choosing the title *News Culture* for this book, it is my intention to signal from the outset a commitment to establishing a rather unconventional agenda for the study of the institutions, forms, practices and audiences of journalism. To the extent that one can safely generalize about the wide variety of existing examinations of the news media within the humanities and social sciences, I think it fair to suggest that many of these analyses share a distinguishing feature. That is to say, they usually prioritize for examination a media–society dichotomy which treats the respective sides of this relationship as being relatively exclusive. Studies tend to focus on either the media themselves, so as to ask questions about how they affect society (the findings usually make for grim reading) or they centre on the larger society in order to explore how it affects the media ('the public gets the media it deserves'). In both instances, the relationship implied by the media–society dichotomy is often simply reaffirmed as one consistent with the role 'everyone knows' the news media play in a democratic society. To borrow an old maxim, the news media are assumed to be afflicting the comfortable while, at the same time, comforting the afflicted.

A key aim of this book is to render problematic this media–society dichotomy. I want to suggest that the invocation of such a dichotomy is placing severe limits on the sorts of questions that can be asked about the news media in our society (or, for that matter, just how democratic our society is in the first place). Should the news media be removed, in analytical terms, from the social, economic and political contexts within which they operate, we run the risk of exaggerating their power and influence. Similarly, any inquiry into how modern societies are 'made and remade in every individual mind' on a daily basis, to use Williams's (1958) apt turn of phrase, needs to account in one way or another for the efficacy of the news media. In other words, then, I want to argue that we need to break down this media–society dichotomy so that we may better grapple with all of the messy complexities, and troublesome contradictions, which otherwise tend to be neatly swept under the conceptual carpet. It is important that we take sufficient care to avoid losing sight of how the news media are embedded in specific relations of power and control while, at the same time, recognizing the ways in which they are working to reinflect, transform and, if only infrequently, challenge these same relations over time.

It is with this concern in mind that I have introduced the notion of 'news culture' as a means to help facilitate critical efforts to transcend the media–society dichotomy. A closer inspection of this dichotomy reveals some of the ways in which it shapes different modes of inquiry into news as a distinctive research object. Three such lines of investigation may be briefly sketched as follows:

- *News as an object of policy formation*: for approaches giving priority to the governmental sphere, news is treated as an agent of representative democracy. Questions are raised about state regulation of the news media, including issues such as 'due impartiality' or 'fairness', official secrets (such as where national security is concerned), censorship, libel and defamation, freedom of information, privacy, doorstepping and 'cheque-book journalism'. Members of the news audience tend to be conceived of primarily as voters possessing rights, which require protection through agencies such as the Office of Communications (Ofcom) in Britain and the Federal Communications Commission (FCC) in the US.
- *News as an object of commodification*: viewed from the vantage point of an economic approach, the status of news as a commodity to be bought and sold is emphasized. Audience members are primarily thought of as current (or potential) consumers, the attention of whom may be purchased in turn by advertisers (or, in the case of public news broadcasting, quantified in order to justify public subsidy or licence fees). The changing dynamics of news media ownership are scrutinized (e.g. questions of concentration, conglomeration and globalization), particularly as they pertain to relations of profit accumulation and maximization at local, national or international levels.
- *News as an object of public opinion*: still another approach situates news as an object of 'rational-critical debate' within the realm of the public sphere (the writings of Habermas (1989, 1992) are particularly applicable here). Attention focuses on the decisive role the news media play in establishing a

discursive space, one framed by the state and economic domains on either side, for public deliberations over social issues. The formative influence of the news on popular attitudes is accentuated by conceiving of the news audience as citizens engaged in public dialogue, bringing to bear the force of public opinion upon authority relations.

Each of these approaches has proven to be important in generating vital insights into how the news media operate in modern societies such as those of Britain and the US. Nevertheless, each is also necessarily partial and selective in what it identifies as being relevant to its concerns. This book will attempt to dwell on those aspects which tend to fall between the cracks of these more familiar types of approaches.

The concept of 'news culture', I shall argue, resists the analytical separation of the 'cultural' from the 'economic' and the 'political' prefigured by the media–society dichotomy. In so doing, it may be employed to help rethink the ideological assumptions, modes of perception, and even unconscious expectations that need to be sustained by journalist and audience member alike if a news account's claim to be a factual representation of reality is to be upheld. As a form of social knowledge, a discourse identified as 'news' exhibits certain evolving yet characteristic features which are shaped in accordance with cultural rules or conventions about what constitutes 'the world out there'. That is to say, while journalists typically present a news account as an 'objective', 'impartial' *translation* of reality, it may be understood to be providing an ideological *construction* of contending truth-claims about reality. This is to suggest that the news account, far from simply 'reflecting' the reality of an event, is effectively providing a codified definition of what should count as the reality of the event. This constant, always dynamic process of mediation is accomplished primarily in ideological terms, but not simply at the level of the news account *per se*. Instead, the fluidly complex conditions under which the account is both produced and consumed or 'read' will need to be accounted for in a critical approach to news culture.

It will be my objective over the course of this book to discern the contours of news culture with an eye to mapping several of the more prominent features of its terrain. Accordingly, a brief overview of the different chapters is as follows:

- The discussion commences in Chapter 1, a new contribution to this edition, by focusing on Habermas's (1989) notion of a 'public sphere' (mentioned above) and its importance for journalism. In his words, the public sphere represents a space for 'rational-critical debate' amongst citizens, one where 'a time consuming process of mutual enlightenment' may take place 'for the "general interest" on the basis of which alone a rational agreement between publicly competing opinions could freely be reached' (1989: 195).

Next, we turn to the political economy of news organizations – including Herman and Chomsky's 'propaganda model' – before considering how ownership dynamics influence life in the newsroom.

- In Chapter 2, we take a step back, tracing the emergence of 'news' as a form of discourse from the earliest days of human civilization up to and including the early twentieth-century newspaper press. Special attention is given to the rise of 'objective' reporting methods, showing how by the 1920s they had been formally legitimized by many news organizations in Britain and the US as being consistent with professionalism. It was only by placing an emphasis on 'accomplished facts', the journalist Walter Lippmann (1922) argued at the time, that news could 'separate itself from the ocean of possible truth'.
- The focus shifts in Chapter 3 to examine the early days of radio and television news in Britain and the US. Of particular interest are the ways in which the narrative forms and devices of broadcast news were conventionalized. Many of the news formats and reporting practices familiar to us today are shown to have been the subject of considerable discussion and debate, their larger significance for the coverage of public affairs being anything but clear at the time.
- Chapter 4 returns us to the current 'mediasphere', to borrow Hartley's (1996) term, in the first instance by engaging with competing conceptions of news values and the journalistic process of framing. Next, an evaluative assessment is offered of a variety of studies concerned with the routine, day-to-day practices of news production or newswork. Particular attention is devoted to journalists' interactions with their sources, together with the attendant implications for news access.
- In Chapter 5, the textual features of news as a distinctive form of discourse are centred for investigation in relation to newspapers, photographs, radio and television. Special priority is given to the question of 'hegemony' as it informs critical research into the ways in which these different genres of news *naturalize* or *depoliticize* certain definitions of reality as being representative of 'common sense', of what 'everyone knows to be true'.
- Following next in Chapter 6 is an exploration of how news discourses are actually 'decoded' or 'read' by viewers, listeners and readers. The varied uses of news, particularly in the household, will be considered so as to discern the lived materiality of the daily practices, rituals, customs and techniques shaping the negotiation of its meanings within the context of everyday life. Young people – or 'digital natives', to use Rupert Murdoch's phrase – and their relationship to news on the internet similarly receive attention in this regard.
- Insights provided by feminist and gender-sensitive critiques of news form the

basis of Chapter 7. Beginning with an analysis of the gender politics of 'objective' reporting, the discussion proceeds to show how the norms and values of white, middle-class male journalists typically sustain a 'macho culture' in the newsroom. Attention then turns to the often sexist ways in which women are represented in the news media, particularly with regard to news coverage of incidents of male violence committed against them.

- Chapter 8 develops Hall's (1990) distinction between 'overt' and 'inferential' racism so as to deconstruct the racialized projection of an 'us and them' dichotomy in the news. The ways in which this dichotomy is maintained, reinforced and contested are examined in relation to the reporting of 'law and order' issues. Next, the chapter scrutinizes the pressures routinely placed on ethnic minority journalists to 'write white', that is, to produce news accounts which conform to a predominantly white audience's preconceptions about the social world.
- Chapter 9, a new chapter for this edition, examines war reporting. It begins with a brief survey of the evolving role of the war correspondent, looking at different conflicts – Vietnam, the Falklands crisis, and the first Gulf War – before focusing more closely on the current war in Iraq. There a diverse ecology of reportorial forms and practices, including those of the Al-Jazeera network as well as those of bloggers relaying the horrific events around them, receive attention.
- Chapter 10, also a new chapter, addresses citizen journalism, with a particular emphasis placed on ordinary people's vital contribution to covering crisis events. Examples include their first-hand, eyewitness reporting of natural disasters such as earthquakes and hurricanes (including the South Asian tsunami, when the phrase 'citizen journalism' first entered the journalistic lexicon), political scandal, and the tragedies of terrorism and conflict, amongst others.
- The book draws to a close in Chapter 11. It focuses, in the first instance, on various critiques of the news media, not least those that contend that 'real journalism' is at risk of disappearing into a 'sleazoid infotainment culture'. In this context, the chapter proceeds to examine television news, before engaging directly with issues around 'newszak', celebrity and 'tabloidization'. In calling into question familiar types of assumptions ordinarily made about news culture by both journalists and their critics alike, we look to the future with a view to considering afresh strategies for change and improvement.

1 NEWS, POWER AND THE PUBLIC SPHERE

> The inhibited judgments were called 'public' in view of a public sphere [. . .] now casting itself loose as a forum in which the private people, come together to form a public, readied themselves to compel public authority to legitimate itself before public opinion.
>
> (Jürgen Habermas, philosopher and sociologist)

One can be forgiven for pausing to reminisce about a time when the future of journalism seemed confident, if not assured. Today, in these troubled times of ours, the news industry finds itself, paradoxically, subjected to intense journalistic scrutiny for all of the wrong reasons. Grim headlines document the agonizing twists and turns of news organizations caught up in a desperate struggle to remain financially viable under severe, seemingly inexorable market pressures. Newspapers, in particular, are buckling under the strain. Some are collapsing altogether – their hard-won reputations for reportorial integrity, earned over generations, consigned to history's dustbin – while others dramatically refashion themselves with an unwavering eye to bottom-line profitability. While managers talk of 'reorganization', 'downsizing', 'layoffs', 'cutbacks', 'concessions' and the like (while striving to avoid the word 'bankruptcy'), news and editorial posts are being 'concentrated', with remaining staff members compelled to 'multi-task' as they adopt greater 'flexibility' with regard to their salary and working conditions. 'Converged' content is being 'repackaged', a polite way of saying that its quantity – and, too often, quality – is shrinking as 'efficiencies' are imposed. The closing of local news beats, like the foreign bureau before them, is a price too high to pay for some, leading them to merge operations with former competitors in order to save revenue by sharing coverage.

For others, forced to think the unthinkable, the decision has been made to abandon the print edition entirely, focusing remaining resources on transforming into internet-only news sources. Even here the language of 'innovation' and 'experimentation' can fail to conceal the unspoken fear that such a bold 'initiative' may soon prove to be too little, too late.

At a time when this ominous trend appears to be gathering momentum, it is readily apparent that optimism is in short supply. And yet, some are convinced that a new business model for news organizations is in the process of emerging, one sufficiently robust to support high-quality coverage across a diverse range of delivery platforms. Declarations about the 'death of newspapers', they contend, are wide of the mark. While decidedly anxious about the prospect of managing the changes ushered in by the internet, they nevertheless see a potential for new, enriched types of news reporting to flourish in the digital age. The imperatives transforming what counts as journalism present opportunities for progressive change, they believe, quite possibly in ways that will empower ordinary citizens to reassert their claim on it in the name of democratizing media power. 'News organizations do not own the news any more', the BBC's Director of Global News, Richard Sambrook (2006), has publicly proclaimed. 'They can validate information, analyse it, explain it, and they can help the public find what they need to know.' However, and this is the crucial point in his view, 'they no longer control or decide what the public know. It is a major restructuring of the relationship between public and media.'

The implicit suggestion that there was once a time when news organizations actually did 'own the news' is open to debate, of course, but there is little doubt that Sambrook is on firm ground when he argues that the 'information revolution' now under way 'has the potential to alter the dynamics of public debate, and the interaction between politics, media and the public, beyond recognition.' Vanishing before our eyes is the world where a select number of powerful news organizations could direct the primary flow of information so long as certain regulatory parameters were respected. In its place today, he maintains, is a world where unlimited information is readily available. For the price of a laptop and an internet connection, it has been commoditized and democratized. 'Thanks to the internet, the role of media gatekeeper has gone', he continues. 'Information has broken free and top-down control is slipping inexorably away.' And, at same time, the former gatekeepers – not least the BBC – are discovering that they are being repositioned beneath a bright spotlight, which can be rather uncomfortable at times. 'We are watched and assessed more closely now by those whom we serve', Sambrook (2006) acknowledges. This is the new reality, he adds, and 'we'd better get used to it. Transparency about the news selection and editing process is now as important as the journalism itself in retaining public trust.'

These comments are interesting for the compelling insights they offer, but also because they are indicative of what appears to be a fast-growing consensus amongst senior news executives that journalism must dramatically refashion its relationships with its publics. In taking this priority as its point of departure, this chapter begins its discussion by elucidating the notion of the 'public sphere' as it has been developed in the historical writings of Jürgen Habermas (1989, 1992). His account of the decisive role the newspaper press played in helping to establish a discursive space for critical deliberations over public issues has proved to be highly influential, and has much to offer enquires into the questions at hand.

The public sphere

'The usage of the words "public" and "public sphere" betrays a multiplicity of concurrent meanings.' So begins Jürgen Habermas's (1989) path-breaking study *The Structural Transformation of the Public Sphere* (translated from the 1962 publication, *Strukturwandel der Öffentlichkeit*). In the course of this enquiry into the establishment of the 'bourgeois public sphere' in the early modern period of European history, Habermas proceeds to outline the basis for a radical reconsideration of the factors informing the emergence of 'public opinion' as a social phenomenon.

Briefly, it is Habermas's contention that the initial appearance of a popular notion of 'public opinion' took place in Britain during the late seventeenth century. The middle of that century had witnessed the partial displacement of terms such as 'world' or 'mankind' in popular discourse by talk of a 'public', followed by the arrival of the word 'publicity', which had been borrowed from the French *publicité* shortly thereafter (1989: 26). The features of this emerging lexicon were being swiftly redrawn as the 'world of letters', that is, the literary field with its capacity for 'rational-critical debate' amongst private individuals, was being transformed in relation to the imperatives of the privatized domain of a market economy on the one hand, and the directives of state-governed institutions on the other.

More specifically, the usage of 'public opinion', a phrase to be differentiated at the time from 'general opinion', was contingent upon a new conception of a sphere of social life where citizens met to articulate criticisms of established authority. In Habermas's words:

> With the rise of a sphere of the social, over whose regulation public opinion battled with public power, the theme of the modern (in contrast to the ancient) public sphere shifted from the properly political tasks of a

> citizenry acting in common (i.e. administration of law as regards internal affairs and military survival as regards external affairs) to the more properly civic tasks of a society engaged in critical public debate (i.e. the protection of a commercial economy). The political task of the bourgeois public sphere was the regulation of civil society.
>
> (Habermas 1989: 52)

By the turn of the eighteenth century, then, a distinctive constellation of forces had arisen in Britain which led, in turn, to the advent of a public sphere of reasoned discourses circulating in the political realm independently of both the Crown and Parliament. The fledgling circumstances of this development, according to Habermas, may be linked to three key events which occurred between 1694 and 1695: the founding of the Bank of England by a group of London merchants, the inauguration of the first cabinet government and, most importantly for our purposes here, the elimination of the institution of censorship 'which made the influx of rational-critical arguments into the press possible and allowed the latter to evolve into an instrument with whose aid political decisions could be brought before the new forum of the public' (1989: 58).

Accordingly, in tracing the evolution of the conditions which would come to underpin the appearance of these 'unique liberties' enjoyed by the British press, Habermas focuses on the emergence of a new stage of capitalist development in the seventeenth century. Specifically, he contends that the enlarged spatialization of early capitalist commercial relations necessitated the distribution of news in a far more public form than that which had been provided by the 'news letters' printed in political journals (this otherwise private correspondence offered current news about 'Imperial Diets, wars, harvests, taxes, transports of precious metals, and, of course, reports on foreign trade') since mid-century (1989: 20). These journals, which were increasingly being established as commodities in their own right for the 'educated classes' (who also found news in broadsheets, learned periodicals, pamphlets and so forth), were also frequently used as devices in the service of public administration.

The steadily growing intertwinement of the interests of state officials with those of the 'capitalists' (the merchants, bankers, entrepreneurs and manufacturers) was leading, in turn, to a shared recognition that social stability could be enhanced through an appropriately informed citizenry. A burgeoning traffic in printed materials, Habermas argues, thus developed alongside that of other goods such that, by the end of the century, there was a regular supply of news that was accessible to the general public – thereby prompting considerable discussion and debate, often in the coffee houses of the time.

The creation of public opinion

The importance of coffee houses for the emergence of what may be described as an embryonic public sphere in various European countries has been the subject of much scholarly attention. For Habermas, the coffee house – with its idealized projection of 'a kind of social intercourse that, far from presupposing equality of status, disregarded status altogether' (1989: 36) – evolved into the central institution of the English public sphere. Its ascendant popularity corresponded to the celebrated ambience it enjoyed as an establishment open, in principle at least, to any ordinary citizen inclined to 'learn the news and discuss it'. Individual premises served as meeting places, usually for a specific type of clientele sharing an interest in a particular kind of news or information (newspapers, along with broadsides, pamphlets, journals and similar tracts, were distributed via coffee houses, where they were passed about from one patron to the next).

The purchase of a single 'dish' of coffee entitled the customer to a seat around a communal table, to be occupied for several hours if so desired. Virtually every type of interest, trade or profession was catered for by one coffee house or another, with particular establishments associated with politics, law, medicine, religion, science, arts, literature or wit, amongst other topics. The term 'penny university', derived from a well-known rhyme of the day, highlighted their educational qualities. A further use revolved around the conduct of business (including insurance, shipping, stock and commodity dealing), where regular hours were kept at certain rooms for negotiations and transactions. Similarly pertinent here was the way coffee houses supported the fledgling postal system via the collection and delivery of letters and newspapers, while others facilitated alternative – even at times surreptitious – purposes, such as auctioneering, matrimonial services, masonic meetings, gambling and prostitution (see also Pincus 1995; Raymond 2002; Clayton 2003; Cowan 2005).

Apparent from the outset was the formative role coffee house sociability played in the creation of public opinion, the collective force of private individuals' deliberations wielding considerable influence. The remarkable appetite of participants for news – as well as for political discussion of its significance – recurrently attracted the attention of authorities concerned with controlling the flow of information. Habermas (1989) observes that coffee houses were sometimes castigated as seedbeds of political unrest. On these grounds, Charles II's government responded to the 'great complaints' that were being 'daily made' of the 'license that was taken in coffee houses to utter most indecent, scandalous and seditious discourses' (Pincus 1995: 828) by seeking to suppress them by proclamation on 29 December 1675. This attempt was abandoned shortly thereafter, however, when it became apparent that the order was being ignored. In addition to government proclamations, other efforts mobilized against coffee houses over the years included Christian authorities convinced that free speech was helping to cultivate atheism, purveyors of rival beverages (including critics fearful that the demand for English grain used in ale would be undercut), and also women alarmed by the amount of time their idle spouses spent newsmongering.

This last point underlines a significant issue. Although egalitarian in theory, actual participation in the typically boisterous, uninhibited discussions of the coffee house was largely confined to middle- and upper-class men with enough money – and conspicuous leisure time – to indulge their coffee-drinking habit on a regular (frequently daily) basis. In contrast with the salons of France, women were seldom welcomed to partake in conversation in this milieu, their custom tending to be discouraged for entirely sexist reasons characteristic of the period. Records indicate that some were present in the role of proprietor (a 'coffee woman', who was often a widow), or more typically in a service capacity, but in any case were ordinarily excluded from taking part in 'rational-critical debate' (Habermas 1989) due to the gendered culture of what was a predominantly masculinized space.

If the 'decisive mark' of this new domain of the public sphere was the published word, as Habermas suggests, this is not to deny that at the outset of the eighteenth century there remained in place a range of institutional impediments to the realization of 'press freedom'. This was despite an improvement in the degree of press autonomy being permitted, following the abolition in 1695 of the forms of censorship previously authorized by the Licensing Act of 1662 (despite the pressures brought to bear on Parliament to renew the Act by the monarchy). The law of personal libel, for example, was a severe constraint on the reporting process, not least because of its arbitrary redefinition in prosecutions for seditious libel. Similarly, the dictates of Crown and Parliament, often enforced on grounds of breach of privilege, ensured that further legal restrictions could be imposed on a case-by-case basis. The year 1712 saw the enactment of what were called 'the taxes on knowledge', the most important being the stamp tax, which were implemented not only to bolster revenues for the Crown but also to control the right of publication. These measures had the desired effect of forcing the more marginal – and often the more radical in political terms – titles out of business (the stamp duty would be substantively reduced in the 1830s, but not be eliminated until 1855; here the selective use of subsidies by the state was a further means to counter the radical press).

Nevertheless, over the course of the first half of the eighteenth century, an extensive array of critical, if almost exclusively bourgeois voices were heard in the news journals. These voices were willing and able to take issue with the

Crown's conduct and Parliament's legislative performance. Habermas argues that these commercially based journals were constitutive of a growing 'public spirit', one which was beginning to replace what had been until then a 'party spirit'. If this challenging, often enraged temperament found its expression in publications such as John Tutchin's *Observator* (1702), Daniel Defoe's *The Review* (1704), and Jonathan Swift's *Examiner* (1710), for Habermas (1989: 60) it is Nicholas Amhurst's *Craftsman* (1726), together with Edward Cave's *Gentleman's Magazine* (1731), which signalled that 'the press was for the first time established as a genuinely critical organ of a public engaged in critical political debate: as the fourth estate'. Indeed, with the decline of the clubs and the coffee houses, the latter being a principal forum for the circulation of news (their golden age being between 1680 and 1730), as noted above the public was now largely being 'held together' through an independent, market-based newspaper press subject to 'professional criticism' (1989: 51; see also Hampton 2009).

Similarly, Habermas singles out for attention the anonymously written letters attributed to 'Junius', published in the *Public Advertiser* from 21 November 1768 through to 12 May 1772, for in his view they should rightly be called 'pioneers of the modern press'. In these letters, he maintains, 'the King, the ministers, top military men, and jurists were publicly accused of political machinations, and secret connections of political significance were thereby uncovered in a manner that ever since has been exemplary of a critical press' (1989: 61). This enhanced climate of criticism, being derivative of a wide range of different confrontations between an emboldened press and both the monarchy and government, was profoundly recasting the norms of the public sphere. Private citizens, encouraged to redefine themselves as part of a larger public force, became intent on regulating the conduct of government officials, as well as on contributing to the shaping of the direction of policy initiatives.

This transformation was made particularly visible with regard to what became a public controversy over the right to report on Parliamentary proceedings. The politicians, in seeking to preserve their general privilege of secrecy (the publication of the 'votes' had been authorized in 1681), would successfully resist efforts to formally overthrow the injunction against reporting until 1803. In that year, the Speaker made available a place in the gallery for journalists, but it would not be until after a new House of Parliament had been built after the fire of 1834 that stands would be erected for journalists. 'For a long time the target of critical comment by public opinion', Habermas (1989: 62) comments, Parliament was now being remade 'into the very organ of this opinion'. By fostering a critical engagement with the issues of the day, then, the press helped to underwrite a consensual (albeit informal) process of surveillance whereby the activities of the government could be made more responsive to the dictates of public opinion.

From Habermas's vantage point, popular participation in the public sphere as a neutral space situated between the state and the market relations of the official economy was reaching its highest point at the dawn of the nineteenth century. As the arena where citizens could congregate in order to deliberate over public affairs amongst themselves, the public sphere constituted a discursive site embedded in a particular politics of representation. This site encompassed the conditions required for the formation of diverse opinions to first circulate and then, where necessary, to challenge through mediation the rationality of institutional decision-making processes (the 'general interest' serving as the criterion by which this rationality was to be judged). In principle, access to the public sphere was open to each and every private individual willing to assent to the legitimacy of the 'rule of the best argument'. Journalism, as a result, was charged with the crucial role of ensuring that these individuals were able to draw upon a diverse spectrum of information sources to sustain their views, a responsibility which placed it at the centre of public life.

The maintenance of this critically reasoning public was therefore dependent upon a news media capable of lending expression to a richly pluralistic range of often sharply conflicting opinions. This expression of views of a critical intent *vis-à-vis* established authority relations was similarly contingent, in principle, upon discursive relations free of any form of coercion associated with power and privilege. Not surprisingly, Habermas concedes that these conditions were not entirely fulfilled: formal rights should not be confused with actual, lived experiences of inequality. Even at the zenith of its inclusionary politic, participation was restricted to relative elites, namely the propertied and educated (and thus primarily white males) members of society. Nevertheless, he argues, 'the liberal model sufficiently approximated reality so that the interest of the bourgeois class could be identified with the general interest [. . .] the public sphere as the organisational principle of the bourgeois constitutional state had credibility.' It is thus the public sphere, to the extent that it facilitates the formation of public opinion, which makes democratic control over governing relations possible.

Structuring public debate

In the concluding sections of *The Structural Transformation of the Public Sphere*, however, Habermas offers a grim assessment of this prospect. There he contends that the electronic media have become systematically implicated in the public sphere's rapid state of decline over the course of the twentieth century. More specifically, he writes:

> The communicative network of a public made up of rationally debating private citizens has collapsed; the public opinion once emergent from it has partly decomposed into the informal opinions of private citizens without a public and partly become concentrated into formal opinions of publicistically effective institutions. Caught in the vortex of *publicity that is staged for show or manipulation* the public of nonorganized private people is laid claim to not by public communication but by the communication of publicly manifested opinions.
>
> (Habermas 1989: 247–8, original emphasis)

His description of the conditions by which the public sphere has all but disappeared places an important emphasis on how the commercialization of mass communication networks has virtually displaced 'rational-critical debate' into the realm of cultural consumption. This 'refeudalization of the public sphere', as he typifies it, has not only transformed the active citizen into an indifferent consumer, it has ensured that she or he is all but excluded from participation in public debates and decision-making processes in any meaningful sense.

Habermas's account is deeply pessimistic about the possibility of ever reversing the current role the mass media play in controlling (in broad alignment with corporate and state interests) the public articulation of different opinions. The growing concentration and conglomeration of ownership in the media sectors of most industrialized societies, increasingly justified by state officials and corporate spokespeople in the name of 'global competitiveness', continues to repoliticize the public sphere in ways which are detrimental to public surveillance and accountability. While today we may point to the new opportunities for access to public communication provided by an array of emergent institutions and technologies (ranging from community access television to the internet), it is evident that the social divisions between those with 'information capital' and those without it are widening. Moreover, precisely what counts as 'rational debate' in the age of 'spin' or 'public opinion management' is a matter of continuous dispute between unequal discourses of citizenship, only some of which are having their definitions of reality reinflected as appropriate, credible or authoritative by the media. Meanwhile, as Habermas (1992: 437) writes, the mass media are developing the public sphere 'into an arena infiltrated by power in which, by means of topic selection and topical contributions, a battle is fought out not only over influence but over the control of communication flows that affect behaviour while their strategic intentions are kept hidden as much as possible'.

For researchers seeking to develop Habermas's thesis in this regard, now is the time to engage with these 'strategic intentions' precisely as they attempt to define the contours of 'public opinion' within the limits of corporate mainstream journalism. Many of them call for a radical reconsideration of what constitutes 'professional' news reporting today, believing that it is the internet – and the types of citizen-led journalism flourishing there – that holds the best hope for a truly democratized public sphere. We shall return to this discussion in later chapters. Here we shall focus on the belief that the citizen's right to freedom of speech is best protected by a market-based mass media system, a conviction that is at the core of the liberal pluralist conception of the journalist's role in modern society. Many of its advocates, who arguably include most journalists themselves, maintain that the news media represents a fourth estate (as distinguished, in historical terms, from the church, the judiciary and the commons). Journalism, as a result, is charged with the crucial mission of ensuring that members of the public are able to draw upon a diverse 'market place of ideas' to both sustain and challenge their sense of the world around them. This responsibility for giving expression to a richly pluralistic spectrum of information sources places the journalist at the centre of public life, as noted above, thereby underscoring the conviction that democracy is impossible without journalism to support it.

The performance of this democratic function is contingent upon the realization of 'press freedom' as a principle safeguarded from any possible impediment associated with power and privilege. The news media, according to the liberal pluralists, must carry out the crucial work of contributing to the 'system of checks and balances' popularly held to be representative of democratic structures and processes. More specifically, by fostering a public engagement with the issues of the day, they are regarded as helping to underwrite a consensual (albeit informal) process of surveillance whereby the activities of the state and corporate sectors are made more responsive to the dictates of public opinion. As arenas of arbitration, the news media are said to allow for clashes over decision making to be expressed, adjudicated and ultimately reconciled in such a way as to ensure that neither cumulative nor continuous influence is accorded to a single set of interests (see also McQuail 1992; O'Neill 1992; Carper 1997; Wheeler 1997). Liberal pluralist researchers insist that the capacity of a particular news organization to present the necessary 'plurality of viewpoints' is preserved 'by virtue of the clash and discordancy of interests which exist between owners, managers, editors and journalists' (Bennett 1982: 41; see also Golding and Murdock 1996).

Opposition to the liberal pluralist position, despite its continued salience in public debates about the news media, has been advanced from a number of different angles by researchers adopting a much more critical stance. For these alternative approaches, many of which rely on a political economy framework for their analyses, the basic tenets of liberal pluralism are in need of serious revision. The writings of Karl Marx have provided an important starting point for several of these lines of critique, including a celebrated passage which he co-wrote with Frederick Engels in *The German Ideology* around 1845:

> The ideas of the ruling class are in every epoch the ruling ideas, i.e. the class which is the ruling *material* force of society, is at the same time its ruling *intellectual* force. The class which has the means of material production at its disposal, has control at the same time over the means of mental production, so that thereby, generally speaking, the ideas of those who lack the means of mental production are subject to it . . . In so far, therefore, as they rule as a class and determine the extent and compass of an epoch, it is self-evident that they . . . among other things . . . regulate the production and distribution of the ideas of their age: thus their ideas are the ruling ideas of the epoch.
>
> (Marx and Engels 1970 [1845]: 64–5)

This passage clearly challenges several of the assumptions underlying liberal pluralist arguments. The 'ruling ideas of the epoch', to be loosely understood as the representations of a 'dominant ideology', are not forced on the subordinate classes, nor are they to be reduced (conspiratorially) to 'useful fictions'. Rather, the Marxist position maintains that the capitalist ruling class must work to advance its particular class-specific interests by depicting its ideas, norms and values in universal terms. That is to say, these 'ruling ideas' need to be mobilized as being consistent with the beliefs of ordinary people, as being the only correct, rational opinions available to them (Marx and Engels 1970 [1845]: 65–6). Mass media institutions, whether publicly or privately owned, are controlled by members of this ruling class. Each one of these institutions reproduces these 'ruling ideas', to varying degrees, so as to lend justification to the class inequalities engendered by capitalist society as being *reasonable* or *commonsensical*. In this way, the media help to ensure that the danger of radical protests emerging to disrupt the status quo is sharply reduced.

Marx's personal knowledge of journalism was shaped by the ten years he spent, while living in London, as a European correspondent for the *New York Tribune*. An impassioned advocate of a free press, who regarded it as a means to counter forces of oppression for the greater welfare of society, he nevertheless did not write at length about the news media. For political economists engaged with these issues today, then, Marx's preliminary insights need to be recast in relation to journalistic institutions the likes of which he could not have even anticipated in the nineteenth century. Broadly speaking, modern political economists have retained Marx's focus on class power as a determinant factor of social control in order to document the impact of changing patterns of news media power and influence within local, national and (increasingly) global contexts (see also McNair 2005; Rantanen 2005; Volkmer 2005; Thussu 2009). Of particular concern are the growing levels of concentration, conglomeration and integration of ownership in this sector, for these dynamics are directly linked to a range of issues associated with control over journalistic content.

For example, many political economists argue that news media power is being restricted to an ever smaller number of (usually white and male) hands; that the corporate priority of profit maximization is leading to increasingly superficial news formats where content becomes ever more uniform and the spaces available to report on controversial issues sharply reduced; and that corporate fears over 'the bottom line' are reshaping judgements about newsworthiness in ways which frequently all but silence alternative or oppositional voices. Such voices – including those in the labour movement, trade unions, feminists, anti-racists, environmentalists, anti-poverty activists and other groups committed to progressive social change – are routinely characterized as representing a threat to the interests of 'market-sensitive' news organizations.

Thus the implications of reducing news to just a commodity form like any other are profound, particularly when these types of critical voices are struggling just to be heard within the confines of ideological parameters conditioned by the drive for 'efficiency gains' (and with them greater advertising profits). It is with these kinds of concerns in mind that political economists continue to channel their research into campaigns aiming to bring about a fundamental reorganization of the current dynamics of media ownership and control, a process to be achieved primarily through the radical restructuring of state regulatory policies.

Filtering propaganda

In seeking to provide a conceptual framework to account for the interrelation of these types of dynamics at the level of news content, Herman and Chomsky (1988) have developed a 'propaganda model'. Writing from a US perspective, they argue that there exists within that country's commercial news media an institutional bias which guarantees the mobilization of certain 'propaganda campaigns' on behalf of an elite consensus (propaganda is deemed to be broadly equivalent with dominant ideology in this analysis). Notwithstanding this 'guarantee', however, the economic power of owners of capital over the media does not culminate in the creation of a political vacuum. Rather, in their view, the news media 'permit – indeed, encourage – spirited debate, criticism and dissent, as long as these remain faithfully within the system of presuppositions and principles that constitute an elite consensus' (Herman and Chomsky 1988: 302). Liberal pluralist treatments of the news media as autonomous institutions are thereby to be countered by examining the systematic subordination of the media *vis-à-vis* the functional requirements of dominant classes. To the degree that the powerful are able to co-ordinate the fluctuating boundaries of public opinion through the exercise of control over what will be found in media content, class power will be successfully reproduced.

Liberal pluralist notions of a 'free', 'independent' and 'objective' news media are thus countered by Herman and Chomsky's (1988: 298) contention that if the news media perform a societal purpose at all, it is to 'inculcate and defend the economic, social, and political agenda of privileged groups that dominate the domestic society and the state'. Propaganda campaigns may be instituted either by the state itself or by one or more of the top media firms (or even in unison), but in all instances the collaboration of the mass media is a prerequisite (1988: 33). In order to specify the 'secret' at work behind the 'unidirectionality of propaganda campaigns', Herman and Chomsky (1988: 33) define its effectivity in terms of a 'multiple filter system'. By drawing attention to these respective 'filters', they are seeking to demonstrate the extent to which journalists reiterate uncritically official positions of the state while, simultaneously, adhering to its political agenda. The resultant news product, they maintain, ultimately makes for 'a propaganda system that is far more credible and effective in putting over a patriotic agenda than one with official censorship' (1988: xiv).

Briefly, five component 'filters' of this model, each of which interact with and reinforce one another, are identified by Herman and Chomsky (1988: 3–31) as follows:

1 The first filter to be accounted for concerns the commercial basis of the dominant news organizations: specifically, the size and the scale of the investment required to run major news outlets, the concentration and conglomeration of ownership and cross-ownership patterns, and the power and wealth of the proprietors and their managers. Close ties between the media elite and their political and corporate counterparts ensure that an 'establishment orientation' is ordinarily maintained at the level of news coverage (here issues of placement, tone, context and fullness of treatment are particularly important). It is this top tier of major news companies which, together with the government and wire services, 'defines the news agenda and supplies much of the national and international news to the lower tiers of the media' (Herman and Chomsky 1988: 4–5). At the same time, the resultant 'profit orientation' of these organizations, many of which are under intense pressure from stockholders, directors and bankers to focus on 'the bottom line', is a further key aspect of this filter shaping news coverage.
2 The second filter pertains to the influence of advertising, the principal income source for commercial news organizations, on media content.

'With advertising,' Herman and Chomsky (1988: 14) write, 'the free market does not yield a neutral system in which final buyer choice decides. The *advertisers'* choices influence media prosperity and survival.' Historically, media relying on revenue from sales alone have found it very difficult to compete with the resources available to their advertising-subsidized rivals. This dynamic typically leads to such outlets being pushed to the margins, where eventually many are forced to close down. Herman and Chomsky also point out that advertisers are primarily interested in affluent audiences due to their 'purchasing power', and thus are less inclined to support forms of news and public affairs content which attract people of more modest means. Moreover, there is a strong preference for content which does not call into question their own politically conservative principles or interfere with the 'buying mood' of the audience.

3 The news media's over-reliance on government and corporate 'expert' sources is cited as the third filter. Herman and Chomsky (1988: 18) describe the symbiotic relationship that journalists have with their information sources, arguing that it is driven both by economic necessity and a reciprocity of interests. These powerful establishment sources provide journalists with a steady, reliable flow of 'the raw material of news', thereby allowing news organizations to expend their resources more 'efficiently'. The relative authority and prestige of these sources also helps to enhance the credibility of the journalist's account. The routine inclusion of such 'experts' not only shapes the news agenda, but simultaneously makes it much more difficult for independent, non-official sources to gain access. 'By giving these purveyors of the preferred view a great deal of exposure', Herman and Chomsky (1988: 24) maintain, 'the media confer status and make them the obvious candidates for opinion and analysis.'

4 Filter number four addresses the role of 'flak' or negative responses to media content as a means of disciplining news organizations. Complaints, including threats of punitive action, 'may take the form of letters, telegrams, phone calls, petitions, lawsuits, speeches and bills before Congress' (Herman and Chomsky 1988: 26). 'Flak' can be produced by individuals, state officials in their ceaseless efforts to 'correct' news coverage, or by various advocacy groups, including politically motivated 'media monitoring' campaigns or 'think tank' operations. Such forms of 'flak' can prove costly for news organizations, not only at the level of legal disputes but also in terms of the potential withdrawal of patronage by advertisers due to organized consumer boycotts. Still, Herman and Chomsky (1988: 28) suggest that these makers of 'flak' receive respectful attention by the media, only rarely having their impact on news management activities explicitly acknowledged.

5 The final filter is the role of the 'ideology of anti-communism' as a 'political control mechanism'. 'This ideology', in Herman and Chomsky's (1988: 29) words, 'helps mobilize the populace against an enemy, and because the concept is fuzzy it can be used against anybody advocating policies that threaten property interests or support accommodation with Communist states [such as China or Cuba in the 1990s] and radicalism.' This 'national religion' of 'anti-communism', they argue, has served to fragment the political left and the labour movements, as well as ensuring that liberals and social democrats are kept on the defensive. Its corresponding influence on the news media has also had far-reaching implications: 'In normal times as well as in periods of Red scares, issues tend to be framed in terms of a dichotomized world of Communist and anti-Communist powers, with gains and losses allocated to contesting sides, and rooting for "our side" considered an entirely legitimate news practice' (1988: 30–1). This ideology retains something of its purchase today – albeit in a markedly diminished capacity – having been supplanted by the 'war on terror' in the aftermath of September 11, 2001 (some critics maintain that a corresponding ideology of Islamophobia has taken the place of anti-communism as a control mechanism).

Overall, then, only the 'cleansed residue', having passed through these successive filters, is pronounced 'fit' to call news. This is not to suggest, however, that the news media are monolithic in their treatment of controversial issues. Rather, Herman and Chomsky (1988: xii) state: 'Where the powerful are in disagreement, there will be a certain diversity of tactical judgments on how to attain generally shared aims, reflected in media debate.' Nevertheless, views which contest the underlying political premises of the dominant state discourse, especially with regard to the exercise of state power, will almost always fall outside of the parameters demarcated by the limits of elite disagreement. The 'filters' identified above are deemed to be working to reinforce these parameters in ways which make alternative news choices difficult to imagine. This process, they contend, 'occurs so naturally that media news people, frequently operating with complete integrity and goodwill, are able to convince themselves that they choose and interpret the news "objectively" and on the basis of professional news values' (1988: 2).

Ownership and control

The 'propaganda model' briefly mapped out above usefully highlights a range of important issues. Here, though, it is important to bear in mind that it is not interpreted so narrowly as to suggest that the news media are to be viewed strictly as purveyors of propaganda coincidental with the interests of ruling class domination. Some interpretations of Herman and Chomsky's approach risk reducing the news media to tired ideological machines confined to performing endlessly, and unfailingly, the overarching function of reproducing the prerogatives of an economic and political elite through processes of mystification. Journalists would then become little more than well-intentioned puppets whose strings are being pulled by forces they cannot fully understand. Meanwhile the news audience – admittedly an unexplored given in this model – would then appear to be composed of passive dupes consistently fooled into believing such propaganda is true.

Any conflation of news with propaganda is, in my view, unsustainable. The propagandist, unlike the journalist (at least under ordinary circumstances), sets out with the deliberate intention of deceiving the public, of concealing 'the truth' so as to direct public opinion in a particular way through manipulative tactics, devices and strategies. To make the point bluntly, then, journalists are not propagandists. 'A journalist who intentionally fabricates or misleads', writes Newkirk (1998), 'is as ill equipped for journalism as a doctor who intentionally mistreats patients is for medicine.' This is not to deny, however, that the factors Herman and Chomsky attribute to 'propaganda' with their notion of 'filtering' are crucial determinants shaping the operation of the news media. Their study is also rich with startling evidence of how the US news media have been implicated in official propaganda campaigns at the level of 'foreign' news (examples of reporting examined range from Central America to Indo-China). I wish to suggest, however, that its more compelling insights regarding the determinants of news coverage need to be further developed, in the first instance by taking account of the ways in which the power of media owners shapes the everyday cultures of the news organizations they control.

Alarm bells have long been sounded about the dangers for independent journalism posed by the growing concentration, conglomeration and globalization of news media ownership. Some have aptly likened the control over information exercised by these companies as 'the new censorship', especially where the interests of public service collide with the private ones of shareholders. Even a glance at their respective company reports and financial statements (most of which are available online) reveals the ways in which 'market-friendly' regulatory authorities have greased the wheels of corporate capital. 'When policy is left to be fought over by powerful commercial interests behind closed doors with no public awareness or participation – by what self-interested commercial parties call "experts" – one gets what one would expect', Robert W. McChesney (2004) remarks. That is, 'a media system that serves powerful corporate interests first and foremost' (2004: 252; see also Boyd-Barrett 2005; Hackett 2005; Klaehn 2005).

The often subtle, seemingly 'commonsensical' ways in which corporate interests influence news content can be rendered discernible for analysis with careful scrutiny. The process of commodification described above encourages journalists to internalize the values of media owners as being consistent with professionalism. In the case of Rupert Murdoch, for example, who is arguably the world's foremost media mogul, news values are narrowly defined within the corporate culture of his companies. At the time of writing, this billionaire's empire encompasses – through the controlling interests of News Corp. – media such as newspapers (including *The Times*, the *Sun* and the *News of the World* in the UK and the *Wall Street Journal* and the *New York Post* in the US, amongst many more around the world), television (Sky News in the UK, Fox News in the US, Star News in Asia, amongst others), film (including Twentieth Century Fox), book publishing and magazines (including HarperCollins), and online websites (such as the social network MySpace.com). 'For Murdoch,' John Lloyd (2004) of the *Financial Times* argues, 'news is a business like any other: standards, balance and fairness are something the market can take care of' (2004: 118). His commitment to 'openly biased media' (Fox TV, the *Sun*, talk radio stations and so forth), Lloyd adds, is due to his conviction that it is what people want to purchase. His share of media markets goes some distance toward explaining why Presidents and Prime Ministers listen so carefully to what he has to say.

Financial dynamics such as these can provide only part of the picture, though. Particularly challenging to document is the lived materiality of news culture, such as the manner in which ownership dynamics give shape to a given news organization's journalistic ethos. While some owners favour regular 'hands-on' interventions where key decisions are concerned, more typical are those owners who rely upon certain trusted subordinates to anticipate their preferences. A former reporter on *The Australian*, a Murdoch title, recalls: 'Journalists on Murdoch's papers aren't given the freedom to operate as journalists should operate.' This is less a matter of certain subjects being off limits apparently, more a question of a certain stance having to be taken regarding how they are reported. 'Murdoch doesn't have to spell it out', he maintains. 'He doesn't send memos, to my knowledge, on the attitude his editors should take. The people who become Murdoch editors just know instinctively what is acceptable, what is not' (cited in Coleridge 1993: 489). What has been 'instinctively acceptable' for Fox News during the war in Iraq, for example, has been the stridently right-wing, pro-war stance informing its reporting and commentary. 'By the time US soldiers were headed across the desert to Baghdad,' David J. Sirota (2004) of *Salon* maintained, 'the "fair and balanced" network, owned by media mogul Rupert Murdoch, looked like a caricature of state-run television, parroting the White House's daily talking points, no matter how unsubstantiated.' For Jim Rutenberg (2003), writing in *The New York Times*, the 'Fox formula' proved that there were significant ratings to be gained in 'opinionated news with an America-first flair'. Fox, he pointed out, represents a new approach to television journalism, one that 'casts aside traditional notions of objectivity, holds contempt for dissent and eschews the skepticism of government at mainstream journalism's core' (see also Bennett *et al.* 2007).

A former editor of Murdoch's *Sunday Times* in London, Andrew Neil, recalls in his memoirs how the views of his proprietor set limits on editorial freedom in the newsroom. Reaffirming the point made about 'instincts' above, Neil writes that Murdoch 'picks as his editors people like me who are generally on the same wavelength as him: we started from a set of common assumptions about politics and society, even if we did not see eye to eye on every issue' (1996: 164). Evidently Neil felt that he was left to 'get on with it' in the main, although he highlights several colourful exceptions to the rule. Tellingly, however, when describing Murdoch as a 'highly political animal', he remarks:

> Rupert expects his papers to stand broadly for what he believes: a combination of right-wing Republicanism from America mixed with undiluted Thatcherism from Britain and stirred with some anti-British establishment sentiments as befits his colonial heritage [Murdoch was born near Melbourne, Australia]. The resulting pottage is a radical-right dose of free-market economics, the social agenda of the Christian Moral Majority and hardline conservative views on subjects like drugs, abortion, law and order, and defence.
>
> (Neil 1996: 165)

In the case of another Murdoch title, the *New York Post*, journalist Danny Schechter (1999) observes that it 'becomes an unapologetic and blatant Republican campaign sheet at election time, with little pretence at nonpartisanship or even conventional journalism. The traditional separation of the editorial pages and the news pages all but disappears once Murdoch picks his candidate' (1999: 378). On the few occasions when Murdoch has paused to characterize his political views, he has typically claimed that they are of little consequence. Rather disingenuously, he insists that all he does is ensure that his news organizations merely reflect what are already widespread, popular opinions. In any case, there can be little doubt that his shifting alignments with different political parties over the years demonstrate a strong pragmatic commitment to advancing his own corporate interests whichever way decisions happen to unfold at the ballot box (see also Allan 2005).

Michael Wolff's (2008) biography of Murdoch, evidently based on more than fifty hours of interviews with him in addition to those with his associates, helps to illuminate these dynamics further. In describing Murdoch as a 'Machiavellian titan', he writes:

> If you work for Rupert, you do his bidding. You submit to Rupert. He gets his newspapers wherever he is in the world, gets out his red pen – just like his father before him – and puts a cross through stories that shouldn't have run, circles a photo and draws an arrow to show where it should have been placed, notes a headline that should have been two lines rather than one, and so on.
>
> (Wolff 2008: 225–6)

Murdoch justifies his involvement in unequivocal terms; it is a right earned on the basis of his financial investment. 'The way he sees it, he is strong, direct, practical and strategically deploying his own money' Wolff observes; 'journalists, given their natural inclinations, are weak, self-indulgent, and, given the opportunity, absolutely sanguine about wasting his money' (2008: 231). What some would regard as an unacceptable degree of interference, a compromising of editorial integrity and independence, is effectively concealed to the extent this managerial control is exercised indirectly. In this way, it is arguably all the more insidious – and effective, presumably, from Murdoch's perspective. Wolff argues:

> Murdoch's management style is oddly unpredictable, partly because of his spectral quality. He's almost never there – except when he is, overwhelmingly, there. Hence, when he's not there, he's there as a palpable absence. Given the hundreds of separate news organizations he's running (together with the hundreds of other non-news organizations) at any given time, you never know when you're on his mind; you never know when he's going to walk through your door.
>
> (Wolff 2008: 237)

Rather tellingly, Woolf suggests that this 'palpable absence' does not generate hostility to the owner amongst the 'News Corp. faithful' so much as a sense of self-doubt intermixed with fear for one's position. To remain employed by him, it follows, 'is to do his bidding, to follow his line, to execute his desires, to support his needs, to grind his axes, to act on behalf of his empire, to carry out his policies, to be a citizen of his nation-state with all its demanding nationalism' (2008: 243). Managerial influence is that much more powerful, it seems, for leaving day-to-day dictates largely unspoken – a question of correct anticipation, rather than a response to direct orders issued from above.

In the next chapter, we take a step back, pausing to consider the economic, political and cultural factors that gave rise to contemporary forms and practices of news reporting in the first place.

2 THE RISE OF 'OBJECTIVE' NEWSPAPER REPORTING

> When a dog bites a man that is not news, but when a man bites a dog, that is news.
>
> (Charles Anderson Dana, editor and proprietor, *New York Sun*, 1882)

> Its primary office is the gathering of news. At the peril of its soul it must see that the supply is not tainted. Neither in what it gives, nor in what it does not give, nor in the mode of presentation, must the unclouded face of truth suffer wrong. Comment is free but facts are sacred.
>
> (C.P. Scott, editor and proprietor, *Manchester Guardian*, 1922)

This chapter's discussion is devoted to the rather daunting task of sketching several broad contours of newspaper history in Britain and the US. Of course, even a book-length study could only begin to meet such a challenge, so I shall be necessarily selective in my approach here. A reasonable place to start, it seems to me, is by trying to cast the question 'what is a newspaper?' in historical terms. As we shall see, such an inquiry needs to stretch back far beyond the invention of the printing press to a time when news was simply spread by word of mouth. It is in the nineteenth century that our discussion really begins, however, as I shall seek to prioritize for consideration the ways in which modern newspaper journalists have endeavoured to professionalize their methods of reporting over the years. More specifically, attention will focus on the historical factors that gave rise to the practice of 'objective' newspaper reporting as a means to promote new definitions of 'the public interest'.

Following a brief overview of the origins of the newspaper and its development across the centuries, this chapter turns to examine 'popular journalism' as it was represented by the 'pauper press' in Britain and the 'penny press' in the US in the 1830s. Of particular importance, in my view, is the need to trace the ascent of the various economic, political and technological factors which together were helping to consolidate the cultural norms of 'neutral', 'non-partisan' reporting. Accordingly, this assessment proceeds to consider, among other issues, the introduction of the electric telegraph in the 1840s, the intensification of varied appeals to professionalism among journalists by the 1890s, and the widespread endorsement of the ideological values of 'unbiased' reporting by journalists following the First World War. It will be argued that it was around this time that the key features of 'objective' journalism, as we recognize it today, were slowly becoming conventionalized for reporters and their readers alike.

From smoke signals to daily newspapers

Before exploring several issues in the history of newspaper journalism relevant to our discussion of modern news culture, it is advantageous to pause and consider some of the more salient factors that led to the emergence of the newspaper itself (see also Smith 1979; Innis 1986; Stephens 1988; Sreberny-Mohammadi 1990; Craven 1992; Schudson 1995, 2008; Thompson 1995; Fang 1997).

Difficulties in defining precisely what should count as a news account date back over five hundred years, since it was during the fifteenth century that the English word 'news' broadly assumed the meaning familiar to us today by displacing the Old English notion of 'tidings'. This is not to suggest, of course, that the concept of news was not already in public use. Indeed, we can assume that it has its ultimate origins in the very development of language in oral or preliterate communities thousands of years ago. Spoken news, whether in the form of gossip, sermons, ballads or tales, was an effective form of communication. Still, it was always at risk of possible misinterpretation (deliberate or otherwise), to say nothing of faulty memories. Nevertheless, this type of information helped to sustain a shared sense of social order. Such communities often had their own, usually highly ritualized, customs for disseminating news at a distance, typically relying on strategies such as messengers running relays, fires, smoke signals or the banging of drums.

Not surprisingly, communicating news over vast expanses of time and space became much easier with the advent of writing. Today's researchers, particularly archaeologists and anthropologists, continue to uncover evidence concerning the advent of a range of different writing devices. Examples include the 'pictographs' written on clay tablets by the Sumerians (who would later invent numerals and, along with the Akkadians, develop 'ideographs') for the purposes of record keeping in southern Mesopotamia around 3500 BC. Another crucial advance came with the use of papyrus reeds by the Egyptians in about 2200 BC. While papyrus lacked the durability of clay, stone or wood, it was possible to inscribe symbols on it much more readily and its lighter weight ensured that it could be more easily transported. These advantages were not lost on the Greeks, who were quick to exploit papyrus, together with their elaboration of the Phoenician alphabet, in the larger interests of trade and commerce, as well as education, literature and science. A few centuries later in China, writing would be committed to bamboo (about 500 BC), then on to silk, and finally on to paper following its invention, reportedly by a eunuch named Ts'ai Lun, in about AD 105, toward the end of the Han dynasty. Significantly, paper would not begin its slow journey to the world beyond China for another five hundred years, when Buddhist priests initially took it to Korea and Japan.

The invention of paper in Europe, which according to many historians was an event that arose independently from developments in China, would not take place until the twelfth century (paper was first used in Britain in 1309). Even then, its popularity did not overtake that of parchment until printing was firmly established. Although credit for the invention of movable type also belongs to the Chinese, Western accounts typically cite Johann Gutenberg of Mainz, Germany, as its originator. Whether or not he was influenced by the evolution of typesetting in China, or the use of metal type in Korea, is a matter of dispute among some historians. In any case, Gutenberg, a goldsmith, succeeded in introducing a typographical system in the 1440s that quickly revolutionized printing throughout Europe. By utilizing a process whereby each letter was moulded individually, and was then continuously reused, he was able to produce texts – most famously a 42-line Bible of 1282 two-column pages around 1457–8 – with a wine press converted for the task. The first printing press in Europe astonished members of the public, even frightening some who regarded its capacity to make near perfect copies of texts as the 'black art' of the devil. From then it was a race among printers in different European cities to further refine this technology, leading Thomas Carlyle to state over three hundred years later: 'He who first shortened the labour of copyists by device of Moveable Types was disbanding hired armies, and cashiering most Kings and Senates, and creating a whole new democratic world; he had invented the art of printing' (cited in Fleming 1993: 227).

The stage was now set for the development of the forerunners of today's newspapers. Although handwritten notices about government affairs appeared in the days of Julius Caesar who, in 59 BC, had decreed that they be publicly displayed on a daily basis, the printing press facilitated the circulation of news throughout society in a way never witnessed before (the first in England was set up in 1476). As historian Mitchell Stephens (1988) writes:

> In 1483 the owner of one press charged three florins for each twenty pages to print a book that a scribe might have copied for one florin for twenty pages. But that press could produce 1,025 copies for the money, the scribe one copy – three times the expense, a thousand times the audience . . . And each printed copy that marched off a press had a crucial advantage: it was an exact replica. Those thousands of readers would each receive the same story, with no *added* errors, distortions or embellishments.
>
> (Stephens 1988: 84–5)

Printed pamphlets or broadsides, which sometimes presented news narratives in the form of prose or a rhyming ballad, were slowly beginning to replace newsletters copied by hand by the start of the sixteenth century. Newsbooks followed next, the more sensational of which were often referred to as *canards*, which consisted of several pages of news usually about the same topic. Items of public interest included news of state announcements, victories in battle, royal marriages, executions of witches and the like, as opposed to accounts of everyday events.

Many historians of the press have argued, though, that the roots of the modern newspaper are most clearly discernible in the weekly news-sheets which originated in Venice close to the end of the sixteenth century (the first of which were still being written by hand). Referred to as a *gazette* after the name of the coin (*gazetta*) used to pay for a copy, they typically consisted of a single sheet of paper folded over to form four pages. These gazettes reported on events from across Europe, largely of a political or military nature, mainly by drawing upon the accounts of travelling merchants and diplomats. As their popularity grew, they began to expand in the range of their news coverage until, by the 1600s, they were beginning to resemble a form broadly consistent with today's newspaper.

Disputes continue to surface among press historians regarding which publication deserves to be acknowledged as the world's first newspaper, with different titles from Germany, the Netherlands and Switzerland usually receiving the most attention. This controversy stems, in part, from disagreements over how best to define what constitutes a newspaper as distinct from other, related types of publication. In a European context, Anthony Smith (1979: 9–10) suggests that news publishing passed through four distinct stages over the course of the seventeenth century:

- first, there was the single story (a 'relation' or 'relacioun'), usually published months after the event being reported on
- second, a continuous series of 'relations' were brought together and published on a near weekly basis as a 'coranto' (the first in the English language appeared in Amsterdam in 1620)

- third, the 'diurnall' appeared, which supplied a weekly overview of newsworthy occurrences transpiring over successive days
- the fourth stage in the evolution was the 'mercury', a form of newsbook where the journalist typically spoke in a personal voice, and the 'intelligencer', which addressed its audience in a more formal or official voice.

Throughout the 1600s, then, these and related types of publications spoke to an ever expanding audience as literacy levels underwent rapid improvement. Available in towns and cities in bookshops and coffee houses, and sold in rural areas by hawkers and peddlers, they 'brought sex and scandal, fantasy, sensationalism, bawdiness, violence and prophecy to their readers: monstrous births, dragons, mermaids and most horrible murders; but they also brought items of news' (Craven 1992: 3; see also Boyce *et al.* 1978).

It was not until the early eighteenth century, however, that the daily newspaper, with its wide coverage of subject matter, was fully established in Britain. The first daily was the *Daily Courant* which was launched on 11 March 1702 on premises 'next Door to the King's-Arms Tavern at Fleet Bridge' (see also Harris 1997). Initially composed of a single sheet of two columns, it sold for one penny and offered its readers both domestic and international news (the latter translated from 'the Foreign Paper from when 'tis taken'). The *Daily Courant* was soon joined by a series of new dailies such that, according to Smith (1979), by 1750:

> London had five daily papers, six thrice-weeklies, five weeklies and, on a far less official level, several cut-price thrice-weeklies, with a total circulation between them of 100,000 copies (up to one million readers) a week. The average weekly wage, at ten shillings, was higher in London than in the provinces, and brought the purchase of an occasional newspaper well within the reach of all but the poorest workers.
>
> (Smith 1979: 56–7)

Despite the severity of tax and libel laws, there was a steady increase in the sales of daily newspapers throughout the century. This was attributable, in part, to general population growth, the spread of literacy and the continuing expansion of networks of distribution. In the case of the last factor, the use of new roads in and out of London by stagecoaches and wagons, as well as the growing proficiency of the General Post Office across Britain, were particularly significant (see also Herd 1952; Harris 1978; Jones 1993; O'Malley *et al.* 1997).

The first regularly published newspaper in the American colonies was *The Boston News-Letter*, which was established by the town's postmaster, John Campbell, in 1704 (an earlier title, Benjamin Harris's *Publick Occurrences*, was closed after a single issue by the colonial authorities). Formerly a handwritten newsletter, this weekly newspaper relied heavily on European news obtained from the pages of various London publications. The country's first daily newspaper was not founded until 1783, when the *Pennsylvania Evening Post and Daily Advertiser* appeared in Philadelphia. Months after its launch the publisher, Benjamin Towne, was indicted as a traitor for having lent his support to the Tories during the city's occupation by the British. Journalism, as Schudson (1995: 45) argues, had become intensely political since the Stamp Act controversy had forced printers to choose sides in 1765. While some titles shied away from publishing any form of news that might be regarded as controversial, others made every effort to incite a revolutionary fervour among their readers.

By the close of the eighteenth century, then, the foundations were being laid for a newspaper press which, according to its champions, would come to represent to the world the epitome of democratic power, prestige and influence. Not everyone shared this view, of course, a point expressed rather forcefully in the words of one commentator writing in 1799:

> The American newspapers are the most base, false, servile, and venal publications that ever polluted the fountains of writing – their editors the most ignorant, mercenary and vulgar automatons that ever were moved by the continually rusty wires of sordid mercantile avarice.
>
> (Cited in Innis 1986: 158)

Differing opinions as to its proper role and deserved status apart, by the 1800s the ascension of the newspaper press as a vitally important forum for public discussion, debate and dissent was assured.

The emergence of popular journalism

It is now apparent, in light of the discussion above, that the emergence of a newspaper press committed to advancing 'the public interest' by reporting the reality of the social world in a 'non-partisan' manner has been a fairly recent development. Most historical accounts of the rise of 'objective' journalism, as we shall see, point to a series of crucial developments in the early decades of the nineteenth century concerning the 'pauper press' in Britain and the 'penny press' in the US. Both types of newspapers were launched during this period with the expressed aim of securing a mass readership interested in the kinds of news which the more 'traditional', 'high-minded' newspapers largely neglected to cover.

Turning first to the 'pauper press', as it had come to be known in Britain during the early nineteenth century, it is important to note that it succeeded in attracting a largely working-class readership because of its commitment to delivering a form of journalism these readers wanted to see at a price that they could afford. An emphasis was placed on reporting news events which had a distinct 'human interest' angle, as they were perceived to possess a greater entertainment value. For example, in 1834 the publisher of the *Twopenny Dispatch*, Henry Hetherington, promised readers that they would find on its pages:

> a repository of all the gems and treasures, and fun and frolic and 'news and occurrences' of the week. It shall abound in Police Intelligence, in Murders, Rapes, Suicides, Burnings, Maimings, Theatricals, Races, Pugilism, and all manner of moving 'accidents by flood and field'. In short, it will be stuffed with every sort of devilment that will make it sell.
>
> (Cited in Stephens 1988: 204)

The pauper press, mainly made up of weekly titles, stood in marked contrast to the so-called 'respectable press'. This even though these mainstream titles, as Williams (1978: 46) remarks, were not particularly respectable: 'there had been heavy direct bribery of journalists by Ministers, and official advertising was steered to papers favourable to Government opinion'. Many of the pauper press titles, available for the price of a penny or two, were actively campaigning for radical social change in the face of the Newspaper Stamp Duties Act which had been imposed with the clear intention of destroying them. Evading this politically motivated tax, which had also been extended to advertisements and paper, was a necessity if these titles were to retain their relatively cheap price.

Governments of the day were fearful of the threat radical journalism posed to established relations of power and privilege, while the proprietors of the 'respectable' press wanted to reduce the competition for readership. Both groups therefore saw important advantages to be gained by restricting the ownership of newspapers to fellow members of the propertied class. In the words of one angry parliamentarian at the time:

> Those infamous publications of the cheap press tended to disorganise the very frame of society . . . they inflame their [the poor's] passions and awaken their selfishness, contrasting their present condition with what they contend to be their future condition – a condition incompatible with human nature, and with those immutable laws which Providence has established for the regulation of civil society.
>
> (Cited in Curran 1978: 64)

The stamp duties, like the ongoing prosecutions for seditious and blasphemous libel, helped to realize this aim, but did not succeed in curbing the influence of the illegal unstamped press entirely. Rather, it was the convergence of these interests with those of advertisers that proved to be even more effective in silencing oppositional voices.

Two factors were particularly significant here: first, advertisers were typically anxious to avoid any association with controversial publications, especially if it meant the risk of incurring the wrath of the Crown. Second, they were willing to place their advertisements only with those titles which attracted an audience made up of people possessing the financial means to purchase their products. By this logic, the 'lower orders' of society inclined to support the campaigning press were, by definition, all but excluded. As a result of these and related factors, few radical titles could match the editorial content of their 'respectable' rivals. Nor could they afford to invest the capital required to stay up to date with the latest improvements in press and ink technologies. Consequently, far from inaugurating a new era of press freedom and liberty, this period witnessed the introduction of a much more effective system of press censorship: 'Market forces,' as Curran and Seaton (1997: 9) argue, 'succeeded where legal repression had failed in conscripting the press to the social order' (see also Asquith 1978; Boyce *et al.* 1978; Koss 1984; O'Malley 1986; Williams 1998; Curran 2002).

The gradual decline of the radical press in Britain may be mapped in relation to the rapid ascension of a middle-class press following the repeal of the 'taxes on knowledge' (the stamp duty was substantively reduced in 1836, and withdrawn altogether in 1855; the duty on advertising was removed in 1853 and that on paper eliminated in 1861). Of the various titles which became dailies following the abolition of the stamp duty in 1855, the most successful was the *Daily Telegraph*. In contrast with *The Times*, for example, which sold at seven pence, the *Daily Telegraph* moved to drop its price to a penny so as to entice a much wider readership to its pages. Sales underwent a dramatic surge upwards, quickly leading to a point where it assumed a dominant position in the market (by 1877 its daily circulation was the largest in the world). A leader writer on the staff in the 1860s, Edward Dicey, would later outline the basis of the newspaper's commitment to popular journalism in 1905:

> We were given a free hand, as we knew that if we produced something the public would like to read we should not be blamed even if we diverged to some extent from the instructions given us at the morning meetings. We had no great respect for constituted authorities, we cared very little for preconceived opinion, and we were not troubled with too strict reverence for absolute accuracy. We were, if I may venture to say so, the pioneers of the Press today.
>
> (Dicey 1997 [1905]: 105)

The penny dailies like the *Daily Telegraph*, while for all intents and purposes middle-class newspapers, nevertheless saw the potential profits to be gained by stretching their appeal to include working-class readers. In many ways, however, they were simply emulating mass circulation strategies which had been firmly established across the Atlantic since the 1830s (see also Lee 1976; Griffiths 1992; Wiener 1996; Allan 1997a).

In the United States, the penny newspapers championed popular forms of journalism which were very similar to those initially embraced by the pauper press in Britain. The *New York Sun*, which appeared on 3 September 1833, is generally regarded as the first of the penny newspapers, and it was almost immediately followed by the *Evening Transcript* and the *New York Herald* (later by the *New York Tribune* in 1841 and *The New York Times* in 1851). From the city of New York, the penny press quickly spread to the other urban centres, beginning with Boston, Philadelphia and Baltimore. The use of the steam press in the 1830s was followed by the introduction of the Hoe rotary press in 1846, thereby enabling the mass production of newspapers on a scale never seen before. While perhaps too much has been made about these technological changes by some writers who see in them a determining influence, they nevertheless significantly altered the dynamics of commodification for better (newspapers could be sold more cheaply) and for worse (the start-up costs for establishing a title quickly became prohibitive). By the middle of the nineteenth century, as Shi (1995) suggests, the US was 'awash in newsprint'. Specifically, in '1840 there were 138 daily newspapers in the country; thirty years later there were 574; by the turn of the century the total was 2,600' (Shi 1995: 95). During the same period, he adds, overall circulation increased from less than two million to over 24 million. By the end of the Jacksonian era, then, the penny press would succeed in displacing the commercial or mercantile press, as well as the explicitly sectarian press, from the positions of prominence that they had previously enjoyed (the party press would virtually disappear by 1875).

The contours of 'public opinion' were being quickly redrawn by this new type of newspaper which sought to claim for itself the status of being the people's voice in a society undergoing democratization. Due to its reliance on market-based income, namely sales and advertisements increasingly directed at consumer items, the penny press provided its customers with a much less expensive product (about five cents cheaper on average; payment was made to 'newsboys' or 'little merchants' on the street, not via annual subscription; see Bekken 1995; Leonard 1995). As a result, these newspapers offered a different type of access to the public sphere, for they were able to declare a greater degree of political independence from government and party. Indeed, not only did some of these newspapers define themselves as 'neutral in politics', but also many tended to be indifferent to elite political events. According to Schudson (1978: 21), a lead in the 9 December 1833 edition of the *New York Sun* about a 'short item of congressional news' was typical: 'The proceedings of Congress thus far, would not interest our readers.' This when the first issue of the same newspaper had proclaimed that its aim was 'to lay before the public, at a price within the means of everyone, all the news of the day'.

For most of the penny newspapers, then, reporting 'the news of the day' entailed a commitment to a new, distinctive range of news values. In particular, the local 'human interest story' was to be prized above all others, for it best represented the conditions of contemporary life as they touched the experiences of 'the masses'. These newspapers thus tended to restrict their coverage of party politics or issues of trade and commerce to matters of popular interest, electing instead to fill their pages primarily with news about the police, the courts, small businesses, religious institutions and 'high society'. News from the streets and private households, especially suicides, fires and burglaries, had mass appeal (in this way the line between 'public' and 'private' life was effectively blurred: Schudson 1978; Smith 1979; Schiller 1981). As James Gordon Bennett, founder of the *New York Herald*, declared in the 11 May 1835 edition of that penny newspaper: 'We shall give a correct picture of the world – in Wall Street – in the Exchange – in the Police Office – in the Opera – in short, wherever human nature or real life best displays its freaks and vagaries' (cited in Roshco 1975: 32). Thus in presenting to their readers a 'gastronomy of the eye' largely made up of 'the odd, the exotic and the trivial', to use Carey's (1986: 163) terms, these newspapers were expeditiously redefining what could and should qualify as news for 'ordinary people' in the context of their daily lives.

This radical remapping of the public sphere fundamentally transformed not only popular conceptions of what should constitute a news event, but also how that news should be communicated. In seeking to satisfy the needs of a general readership far more encompassing in class terms than that of their more established rivals, the penny newspapers utilized a language of reporting which emphasized the significance of everyday life in a 'realistic' manner. The *New York Herald*, for example, had been launched in 1835 with a pledge 'to record facts, on every public and proper subject, stripped of verbiage and coloring' (cited in Shi 1995: 95). Despite the ongoing criticisms of 'sensationalism' being levelled at the penny press by the six-penny newspapers (especially with regard to crime and scandal, the coverage of which was deemed to be 'morally dubious'), there was a conviction among the editors and journalists of the new titles that there was a growing 'public demand for facts'.

This perception that the appeal of 'facts' was intensifying among newspaper readers, arguably attributable to the ascension of 'realism' in areas as diverse as science, architecture, literature and the fine arts, encouraged journalists to strive even harder to present the information on their pages in the most literal way possible. The penny press thus began to reflect a marked preference for factual news coverage (at its most literal this would simply consist of verbatim transcripts of official statements) over ('subjective') editorial explanation.

Ironically, then, as an elite press previously preoccupied with partisan interests gave way to a popular one which sought to prioritize a public interest, the goals of explanation and critique were increasingly being played down in favour of a panorama of facts ostensibly devoid of evaluative comment.

Separating 'facts' from 'values'

The introduction of the electric telegraph in the 1840s is also typically cited by newspaper historians as a crucial contributory factor informing the emergence of journalistic 'objectivity' as a professional ideal, one based on the presentation of 'unvarnished facts'. Credit for the world's first telegraphic patent belongs to two British physicists, William F. Cooke and Sir Charles Wheatstone, who together in 1836 created a prototype system. The first fully working version was patented the following year by Samuel F.B. Morse in the United States. It would take about another six years, and a substantial financial investment from the US Congress, before an experimental telegraphic line was ready to be tested before the public. This successful demonstration, which took place on 1 May 1844, relayed the news from Baltimore that the Whig Party had nominated Henry Clay for President and Theodore Frelinghuysen for Vice-President to an anxious Morse waiting at the other end of the line in Washington, DC. Later that same month, Morse used his sending device in the Supreme Court chamber to tap out the first official telegraph message, 'What hath God wrought?' The second message was 'Have you any news?'

Four years later, six New York newspapers organized themselves into a monopolistic co-operative to launch the Associated Press (AP), a wire service devoted to providing equal access for its members to news from one another and, more importantly, from sources in distant sites (the Mexican War, and later the American Civil War, being prime examples). News reports, which had previously travelled by horse and boat (carrier pigeons were used only infrequently), took on an enhanced degree of timeliness which had far-reaching implications for the redefinition of a public sphere. This point was underscored by Bennett of the *New York Herald* when he commented on the significance of the telegraph for the political public sphere:

> This means of communication will have a prodigious, cohesive, and conservative influence on the republic. No better bond of union for a great confederacy of states could have been devised . . . The whole nation is impressed with the same idea at the same moment. One feeling and one impulse are thus created and maintained from the centre of the land to its uttermost extremities.
>
> (Cited in Stephens 1988: 227)

The news values of newspapers were thus being recast by a new language of dailiness, one which promoted a peculiar fascination for facts devoid of 'appreciation' to communicate a sense of an instantaneous present.

Debates regarding the strictures of non-partisan, factual reporting took on a new resonance as AP began to train its own journalists to adopt different norms of reporting. This included the 'inverted pyramid' structure of news accounts, as unreliable telegraph lines made it necessary to compress the most significant facts into the summary 'lead' paragraph. Moreover, because newspapers of very different political orientations were subscribing to its service, the 'impartiality' of AP's 'real time' news accounts became a further selling feature. 'Opinions' were left for the client newspaper to assert as was appropriate for their 'political stripe'. In the words of the head of the AP Washington bureau, an individual who had worked for the service since its inception:

> My business is to communicate facts; my instructions do not allow me to make any comment upon the facts which I communicate. My dispatches are sent to papers of all manner of politics, and the editors say they are able to make their own comments upon the facts which are sent them. I therefore confine myself to what I consider legitimate news. I do not act as a politician belonging to any school, but try to be truthful and impartial. My dispatches are merely dry matters of fact and detail. Some special correspondents may write to suit the temper of their organs. Although I try to write without regard to men or politics, I do not always escape censure.
>
> (Cited in Roshco 1975: 31)

These emergent conventions of wire service reporting, apparent as they were not only in a 'dry' language of facts but also in the routinization of journalistic practices, were clearly helping to entrench the tenets of 'objectivity' as a reportorial ideal (see also Kaplan 2009).

In Britain, the first news received by telegraph to appear in the newspaper press occurred on 6 August 1844 in the form of a telegram from Windsor Castle announcing the birth of Queen Victoria's second son. This development set in motion a series of events which would enable news to travel at breathtaking speeds. By the early 1850s, British engineers had succeeded in stretching a submarine telegraph cable across the English Channel to France, as well as one between England and Ireland. It would take several attempts before a viable transatlantic telegraph connection was established, but in 1866 a British steamship laid down a submarine cable between Valentia, Ireland and Heart's Content, Newfoundland (it was the first of 15 such cables that would be laid by 1900). Using combinations of terrestrial and submarine cables, Britain was linked by the early 1870s with South-East Asia, China and Australia, and later Africa and

South America. As Thompson (1995) points out, the advent of the telegraph was leading to the uncoupling of space and time:

> Up to the 1830s, a letter posted in England took five to eight months to reach India; and due to monsoons in the Indian Ocean, it could take two years for a reply to be received. In the 1870s, a telegram could reach Bombay in five hours, and the answer could be back on the same day . . . Rapid communication on a global scale – albeit along routes that reflected the organisation of economic and political power – was a reality.
>
> (Thompson 1995: 154)

Most of the information being transmitted along these lines was of a commercial nature, often consisting of financial data such as forecasts about commodity trading. Various governments were also quick to exploit the technology, primarily for political (and, as in the case of the Boer War, military) advantage. News of interest to the public made up only a small part of the messages, but its significance for how newspaper organizations 'covered' the world was profound.

'Telegraphic journalism', as it was sometimes called at the time by commentators, dramatically transformed how newspaper readers perceived the world around them. The 'latest telegrams' were rapidly becoming a regular feature of most dailies, thereby creating a sense of immediacy which was making 'news' and 'newspapers' synonymous. Just as was the case with their counterparts in the US, British journalists were placing a greater emphasis on processing 'bare facts' in 'plain and unadorned English'. Each word of a news account had to be justified in terms of cost, which meant that the more traditional forms of news language were stripped of their more personalized inflections. This development was particularly pronounced in relation to 'foreign' news, where the public demand for it was growing (especially with respect to the British Empire) in direct relation to increases in the costs associated with providing it. Of the mid-century daily newspapers, only *The Times* was willing and able to meet the expense of an extensive network of correspondents and 'stringers' to telegraph news from around the world. For its rivals, an alternative source of foreign news were the daily reports being relayed by the European news agencies, the most important of which for British newspapers was Reuters (Havas of France and Wolff of Germany were the other two main ones; see also Boyd-Barrett 1978; Palmer 1978; Read 1992; Rantanen 1997).

The telegraphic news coverage generated by the Reuters news agency provided the other leading newspapers in London with the means to compete with *The Times* for a fraction of the price otherwise necessary to set up an independent set of news bureaux. Established as a financial service in London in 1851 by Julius Reuter, a German journalist, by 1858 the agency had evolved into one entrusted to supply news from around Britain and the world with unrivalled speed and accuracy. Considerable pride was taken in communicating the essential facts of 'hard' or 'spot' news free from the distorting influences of personal opinion. Commenting on the constraints which conditioned the norms of telegraphic reporting, Sigismund Engländer, Reuter's chief assistant, declared in 1889:

> I inaugurated myself, nearly thirty years ago, the present service of sober, naked statements of facts for our services, but at that time the newspapers published only a few sober telegraphic announcements of facts, and telegraphy itself was in its infancy: but your Editors still shrink from developing any light and colour in the service, and believe the dull skeleton of telegrams alone to be acceptable.
>
> (Cited in Read 1992: 103)

More than one newspaper editor shared Engländer's concern about this over-reliance on 'naked statements of facts'. For example, Lord Burnham of the *Daily Telegraph* wrote:

> On 9th May 1864, a naval battle took place between the fleet of Denmark and the combined fleets of Austria and Russia. If there be anything in which the British public takes deep interest, it is a sea fight; yet here was a battle almost within earshot of our own eastern seaboard, and the London press on the following morning published less than a quarter of a column of details, supplied by Reuter's agency. There was no special correspondence, no graphic narrative.
>
> (Cited in Palmer 1978: 207)

Burnham proceeded to argue that this problem would eventually improve by the next century, but it was becoming apparent to many at the time that the near fetishization of facts for their own sake was the driving logic of telegraphic journalism. Indeed, this logic was neatly pinpointed when, in 1894, a correspondent for *The Times* was informed that 'telegrams are for facts; appreciation and political comment can come by post' (cited by Stephens 1988: 258).

The toil of ink-stained hacks

Current debates over whether or not journalism properly constitutes a fully-fledged profession, one with specialized rules of method and ethical conduct (like medicine, law or engineering), date back at least to the early nineteenth century. It was about that time when the term 'journalist' was becoming widely used, although journalism itself was not held to be worthy of the efforts of a gentleman, let alone a gentlewoman, with the possible exception of the writing of editorial leaders for *The Times*. Its gradual climb to 'respectable', if not prestigious, status encountered several difficulties along the way. An example of the sort of attack launched by critics includes that expressed by the philosopher John Stuart Mill:

> In France the best thinkers and writers of the nation write in the journals and direct public opinion; but our daily and weekly writers are the lowest hacks of literature which, when it is a trade, is the vilest and most degrading of all trades because more of affectation and hypocrisy and more subservience to the baser feelings of others are necessary for carrying it on, than for any other trade, from that of the brothel-keeper up.
>
> (Cited in Elliott 1978: 177)

Efforts to organize journalism as a profession took a significant step forward when the National Association of Journalists was founded in 1884 (it would become a royal chartered institute six years later: see Underwood 1992). Its main aim, according to Elliott (1978: 175), was 'to achieve professional status for journalists by promoting the interests of journalists, raising their status and qualifications, supervising their professional duties and testing qualifications for membership'. An alternative definition of professionalism, this one based upon unionism, was mobilized in 1907 when the National Union of Journalists (NUJ) became the world's first trade union for journalists (Ecclestone 1992). Primarily concerned with enhancing the living conditions of its members, the NUJ fought for a national agreement on minimum wages which was eventually achieved in 1919 (see also Bromley 1997).

Several historians, in examining evidence of the day-to-day routines of news writing in the nineteenth century, have highlighted the significance of certain reporting practices for attempts to justify a claim to professional status. The fundamental virtues of the 'respectable' journalist, according to this emergent ethos, were speed, accuracy and the ability to work under deadline pressure (here 'respectable' typically meant male, as by sexist reasoning women were deemed to be 'unsuited' for the task; see Mills 1990; Sebba 1994; see also Chapter 7). The temporal constraints of periodicity meant that journalists were now favouring those types of 'news events' which were likely to change on a daily basis. As well, the growing public demand for facts meant that accounts had to be double-checked in order to ensure an 'unblemished version of events'. Here the significance of the practice of shorthand as part of the journalist's craft comes into play, as Smith (1978) writes:

> The acquisition of various systems of shorthand, leading up eventually to the universally applicable system perfected by Pitman, gave reporters their true mystery. It separated the correspondent from the reporter. It meant that a man [*sic*] could specialise in observing or hearing and recording

> with precision . . . It gave the reporter an aura of neutrality as he stood between event and reader; it gave him the chance to feel that he represented the interests of the newspaper's clients; it connected the task of reporting to the perspective of experimental science; and it gave the writer a tool which enabled him to aspire to the status of the engineer and the philosopher.
>
> (Smith 1978: 162)

By the end of the nineteenth century, journalists recognized that a knowledge of shorthand was crucial if the rudimentary standards of 'objectivity' were to be upheld as being representative of professionalism.

Appeals to professionalism, as noted above, have always been hotly contested among journalists in the US. Some historians maintain that journalists began referring to their craft as a profession as early as the Civil War, while others eschew the idea of professional status altogether. In any case, there seems little doubt that it was the penny press in the 1830s which firmly established the institution of paid reporters, although it would still take several more decades for salaried positions to become the norm. By mid-century, various social clubs and press societies were being created as informal, shared spaces for journalists to meet to discuss their concerns about what was rapidly becoming – in the eyes of many of them – a 'profession' (this when the drinking of toasts from skulls was not an unknown practice at some of these clubs). These spaces were formally inaugurated after the Civil War with the opening of the New York Press Club in 1873. It was in this period, just as the newspaper was being redefined as a big business requiring financial investment on a large scale, that journalists' formal claims to a professional status deserving of public esteem were becoming widespread. As Schudson (1978) points out, this status was contingent upon the public recognizing certain differences between the so-called 'old-time reporter' and the 'new reporter':

> The 'old reporter', according to the standard mythology, was a hack who wrote for his [*sic*] paycheck and no more. He was uneducated and proud of his ignorance; he was regularly drunk and proud of his alcoholism. Journalism, to him, was just a job. The 'new reporter' was younger, more naïve, more energetic and ambitious, college-educated, and usually sober. He was passionately attached to his job.
>
> (Schudson 1978: 69)

Concomitant with this shift from reporting as a provisional occupation like any other to a 'respectable, professional career' was a growing perception among journalists themselves that they were assuming, at the same time, a responsibility to contribute to the general welfare of an increasingly democratic society (see also Hardt and Brennen 1995; Leonard 1995; Matheson 2003; Donsbach 2009; Örnebring 2009).

In common with certain other occupational groups, such as those of medicine or law, many British and US journalists sought to legitimize their claim to professional status with reference to a larger sense of 'public responsibility'. More specifically, this affirmation of a specific obligation to the reader was typically framed on the basis of a commitment to exposing the 'truth' about public affairs, regardless of the consequences, and no matter how unpalatable. These and related developments were informing the emergence of newspaper titles determined to adopt a progressive 'crusading' role in the name of public service. Leading the way in the US was *The New York Times*, a daily generally held by 'opinion leaders' to be the embodiment of reasoned, factual news coverage. Illustrative of this endorsement of 'straight' reporting is a statement made by the publisher Adolph Ochs, who purchased the title in August 1896. In the course of outlining the newspaper's policies following his acquisition of the title, Ochs declared:

> It will be my earnest aim that *The New York Times* give the news, all the news, in concise and attractive form, in language that is parliamentary in good society, and give it as early, if not earlier, than it can be learned through any other reliable medium; to give the news impartially, without fear or favor, regardless of any party, sect or interest involved; to make the columns of *The New York Times* a forum for the consideration of all questions of public importance, and to that end to invite intelligent discussion from all shades of opinion.
>
> (Cited in Schudson 1978: 110–11)

This quotation highlights a convergence of the discourses of factual journalism with those of professional responsibility *vis-à-vis* the public sphere in general, and the interests of its affluent readers in particular. With its new motto of 'All the news that's fit to Print', the *New York Times* sought to claim for itself the status of an open forum for debating public affairs. This when the boundaries of its definition of 'serving the public' were recurrently projected in a way which justified existing relations of power and privilege, namely those of wealthy white males, as being consistent with American democracy.

'Objectivity' as a professional ideal

In the years immediately following the close of the First World War in Europe, the necessary conditions were in place for a general affirmation of the tenets of 'objectivity' among both journalists and their critics. Popular disillusionment not only with state propaganda campaigns but also with the recent advent of 'press agents' and 'publicity experts' had helped to create a wariness of 'official' channels of information. For those journalists alert to the danger of equating reality with official definitions of truth, the need for more 'scientific' methods to process facts was increasingly being recognized.

There is sufficient evidence to suggest that over the course of the 1920s the ideal of 'neutral' reporting gradually became synonymous with the invocation of the 'public interest' for many news organizations. While in Britain this ideal tended to be left implicit to most definitions of journalistic practice, in the US it was formally enshrined as a professional standard by a number of different bodies. By way of example, in April 1923 the American Society of Newspaper Editors announced their 'canons' of journalism, the fifth one of which reads, in its entirety, as follows:

> Impartiality – Sound practice makes clear distinction between news reports and expressions of opinion. News reports should be free from opinion or bias of any kind.
>
> 1. This rule does not apply to so-called special articles unmistakably devoted to advocacy or characterized by a signature authorizing the writer's own conclusions and interpretations.
>
> (Cited in Roshco 1975: 46; see also Willis 1991; Salcetti 1995; Matheson 2000)

In other words, 'impartiality' demanded of journalists that they distinguish 'facts' from 'values' if their respective newspaper was to be recognized as a free arbiter of truth. As many of these journalists quickly discovered, however, such a commitment to 'value-free' reporting frequently had disturbing implications in professional terms. Specifically, many of the most passionate advocates of 'objective journalism' were the very editors and publishers intent on opposing the unionization of their newspapers. From this self-serving perspective, a journalist could hardly be a dispassionate, non-partisan observer while, at the same time, belonging to such a 'controversial' organization as a union.

Interestingly, the near-obsession with 'objectivity' indicative of most US newspapers often encountered criticism from abroad. According to one historian, for example, the French 'condemned a worsening quality of journalism, which put facts before ideas, and attributed it to "americanisation" ' (Lee 1976: 231). Then again, in somewhat stronger language, the US press baron Joseph Pulitzer declared: 'In America, we want facts. Who cares about the philosophical speculations of our correspondents?' (cited in Chalaby 1996: 311). In any case, this appeal to 'objective', non-'biased' reporting was slowly becoming institutionalized, to varying degrees, throughout the 1920s in the growing professional culture of US and British (albeit to a lesser extent) journalism. Evidence of this gradual process of institutionalization is apparent in factors such as the following:

- more reporters began to specialize in relation to distinct news topics (labour, science, agriculture, and so forth) using 'impersonal', fact-centred techniques of observation
- there was further refinement in news interview conventions, leading to more aggressive questions being asked of public figures (the interview itself being a relatively recent invention)
- more prominence was given to the by-lined news account
- greater emphasis was placed on new genres of 'investigative' and 'interpretative' reporting, the latter being increasingly displaced from 'hard news' into political columns
- there was a more pronounced reliance on quotation marks for source attribution
- finally, improvements in the relative degree of autonomy from the day-to-day control of both proprietors and editors were being secured.

Each of these developments spoke in a different way to public scepticism about the ideal of realizing 'the plain truth' on the pages of a newspaper. By dispensing with the language of 'truth' in favour of that of 'objectivity', journalists underscored the necessity of discerning how 'the world out there' was being represented from an interested or 'biased' viewpoint. That said, however, even if each and every statement of fact was to be subject to verification, the professionally validated rules and procedures of 'objective' reporting did not directly call into question the existence of absolute truth. 'Objectivity' demanded of journalists only that their role be delimited to one of facilitating the public's right of access to facts free from partisan values.

One of the most influential journalists writing in the US in the 1920s, Walter Lippmann, gave voice to this redefinition in his book *Liberty and the News*. 'Merely to talk about the reporter in terms of his [or her] real importance to civilization will make newspaper men laugh', Lippmann (1920) observed. 'Yet reporting is a post of peculiar honor. Observation must precede every other activity, and the public observer (that is, the reporter) is a man [or woman] of critical value' (1920: 79–80). At stake in this process was nothing less than the very health of democratic society itself, he believed. The 'objective information' required for governing institutions to operate effectively necessitates that the press supply 'trustworthy news', a role demanding that the 'newspaper enterprise' be transformed from 'a haphazard trade into a disciplined profession'. In his next book, *Public Opinion*, published two years later, he further clarified this point. 'The function of news,' he wrote, 'is to signalize an event, the function of truth is to bring to light the hidden facts, to set them into relation with each other, and make a picture of reality on which men [*sic*] can act' (1922: 226). It was his view that only through 'accomplished facts' would news be able to 'separate itself from the ocean of possible truth'.

Chapter 3 extends this discussion of objectivity by investigating how these types of issues were dealt with in the early days of both radio and televisual news broadcasting in Britain and the US.

3

THE EARLY DAYS OF RADIO AND TELEVISION NEWS

> Television newsreels will, of course, continue to develop and be of the greatest interest and attraction, but there is surely not the least possibility that they will ever replace the news on sound.
>
> (Lord Simon of Wythenshawe, Chair of the BBC Board of Governors 1947–52)

> Before you leave home in the morning, even before you finish your second cup of coffee, you are going to become an ear and eyewitness to every major world event – as it happened while you slept, as it happens *now* . . . This is the morning briefing session that will arm you with information to meet the day more fully than any citizen has ever been armed before.
>
> (Announcement made at the launch of NBC morning news programme 'Today', 14 January 1952)

The thorny issue of whether or not journalists are capable of providing a 'duly impartial' account of the social world has long preoccupied many researchers interested in the operation of the news media in modern societies. As we saw in Chapter 2, the norms and conventions broadly held to be indicative of news factuality have undergone a series of important changes since the arrival of the daily newspaper in the eighteenth century. In this chapter, our discussion carries on from the 1920s, where we left off, but initiates a turn to consider the early days of radio and television news broadcasting.

Once again, we shall retain a dual focus on developments in reportage in both Britain and the United States. Such an approach, it is hoped, will enable a number of comparisons to be made by highlighting points of similarity and difference between their respective news cultures. Moreover, it is important to bear in mind that at the time, as is the case now, these two models of broadcasting provided many journalists located around the world with formative sources of alternative ideas, strategies and tactics to use when defining what should count as a proper, authoritative 'newscast'. On this basis, it will be shown how notions such as 'impartiality', 'balance' and 'fairness' were encodified as guiding principles for broadcast journalism in these two countries in surprisingly different ways. I shall argue that despite these differences, however, there was a shared desire on the part of broadcasters to offset fears, both governmental and corporate, about the dangers these new forms of journalism might pose *vis-à-vis* the articulation of popular dissent across the public sphere.

BBC News on the 'wireless'

When the British Broadcasting Company began its General News bulletins from London on 23 December 1922, it did not have in its employ a single journalist engaged in reporting the day's news. The cries of alarm expressed by newspaper proprietors about unfair competition from the wireless had been taken so seriously that a prescriptive injunction was inserted in the company's licence. BBC news reports were to be strictly limited to summaries prepared by a consortium of news agencies (Reuters, the Press Association, Exchange Telegraph and Central News) and then broadcast only after 7:00 pm, so as to minimize any potential harm to the sales figures of the daily press.

Improvements in this situation were achieved only gradually, even though John Reith, the managing director-general of the BBC (he would later be the first director-general of the corporation from 1927 to 1938), consistently petitioned the postmaster-general to reduce the restrictions on news coverage. In 1924, for example, he wrote a letter requesting 'permission to handle controversial subjects, providing we can guarantee absolute impartiality in the act' (cited in Scannell and Cardiff 1991: 27). His request was flatly denied; 'controversial' matters continued to be prohibited for fear of their potentially dangerous influence on public opinion.

About two years later, during the General Strike of May 1926, the BBC was provided with a remarkable opportunity to proclaim its independence while, at the same time, demonstrating its willingness to obey government instructions behind the scenes. The strike having temporarily closed almost all of the newspapers, the public turned to the wireless for reports on the crisis; the BBC responded with up to five bulletins a day, most of which included at least some material it had gathered itself. At stake was the BBC's political loyalty, an issue which was framed in terms of its capacity to uphold the tenets of 'responsible' (that is, non-controversial) reporting in the name of 'impartiality'. As Reith wrote in a memorandum to Stanley Baldwin, the Prime Minister, the BBC could be trusted to endorse the government's position against that of the trade union movement. In his words: 'Assuming the BBC is for the people and that the Government is for the people, it follows that the BBC must be for the Government in this crisis too' (cited in Burns 1977: 16–17). Government ministers were therefore given direct access to BBC microphones in order to advance their definitions of the crisis, while voices from the opposition parties and the trade unions were virtually silenced. Many listeners who were disgruntled with the 'one-sided' radio coverage, as one historian notes, took to using the term BFC (British Falsehood Corporation) to express their indignation (Pegg 1983: 180).

This 'baptism of fire' for the BBC, as it was later characterized by some newspaper commentators, underlined how the direct line of control held by the state over the company under the legal authority of the Wireless Broadcasting Licence was being translated into self-censorship. At the same time, however, the strike proved that a national audience could be created for broadcasting. In the words of Hilda Matheson, the first head of the Talks Department, writing in 1926: 'The public and wireless listeners are now nearly synonymous terms' (cited in Curran and Seaton 1997: 141; see also Briggs 1961–95; Davies 1994; Crisell 1997).

In the years immediately following the General Strike, Reith sought to further enhance public trust in the BBC's 'authentic impartial news'. He recognized that a greater degree of independence would have to be established for the company from direct government surveillance, even if the use of such pressure was the exception rather than the rule. His efforts were largely in vain, although he did achieve some success in advancing a revisioning of the BBC, in institutional terms, as a national service in the public interest which was deserving of a more prominent reportorial role. By January 1927, when the BBC had achieved corporation status by royal charter, an earlier time slot of 6:30 pm had been secured for the news bulletins. Further concessions had also been won with regard to the use of live 'eyewitness accounts' (especially in the case of sporting contests and public events, such as the coronation of 1937).

Still forced under its licence conditions to avoid any type of programming that could be regarded as controversial, which was also taken to apply to the proceedings of Parliament, the corporation nevertheless began to grant itself more latitude in the imposition of self-censorship despite the postmaster-general's veto power. The government's confidence in the BBC's willingness to be respectful of the limits of its 'independence' was slowly being reinforced, and the ban on controversial broadcasts was lifted in 1928 (if only experimentally at first). There was also at this time a growing sense that the mutual interests of the Post Office, the newspaper proprietors and the press agencies were inhibiting the introduction of the more interesting and informative news formats being offered by broadcasting systems in other countries. By way of an example, the BBC's extremely narrow definition of what were appropriate 'news values' meant that on Good Friday 1930, its news editors declared that in their view 'there was no news of the normal type or standard for broadcasting, and as a result no news bulletin was given' (cited in Scannell and Cardiff (1991: 118) who observe, in turn, that the announcer simply declared that 'there is no news tonight'). While this 'no news' news bulletin cannot be regarded as typical, it does provide a telling illustration of the relative rigidity of the topical parameters (and their attendant 'news values') within which the corporation was attempting to operate in order to placate its administrators.

By the end of 1934, changes were under way to turn BBC News into an independent department, a move designed, in part, to further encourage public confidence in its corporate ethic of neutrality. The separation of News from the Talks Department was linked, in part, to charges of 'bias' being made against the latter department. If newspaper commentators framed the new division as the BBC's 'Answer to Tory Suspicions of Radicalism', within the corporation 'it was seen as a result of a sustained campaign by the right-wing press against alleged BBC "redness" ' (Scannell and Cardiff 1991: 118). Also under way at this time was a gradual shift to embrace more accessible, if not popularized, norms of reporting, particularly with respect to questions of style, tone and format. In 1936, the journalist Richard Dimbleby, who would later be recognized as perhaps the most influential radio reporter ever to work for the BBC, proposed a radical redefinition of what should constitute radio news:

> It is my impression, and I find it shared by many others, that it would be possible to enliven the News to some extent without spoiling the authoritative tone for which it is famed. As a journalist, I think I know something of the demand which the public makes for a 'News angle', and how it can be provided. I suggest that a member or members of your staff – they could be called 'BBC reporters or BBC correspondents' – should be held in readiness, just as are the evening paper men [*sic*], to cover unexpected News for that day. In the event of a big fire, strike, civil commotion, railway accidents, pit accidents, or any other major catastrophes in which the public, I fear, is deeply interested, a reporter could be sent from Broadcasting House to cover the event for the bulletin.
>
> (Cited in Scannell and Cardiff 1991: 122)

This configuration of a public audience for the bulletins which is demanding a 'news angle', and one which is 'deeply interested' in catastrophes (perhaps regrettably so in Dimbleby's eyes), cut against the grain of previous conceptions of the BBC's audience. Moreover, it brought to the fore the issue of what type of newscast would be best suited to presenting the news (see also Miall 1966). Interestingly 1936 would also see the BBC undertake its first rudimentary forms of audience research.

The corporation's self-declared responsibilities *vis-à-vis* the listening public were posited within the dictates of government influence, notwithstanding its occasional assertion to the contrary. For this and related reasons, it would be years before Dimbleby's vision was realized. In the meantime, the news bulletin's authoritative claim to impartiality relied almost exclusively on material acquired via the news agencies, even in those instances where the newer forms of technology made 'on the spot' reports possible. Deviations from this general pattern would occur only rarely until the outbreak of war, clearly the most important of which was the live broadcast (on both radio and television) of Prime Minister Neville Chamberlain's return to London from his meeting with Adolph Hitler in Munich. Still, when Britain declared war against Germany in September 1939, the BBC possessed only a tiny staff of reporters, of whom one was Dimbleby, to call into action.

Over the course of the early years of the war, a variety of reportorial innovations would rewrite the conventions of radio journalism. In rounding out this section, our attention turns to the events of D-Day, the first major test of the BBC's newly fashioned War Reporting Unit. Just past dawn on the morning of 6 June 1944, when hundreds of ships began approaching the Normandy coastline of France, the Unit was primed to cover the event. The Corporation broke the news to its listeners at 8:00 am that morning, with announcer Freddy Allen reading the statement: 'Supreme Allied Headquarters have issued an urgent warning to inhabitants of the enemy-occupied countries living near the coast. The warning said that a new phase in the Allied Air offensive had begun' (cited in Nicholas 1996: 211–12). It was followed by a short extract drawn from a 'flash' from a monitored German source, the Transocean news agency, reporting that Allied paratroops had landed in France. At 9:32 am, a special bulletin declared the official news that 'D-Day has come . . .', citing as its source Communiqué No. 1 from Supreme Headquarters Allied Expeditionary Forces (SHAEF). The Communiqué simply stated: 'Under the command of General Eisenhower, Allied Naval Forces, supported by strong Air Forces, began landing Allied Armies this morning on the northern coast of France' (cited in Hibberd 1950: 253).

More substantive details would emerge in news bulletins over the course of the day, supplemented by eyewitness perspectives provided by the Corporation's correspondents (no longer described as 'observers'). In anticipation of the invasion, 48 of these correspondents had been assembled into the War Reporting Unit in May of the previous year. Each of them was experienced in providing 'actuality' in vivid terms, making effective use of the 'midget' recorders devised by BBC engineers. These recording machines were lightweight (or, at 40 lbs, relatively so) and portable, enabling the correspondent to record one hour's worth of material on 12 double-sided discs stored in the lid (Cumberlege 1946; Royle 1987). The resultant forms of 'on the spot' field reporting, engendering at times a breathtaking quality of immediacy, were intended to furnish the listener with 'pictures in sound'.

Interestingly, it was the launch of a new programme on D-Day, the 30-minute *War Report*, which formally marked a turning point in the BBC's war reportage. It was announcer John Snagge who introduced *War Report* to listeners immediately after the Nine O'Clock News, its regular timeslot from that day forward. This first edition of the programme highlighted radio's technological reach with on-the-spot actuality material – both live and recorded – from a range of correspondents reporting events at first hand. Included that day were dispatches recorded 'live' the night before by correspondents awaiting embarkation with the Allied forces, as well as Richard Dimbleby (the Corporation's first accredited war correspondent), Frank Gillard and Howard Marshall from the shores of Normandy. In the hours to come, some 17 BBC correspondents 'sailed with the navies, flew with the bombers, jumped with the paras, landed with the gliders and hit the beaches with the US and British armies' (Hudson and Stanier 1997: 69–70). Evidently Snagge's words, 'and now over to Normandy', were long remembered afterwards (Miall 1994: 26).

By making extensive use of actuality material, a new approach to radio journalism was being fashioned with an extraordinary appeal for audiences demanding 'authentic' news. Adopting an 'essentially personal and informal' style, this 'news magazine' went to the air every night in the months to come as the invasion continued apace, regularly attracting 10 to 15 million listeners in Britain (and millions more overseas). *War Report*, in the BBC's own words, promised to deliver the 'latest and fullest picture of the war' to the listener. It 'took the microphone to places where things were happening, and let it listen – as one would one's self like to listen – to the sounds of battle, to the voices of men just returned from the fighting line, to observers who spent that day touring the scene of action' (cited in Briggs 1970: 662).

In the case of correspondent Frank Gillard, for example, the opportunity to report from Normandy finally came when he scrambled ashore with troops in an assault craft. His first-hand observations, recorded from the beach at Arromanches, stated:

> At first sight everything round the beaches still looks chaotic – there's still so much wreckage and litter lying about. Smashed-up buildings, tangles of wire, heaps of driftwood, enormous bomb-craters, waterlogged landing-craft just pushed out of the way . . . wrecked vehicles piled one on top

> of another . . . but despite appearances everything is thoroughly under control. To prove it there are those unending columns of men and vehicles pouring inland in perfect order . . .
>
> (Cited in Stroud 1969: 35)

Reporting under near-constant artillery fire and bombing, Gillard made the best of a difficult situation on the beach area, before finally being able to move inland with the advancing troops. Movement was difficult, not only because of the enemy counterattack, but also because of the cumbersome weight of the recording equipment. Even when a set of recordings was complete, ensuring its safe return to Britain was at times a formidable challenge. 'You just took your chance,' he later recalled, 'and gave them to anybody who was going back. I was always going down to the beaches hoping to find a destroyer or other craft that was making a return journey' (cited in Stroud 1969: 36). It was only on the third day, when landing-strips had at last been secured, that matters improved. Gillard was able to arrange with pilots to take the heavy discs back for the BBC to broadcast. It would be the Royal Signals, however, who provided a more practical long-term solution, namely by making available a truck with a VHF transmitter perched high on the seafront's cliffs. Once given the official go-ahead, he was able to speak – subject to the constraints of censorship – directly to the BBC.

Public recognition of the BBC's reportorial achievements registered on both sides of the Atlantic, and beyond. In the US, for example, some 725 radio stations had rebroadcast BBC invasion news. The 'actuality' recordings of the sounds of warfare, like the voices of the soldiers, were said to have made a particularly deep impression with members of the public. 'Beginning at 12:40 am last Tuesday, and on through the day you had a feeling that radio, in its capacity as an informant, had grown up', observed *The New York Times*. 'The service of the British Broadcasting Corporation, as D-Day listeners know, was not less than superb. [Its actuality broadcasts] came over bringing a sense of reality and on-the-spot realism beside which the contrived studio program seemed virtually static' (*The New York Times*, 10 June 1944; see Cumberlege 1946: 52–3; Briggs 1970: 637).

The start of radio news in the US

It is difficult to say precisely when radio news broadcasting began in the United States. This is partially a problem of defining what constitutes a fully fledged newscast, but also a recognition of how dispersed the array of different radio stations was compared with a centralized BBC network (a situation aptly described by one commentator as 'chaos in the ether'). News had been relayed by 'wireless telegraphy' since the earliest experimental broadcasts, but the audience was almost entirely restricted to those 'ham' or 'amateur' operators who happened to be listening in on their crystal sets with earphones. One early event of note was the decision made by a Detroit newspaper, the *News*, to announce the returns from the local, state and congressional primary elections on 31 August 1920. The next day's edition of the newspaper declared:

> The sending of the election returns by the Detroit *News* Radiophone Tuesday night was fraught with romance, and must go down in the history of man's [*sic*] conquest of the elements as a gigantic step in his progress. In the four hours that the apparatus, set up in an out-of-the-way corner of the *News* building, was hissing and whirring its message into space, few realized that a dream and a prediction had come true. The news of the world was being given forth through this invisible trumpet to the waiting crowds in the unseen market place.
>
> (Cited in McLauchlin 1975: 111)

Evident in this quotation are a number of interesting points, not least of which is the configuration of the public sphere as an 'unseen market place'. Rather tellingly, and in sharp contrast with notions of public service broadcasting developing in Britain and elsewhere at the time, this commercialized rendering of the audience for radio underscored its profit potential.

Historians more typically identify a scheduled broadcast made in Pittsburgh on 2 November 1920 as deserving particular attention. That night, station KDKA (operated by the Westinghouse Corporation) went on the air to relay news of the Harding–Cox presidential election returns, an event which attracted thousands of wireless enthusiasts. The broadcast, using a 100-watt transmitter, took place in a shack built atop of one of Westinghouse's taller buildings as a temporary studio. To help fill the gaps between returns, a hand-wound phonograph was used. The resultant 'radio mania' sparked by this 'national sensation' spread far and wide, to the extent that sales of receiving sets reached about 100,000 by 1922, and over half a million in 1923 (Lichty and Topping 1975; Czitrom 1982; Fang 1997). By 1925, 'five and a half million radio sets were in use in the United States,' according to Stephens (1988: 276), 'nearly half the number in use in the world.'

It was the financial imperative of increasing radio equipment sales which led the manufacturing companies to introduce regular forms of programming on their stations. KDKA was soon joined in broadcasting news bulletins by a number of stations situated across the US. The station WJAG in Nebraska, owned by the Norfolk *Daily News*, was arguably the first to inaugurate a daily noon-time news broadcast on 26 July 1922, while the New York *Tribune* aired a daily fifteen-minute news summary via WJZ beginning 3 February 1923 (Danna 1975a). It was typically the case that these stations derived the content for these bulletins from newspaper accounts, namely because it was far cheaper to have the announcers read 'borrowed' extracts than it was to employ reporters to generate news.

By the early 1930s, the public was becoming accustomed to the idea of this new medium as a 'hard' news channel. NBC, with Lowell Thomas, had been the first to launch a fifteen-minute newscast five times a week in 1930, with the other networks following in step by 1932. Two news events occurred in 1932 which highlight, from the vantage point of today, several aspects of what was becoming distinctive about radio news. The first was the tragic kidnapping of the infant son of Charles and Anne Morrow Lindbergh in New Jersey on 1 March of that year. Charles Lindbergh was a world-famous aviator, having been the first person to make a solo non-stop flight across the Atlantic Ocean on 20–21 May 1927. Reporters with NBC News were among the first to learn of the kidnapping, yet the network evidently refused to broadcast the story because it was judged to be 'too sensational'. This decision was reversed hours later as NBC joined other stations in clearing its evening schedules for several days as news flashes brought fresh details to light (the child's body would not be discovered for about ten weeks). The sheer volume of the news reports was unprecedented, leading some to argue at the time that it represented 'perhaps the greatest example of spot news reporting in the history of American broadcasting' (cited in Bliss 1991: 31). In their relentless coverage of the story, radio journalists were seeking to out-manoeuvre their newspaper rivals so as to be recognized as the best sources of information for a public desperate for the latest revelation. And they succeeded.

The second formative event of 1932 was the election of President Franklin Delano Roosevelt who, in the words of one newscaster at the time, 'humanized radio in a great governmental, national sense as it had never before been humanized' (cited in MacDonald 1979: 300). The use of radio by politicians was not a new development: one of the earliest of such events had been William G. Harding's Armistice Day speech in 1921. Republican Calvin Coolidge won the first 'radio campaign' in 1924, and his inaugural address was the first to be broadcast by radio on 4 March 1925. Roosevelt, however, would be the first to fully exploit the medium as a means to decisively reshape public opinion. Shortly after his victory, he initiated a series of 'fireside chats' where he spoke in a relaxed, informal manner to the radio audience about matters of national policy. Radio, according to one commentator, was now able to 'bring the people right into the White House'. Elsewhere, it was pointed out that: 'Perhaps for the first time in American history the people of the nation were made to feel that they knew their President personally and that they were receiving inside information firsthand on important events' (cited in Lichty and Topping 1975: 302). Still, radio journalists were prohibited from attending the Senate and House press galleries, and instead were forced to use the visitors' galleries as their workplace.

Election night in 1932 had also provided radio with the opportunity to show how easily it could 'scoop' the press by reporting election returns swiftly and comprehensively. For the newspaper industry, this was the last straw. The public's growing interest in radio news programming had been worrying industry executives for some time. They were anxious about the competition for audiences that it posed, particularly where advertising revenues were concerned (several newspapers had reacted by purchasing radio stations). Nor had the broadcasters' practice of selectively 'lifting' news from the press escaped their attention. If initially they had been satisfied with on-air credit for being the source of the news items (many of which were produced via the wires services they effectively controlled), in the aftermath of the election the situation had deteriorated to the point of an all-out 'press–radio war'. In April 1933 the Newspaper Publishers' Association, the principal organization of newspaper executives, together with the major news wire services, sought to bring any further encroachment on their profitability to a halt through a variety of tactics. These tactics included, among others, charging an advertising fee for printing daily radio schedules on their pages, intimidating the sponsors of radio newscasts into placing their advertisements exclusively in the press, and denying broadcasters access to wire service bulletins.

Before 1933 came to a close, however, the combatants in the 'press–radio war' had agreed to a compromise in what one writer called the 'smoke and hate-filled rooms' of the Hotel Biltmore in New York City (cited in Danna 1975a: 343). The so-called Biltmore Agreement meant that radio stations such as those operated by NBC and CBS could broadcast only two five-minute newscasts per day (one at 9:30 am and another at or after 9:00 pm) in order to 'protect' both morning and evening newspapers; were to ensure that only news summaries provided by the Press–Radio Bureau were used (which began on 1 March 1934); had to refrain from engaging in their own news-gathering activities; and, finally, avoid including advertisements in newscasts, although sponsorship of commentary was permitted (Danna 1975b; Sterling and Kittross 1978: 123; Bliss 1991: 42–3). This arrangement did not hold for very long, primarily because independent ('non-chain') stations, many of which were locally based, began to gather and report their own news. Moreover, the news agency Transradio had also stepped in to fill the 'news blackout gap' left behind by the Associated Press, United Press and International News Service. In about a year's time, the main tenets of the Biltmore Agreement were being openly transgressed to the point that it had been effectively rendered defunct. Other attempts to limit radio news would be launched by print media groups throughout the 1930s, but none would prove successful.

In marked contrast with the political climate in which the BBC was operating at the time, there was no corresponding attempt on the part of government regulators to enforce a definition of 'impartiality' on broadcasters. The Federal Communications Commission was established by Roosevelt's administration in 1934 to co-ordinate the use of radio (as well as the telegraph and telephone). It possessed the powers to revoke, or refuse to renew, a licence where it determined that a station's policies and programmes were inconsistent with 'the public interest, convenience and necessity' (fines could also be imposed). Such action was extremely rare, however, leading to charges being made that the FCC was little more than a 'paper tiger'. In the eyes of broadcast reformers fearful about the growing network control of radio, the FCC was failing to meet its public responsibility to ensure access to the airwaves for those groups who felt that their right to free speech was being denied (they included educators, agricultural interests, the labour movement, civil libertarians and religious groups: see Engelman 1996). Any notion of public service broadcasting, they maintained, was incompatible with the conformity of opinion represented by an advertising-dominated commercial system.

Such claims were countered by organizations such as the National Association of Broadcasters (NAB), a powerful lobbying group capable of bringing formidable pressures to bear on the FCC in order to protect the interests of commercial radio. The NAB sought to discourage the airing of 'controversial' viewpoints by imposing on its membership what it considered to be a new ethical code of practice. This code prohibited the discussion of issues deemed to be controversial outside of those news and related programmes specifically devoted to the expression of opinions. In this way, the NAB argued, it was ensuring that radio stations would be self-regulating so as to reduce the likelihood of the federal government intervening to monitor the content of programming. Although the code was legally unenforceable, it succeeded in severely restricting the diversity of voices being heard. Most broadcasters were content to interpret the code in such a manner as to virtually rule out the exploration of any subject which even had the potential to upset programme sponsors.

Critics of the NAB argued that while newscasts were not formally placed under the same restrictions, they were nevertheless being made to conform to the spirit of the code. That is to say, the values endorsed by the code affixed broadcasting's proclaimed commitment to public service within strictly commercial imperatives. The boundaries of journalistic 'impartiality' were thus being defined, in part, by a conception of the audience not as citizens in need of a public forum for argument and debate, but rather as potential consumers in search of entertaining diversions from everyday life. The implications were startling when one considers, for example, that according to a 1939 *Fortune* survey: '70 percent of Americans relied on the radio as their prime source of news and 58 percent thought it more accurate than that supplied by the press' (Czitrom 1982: 86).

The limits of 'impartiality': British television news

Although Britain's first experimental televisual programme had been transmitted from Broadcasting House on 22 August 1932, and news had made its appearance on 21 March 1938 (a recording of radio news presented without pictures), newscasts would not be a daily feature on television until 1954. The television service had returned on 7 June 1946, having been closed down during the war years, in part because of fears that enemy bombers would home in on the transmitters. The radio news division prepared a nightly summary of the news to be read on television by an unseen announcer, while a clock-face appeared as the visual component. Newsreels were now manufactured in-house, due to the refusal of the cinema newsreel companies to supply them, and outside broadcasts were also regularly featured.

The BBC, always fearful of the charge that its views were being broadcast in its newscasts, took elaborate care to ensure that it observed a commitment to 'impartiality' as a professional and public duty. Given its responsibilities as a trustee in the national interest, the corporation could not be seen to be expressing a partisan position, especially in matters of public policy. Indeed, anxieties expressed by members of the main political parties that the BBC could ultimately appropriate for itself the status of a forum for national debate to match that of Parliament led, in turn, to the implementation of the 'fourteen-day rule' beginning on 10 February 1944 (it would stay in place until 1957). By agreeing (at first informally) not to extend its coverage to issues relevant to either the House of Commons or the House of Lords for fourteen days before they were to be debated, the BBC succumbed to pressures which severely compromised its editorial independence. No such restrictions were requested *vis-à-vis* the newspaper press, nor would their imposition likely to have proven to be successful.

By the early 1950s, with Britain engaged in the war in Korea (filmed coverage of which sparked public interest in television reports), the arrival of competition from the commercial sector in the form of the Independent Television (ITV) network was imminent. BBC officials scrambled to get a daily newscast on the air prior to the launch of the new, commercial rival. Two weeks before the Television Act received the royal assent, the first edition of the BBC's *News and Newsreel* was broadcast on 5 July 1954. While the 7:30 pm programme had been heralded as 'a service of the greatest significance in the progress of television in the UK', Margaret Lane, a critic in the corporation's own journal, *The Listener*, was not convinced:

> I suppose the keenest disappointment of the week has been the news service, to which most of us had looked forward, and for which nobody I encountered had a good word. The most it can do in its present stage is to improve our geography, since it does at least offer, in magic lantern style, a series of little maps, a pointer and a voice . . . The more I see of television news in fact the more I like my newspaper.
>
> (Cited in Cox 1995: 38)

Shortly thereafter, Gerald Barry would comment in his television column in the *Observer* newspaper:

> The sad fact has to be recorded that news on television does not exist. What has been introduced nightly into the TV programmes is a perfunctory little bulletin of news flashes composed of an announcer's voice, a caption and an indifferent still photograph. This may conceivably pass as news, but it does not begin to be television.
>
> (Cited in Davis 1976: 13)

By June 1955, the title *News and Newsreel* was dropped in favour of *Television News Bulletin*. The ten minutes of news was read by an off-screen voice in an 'impersonal, sober and quiet manner', the identity of the (always male) newsreader being kept secret to preserve the institutional authority of the BBC, to the accompaniment of still pictures (as the title suggests, the news was then followed by a newsreel). Only in the final days leading up to the launch of its 'American-style' rival on the new commercial network did this practice change, and then only partially. In the first week of September 1955, the BBC introduced the faces of its newsreaders to the camera, but not their names. The danger of 'personalizing' the news as the voice of an individual, as opposed to that of the corporation, was considered to be serious enough to warrant the preservation of anonymity. This strategy, which had its origins in radio, arguably communicated an enhanced sense of detached impartiality for the newscast, and would last for another eighteen months (the policy of anonymous newsreading would continue for BBC radio until 1963: Goldie 1977; Schlesinger 1987: 37; see also Briggs 1961–95; Winston 1993; Camporesi 1994).

The Television Act (1954), introduced by Winston Churchill's Conservative Party government after two and a half years of often acrimonious debate, had set up the Independent Television Authority (for a flavour of the opposition's attacks, see Reith 1974). The ITA established, in turn, Independent Television News (ITN) as a specialist subsidiary company in February 1955. Contained in Clause 3 of the Act were the following instructions:

> 3.–(I) It shall be the duty of the Authority to satisfy themselves that, so far as possible, the programmes broadcast by the Authority comply with the following requirements, that is to say:
>
> (a) that nothing is included in the programmes which offends against good taste or decency or is likely to encourage or incite to crime or to lead to disorder or to be offensive to public feeling or which contains any offensive representation of or reference to a living person;
> (b) that the programmes maintain a proper balance in their subject-matter and a high general standard of quality;
> (c) that any news given in the programmes (in whatever form) is presented with due accuracy and impartiality; . . .
> (f) that due impartiality is preserved on the part of the persons providing the programmes as respects matters of political or industrial controversy or relating to current public policy; and
> (g) subject as hereinafter provided in this subsection, that no matter designed to serve the interests of any political party is included in the programmes.

The imposition of these prohibitions on to the independent programme companies, especially with respect to the formal obligation to observe 'due accuracy and impartiality', was broadly consistent with the general editorial policy of the BBC. Still, an important difference with respect to how impartiality was to be achieved had been signalled, if not clearly spelt out. Where the BBC generally sought to reaffirm its impartiality over a period of time, ITN would have to demonstrate a 'proper balance' of views within each individual programme.

At 10:00 pm on 22 September 1955, ITN made its début on the ITV network. The 'newscaster' for that evening, as they were to be called, was Christopher Chataway, a one-time Olympic runner who had been working as a transport officer for a brewery. The other 'personalities' hired by the network included the first female newscaster on British television, Barbara Mandell (a former radio news editor in South Africa), who presented the midday bulletin, and Robin Day, then an unknown barrister with little journalistic experience, who fronted the 7:00 pm bulletin. 'News is human and alive,' declared Aidan Crawley, ITN's first editor, 'and we intend to present it in that manner' (cited in Hayward 1998; see also Crawley 1988). This view was reaffirmed by Geoffrey Cox, who assumed the role of editor just months after the launch following the resignation of Crawley over budget disputes with the networking companies. It was Crawley and Cox's shared opinion that 'the power of personality' in presenting the news was a crucial dimension of the effort to attract public attention away from the BBC and on to ITN as a distinctive news source (see also Paulu 1961;

Sendall 1982). Here it is also interesting to note that Cox came from a newspaper tradition, namely the London *News Chronicle*, which presumably gave him a different approach to television news values than his counterparts at the BBC for whom radio news was the norm.

In contrast with the BBC's anonymous newsreaders, ITN's newscasters were given the freedom to rewrite the news in accordance with their own stylistic preferences as journalists, even to the extent of ending the newscast with a 'lighter' item to raise a smile for the viewer. Cox was well aware, though, that the advantages to be gained by having newscasters who were 'men and women of strong personality' (who also tended to be 'people of strong opinions') had to be qualified in relation to the dictates of the Television Act concerning 'due accuracy and impartiality'. Given that ITN was a subsidiary company of the four principal networking companies, lines of administrative authority were much more diffuse than was the case in the BBC or, for that matter, in the newspaper press. Still, pressure from the networking companies to increase the entertainment value of the newscasts was considerable.

Consequently, Cox (1995: 75) saw in the Act's requirements the means to negotiate an even greater degree of day-to-day autonomy from institutional constraints:

> Impartiality, if it was interpreted actively, and not passively, could be a means both of protecting our independence and of strengthening our power to gather and interpret news, to arrive at the truth. It was a safeguard against pressures not only from the Government or other people of power, but also against the views and whims of the programme companies who owned us . . . These few words [Clause 3] could free a television news editor from the proprietorial pressures which were then widespread in Fleet Street – much wider than is the case today. They could give him [*sic*] the freedom to create something new in popular journalism.

Robin Day (1995: viii), who would eventually become one of Britain's best-known journalists, has credited Cox's editorial standards at the time for securing 'vigorous, thrusting news coverage, responsibly and impartially presented in popular style' (see also Day 1989).

The question of how best to ensure that the newscast conveyed a commitment to impartiality for its audience was a serious challenge. As Day (1995) has since recalled:

> In the early formative days, he [Cox] had to inculcate a belief in impartiality into the mixed group who came together in 1955 to form the first television journalists of ITN. There was a small core of newsmen, mostly ex-BBC, headed by Arthur Clifford, the brilliant News Editor, who were

> trained in the discipline of impartiality. Others had no such background. There were cameramen and film editors from the cinema newsreels, where coverage had often been blatantly propagandist. There were journalists from Fleet Street, where proprietors expected their views to shape the contents as well as the policies of their newspapers. There were writers who believed that news should be seasoned by opinion.
>
> (Day 1995: viii)

In Day's view, Cox possessed a 'profound belief' in the principles of 'truth and fairness', qualities which meant that under his editorship 'ITN succeeded in combining the challenge and sparkle of Fleet Street with the accuracy and impartiality required by the Television Act' (Day 1995: ix). If this assertion is a somewhat boastful one, it nevertheless reaffirms how, from a journalistic point of view, the tenets of impartiality tend to be rendered as being consistent with professionalism.

This 'discipline of impartiality', with its appeal to the separation of news and opinion, also had implications for ITN's configuration of 'the public' for its newscasts. In its first year, ITN dramatically redefined the extent to which so-called 'ordinary' people could be presented in a television news account. Street-corner interviews, or vox pops as they were often called by the newscasters, began to appear on a regular basis. Moreover, at a time when 'class barriers were more marked', Cox (1995) recalls that ITN sought to portray the news in 'human terms' through reports which

> brought onto the screen people whose day to day lives had not often in the past been thought worth reflecting on the air. It gave a new meaning to the journalistic concept of the human interest story. In Fleet Street the term meant stories which were interesting because they were of the unusual, the abnormal, the exceptional. But here the cameras were making fascinating viewing out of ordinary everyday life, bestriding the gap between the classes – and making compulsive television out of it. Whether the story was hard news or not did not seem to matter. It was life, conveyed by the camera with honesty and without condescension, adding interest and humanity to the bulletins in a way unique to this new journalistic medium.
>
> (Cox 1995: 57)

Cox maintains that his sense of ITN's audience at the time was that it was 'largely working class', yet this assumption could not be allowed to 'bias' the network's news agenda. ITN's preferred definitions of 'news values', if not quite as restrictive as those of the BBC, still ensured that a potential news source's 'credibility' or 'authoritativeness' would be hierarchically determined in relation to class (as well as with regard to factors such as gender and ethnicity).

The news agenda was similarly shaped by a principle of 'impartiality' which dictated that analysis and interpretation were to be scrupulously avoided in both the spoken news and film report segments of the newscast. However, expressions of opinion could be included in the newscast through studio interviews. These 'live' segments facilitated a stronger sense of immediacy, for spontaneous or 'off the cuff' remarks added a degree of excitement that might have otherwise been denied in the name of editorial fairness or balance. Perhaps more to the point, though, they were also more 'cost-efficient' than film reports.

By 1956, the BBC had elected to follow ITN's lead. In seeking to refashion its television newscasts to meet the new 'personalized' standards of presentation audiences were coming to expect, the corporation began to identify its newsreaders by name. It also emulated ITN by allowing them to use teleprompters in order to overcome their reliance on written scripts. Further technological improvements, most notably in the quality of film processing, similarly improved the visual representation of authenticity. That said, however, the question of whether or not to use dubbed or even artificial sound to accompany otherwise silent film reports posed a particularly difficult problem for journalists anxious to avoid potential criticisms about their claim to impartiality. Much debate also ensued over what circumstances justified imitating ITN's more informal style of presentation, particularly with regard to the use of colloquial language, to enhance the newscast's popular appeal (previously BBC news writers had been told to adopt a mode of address appropriate for readers of the 'quality' press). ITN had also shown how the new lightweight 16mm film camera technology could be exploited to advantage 'in the field' for more visually compelling images (complete with 'natural sound') than those provided by the newsreel companies with their bulky 35mm equipment. Indeed, through this commitment to 'bringing to life' news stories in a dramatic way, as well as its more aggressive approach to pursuing 'scoops' (exclusives) and 'beats' (first disclosures), ITN was stealing the march on the BBC with respect to attracting a greater interest in news among viewers.

The same year also saw the range of newsworthy topics for both the BBC and ITN substantively extended with the suspension of the so-called fourteen-day rule (it would be formally withdrawn by Prime Minister Harold Macmillan in July 1957). In the absence of this form of government control, both the BBC and ITN networks were able to redefine what could count as legitimate political coverage. It was at this point, then, that they were at last effectively positioned within the public sphere to realize their current status, arguably that of alternative forums of debate to Parliament. If for some politicians their worst fears were being realized, others saw in these same developments the potential for further enhancements to the structures of democratic accountability. In any case, as Robin Day (1989: 92) would later recall in his memoirs: 'It is an incredible fact of broadcasting history that in the very year that ITN began (1955) there had been a general election in which there was no coverage by BBC broadcasters of the campaign, *not even in the news bulletins*.'

US television news begins

In December 1941, a time when war had been raging across Europe for over two years, life was close to normal for most people living in the US. That normality was abruptly shattered one Sunday, however, by a news flash from station KGU in Hawaii. Programming on the NBC radio network was interrupted as an announcer hurried on to the air to reread it to a national audience:

> BULLETIN: We have witnessed this morning the attack of Pearl Harbor and the severe bombing of Pearl Harbor by army planes that are undoubtedly Japanese. The city of Honolulu has also been attacked and considerable damage done. This battle has been going on for nearly three hours. One of the bombers dropped within fifty feet of Tanti Tower. It's no joke – it's a real war.
>
> (Cited in Rose 1975: 354–5)

This radio bulletin, complete with its errors in detail concerning the bombing of Honolulu (it would later be revealed that all but one of the explosions in the city were caused by US anti-aircraft fire) and the duration of the attack, sparked near panic across the country (Rose 1975). Everyone, it seemed, was instantly turning to radio for the latest developments; everyone, that is, with the exception of a tiny audience of people who were watching television's first 'instant special' on CBS in New York.

CBS had begun a regular television service only months earlier, providing two fifteen-minute news programmes on each weekday (described by the station as a 'roundup of news, together with the latest bulletins and background developments': cited in Nielsen 1975: 421). The news staff consisted of two people, Richard Hubbell as the newsreader and Robert Skedgell as the writer. As Skedgell would later recall: 'The newsroom, if it could be so called, was an open space just large enough to hold two desks, one UP radio wire, and a couple of filing cabinets. It looked like an insurance office' (cited in Bliss 1991: 219). The shocking news from Pearl Harbor on 7 December 1941 compelled Hubbell and Skedgell, together with the help of 'various regular radio correspondents', to broadcast their programme for the first time on a Sunday. In Skedgell's words:

> I believe we were on air at about 3:30 and continued non-stop until 1:30 the next morning . . . There was not very much hard news that Sunday night,

> so much of our report was speculative: where the Japanese fleet was, what the Japanese intentions were, where the US fleet had gone, how much damage it had suffered. Of course, the maps were brought into considerable use, along with our usual graphics ['symbols of tanks, planes, bomb bursts, sinking ships, and so forth – no film, no switches anywhere'], during the long hours.
>
> (Cited in Bliss 1991: 219–20)

In the hours following the catastrophe, as military censors turned the stream of 'hard facts' into a meagre trickle, journalists of every type were turning to official sources to add substance to conjecture. President Roosevelt's address to a joint session of Congress the following day reached an estimated 79 per cent of US radio homes, while the next evening's 'fireside chat' registered a rating of 83 per cent (Lichty and Topping 1975: 454). The television coverage, in contrast, was less than satisfactory. Due to its inability to establish a video line to Washington, CBS was reduced to providing an audio feed accompanied by a studio camera shot of a US flag, gently waving in a breeze generated by an electric fan.

Television news, which had first appeared in the US during the 1930s on several experimental stations, did not get fully under way until after the Second World War. The first regularly scheduled network newscast to adopt the general characteristics familiar to us today was *The CBS-TV News with Douglas Edwards*, which appeared in a fifteen-minute slot each weekday evening beginning in August 1948 (newscasts would not be lengthened to half an hour until September 1963). It was sponsored by the car manufacturer Oldsmobile. NBC was next with *The Camel News Caravan* beginning in February 1949, sponsored by Winston-Salem, makers of Camel cigarettes. Advertisements formed a part of each newscast, and in the case of *The Camel News Caravan* went even further. The newsreader, John Cameron Swayze, sat at a desk to read the news, a packet of Camel cigarettes and an ashtray (the word 'Camel' on its side in clear letters) strategically placed beside him. Further sponsorship 'distortions' took many forms, as Barnouw (1990) elaborates:

> Introduced at the request of the sponsor, they were considered minor aspects of good manners rather than news corruption. No news personage could be shown smoking a cigar – except Winston Churchill, whose world role gave him special dispensation from Winston-Salem. Shots of 'no smoking' signs were forbidden.
>
> (Barnouw 1990: 171)

The pace of the newscast was brisk, with the 'breezy, boutonniered' Swayze moving it forward each day with the line 'Now let's go hopscotching the world for headlines!' before bringing it to a close with his customary 'That's the story, folks. Glad we could get together!' (cited in Barnouw 1990: 102–3). Rival newscasts followed shortly thereafter on the ABC (formerly NBC's 'Blue Network') and DuMont networks (the latter collapsed in 1955).

Most of the editors and reporters who found themselves working in television news had backgrounds in newspapers, the wire services or radio news organizations. Such was likewise the case for the producers and production people, although they also tended to be drawn from wire service picture desks, newsreels and picture magazines (Nielsen 1975). The significance of these disparate backgrounds is apparent in the types of debates which emerged regarding how best to present news televisually. In essence, the television newscast represented a blending of the qualities of radio speech with the visual attributes of the newsreel. With little by way of precedent to draw upon, a number of variations on basic newscast formats were tried and tested during these early years.

If the techniques of radio news provided a basis for anchoring the authority of the voice-over, it was the newsreel which supplied a model for the form that television news might take. Aspects of this model included 'the fragmented succession of unrelated "stories", the titles composed in the manner of front page headlines, and the practice of beginning each issue with the major news event of the day, followed by successively less important subject matter' (Fielding, cited in Winston 1993: 184). Newsfilm items tended to be the principal component of the newscast (video tape was first used in network news in 1956), although switches to reporters in other cities were by now a regular feature. The performative role of the 'anchorman' (women were almost always denied this status: see Chapter 7) was also firmly established by the mid-1950s. One exception to the general rules in play was the early morning *Today* programme on NBC. Its mix of news, features and variety show elements enjoyed wide popular appeal, the latter leading to the inclusion of a charismatic chimpanzee named J. Fred Muggs as a regular member of the presenting team for several years (Barnouw 1990: 147–8, 168).

By 1954, television had displaced radio in the daily audience figures for usage of each medium, registering just under 3 hours to radio's 2.5 hours according to various surveys (Bianculli 1992: 58). Newscast formats had become relatively conventionalized from one network to the next by this time, although the question of how journalistic notions of 'impartiality' and 'fairness' were to be achieved in practical terms was the subject of considerable dispute. The determined search for ever larger ratings figures, due to the higher sponsorship revenues they could demand, made television news increasingly image-oriented in its drive to attract audiences. An emphasis was routinely placed on staged events, primarily because they were usually packaged by the news promoters behind them (whether governmental or corporate) with the visual needs of television in mind. News of celebrities, speeches by public figures, carnivals and fashion shows made for 'good television', and such coverage was less likely to conflict with sales of advertising time.

Significantly, then, the very features of television news which some critics pointed to as being vulgar, banal or trivial were often the same ones which advertisers believed created an appropriate tone for the content surrounding their messages. Pressure was recurrently brought to bear on the networks to ensure that their viewers, as potential consumers, would not be offended by newscasts presenting the viewpoints of those from outside the limits of pro-business 'respectability'.

At the same time, the networks were also under increasing pressure from the Federal Communications Commission to observe the tenets of what would eventually evolve into a fully fledged 'Fairness Doctrine' as part of their licence obligations. Attempts had been made by the FCC even before a statutory basis for the doctrine was established in 1959 to enforce a principle whereby the right of stations to 'editorialize' on the air would be strictly limited. These attempts at regulating fairness, promoted under the FCC's 1949 report *In the Matter of Editorializing by Broadcast Licensees*, revolved around a declaration that:

> Only insofar as it is exercised in conformity with the paramount right of the public to hear a reasonably balanced presentation of all responsible viewpoints on particular issues can such editorialization be considered to be consistent with the licensee's duty to operate in the public interest.
>
> (Cited in Sterling and Kittross 1978: 305)

In general, the FCC's efforts met with little success throughout the 1950s, partly due to its inability to adequately police the requirements. A further contributory factor was the commission's internal confusion over how best to delimit a balance between advocacy on the part of the broadcaster on the one hand, and the rights of those expressing opposing views on the other (these issues were clarified to some extent in the Communications Act (1960), although not to the satisfaction of any of the parties involved). The net effect of the fairness requirements, then, was to encourage the makers of news programmes to avoid reports which were likely to attract the attention of the FCC even if, as was likely the case, its strictures would lack sufficient bite to be meaningful.

Daily newscasts in the 1950s were regularly supplemented with special event news coverage. One of the most significant examples, at least in terms of the sensational viewing figures it generated, was the televising of the 1950–1 Senate hearings into organized crime. Chairing the hearings, which were held over a period of weeks across the US, was Estes Kefauver, a Democratic senator from Tennessee. His skill in posing penetrating questions propelled him to national prominence as he was widely credited with unravelling many of the intricate webs of deceit being spun in the testimony of certain witnesses (at times, according to one ratings service, New York City's entire viewing audience was watching the proceedings: Bliss 1991: 252). For most commentators, the testimony of reputed gangster leader and 'big-time gambler' Frank Costello signalled the highpoint of the coverage. Due to his angry refusal to allow his face to appear on screen, the cameras focused instead on his nervously twitching hands; in so doing, one of the most talked about television images to date was created. Many commentators were quick to observe that television had provided a revealing close-up of psychological tension that could only be described on radio. A *Broadcasting* magazine editorial published later that year declared that this coverage of the hearings had 'promoted television in one big swoop from everybody's whipping boy – in the sports, amusement, and even retail world – to benefactor, without reservations. Its camera eye had opened the public's' (cited in Bianculli 1992: 57; see also Sterling and Kittross 1978: 288).

The public's eye was similarly pried open on a more regular basis by a range of public affairs programmes, the first of which on network television was *See It Now* on CBS. Hosted by one of the most respected broadcast journalists in the US, Edward R. Murrow, this weekly half-hour programme did not shy away from controversy. Perhaps most famously, it was widely regarded as having played an instrumental role in exposing the pernicious underpinnings of McCarthyism. Nevertheless, and as noted above, on a much more typical, day-to-day level, newscasts of the 1950s did their best to avoid controversy for fear of offending advertisers on the one hand, or the FCC on the other. As a result of these and related factors, the ideological limits represented by 'fair' and 'balanced' reporting were extremely narrow. That is to say, the shallowness of much of what passed as reporting was directly linked to these anxieties over precisely where 'impartiality' ended and 'editorialization' began. Such apprehensions routinely led to self-censorship, thereby severely compromising the network's proclaimed commitment to providing journalism consistent with the public interest. It would be only in the course of the next decade that television reporters would truly begin the long process toward realizing the ideal of 'free speech' more closely associated with their rivals in the newspaper press.

By the early 1960s, public opinion surveys were routinely indicating that television was beginning to displace both radio and the newspaper press as the principal source of news for audiences in Britain and the United States. Many commentators were asserting that the capacity of broadcast news and current affairs programming to shape 'the public agenda' signified that the electronic media were providing a progressive, even democratizing function with regard to public enlightenment about social problems. Other commentators were far more pessimistic, arguing that the lack of democratic accountability over broadcasting institutions was ensuring that commitments to journalistic integrity would always be rendered subordinate to the interests of state and corporate elites.

It is precisely this dispute over the proper role and responsibilities of the news media in a democratic society – specifically, with regard to reporting the truth – which serves as the starting point for our discussion in Chapter 4.

4 MAKING NEWS, REPORTING TRUTHS

> The fundamental obligation of the reporter is to the truth.
>
> (Fergal Keane, BBC journalist)

> News may be true, but it is not truth, and reporters and officials seldom see it the same way.
>
> (James Reston, US journalist)

Truth, according to an old journalistic saying, is the news reporter's stock-in-trade. This principle was reaffirmed by Fergal Keane, a widely respected BBC foreign correspondent, in a televised Huw Weldon Memorial Lecture (broadcast 20 October 1997 on BBC 1). In his words:

> The art of the reporter should more than anything else be a celebration of the truth . . . The reason millions of people watch and listen is because we place the interests of truth above everything else. Trust is our byword. That is the unalterable principle. It is our heritage and our mission, and I would rather sweep the streets of London than compromise on that . . . The fundamental obligation of the reporter is to the truth. Start messing with that for any reason and you become the moral accomplices of the secret policemen.

These are powerful words, eloquently spoken. At one level, it seems to me, the implications of Keane's argument are clear: a journalism resolutely committed to 'the truth' must never hesitate to uncover and expose lies, deceit and misrepresentation regardless of the consequences.

At another, more subtly complex level, however, the implications of Keane's declaration quickly prove to be much more challenging to discern. This reference to 'the truth' begs a rather awkward question: namely, whose definition of what is true is being upheld as 'the truth'? The answer to that question goes to the heart of ongoing debates over whether or not the news media 'reflect' social reality truthfully, or the extent to which journalists can produce a truthful news account. These debates typically restrict the discussion to one regarding how best to separate 'facts' from 'values'. The assumption that 'the truth' resides entirely in the former leaves to one side the problem of whether or not such a separation is actually possible in the first place. In light of these types of issues, then, this chapter will examine how the news media work to define the ideological limits of 'truth' by exploring how journalists produce news accounts which claim to be 'objective' reflections of reality.

More specifically, we examine a range of insights generated by researchers attempting to explore the ideological dynamics of newswork practices, that is, the day-to-day routines of news production which inform the cultural construction of news as an 'impartial' form of social knowledge. Here the focus is on the extent to which the codified conventions of newswork contribute to the *naturalization* of the various social divisions and inequalities indicative of modern society, principally by helping to reaffirm these inequalities as being *appropriate, legitimate* or *inevitable* in ideological terms.

News values

For many of the critical researchers focusing squarely on the dynamics of news production, it is the culture of routine, day-to-day interactions within specific news institutions which has warranted particular attention. From a variety of different conceptual perspectives, notably those associated with cultural and media studies, sociology, criminology and ethnomethodology among others, they have sought to investigate the ideological imperatives embedded in the work of constructing news as a truthful representation of reality. An effort is made by these researchers to problematize or 'make strange' the everyday activities of journalists, or newsworkers as they are often called in these studies, as they go about performing their job. Drawing upon a range of research strategies, including questionnaires, in-depth interviews, participant observation and ethnography, these investigations have endeavoured to document the fluidly contingent means by which the ideological character of news is encoded through the professionalized norms and values of reporting.

Even a glance at the front pages of different national newspapers on a given day, or the national news broadcasts on rival networks, typically reveals a broad similarity in the 'stories' being covered, and the hierarchical order in which they have been organized. Journalists, as well their editors and all of the other individuals involved in the work of processing news in a particular news organization, bring to the task of making sense of the social world a series of 'news values'. These news values are operationalized by each journalist, as Hall (1981) suggests, in relation to her or his 'stock of knowledge' about what constitutes 'news'. If all 'true journalists', he argues, are supposed to know instinctively what news values are, few are capable of defining them:

> Journalists speak of 'the news' as if events select themselves. Further, they speak as if which is the 'most significant' news story, and which 'news angles' are most salient, are divinely inspired. Yet of the millions of events which occur every day in the world, only a tiny proportion ever become visible as 'potential news stories': and of this proportion, only a small fraction are actually produced as the day's news in the news media.
>
> (Hall 1981: 234)

Hence the need to problematize, in conceptual terms, the operational practices in and through which news values help the reporter to justify the selection of certain types of events as 'newsworthy' at the expense of alternative ones. To ascertain how this process is achieved, researchers have attempted to explicate the means by which certain 'news values' are embedded in the very procedures used by reporters to impose some kind of order or coherence on to the social world. After all, the world has to be rendered 'reportable' in the first place, a point succinctly made by Barthes (1973) who once observed: 'What is noted is by definition notable.'

There is an extensive research literature concerned with 'news values', much of which elaborates upon an innovative study conducted in the mid-1960s by Galtung and Ruge (1981) on the structure of foreign news in the Scandinavian press (see, for example, Epstein 1973; Roshco 1975; Tuchman 1978; Gans 1979; Fishman 1980; Hartley 1982; Ericson *et al.* 1987; Bell 1991; Dayan and Katz 1992; Zelizer 1992). In selectively drawing upon these attempts to specify the informal (largely unspoken) rules or codes of *newsworthiness*, the following factors may be regarded as being significant:

- *Conflict*: 'balanced' journalism dictates that 'each story has two sides'; when these 'sides' are in dispute, a sense of *immediacy* is likely to result at the same time that potential *interest* is enhanced through *dramatization*.
- *Relevance*: the event should be seen to impinge, however indirectly, on the news audience's lives and experiences. The *proximity* of the event is a related factor.

- *Timeliness*: recent events are favoured, especially those that have occurred in the previous 24 hours and which can be easily monitored as they unfold in relation to institutional constraints and pressures.
- *Simplification*: the significance of an event should be relatively unambiguous; the diversity of potential interpretations may then be kept to a minimum.
- *Personalization*: an emphasis on human actors 'coping with life on the ground' is preferred over abstract descriptions of 'faceless' structures, forces or institutions.
- *Unexpectedness*: an event which is 'out of the ordinary' is likely to be 'novel' or 'new', thereby enhancing its chances of being caught in the news net. As an old cliché goes: 'Dog bites man isn't news; man bites dog is.'
- *Continuity*: an event should allow for the projection of a sense of where it 'fits in' so as to allow for prescheduling, a significant consideration for a news organization allocating its resources. A related factor is its *consonance* or conformity to the journalist's (and audience member's) preconceptions about what type of 'news story' it is likely to resemble.
- *Composition*: a mixture of different types of events must be processed on any given day, thus events are chosen in relation to fluctuations in the 'news hole' to be filled. Divisions between, for example, international, national and local news are usually clearly marked in regional newspapers and newscasts.
- *Reference to elite nations*: a hierarchy is often discernible here which gives priority to events in those countries which are regarded as 'directly affecting the audience's well-being', such as the US and other members of the 'first world'. This is at the expense of those events taking place in other places, particularly developing or 'third world' countries which only infrequently receive newsworthy status (and then only under certain terms: see Chapter 8).
- *Reference to elite persons*: activities performed by politicians, members of the monarchy, entertainment and sporting celebrities, corporate leaders and so forth, are far more salient in news terms than those of 'ordinary people'.
- *Cultural specificity*: events which conform to the 'maps of meaning' shared by journalist and news audience have a greater likelihood of being selected, a form of ethnocentrism which gives priority to news about 'people like us' at the expense of those who 'don't share our way of life'.
- *Negativity*: 'bad news' is ordinarily favoured over 'good news', namely because the former usually conforms to a higher number of the above factors. As the celebrated media theorist Marshal McLuhan once remarked, advertisements constitute the only 'good news' in the newspaper.

The news culture indicative of one news organization will be at variance with that of others, of course, but researchers have been able to identify a variety of shared assumptions which recurrently underpin these daily negotiations (see also Harrison 2006; Brighton and Foy 2007; Harcup 2007; Preston 2008; Meikle 2009). Thus while news values are always changing over time and are inflected differently from one news organization to the next, it is still possible to point to these and related news values as being relatively consistent criteria informing these assignments of significance. News accounts, then, may be deconstructed in ideological terms so as to elucidate how these news values help to rule in certain types of events as 'newsworthy' while, at the same time, ruling out alternative types.

Framing events

At the heart of these processes of inclusion and exclusion are certain 'frames' which work to impose order on the multiple happenings of the social world so as to render them into a series of meaningful events. The concept of 'frame' enjoys considerable currency in a variety of analytical contexts. Definitions of its component elements vary accordingly, although most share some degree of commitment to a phenomenological understanding of social life where any corresponding notion of 'reality' is rendered problematic. In the social sciences, its central tenets were outlined by the sociologist Erving Goffman in a series of writings from the early 1950s onwards, although his 1974 text *Frame Analysis* is typically cited for its formative influence today.

Over the course of *Frame Analysis*, Goffman (1974) aims to 'isolate some of the basic frameworks of understanding available in our society for making sense out of events' while, at the same time, analysing 'the special vulnerabilities to which these frames of reference are subject' (1974: 10). Given that a social event will entail any number of situations transpiring simultaneously, much will depend upon how it is characterized – either at the time or retrospectively – from an individual's particular point of view. Goffman, drawing on Gregory Bateson's (1972) use of the term 'frame' in this regard, proceeds to contend that 'definitions of a situation' are effectively 'built up in accordance with principles of organization which govern events – and our subjective involvement in them' (Goffman 1974: 10–11). To the extent that the basic elements of these principles can be discerned, the word 'frame' is intended to capture something of their complexity. The structure of experience an individual possesses at any one moment may be fraught with ambiguity, eluding any attempt to firmly categorize it, and yet it necessarily entails a process whereby ostensibly meaningless aspects of an event are made meaningful.

Meaning making, in other words, implies one or more primary frameworks – or schemata of interpretation – upheld by the individual striving to make sense of the event. These frameworks, Goffman argues, vary markedly in the relative degree of their organization. 'Some are neatly presentable as a system of entities, postulates, and rules,' he writes, 'others – indeed, most others – appear to have no apparent articulated shape, providing only a lore of understanding, an approach, a perspective' (1974: 21). In any case, however, 'each primary framework allows its user to locate, perceive, identify and label a seemingly infinite number of concrete occurrences defined in its terms' (1974: 21). The individual, in everyday circumstances, will be largely unaware of a given framework's features (if called upon, he or she may not be able to describe it in a methodical manner), let alone its purchase on their perceptions. Nevertheless, such frameworks equip the individual with background understanding of events. Not only do 'we tend to perceive events in terms of primary frameworks,' Goffman maintains, 'the type of framework we employ provides a way of describing the event to which it is applied' (1974: 24).

Precisely how a particular news event is 'framed' by the journalist claiming to be providing an 'objective' or 'balanced' account thus takes on a distinct ideological significance. Gitlin (1980) extends this notion of 'frame' to argue for a consideration of how the daily routines of journalism strive to *naturalize* the social world in accordance with certain discursive conventions. News frames, he argues, make the world beyond direct experience look natural; they are 'principles of selection, emphasis, and presentation composed of little tacit theories about what exists, what happens, and what matters' (Gitlin 1980: 6). The subject of often intense negotiation between journalists and their editors, as well as their sources, frames help to render 'an infinity of noticeable details' into practicable repertoires. Frames thereby facilitate the ordering of the world in conjunction with hierarchical rules of inclusion and exclusion. As Gitlin (1980) contends:

> largely unspoken and unacknowledged, [frames] organise the world both for journalists who report it and, in some important degree, for us who rely on their reports. Frames enable journalists to process large amounts of information quickly and routinely: to recognise it as information, to assign it to cognitive categories, and to package it for efficient relay to their audiences. Thus, for organisational reasons alone, frames are unavoidable, and journalism is organised to regulate their production.
>
> (Gitlin 1980: 7)

Once a particular frame has been adopted for a news story, its principles of selection and rejection ensure that only 'information' material which is seen to be *legitimate*, as *appropriate* within the conventions of newsworthiness so defined, is to appear in the account. 'Some of this framing,' Gitlin (1980: 28) argues, 'can be attributed to traditional assumptions in news treatment: news concerns the *event*, not the underlying condition; the *person*, not the group; *conflict*, not consensus; the fact that "*advances the story*", not the one that explains it.'

The invocation of a news frame is not to be viewed, however, as a means to preclude the encoding of 'information' which might explicitly politicize the seemingly impartial definitions of social reality on offer. Rather, the very authoritativeness of the frame is contingent upon its implicit appeal to 'objectivity', which means that it needs to regularly incorporate 'awkward facts' or even, under more exceptional circumstances, voices of dissent. The news frame's tacit claim to comprehensiveness dictates that it must be seen as 'balanced' and 'fair' in its treatment of counter-positions. Indeed, after Gitlin (1980: 256), 'only by absorbing and domesticating conflicting values, definitions of reality, and demands on it, in fact, does it remain hegemonic.' Accordingly, it is through repetition, through the very everydayness of news discourse, that the prevailing frames (once again, neither arbitrary nor fixed) acquire an ostensibly *natural* or taken-for-granted status.

It is precisely this capacity of the frame to shape the articulation of reality, to help set down rules of inclusion (and thus, by definition, exclusion), that has attracted the interest of scholars endeavouring to elucidate the social organization of perception. Frames focus attention, privileging certain areas of emphasis over and above alternative possibilities in a manner held to be appropriate within its own terms of reference. Entman (1993), extending Goffman's thesis, neatly pinpoints several key aspects of this process:

> Framing essentially involves selection and salience. To frame is to *select some aspects of perceived reality and make them more salient in the communicating text, in such a way as to promote a particular problem definition, causal interpretation, moral evaluation and/or treatment recommendation* for the item described. Frames, then, *define* problems – determine what a causal agent is doing and costs and benefits, usually measured in terms of cultural values; *diagnose* causes – identify the forces creating the problem; *make moral judgments* – evaluate causal agents and their effects; and *suggest remedies* – offer and justify treatments for the problem and predict their likely effects.
>
> (Entman 1993: 55, original emphasis)

Whilst suitably cautious about its utility as a fully-fledged theory in its own right, Entman's elaboration of frame analysis operationalizes Goffman's metaphor in a nuanced, enabling manner. The framing of certain facets of events or issues, he stresses, will facilitate the making of connections among them; the deeper the cultural resonance, it follows, the greater the potential for influence (see also Entman 2004).

Stephen D. Reese (2001) suggests that frames are best thought of as '*organizing principles* that are socially *shared* and *persistent* over time, that work *symbolically* to meaningfully *structure* the social world' (2001: 11). To clarify, he outlines a frame's compositional features as follows:

- *Organizing*: Framing varies in how successfully, comprehensively, or completely it organizes information.
- *Principles*: The frame is based on an abstract principle and is not the same as the texts through which it manifests itself.
- *Shared*: The frame must be shared on some level for it to be significant and communicable.
- *Persistent*: The significance of frames lies in their durability, their persistent and routine use over time.
- *Symbolically*: The frame is revealed in symbolic forms of expression.
- *Structure*: Frames organize by providing identifiable patterns or structures, which can vary in their complexity.

(Reese 2001: 11–12)

Reese (2007), in a later essay, explains what he hoped to achieve with this definition. Discernible within it, he writes, were 'a number of variables that I meant to help generate some research questions, such as the extent to which frames organize, are shared, persist, and [so] forth.' More than a 'stance' or a 'position' *vis-à-vis* a 'dominant theme', a frame works through texts – such as news reports – to structure social meaning in accordance with various interpretive principles. Further questions thus arise with respect to the embeddedness of frames in ideology, given their capacity to support certain political interests (even if not intentionally so, he hastens to add). In this way, Reese's definition also highlighted what he regards as the most interesting aspect of frames: namely, 'their dynamic quality, their ability to project knowledge ahead as they guide the structure of incoming experience' (2007: 150).

Framing, then, is the subject of intense negotiation, and as such frequently proves to be a contested process – not least between journalists and their sources (as well as between journalists and their editors within a news organization, where decisions about placement, headlines, images, captions, and the like, become important). Indeed, in addition to helping to define what is significant to know, frames have far-reaching implications for how claims made by sources are selected (or not) as newsworthy, the narrative conventions guiding the ways in which they are reported, and the possible consequences for influencing public perceptions.

Routinizing the unexpected

In discussing the day-to-day activities of reporting, journalists and their critics alike often draw upon the metaphor of a 'mirror' to describe how the social world is 'reflected' in news accounts. The pioneering US broadcast reporter Edward R. Murrow once famously stated, for example, that journalism 'must hold a mirror behind the nation and the world' and that, moreover, 'The mirror must have no curves and must be held with a steady hand' (cited in MacDonald 1979: 310). This language of reflection is similarly employed in critiques of news coverage to pinpoint evidence of 'bias', that is, to question whether journalists have mirrored reality in an 'objective' manner or, failing that, the extent to which they have allowed certain 'distortions' to creep into the reporting process.

Not surprisingly in light of the issues raised in the discussion above, many critical researchers have dismissed the 'mirror' metaphor for being too simplistic. Even its advocates, they point out, have to acknowledge the vast number of 'blind spots' which render certain types of events virtually invisible. The mirror metaphor is also difficult to sustain due to its inability to account for the ideological dynamics embedded in the journalist's mediation of the social world. This process of mediation involves not only a series of procedures for knowing the world but, equally importantly, for not knowing that world as well. As Hallin (1994) writes of the 'mirroring' qualities of so-called 'objective reporting' of governmental affairs in the US:

> A form of journalism which aims to provide the public with a neutral record of events and which, at the same time, relies primarily on government officials to describe and explain those events obviously has the potential to wind up as a mirror not of reality, but of the version of reality government officials would like to present to the public.
>
> (Hallin 1994: 52)

In light of these types of criticisms, Tuchman's (1978) concept of a 'news net' has been widely regarded as a much more suitable metaphor than that of a reflective 'mirror'. Introduced following her research into newswork practices, the idea of a news net is a more useful way of conceptualizing this imposition of order on the social world. News, in her analysis, is a social resource which, through its very construction, implies a series of particular constraints or limits on the forms of knowledge which can be generated and called 'reality'.

Tuchman's study, which draws on data gathered by participant observation and interviews with reporters and editors over a ten-year period in the US, documents how news organizations disperse a news net that intertwines time and space in such a way as to allow for the identification of 'newsworthy' events. If the news net is intended for 'big fish', as she argues, then at stake in conceptual terms is the task of unravelling this 'arrangement of intersecting fine mesh (the stringers), tensile strength (the reporters), and steel links (the wire services) supposedly provid[ing] a news blanket, ensuring that all potential news will be found' (Tuchman 1978: 22). That is to say, the bureaucratic threads of the news net are knitted together so as to frame certain preferred types of occurrences as 'news events' while, concurrently, ensuring that others slip through unremarked.

A news net stretched to encompass certain centralized institutional sites, ones where news is 'likely to be made today', reinforces a myriad of normative assumptions about what should constitute the public agenda. The problem of defining what counts as an 'appropriate news story' is directly tied to journalistic assumptions about what the news audience is interested in knowing. Tuchman's (1978: 25) study discerned three general premises incorporated into the news net: first, readers are interested in occurrences at certain localities and not others; second, readers are concerned with the activities of only specific organizations; and third, readers find only particular topics to be worthy of attention.

Bearing in mind this set of working assumptions, Tuchman (1978: 25–31) maintains that three interrelated methods of dispersing reporters can be described using the following criteria: geographic territoriality, organizational specialization and topical specialization.

First, 'geographic territoriality' is the most important of the three methods basic to the news net. Each news organization divides the social world into distinct areas of territorial responsibility so as to realize its respective 'news mission'. Assessments can then be made as to where news is most likely to happen – in effect, as McQuail (1992) notes, a self-fulfilling tendency – thereby allowing for a considerable degree of pre-planning. The news mission is a double-sided dynamic: on the one hand, it conforms to certain presumptions regarding what the audience 'wants to know', while on the other hand, it sets these presumptions against pre-given financial and technological constraints (on the importance in this regard of the international news agencies, such as Reuters, Associated Press, United Press International and Agence France Presse; see Wallis and Baran 1990; Reeves 1993; Herman and McChesney 1997; Boyd-Barrett and Rantanen 1998; van Ginneken 1998).

Second, 'organizational specialization' is another method for dispersing reporters. Beats and bureaux need to be set up in connection with the numerous organizations that are regularly 'making news' in that specific territory. Examples range from the 'crime beat', including such places as the police station, courts or prisons, to other sites routinely generating news like the city council, the fire and rescue services, the health authority, and so forth. Due to their formal status as sources of centralized information, these sites are legitimized as the preferred places for journalists to collect the 'facts' they require. The coding of a given news item as 'belonging' to a particular site is not always a straightforward decision, however, and can lead to conflict within the news organization (see Roshco 1975; Gans 1979; Fishman 1980; Zelizer 1992; Reeves and Campbell 1994; Glover 1999; Palmer 2000).

Third, 'topical specialization' is the final method; at issue here is the extent to which topical specialities, such as consumer affairs, finance, education, environment, health, arts, science, the 'women's page' (see Chapter 7), travel, gardening, motoring or sports, bypass the territorial desks. Usually each topic is associated with its own department which will possess a budget to be spent on the preparation of material. A decision on the quantity of material can be made only after the territorial editors announce how much space has been left over for each of them to use (see also Epstein 1973; Norris 1997a, b; Gavin and Goddard 1998; van Zoonen 1998; Allan *et al.* 2000; Allan 2002; Bromley 2005; Priest 2005; Anderson *et al.* 2009).

Evidently, the amount of movement in and across the three methods involves considerable negotiation, and thus flexibility, as each pulls the news net in different directions. Attention may then shift to consider, among other concerns, the following:

- The economic pressure to maintain a cost-efficient, profitable news organization, in part by avoiding expenses which may not result in a final news story, means that investigative reporting is often disallowed on these terms (see Williams 1996; Bagdikian 1997; Franklin and Murphy 1998; Hackett and Zhao 1998; Pilger 1998; Marjoribanks 2000; Bromley 2005; Barnett 2005; de Burg 2008; Matheson and Allan 2009).
- There is a need to conform to the news organization's daily production schedule, especially where deadlines are concerned. Schlesinger (1987) uses the phrase 'stopwatch culture' to pinpoint how these relations are interwoven throughout the production process (see also Gans 1979; Curran 1990; A. Bell 1991, 1998; Willis 1991; Steiner 1998).
- Being able to routinize the uncertainty of future happenings is considered to be of critical importance as the journalist's obligation to produce sufficient copy to fulfil 'story quotas' must be met. In contrast with 'hard' news, so-called 'soft' news or 'human interest' stories are usually less dependent on notions of 'timeliness' (see Tiffen 1989; Jacobs 1996; Kitzinger 1998; Skidmore 1998).
- This practical need to anticipate or pre-plan news-as-events, Tuchman (1978) argues, leads to the further sub-classification of three types of 'hard' news: namely, 'spot' news, 'developing' news and 'continuing' news.

'Continuing' news usually revolves around events which are prescheduled well in advance, thereby making them highly sought after by reporters and editors alike (see Fishman 1980; Dayan and Katz 1992; Miller 1993, 1994; Becker 1995).

- The implementation of new technologies (each have their own varying 'time–space rhythms') to enhance speed, flexibility and, thereby, professionalism (see Cottle 1995; Schudson 1995; Tunstall 1996; McNair 1998; Shingler and Wieringa 1998).

Professional ideals, such as those of 'impartiality' and 'objectivity', are thus likely to be operationalized in ways which privilege the (largely internalized) 'journalistic standards' appropriate to the news organization's ethos and its priorities.

A hierarchy of credibility

The very basis upon which the journalist is able to detect 'news events', according to Fishman (1980: 51), rests on a commonsensical understanding that society is bureaucratically structured. It is this perspective which provides specific procedures for locating knowledge of occurrences. Specifically, it furnishes the reporter with a 'map of relevant knowers' for newsworthy topics. A journalist covering a story concerning, say, the possible effects of a nuclear power plant on the health of children in a local community knows that information officers at the plant, as well as politicians, scientists, nuclear energy lobbyists, health officials, social workers and environmental groups, among others, will be positioned to offer their viewpoints (see also Anderson 1997; Campbell 1999; Allan 2002; Anderson *et al.* 2005). 'Whatever the happening,' writes Fishman (1980: 51), 'there are officials and authorities in a structural position to know.' This 'bureaucratic consciousness', to employ his phrase, indicates to journalists precisely where they will have to position themselves to be able to follow the time-line or 'career path' of events as they pass through a series of interwoven, yet discernible phases.

To clarify, Becker (1967) employs the notion of a 'hierarchy of credibility' to specify how, in a system of ranked groups, participants will take it as given that the members of the highest group are best placed to define 'the way things really are' due to their 'knowledge of truth'. Implicit in this assumption is the view that 'those at the top' will have access to a more complete picture of the bureaucratic organization's workings than members of lower groups whose definition of reality, because of this subordinate status, can be only partial and distorted. As Becker (1967: 241) writes, 'any tale told by those at the top intrinsically deserves to be regarded as the most credible account obtainable . . . Thus, credibility and the right to be heard are differentially distributed through the ranks of the system.' By this rationale, then, the higher up in this hierarchy the news source is situated, the more *authoritative* his or her words will be for the journalist processing the bureaucratic account. Newsworkers are thus predisposed to treat these accounts as factual, according to Fishman (1980: 96), 'because journalists participate in upholding a normative order of authorized knowers in society [and] it is also a position of convenience'. After all, the 'competence' of the source should, by this logic, translate into a 'credible' news story.

Of interest in this context is Hallin's (1986, 1994) analyses of how the dictates of 'objective' reporting serve to ratify a normative order of 'credible' sources, especially when challenges to the status quo are being mobilized. The journalist's world, he argues, can be usefully characterized as being divided into three regions, each governed by different standards of reporting (1986: 116–18). These regions may be represented as concentric circles (see Figure 4.1).

1 *Sphere of consensus*: this sphere, Hallin (1986) proposes, can be defined as representing 'motherhood and apple pie'. That is to say, it encircles those social issues which are typically regarded by journalists (and, they are likely to assume, most members of the public) as being beyond partisan dispute and, as such, non-controversial. Consequently, '[w]ithin this region journalists do not feel compelled either to present opposing views or to remain

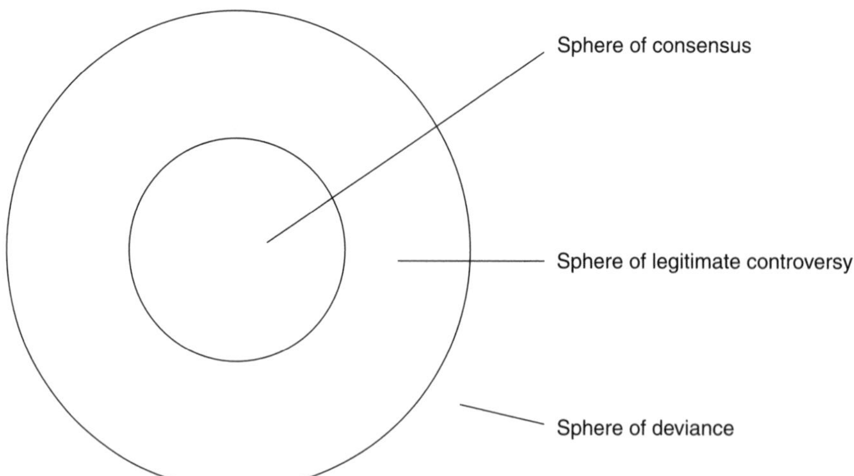

Figure 4.1 Spheres of consensus, controversy and deviance

Source: Hallin (1986: 117)

disinterested observers. On the contrary, the journalist's role is to serve as an advocate or celebrant of consensus values' (Hallin 1986: 116–17).

2 *Sphere of legitimate controversy*: in this sphere, there are a range of social issues which are framed by journalists as being the appropriate subject of partisan dispute. The typical types of controversies which unfold during electoral contests or legislative debates, for example, are situated here, the ideological parameters of which are represented by the positions articulated between and within the main political parties (as well as the bureaucracies of the state or civil service). 'Within this region,' Hallin (1986: 116) writes, 'objectivity and balance reign as the supreme journalistic values.'

3 *Sphere of deviance*: the realm located beyond the above sphere is occupied, according to Hallin (1986: 117), by 'those political actors and views which journalists and the political mainstream of the society reject as unworthy of being heard'. Virtually any pretence of journalistic 'neutrality' falls away, he argues, as news organizations perform the work of boundary maintenance. In this sphere, journalism 'plays the role of exposing, condemning, or excluding from the public agenda those who violate or challenge the political consensus. It marks out and defends the limits of acceptable political conflict' (Hallin 1986: 117).

These respective spheres, Hallin is quick to acknowledge, each contain internal gradations, and the boundaries distinguishing them are relatively fluid and changeable. Nevertheless, this model suggests that 'gut instincts' about source credibility are politicized, as the further away a potential source is from the political consensus the less likely it will be that the source's voice will gain media access.

One of the most noteworthy attempts to document the importance of these types of dynamics in Britain was a project co-authored by Hall, Critcher, Jefferson, Clarke and Roberts (1978), entitled *Policing the Crisis: Mugging, the State, and Law and Order*. Their investigation examines how journalistic conceptions of 'competence' and 'credibility' help to ensure that news statements are almost always dependent upon 'objective' and 'authoritative' statements from 'legitimate' institutional sources. For journalists, Hall *et al.* (1978) write:

> This means constantly turning to accredited representatives of major social institutions – MPs for political topics, employers and trade-union leaders for industrial matters, and so on. Such institutional representatives are 'accredited' because of their institutional power and position, but also because of their 'representative' status: either they represent 'the people' (MPs, Ministers, etc.) or organised interest groups.
>
> (Hall *et al.* 1978: 58)

It follows that the 'professional rules' indicative of the routine structures of news production are typically serving to represent the 'opinions of the powerful' as being consistent with a larger 'public consensus'. Here Hall *et al.* (1978: 58) proceed to note the irony that 'the very rules which aim to preserve the impartiality of the media, and which grew out of desires for greater professional neutrality, also serve powerfully to orientate the media in the "definitions of social reality" which their "accredited sources" – the institutional spokes-[persons] – provide'.

The journalist's daily struggle to negotiate the professional demands of newswork, with all of the attendant pressures, produces in Hall *et al.*'s (1978: 58) view 'a systematically structured *over-accessing* to the media of those in powerful and privileged institutional positions'. It is precisely this issue of how the definitions of certain sources are routinely 'over-accessed' to the detriment of alternative viewpoints which is crucial. Sources who enjoy high status positions in society can assume, in turn, that they are much more likely to become what Hall *et al.* (1978) call 'the *primary definers*' of controversial topics.

Accordingly, the structured relationship between the news media and this hierarchy of institutional definers permits the most powerful of the latter to set down the initial definition or primary interpretation of the news topic to be processed. It is recurrently the case that this interpretation will then be mobilized to 'command the field' with the likely result that it will, in turn, establish the terms of reference within which all further coverage (as well as any subsequent 'debate') takes place. 'Arguments *against* a primary interpretation,' Hall *et al.* (1978: 58) stress, 'are forced to insert themselves into *its* definition of "what is at issue" – they must begin from this framework of interpretation as their starting-point.' Moreover, this 'initial interpretative framework is extremely difficult to alter fundamentally, once established' (Hall *et al.* 1978: 58–9).

In this way, then, the news media are regarded as playing a vital ideological role in reaffirming the iniquitous power relations underlying society's institutional order.

Challenges to the concept of 'primary definition' have emerged from a variety of different perspectives. For many liberal pluralists, for example, Hall *et al.* (1978) are guilty of overemphasizing the capacity of the news media to structure public debate in ways consistent with the interests of the powerful. In their view, journalists almost always enjoy a sufficient degree of autonomy from these types of influences, thereby ensuring that their reportage is 'balanced' and 'objective'. More usefully, other researchers have sought to extend the approach introduced by Hall *et al.* through a more rigorous assessment of the institutional imperatives of source competition.

One such intervention has been advanced by Schlesinger and Tumber (1994) in their book *Reporting Crime: The Media Politics of Criminal Justice*. Although they endorse the general argument that newswork practices typically promote the views of authoritative sources, they proceed to provide six specific points of criticism (Schlesinger and Tumber 1994: 17–21). These points, together with illustrative references to other studies, may be briefly outlined as follows.

First, the notion of 'primary definition' fails to recognize possible disputes between official sources struggling to influence the production of a news account. In the course of such a conflict it may not always be clear who is actually the *primary* definer (or by which criteria such primacy is to be defined) in a given instance.

A telling illustration of this point is documented in Hallin's (1986, 1994: 55) investigations into US news coverage of the Vietnam War: 'The case of Vietnam suggests that whether the media tend to be supporting or critical of government policies depends on the degree of consensus those policies enjoy, particularly within the political establishment.' It then follows, he suggests, that although news content 'may not mirror the facts', media institutions 'do reflect the prevailing pattern of political debate: when consensus is strong, they tend to stay within the limits of the political discussion it defines; when it begins to break down, coverage becomes increasingly critical and diverse in the viewpoints it represents, and increasingly difficult for officials to control'.

Second, the extent to which official sources engage in tactics to pass privileged but unattributable information to journalists under a cloak of confidentiality, such as through the use of 'off-the-record' briefings, is not sufficiently recognized.

Typical examples of statements from non-attributable sources, frequently presented to reporters as 'for background only' comments, include: 'according to a well-placed government source', 'sources close to the Prime Minister say', 'a trusted source has revealed', 'as leaked by an inside source', and so forth. In Britain, a decision made by the Labour government shortly after taking office in May 1997 to formally place lobby briefings by government spokespeople 'on the record' (along similar lines to the US custom) has by no means eliminated the practice. It is often described as a key element of 'spin doctoring' (see also Glover 1999; Palmer 2000).

Third, important questions are being obscured with regard to the means by which the boundaries of primary definition are being drawn, and redrawn, as official sources compete amongst themselves (using different media strategies) over access to the discursive field of debate.

As Deacon and Golding (1994: 201–2) argue in their study of British media coverage of the 'poll tax' disputes, 'the ideological advantages of primary definition can be eroded by political vulnerability, so that an "accredited" source becomes largely "discredited" – consistently on the defensive and increasingly unable to control the direction of public and media debate'. They then proceed to make a further crucial point: 'Not only does primary definition have to be won, it must also be sustained interpretatively and evaluatively through a series of battles, in which its political vulnerability may progressively increase' (Deacon and Golding 1994: 202).

Fourth, the apparent atemporality of Hall *et al.*'s (1978) formulation needs to be highlighted, that is, its inattention to how the structure of access changes over time as new forces, and their representatives, emerge.

This point is underscored by Hansen's (1993b: 151) investigation of the strategies employed by environmental groups, such as Greenpeace, to secure access to media debates (see also Allan *et al.* 2000). In his words: 'It is one thing for environmental groups to achieve massive media coverage for a short period of time and in relation to specific issues. It is quite a different task to achieve and maintain a position as an "established", authoritative and legitimate actor in the continuous process of claims-making and policy-making on environmental matters.'

Fifth, it is the need to account for the ways in which journalists challenge official sources, even to the extent of pursuing campaigns, which is at issue. Schlesinger and Tumber (1994: 19) criticize Hall *et al.*'s (1978) approach for tending to 'overstate the passivity of the media as recipients of information from news sources: the flow of definitions is seen as moving uniformly from the centres of power to the media'. They point out that there are significant variations between different news media which need to be addressed, both in terms of the respective medium (such as between television and the press) and at the level of rival news outlets (such as different newspapers).

An illustration of this point is found in Miller's (1993, 1994) research into media portrayals of the conflict in Northern Ireland during 'the Troubles', where he argues that current affairs and documentary programmes were frequently regarded by government officials as the most difficult to manage:

> It is precisely for this reason that official agencies attempt to elucidate the exact nature of queries and even of proposed programmes before permitting access. The access that is granted is heavily bounded by the interests of the sources, but in the end they are betting on slightly longer odds than with hard news stories, which have less space and time and are less likely to do investigative reports.
>
> (Miller 1994: 109–10)

A final criticism renders explicit Schlesinger and Tumber's (1994) commitment to introducing an alternative logic to Hall *et al.*'s (1978) mode of inquiry. Specifically, they contend that most researchers have been media-centric in their approach to analysing source–media relations, a problem which can be overcome only by granting equal priority to the perspectives of the sources themselves as they work to generate 'counter-definitions'. These complex processes of negotiation or brokerage between power-holders and their opponents need to be brought to the fore.

Overall, then, it is Schlesinger and Tumber's (1994: 20) contention that the approach advocated by Hall *et al.* (1978) is insufficiently curious about 'the processes whereby sources may engage in ideological conflict prior to, or contemporaneous with, the appearance of "definitions" in the media'. Hence the importance of centring the contested dynamics within and between source organizations as they struggle to 'get their message out' through news media which are far from monolithic in their reporting.

Analyses have much to gain, it follows, by examining the precise methods employed by news sources in their efforts to shape media agendas. News promoters anxious to have their voice articulated across the field of the news media are often only too willing to openly cater to the practical needs of newswork. Drawing upon findings derived through an extensive series of interviews with news sources situated across the British criminal justice system, Schlesinger and Tumber (1994) proceed to distinguish a number of conditions typically involved in a source's attempts to realize its goals:

> 1 that the source has a well-defined message to communicate, framed in optimal terms capable of satisfying news values
> 2 that the optimal locations for placing that particular message have been identified, as have the target audiences of the media outlets concerned
> 3 that the preconditions for communicative 'success' have been assured so far as possible by, for instance, cultivating a sympathetic contact or fine-tuning the timing of a leak
> 4 that the anticipated strategies of others (which may include support as much as opposition) are incorporated into ongoing media strategies. Support may be harnessed by coalition-building. Opposition may, for instance, be countered by astute timing or discrediting its credibility
> 5 that means exist for monitoring and evaluating the impact of a given strategy or tactic and for adjusting future action in the light of what is reflexively learned
> 6 that some messages may be as much intended for private as public communication, thus operating on at least two levels.
>
> (Schlesinger and Tumber 1994: 39)

The relative success enjoyed by a potential news source in 'getting its message out' is thus likely to be directly tied to its capacity to routinize its own activities, especially with respect to preparing 'copy-ready' information materials with an eye to the needs of the time-pressured journalist.

Bell's (1991) examination of the principal sources drawn upon by newspaper journalists in New Zealand similarly highlights the significant role played by 'pre-existing text' in journalists' judgements. 'A story which is marginal in news terms but written and available,' he argues, 'may be selected ahead of a much more newsworthy story which has to be researched and written from the ground up' (1991: 59). His observation that most news copy consists of reported speech (even though it is often not attributed as such) underscores the extent to which journalists regularly rely on reprocessing or repackaging source material as news. Specifically, Bell (1991: 57) identifies the following 'input sources' (types of contact journalists have with sources) as being the most salient:

- interviews, either face to face or by telephone
- public addresses
- press conferences
- written text of spoken addresses
- organizationally produced documents of many kinds: reports, surveys, letters, findings, agendas, minutes, proceedings, research papers, etc.
- press releases
- prior stories on a topic, either from own or other media (journalists, as Bell writes, 'feed voraciously off each other's stories')
- news agency copy
- the journalist's notes from all the above inputs, especially the spoken ones.

Forms of text-based contact such as these encourage journalists to see the world through the eyes of their sources, if only because it makes their work that much easier to manage.

Similar types of source–media research provide further examples of some of the preferred tactics employed by news sources or event promoters (see Tiffen 1989; Eldridge 1993; Keeble 1994; Negrine 1996; Niblock 1996; J. Wilson 1996; Franklin 1997; McNair 1998; Palmer 2000; Manning 2001; Varley and Tapsall 2001; Cottle 2003a and b; Anderson *et al.* 2005; Davies 2008a and b; Lewis *et al.* 2008; Franklin *et al.* 2009). These tactics include:

- handing out to journalists advance copies of talks or speeches
- the scheduling of press conferences at convenient hours (safely before deadlines)
- news releases in 'ready-to-go' format, including an 'inverted pyramid style' narrative structure

- prompt access to bureaucratic personnel with pertinent information
- the opportunity to attend 'informal chats' or 'pseudo-events'.

Needless to say, source strategies such as these do not guarantee that journalists will 'stay on message', but they do enhance the likelihood that the source in question will be accorded with a privileged place in the hierarchy of access. This is no small achievement. 'The right to be considered the primary source of authoritative information about world events,' as Hallin (1994: 49–50) suggests, 'should probably be considered a central component of the legitimacy of modern political institutions.' This power, he continues, is 'comparable in a secular age to the right of the church in medieval Europe to interpret the scriptures' (Hallin 1994: 50).

Issues of access

When asked to reflect on how they go about their daily work of identifying those 'newsworthy' sources deserving to be included in a news account, journalists will often claim that they simply follow their 'gut feelings', 'hunches' or 'instincts'. Many insist that they have a 'nose for news', that they can intuitively tell which sources are going to prove significant and which ones are bound to be irrelevant to the news frame. Drawing upon an extensive range of interviews with Canadian newsworkers, Ericson, Baranek and Chan (1987, 1989, 1991) suggest that what guides the journalist in the course of these encounters is a 'vocabulary of precedents'. That is to say, the journalist's previous experience of the rules and organizational constraints characteristic of newswork interactions with sources directs them to visualize the social world in terms of specific types of knowledge.

> The ongoing articulation of precedent in the working culture of journalists provides them with recognition knowledge (that this is a story of a particular type), procedural knowledge (how to get on with contacting and using human and documentary sources), and accounting knowledge (how to frame and formulate the story; how to justify the chosen approach to others).
>
> (Ericson *et al.* 1987: 348)

This 'vocabulary of precedents' therefore profoundly shapes who journalists speak to, what they talk about, and how that discussion is represented. As noted above, journalists typically rely on sources to furnish them with a verbal or written account of their institution's stance or position, thereby saving them the effort of having to undertake an investigation themselves. 'Moreover, even on the rare occasions when journalists do get close to the original source,' write Ericson *et al.* (1987: 352), 'they are usually required to obtain a constructed account from an authorized source rather than be able to provide their own direct interpretation.'

If reporters are generally predisposed to accept the words of authorized sources as being factual, then it follows that statements which differ from one another must be handled in certain prescribed ways. Journalists anxious to avoid potential criticism for anchoring their account on 'biased' sources must take care to frame any conflict outside the realm of competence by foregrounding the interested perspectives of the sources. 'Precisely by conceiving of interested perspectives in social structural terms,' Fishman (1980: 124) writes, 'the reporter is able both to identify a set of competent and relevant interests and to trust that their differing accounts reveal differing factual aspects of the event.' Supplementary evidence may thus be mobilized in the form of conflicting truth-claims. For a news source to be included as part of the constellation of interests being constructed around an event, it must either explicitly or implicitly reaffirm the terms being employed by the journalist in the initial framing of the event itself. To speak 'off topic', or to stray from the perceived area of competence (and thus be demonstrating 'personal bias'), is to risk being positioned outside the ideological limits of newsworthiness.

Accessed voices, as Cottle (1993) found in his study of regional news, must be seen to be 'appropriate', 'articulate' and 'represent a clear point of view' to be deemed relevant. This sense of relevancy, he points out, tends to be 'construed in terms which reflect the programme's bid for popular appeal, typically involving the professional pursuit of immediacy, drama and general human interest' (1993: 89). At the same time, as the study by Deacon and Golding (1994: 202–3) confirms, a key distinction needs to be recognized between sources approached as 'advocates' (associated with a particular position) and those made to serve as 'arbiters' (regarded as non-aligned providers of information):

> Although all news sources can be thought of as 'advocates' – who each have a preferred image or message they would like to convey in the media – some are selected by journalists to act as 'arbiters' on particular issues. The views and opinions of these arbiters – provided they are comprehensible to journalists and, crucially, can be broadly assimilated within their inferential framework – are treated with greater deference than those of even the most senior 'advocates' and play a very important part in shaping media evaluations of the issues upon which they are invited to comment.
>
> (Deacon and Golding 1994: 202–3)

The 'arbiters' of a specific field of discourse, to the extent that their views guide the journalist's engagement with sources explicitly adopting a position of advocacy, are thereby performing a 'legislator' function (Deacon and Golding 1994: 16). In other words, they are helping to establish the (ostensibly non-partisan) criteria by which certain 'advocates' will be granted access to be heard on matters of controversy and, moreover, what aspect of the topic they will be encouraged to address.

Once it is recognized that the truly 'objective' news account is an impossibility, critical attention may turn to the strategies and devices used by journalists to lend to their accounts a factual status. Given that this factual status can never be entirely realized, the notion of a 'will to facticity' pinpoints the necessarily provisional and contingent nature of any such journalistic appeal to truth. Journalists must know, for example, what questions to ask the source in order to get at the right 'facts'. Here the news frame comes back into play, for as Tuchman (1978: 81) contends, 'knowing what to ask influences whom one asks: the choice of sources and the search for "facts" mutually determine each other'. As a general rule, Fishman (1980) maintains, journalists will usually take care when first setting up interviews with a source to inform him or her about what they are to talk about:

> Journalists orient their sources toward a certain way of looking at an event: as a legal–bureaucratic entity, as a moral issue, as a part of a historical trend, and so forth. Thus, they define for their sources the terms of an acceptable account, the terms in which all the various accounts will be framed, and the terms in which the event eventually will be described in the news story.
>
> (Fishman 1980: 131)

During the actual interview, then, this shared narrative framework becomes, in effect, an organizing principle of inclusion and exclusion. The journalist, according to Fishman, sets down the rules which must be obeyed if facticity and newsworthiness are going to intermesh.

A number of research studies show that in order to achieve the recognized 'credibility' required to be a legitimate or trustworthy candidate for the purpose of appropriation within the news net, individuals or groups attempting to mobilize alternative definitions of the situation are often forced to accommodate or adapt to the narrow confines of legitimized topic parameters. Attention has also been directed to how the tempo or rhythm of newswork serves, in turn, to place an enhanced emphasis on 'events', not 'issues'. Where the former have a beginning, a middle and an end, and are therefore easily processed as derivative of the *factual*, the latter implies that the line of demarcation separating the realm of facts from the realm of interpretation and explanation has been crossed. This when objective reporting dictates that this line always be respected. Hence the structural dependence on reliable institutional sources who produce consequential events. These sources, as argued above, allow for certainty to be built into the reporting process, principally through the imposition of predictability (even a certain rationality) *vis-à-vis* the confusion of the social world.

Consequently, those individuals or groups who lack regular access to the news frame (their definitions rarely getting entangled in the news net) have the option of resorting to 'disruptive access'. At stake is the need to force the temporary suspension of the routinized, habitual access enjoyed by others so as to create opportunities for their voices to be processed as newsworthy. As Molotch and Lester (1974: 108) write, these voices 'must "make news" by somehow crashing through the ongoing arrangements of newsmaking, generating surprise, shock, or some more violent form of "trouble" ' (see also Gitlin 1980; McLeod and Hertog 1992; Liebes and Curran 1998). Specific investigations of the interventions mobilized by various individuals, groups and movements to secure access through 'disruptive' means include the following studies concerning news coverage of:

- the women's movement (Tuchman 1978; van Zoonen 1994; Barker-Plummer 1995; Meyers 1997; Norris 1997a; Bradley 1998; see also Carter *et al.* 1998; Gallagher 2001; Ross 2005; Steiner 2005; Chambers and Steiner 2009)
- campaigns against racism (Hollingsworth 1986; Gordon and Rosenberg 1989; van Dijk 1991; Wilson and Gutiérrez 1995; Dennis and Pease 1997; Gabriel 1998; Jacobs 2000; Rhodes 2005; Harker 2009)
- the anti-war, anti-nuclear weapons and peace movements (Halloran *et al.* 1970; Gitlin 1980; Hackett 1991; Young 1991; Jeffords and Rabinovitz 1994; Eldridge 1995; Lynch 2009)
- the environmental and ecological movements (see Hansen 1993a; Neuzil and Kovarik 1996; Anderson 1997; Chapman *et al.* 1997; Adam 1998; Campbell 1999; Allan *et al.* 2000; Allan 2002)
- campaigns over issues of sexuality, including how they pertain to lesbian and gay rights (see Dickey 1987; Gross 1989; Moritz 1992, 2009; Stratford 1992; Fejes and Petrich 1993) as well as the media politics around HIV and AIDS (Watney 1987; Lupton 1994; Miller *et al.* 1998; Critcher 2003, 2005; Castanñeda and Campbell 2006)
- anti-poverty, anti-crime and community rights campaigns (see Curran *et al.* 1986; Cottle 1993, 1994; Deacon and Golding 1994; Meinhof and Richardson 1994; Reeves and Campbell 1994; Devereux 1998; Chavez 2001; Knight 2001; Atton 2009).

News interest is certainly not an end in itself, however, as the ensuing coverage may actually be the antithesis of that which had been initially desired by those individuals or groups struggling to articulate a counter-interpretation of the situation. All too frequently efforts to dislodge primary definitions are ignored, dismissed as 'soft news' novelties, or trivialized in other ways. As several of the above studies suggest, it is recurrently the case that the news frame is organized around the question of how quickly order can be restored to the social world, thereby ensuring that little, if any, attention is directed to the ethical implications of the issues raised through 'disruptive access' (see Belsey and Chadwick 1992; Chaney 1994; Tester 1994; Brants *et al.* 1998; Kieran 1998; Thompson 1998; Berry 2000; Keeble 2005; McNair 2005; Harcup 2007; Jacquette 2009).

This chapter thus comes to a close by posing several points of inquiry to be addressed in subsequent chapters:

- What are the prerequisites to be met before a voice 'deserves' inclusion in media debate as an 'authoritative', 'newsworthy' source?
- In what ways have various alternative or oppositional voices been made to cater their interventionist strategies so as to conform to the routinized imperatives of newswork?
- In what ways do these journalistic inflections of 'respectability', 'competence' and 'prestige' mark the limits of 'acceptable' dissent?
- To what extent does this constant threat of marginalization, of being defined as 'deviant' *vis-à-vis* 'the consensus', condition what can and cannot be said by these critical voices?

These questions take on an added urgency in light of the tectonic shifts reshaping the landscape of journalism as the convergence of 'old' and 'new' media continues apace (see also Patterson and Domingo 2008; Löffelholz and Weaver 2008; Allan and Thorsen 2009). Today's reporter is increasingly expected to be multi-skilled in order to work comfortably across a range of digital platforms while, at the same time, warding off the challenges posed by ordinary citizens – including the bloggers and YouTubers of 'the iPod generation' – threatening to storm the ramparts of the journalistic profession (see Chapter 10). Still, as we have seen above, for journalists willing to rethink familiar issues of access – and thereby embrace new forms of connectivity with their publics – the quality of their insights is certain to be enriched.

5 THE CULTURAL POLITICS OF NEWS DISCOURSE

> A senior politician is only ever a sound-bite away from destruction.
>
> (David Mellor, former Conservative government minister)

> There is a strong argument that unrelieved coverage of death, crisis and disaster gives a misleading picture of what life is like for most of Britain's citizens most of the time . . . that individual news stories become divorced from proper perspective or context . . . The good news is out there, and the media shouldn't be afraid to report it.
>
> (Martyn Lewis, BBC newsreader)

Journalists are among the pre-eminent story-tellers of modern society. Their news accounts shape in decisive ways our perceptions of the 'world out there' beyond our immediate experience. For many of us, our sense of what is happening in the society around us, what we should know and care about from one day to the next, is largely derived from the news stories they tell. Given that we have to take so much on trust, we rely on news accounts to be faithful representations of reality. We are asked to believe, after all, that truly professional journalists are able to set aside their individual preconceptions, values and opinions in order to depict reality 'as it actually is' to us, their audience. This assumption, deeply inscribed in the methods of 'objective' reporting, encourages us to accept these 'reflections' of reality as the most truthful ones available.

In seeking to render problematic this process of representation, this chapter focuses on how news discourses help to *naturalize* a cultural politics of legitimacy so as to lend justification to modern society's distribution of power and influence. More specifically, it is the extent to which these news discourses effectively *depoliticize* the dominant meanings, values and beliefs associated with these inequalities, and in so doing contribute to their perpetuation, that will be addressed. This chapter thus aims to raise important questions regarding the ways in which the language of news encodifies as 'common sense' a hierarchical series of normative rules by which social life is to be understood. It will be argued that it is the very *hegemonic* nature of this representational process which needs to be centred for purposes of investigation so as to discern, in turn, how the parameters of 'the public consensus', and with it 'the moral order', are being affirmed, recreated and contested in ideological terms.

Accordingly, the discussion commences with a consideration of the concept of 'hegemony' as it has been taken up by critical researchers analysing the politics of 'common sense'. Attention then turns to newspaper discourse, and later to radio and televisual newscasts, in order to examine a number of the textual strategies in and through which a range of preferred truth-claims about society are inflected as *authoritative, rational* and *appropriate* – and, in this way, potentially *hegemonic*. Such an approach can be shown to provide fresh insights into the means by which news accounts appeal to apparently common-sense renderings of 'reality' ('conventional wisdom', 'received opinion', 'what every reasonable person knows', and so forth) as being self-evidently true. That is to say, it enables the researcher to denaturalize the very naturalness of the ideological rules governing news discourse's representation of 'what can and should be said' about any aspect of social life.

News and hegemony

For many critical researchers endeavouring to disrupt the seemingly natural tenets of 'common sense' in order to critique them, the concept of 'hegemony' has proven to be highly useful. Most attempts to define the concept attribute its development to Antonio Gramsci, a radical Italian philosopher who died in 1937 after more than a decade in Mussolini's prisons. Very briefly, in his critique of power dynamics in modern societies, Gramsci (1971) describes hegemony as a relation of

> 'spontaneous' consent given by the great masses of the population to the general direction imposed on social life by the dominant fundamental group; this consent is 'historically' caused by the prestige (and consequent confidence) which the dominant group enjoys because of its position and function in the world of production.
>
> (Gramsci 1971: 12)

It is this implied distinction between consent and its opposite, coercion, which Gramsci recognizes to be crucial. In the case of the coercive force of ruling groups, he underlines the point that it is the 'apparatus of state coercive power which "legally" enforces discipline on those groups who do not "consent" either actively or passively' (Gramsci 1971: 12). The exercise of this coercive force may involve, for example, the armed forces of the military or the police, courts and prison system to maintain 'law and order'.

This type of coercive control in modern societies is the exception rather than the rule, however, when it comes to organizing public consent. Power, Gramsci argues, is much more commonly exercised over subordinate groups by means of persuasion through 'political and ideological leadership'. It follows that a ruling group is hegemonic only to the degree that it acquires the consent of other groups within its preferred definitions of reality through this type of leadership. In Gramsci's words:

> A social group can, and indeed must, already exercise 'leadership' before winning governmental power (this indeed is one of the principal conditions for the winning of such power); it subsequently becomes dominant when it exercises power, but even if it holds it firmly in its grasp, it must continue to 'lead' as well.
>
> (Gramsci 1971: 57–8)

Subordinate groups are encouraged by the ruling group to negotiate reality within what are ostensibly the limits of common sense when, in actuality, this common sense is consistent with dominant norms, values and beliefs. Hegemony is to be conceptualized, therefore, as a site of ideological struggle over this common sense.

Gramsci's writings on hegemony have proven to be extraordinarily influential for critical researchers examining the operation of the news media in modern societies. Three particularly significant (and interrelated) aspects of the cultural dynamics of hegemony are the following.

First, *hegemony is a lived process*. Hegemonic ideas do not circulate freely in the air above people's heads; rather, according to Gramsci, they have a material existence in the cultural practices, activities and rituals of individuals striving to make sense of the world around them. That is, hegemony is a process embodied in what Williams (1989b: 57) aptly describes as 'a lived system of meanings and values', that is, as 'a whole body of practices and expectations, over the whole of living: our senses and assignments of energy, our shaping perceptions of ourselves and our world'. It follows that hegemony constitutes 'a sense of reality for most people in the society' and, as such, is the contradictory terrain upon which the 'lived dominance and subordination' of particular groups is struggled over in day-to-day cultural practices.

Second, *hegemony is a matter of 'common sense'*. A much broader category than ideology, common sense signifies the uncritical and largely unconscious way of perceiving and understanding the social world as it organizes habitual daily experience. Gramsci stresses that common sense, despite the extent to which it is 'inherited from the past and uncritically absorbed', may be theorized as a complex and disjointed 'infinity of traces', and as such never simply identical with a class-based ideology. 'Commonsensical' beliefs, far from being fixed or immobile, are in a constant state of renewal: 'new ideas', as he notes, are always entering daily life and encountering the 'sedimentation' left behind by this contradictory, ambiguous, 'chaotic aggregate of disparate conceptions' (Gramsci 1971: 422). In critiquing what passes for common sense as 'the residue of absolutely basic and commonly-agreed, consensual wisdoms', Hall (1977: 325) further elaborates on this point: 'You cannot learn, through common sense, *how things are*: you can only discover *where they fit* into the existing scheme of things' (original emphasis).

Third, *hegemony is always contested*. Far from being a totally monolithic system or structure imposed from above, then, lived hegemony is an active process of negotiation; it can never be taken for granted by the ruling group. In Gramsci's (1971: 348) words, at stake is 'a cultural battle to transform the popular "mentality" and to diffuse the philosophical innovations which will demonstrate themselves to be "historically true" to the extent that they become concretely – i.e. historically and socially – universal'. Consequently, no one group can maintain its hegemony without adapting to changing conditions, a dynamic which will likely entail making certain strategic compromises with the forces which oppose its ideological authority. Dominance is neither invoked nor accepted in a passive manner; as Williams (1989b: 58) points out: 'It has continually to be renewed, recreated, defended, and modified [in relation to] pressures not at all its own.' Hence Gramsci's contention that common sense be theorized as the site upon which the hegemonic rules of practical conduct and norms of moral behaviour are reproduced and – crucially – also challenged and resisted.

Significantly, then, this shift to address the cultural dynamics of hegemony displaces a range of different formulations of 'dominant ideology', most of which hold that news discourse be theorized as concealing or masking the true origins of economic antagonisms, that is, their essential basis in the class struggle. At the same time, this emphasis on the hegemonic imperatives of news discourse allows the critical researcher to avoid the suggestion that the 'effects' of news discourse on its audience be understood simply as a matter of 'false consciousness'. As we shall see, beginning with the next section's discussion of newspaper discourse, an analytical engagement with the cultural dynamics of hegemony provides the researcher with important new insights into how news texts demarcate the limits of 'common sense'.

The common sense of newspaper discourse

'Journalists believe something is reportable,' according to Ericson *et al.*'s (1987: 348) study of Canadian news organizations, 'when they can visualize it in the terms of news discourse.' This process of visualization does not constitute a neutral reflection of 'the world out there'. Rather, it works to reaffirm a hegemonic network of conventionalized rules by which social life is to be interpreted, especially those held to be derivative of 'public opinion' or, at an individual level, 'human nature'. Accordingly, many critical researchers argue that news accounts encourage us to accept as *natural, obvious* or *commonsensical* certain preferred ways of classifying reality, and that these classifications have far-reaching implications for the cultural reproduction of power relations across society.

In order to develop this line of critique in relation to newspaper discourse, critical researchers have 'borrowed' a range of conceptual tools from various approaches to textual analysis. Particularly influential analyses of newspaper texts have been conducted using, among other methodologies, content analysis, semiotics or semiology, critical linguistics, sociolinguistics and critical discourse analysis (for overviews, see Hartley 1982, 1996; Bell 1991; Fowler 1991; Zelizer 1992; Eldridge 1993; Fairclough 1995; Bell and Garrett 1998; Franklin 2008). These text-centred approaches provide a basis to break from those forms of analysis which reduce language to a 'neutral' instrument through which 'reality' is expressed. By foregrounding the textual relations of signification, they suggest fascinating new ways to think through Gramsci's theses concerning the lived hegemony of common sense. Moreover, these approaches allow for the opening up of what has become a rather empty assertion, namely that news texts are inherently meaningful, so as to unpack the *naturalness* of the ideological codes implicated in their representations of reality. Thus the notion of 'codification' may be used to specify the means by which the meanings attributed to a text are organized in accordance with certain (usually so *obvious* as to be *taken-for-granted*) rules or conventions.

This is to suggest that a newspaper account, far from simply reflecting the reality of a news event, is actually working to construct a codified definition of what should count as the reality of the event. In order to examine these processes of codification, the specific ways in which a newspaper adopts a preferred language to represent 'the world out there' need to be opened up for analysis. That is to say, it is necessary to identify the means by which a particular newspaper projects its characteristic 'mode of address', its customary way of speaking to its audience, on its pages from one day to the next. Shaping this mode of address, as argued by Hall *et al.* (1978: 60) in *Policing the Crisis*, are a series of imperatives governing how the 'raw materials' of the social world are to be appropriated and transformed into a news account. An event will 'make sense', they argue, only to the extent that it can be situated within 'a range of known social and cultural identifications' or 'maps of meaning' about the social world. Here a key passage by Hall *et al.* (1978) is worth quoting at length:

> The social identification, classification and contextualisation of news events in terms of these background frames of reference is the fundamental process by which the media make the world they report on intelligible to readers and viewers. This process of 'making an event intelligible' is a social process – constituted by a number of specific journalistic practices, which embody (often only implicitly) crucial assumptions about what society is and how it works. One such background assumption is the *consensual* nature of society: the process of *signification* – giving social meanings to events – *both assumes and helps to construct society as a 'consensus'*. We exist as members of one society *because* – it is assumed – we share a common stock of knowledge with our fellow men [and women]: we have access to the same 'maps of meanings'. Not only are we able to manipulate these 'maps of meaning' to understand events, but we have fundamental interests, values and concerns in common, which these maps embody or reflect.
>
> (Hall *et al.* 1978: 54–5, original emphasis)

It is this seemingly commonsensical belief that 'the consensus' is 'a basic feature of everyday life' that underpins journalistic efforts to codify unfamiliar, 'problematic' realities into familiar, comprehensible definitions about how the world works.

Of primary importance when distinguishing the newspaper's mode of address is its 'professional sense of the newsworthy', an aspect of its 'social personality' conditioned by various organizational, technical and commercial constraints, as well as by its conception of the likely opinions of its regular readers (its 'target audience'). It follows that individual newspapers, even those sharing a similar outlook, will inflect the same topic differently. As Hall *et al.* (1978) point out:

> The language employed will thus be the *newspaper's own version of the language of the public to whom it is principally addressed*: its version of the rhetoric, imagery and underlying common stock of knowledge which it assumes its audience shares and which thus forms the basis of the reciprocity of producer/reader.
>
> (Hall *et al.* 1978: 61, original emphasis)

This form of address, specific to each and every news organization, may thus be advantageously described as the newspaper's distinctive 'public idiom'.

Still, despite the apparent variations in this public language from one title to the next, Hall *et al.* (1978) maintain that it is almost always possible to discern in its usage the 'consensus of values' representing the ideological limits of 'reasonable opinion'. Given that this 'consensus of values' is broadly aligned with the interests of powerful voices which tend to be over-accessed by news organizations, Hall *et al.* (1978) contend that this process of reinflecting a news topic into a variant of public language similarly serves:

> to *translate into a public idiom the statements and viewpoints of the primary definers*. This translation of official viewpoints into a public idiom not only makes the former more 'available' to the uninitiated; it invests them with popular force and resonance, naturalising them within the horizon of understandings of the various publics.
>
> (Hall *et al.* 1978: 61, original emphasis)

In this way, then, the definitions, interpretations and inferences of the powerful are embedded, to varying degrees, into the 'everyday' language of the public. Newspapers, as Hall *et al.* (1978: 62) write, ' "take" the language of the public and, on each occasion, return it to them *inflected with dominant and consensual connotations*' (original emphasis).

In order to further critique this process of inflection, then, it is necessary to disrupt the very *naturalness* of the ideological codes embedded in the language of newspaper discourse. Such a line of inquiry will need to elucidate the conventionalized rules, strategies or devices which make it recognizable as a distinct genre of 'purely factual' narrative. In the case of a 'hard' news account, for example, it is possible to show that there are certain prescribed forms of narrative logic associated with the telling of a 'hard' news story which stand in contrast with those of 'soft' news stories (a good journalist, as Bell (1991: 147) observes, 'gets good stories' or 'knows a good story', while a critical news editor asks: 'Is this really a story?' 'Where's the story in this?'). The 'hard' news account is similarly defined in opposition to other types of account, such as 'editorials' or 'leaders' which foreground matters of 'opinion'. This genre of discourse will narrativize the social world in a particular manner, that is, in a way which organizes 'the facts' within a distinctively hierarchical structure based on notions of newsworthiness.

Potential readers of this 'hard' news newspaper account are likely to anticipate that it will provide them with a highly formalized construction of the social world. Formalized, that is, in the sense that the 'hard' news item, whether it appears in a tabloid or broadsheet newspaper, typically reinflects the following elements in distinctive ways:

Headline: represents the principal topic or 'key fact' at stake in the account. To the extent that it is recognized as performing this function by the readers, it is likely to influence their interpretation of the account to follow. In this way, then, it helps to set down the ideological criteria by which the reader is to 'make sense' of what follows.

News lead: typically the opening paragraph or two providing a summary or abstract of the account's essential 'peg' or 'hook' which projects, in turn, 'the story' in a particular direction or 'angle'. The five Ws and H (the who, what, where, when, why and how most pertinent to the event) will likely be in the lead or first paragraph; however, as Keeble (1994: 100) observes, 'the "why" factor is always more problematic'.

Narrative order and sequence: the 'hard' news account almost always follows an 'inverted pyramid style' format. That is, beginning with the news lead, which presents the information deemed to be most 'newsworthy', the account proceeds to structure the remaining details in a descending order of discursive (and usually ideological) significance. By the latter stages of the account, the material being presented could – at least in principle – be dropped without affecting the narrative coherence or sense of the preceding paragraphs. These narrative strategies have become conventionalized to the point that departures from them are likely to disrupt the reader's expectations, yet there is nothing necessary or natural about the rules governing their (in historical terms, rather recent) deployment.

Vocabulary: the regular usage of certain types of stylistic devices, including metaphors, jargon, euphemisms, puns and clichés, tends to characterize a newspaper's 'social personality', as well as its 'professional sense of the newsworthy'. The most marked contrasts are usually between the 'popular', tabloid press and the 'quality', broadsheet titles. In general, the former are usually much more colloquial in vocabulary and emotive in judgement (often to the point of being sensational in tone): 'A vocabulary of emotional arousal,' Holland (1983: 85) writes, 'summons laughter, thrills, shocks, desire, on every page of the *Sun*.' The so-called serious newspapers, in contrast, use terms more likely to be regarded as 'un-emotive' or 'dispassionate', and thereby more consistent with an authoritative appeal to objectivity (see also Cameron 1996; Matheson 2005).

Forms of address: the terms used to refer to, or identify, different news actors indicate a range of important features, including varying degrees of formality ('Tony' versus 'Prime Minister Blair'), the status or power to be attributed to the actor ('monster' or 'fiend' versus 'defendant' or 'alleged perpetrator') or the presumed relationship between the actor and the implied reader of the account (as noted below, made apparent in use of either personalized or impersonalized terms). In the case of the *Sun*, for example, its form of address is personal and direct; as Pursehouse (1991: 98) argues, it 'seeks a relationship with "folks" (not "toffs") and uses a voice of the everyday vernacular and direct "straight talking" to achieve this connection'. The form of address is associated, in turn, with speech of differing degrees of directness, ranging from words reported in quotation marks to those paraphrased by the journalist, thereby raising questions regarding relative truth-value or modality.

Transitivity and modality: the terms chosen by a journalist to represent the relationship between actors and processes, that is, 'who (or what) does what to whom (or what)', are indicative of transitivity. The journalist's transitivity choices can take on an ideological significance, such as where questions of blame or responsibility are raised (see, for example, Clark's (1992) analysis of tabloid news coverage of rape attacks, showing how the victim (e.g. 'no-sex wife') is recurrently blamed for the crime and not her male attacker (e.g. 'hubby'); or Trew's (1979) analysis concerning responsibility for disturbances being attributed to 'strikers' or unions and not employers or the police; see also Fowler 1991; Montgomery 1995). Intertwined with relations of transitivity are those of modality, that is, the ways in which journalists convey judgements concerning the relative truthfulness (or not) of the propositions they are processing. The apparent 'objectivity' of a news account is enhanced to the extent that modal expressions are minimized, thereby encouraging the reader to believe that the journalist is a dispassionate relayer of facts (as opposed to a subjectively emotive person with opinions).

Relations of time: looking beyond the stated place and time ('dateline') of a news account, it is possible to identify the time structure being imposed via the narrativization of the news event in question. 'Hard' news is a highly perishable commodity which is always in danger of becoming 'out of date'; consequently, such accounts usually contain an explicit temporal reference (such as 'yesterday') in the news lead. In marked contrast with other types of narratives, especially fictional ones, time in the 'hard' news account is typically represented in a non-linear manner. The account which respects a chronological ordering of the events it describes is a rare exception to a general rule which holds that 'effects' or 'outcomes' are prioritized over 'causes'. 'Perceived news value,' as Bell (1991: 153) writes, 'overturns temporal sequence and imposes an order completely at odds with linear narrative point. It moves backwards and forwards in time, picking out different actions on each cycle.'

Relations of space: interwoven with relations of time are those of space, the latter being represented in a series of ways in the 'hard' news account. Hallin (1986) usefully identifies five typical ways in which journalists refer to geographical locations (see also Brooker-Gross 1985; Chaney 1994). Specifically, place as authority (the 'here' identified in the account is often listed in the dateline; news gathered 'on the scene' is likely to be deemed to have greater credibility); place as actionable information (relatively rare in 'hard' news; much more likely to appear in 'Weekend', travel or real estate sections where readers are looking for such information in order to do something); place as social connection (through its construction of place, a newspaper can give readers a sense of participation in a distant event, thereby acting as a creator of community); place as setting (invitations to 'experience' the event through detailed descriptions of setting appear only infrequently in 'hard' news because they tend to be considered inappropriate for 'objective' reporting); and, finally, place as subject (the ways in which places themselves become 'news' are often ideologically charged, especially at the level of international politics).

Implied reader: journalists construct news account against a backdrop of assumptions about the social world which they expect the readers to share. It follows that the journalist's orientation to the implied reader, or imagined community of readers, necessarily shapes the form and content of the account. Necessarily implicated in this projection of this ideal reader, who may bear little resemblance to the actual living and breathing reader, are an array of ideological presuppositions concerning relations of class, gender, race, ethnicity, sexuality, age and so forth. Brookes and Holbrook (1998) suggest, for example, that British tabloid news coverage of 'mad cow disease' consistently addressed women as housewives and mothers (evidently a typical feature where 'food scares' are concerned: see Fowler 1991; Allan 2002). Personal pronouns are almost always absent in the 'hard' news account, with the exception of the 'I' of an eyewitness or investigative item (this is in sharp contrast to the frequent use of 'we' on the editorial leader page when the newspaper assumes its public voice).

Closure: the achievement of closure with respect to the 'hard' news account is always partial and contingent, that is, it is never fully realized. In narrative terms, the account typically comes to an end abruptly without formal markers signalling closure (in contrast with broadcast news). As noted above, the 'inverted pyramid style' format facilitates the work of the copy-editor, who trims the length of accounts, usually starting from the bottom, in relation to the size of the available 'news hole'. Narrative closure is successful when readers achieve a feeling of completeness, that

> is, a satisfactory sense that the account has processed an array of facts sufficient to make clear a reasonable and appropriate interpretation of the situation. Thus ideological closure may be said to have been accomplished where readers identify with this dominant interpretation ostensibly encouraged by the account, regarding it to be adequate and factually consistent – for the moment at least – with their personal understanding of the social world.

It is important to note that critical analyses of newspapers, whether tabloid or broadsheet, usually restrict their examinations to the characteristics of the news coverage being generated. This centring of news accounts as the primary focus of inquiry is at the expense of considerations of other forms of content, particularly those types more likely to be seen as mere diversions due to their perceived entertainment value. 'Insofar as acknowledgement is given to entertainment features in the press,' as Curran *et al.* (1980: 288) argue, 'this tends to be grudging and dismissive, as if such content detracts from the central political role and purpose of the press.' As they proceed to point out in their exploration of the non-current affairs sections of newspapers, it is precisely where content is promoted as being 'apolitical' (such as in the realms of human interest as it relates to sport, royalty, celebrities, gossip, competitions, astrology and so forth) that 'ideological significance is most successfully concealed and therefore demands most analysis' (Curran *et al.* 1980: 305). It is also relevant to note that this type of content is regularly disparaged by 'hard' news journalists who are more likely to express concerns over ideology in a different way, namely as a fear that the quality of reporting is being 'dumbed down' by these types of items in the name of boosting circulation figures.

Further studies of 'human interest' or 'soft' news have similarly highlighted how its apparent neutrality reinforces what might be termed the 'dominant political consensus' by encouraging and constraining readers to see events in particular ways. The implications which news coverage of sporting events have for discourses of popular culture, for example, has been the subject of critical attention (see Boyle *et al.* 2009; Brookes 2002; Rowe 2004, 2005). Similarly, critiques of editorials or 'leaders', feature articles (including 'opposite editorial' or 'op ed' pages or 'backgrounders') and opinion columns have pinpointed a range of issues, including how the inclusion of this 'subjective', 'interpretative' material helps to underwrite the proclaimed 'objectivity' of 'hard' news accounts (see Trew 1979; Love and Morrison 1989; Bell 1991; Fowler 1991; Reah 1998; Coward 2009). Cartoons have also been singled out for scrutiny, with several studies assessing how issues concerning, for example, 'the economy' (Emmison and McHoul 1987), national identity (Brookes 1990) and military conflicts (Aulich 1992), among others, have been subject to political caricature (see also Seymour-Ure 1975). Also of interest are 'letters to the editor', not least in terms of how the criteria of inclusion in play delimit the ideological boundaries of *legitimate* or *fair* comment (see Fairclough 1989; Tunstall 1996; Bromley 1998b; Wahl-Jorgensen 2007).

The objectivity of news photographs

Another element of both 'quality' and 'popular' newspapers which similarly deserves more critical attention than it has received to date is the news photograph. Hall (1981: 232–4), in his analysis of news images, suggests that although editors may select a photograph in terms of its formal news values (such as impact, dramatic meaning, unusualness, controversy, and so forth), they are also simultaneously judging how these values will be best treated or 'angled' so as to anchor the intended interpretation for the implied reader. News photographs proclaim the status of being 'literal visual-transcriptions' of the 'real world'; this when, as Hall contends:

> the choice of *this* moment of an event as against that, of *this* person rather than that, of *this* angle rather than any other, indeed, the selection of this photographed incident to represent a whole complex chain of events and meaning, is a highly ideological procedure. But, by appearing literally to reproduce the event as it *really* happened, news photos suppress their selective / interpretive / ideological function. They seek a warrant in that ever pre-given, neutral structure, which is beyond question, beyond interpretation: the 'real world'.
>
> (Hall 1981: 241)

News photographs, in this way, help to reinforce the newspaper's larger claim to be 'objective' in its representations of the social world. 'Photography is imbued with the appearance of objectively recorded reality,' writes Banks (1994: 119); 'consequently, editors often seek to use photographs to provide the stamp of objectivity to a news story' (see also Zelizer 2005, 2009; Brennen, 2009).

This appeal to 'objectivity' can be sustained, of course, only to the extent that the reader accepts the photograph as an unmediated image of actual events. What must be denied at all costs, as Taylor (1991: 10) argues, is that news images are 'intricately sewn into the web of rhetoric. They are never outside it, and always lend it the authority of witness' (see also Tagg 1988; Becker 1992; Hartley 1992, 1996; Kress and van Leeuwen 1998). Ostensibly grounded in the 'bedrock of truth', the photograph must naturalize its impossible claim to be making visible 'what really happened' as a neutral, 'historically instantaneous' (Hall 1981) record of reality. This process of naturalization, as Schwartz (1992: 107) maintains, is engendered in and through the conceptual rules or frameworks governing the professional practice of photojournalism: 'Conventions of framing, composition, lighting, and color or tonal value guide the translation of newsworthy subjects into the two-dimensional photographic image.' The array of representational devices employed by the photojournalist need to retain their apparent transparency, she argues, if the source of drama is to be located in the subject itself and not in the strategies invoked by the photographer. In her words: 'Photojournalism, cloaked in its mantle of objectivity, offers the viewer a vision of the world easily consumed and digested, while its naturalism perpetuates its legitimacy as an objective bearer of the news' (Schwartz 1992: 108).

Matters are becoming increasingly complicated in this regard, however, due to the ways in which photojournalism is being transformed by digital technologies. The manipulation or 'correction' of news images – the so-called Photoshop effect – has proved to be remarkably controversial at times, raising searching ethical questions about what constitutes acceptable, professional conduct. Disputes over what is permissible by way of alteration revolve, to some extent, over standards set down in relation to a pre-digital medium. That is to say, a language of film permeates normative descriptions of what sort of practical adjustments can be safely regarded as reasonable and appropriate. Techniques such as cropping, tinting, dodging or burning, once painstakingly applied through an elaborate set of procedures in a news organization's darkroom in order to accentuate the news photograph's intended significance (if not 'editorial message'), can now be realized in a matter of minutes through a series of keystrokes and/or clicks of a mouse on a laptop computer in the field. Seemingly straightforward policy statements forbidding 'altering the content of news photographs' thus tend to gloss over the subtle ways in which images are routinely crafted in order to enhance their quality for better reproduction, thereby appearing to make what is really a question of emphasis into a stark either–or proposition. No concession is made for extenuating circumstances, even in wartime. '[It] is precisely because so much of the most important journalism is done under such intense pressure that absolute standards are required', Tim Rutten (2003), media critic at the *Los Angeles Times*, states. 'You don't want reporters with bullets flying over their heads or minutes to their deadlines parsing the moral ambiguities of their craft.'

Rutten's point was made in the aftermath of a crisis revolving around precisely this issue involving one of his then colleagues at the newspaper. For Brian Walski, a staff photographer (or 'shooter') for the *Times*, circumstances meant that he was in a state of near-exhaustion when on assignment in Basra, Iraq in March 2003. In covering the movements of British troops, he came across a scene where a soldier was urging several Iraqi citizens to take cover from hostile gunfire, one of whom was holding a small child in his arms. Shooting digitally, Walski (2003) would later remember:

> Things are happening so fast. You have to watch out for yourself, and look what's going on to be able to compose pictures. I had ten frames of soldier totally cut off. At some point I must have zoomed out. When that guy came up with the baby, I shot off ten more frames. I had just one where you could see the soldier's face. The others he was turned away.
>
> (Walski 2003)

At around 10:00 pm that night, following what had become a 14-hour stint, he sat down with his laptop computer to review the day's work, deciding which photographs to relay back to the newsroom via the company's Newscom network. 'We were in Iraq at that point for six days', he recalled. 'We were sleeping in our car. [. . .] There was no safe haven of any kind where you could kind of relax and get a good night's sleep. It was constant tension.' This tension would later help to explain why Walski proceeded to make a decision that would bring his distinguished career to an abrupt end.

Sifting through the shots taken that day, Walski found himself 'playing around a little bit' in the effort to find a 'better image' in compositional terms. Having occasionally 'tweaked' photographs in the past ('taken out a phone pole') with image editing software, it occurred to him that a merging of two of the shots would produce a more dramatic representation of events. In haste, he made a spur of the moment decision to 'improve' one image by digitally combining it with a second one – 'I put them together and thought, "Looks good," and that was it' – without pausing to think through the ramifications. In the composite version of the image, the British solder appears to be cautioning the man holding the child, the imploring look of the Iraqi ostensibly giving expression to the tragic plight of innocent civilians caught up in the hostilities. Such a resonant photograph, not surprisingly, caught the attention of news editors, many of whom promptly cleared the space to run with it. The *LA Times* placed it on page one, above the fold, while several other papers sharing syndication rights similarly gave it prominent play. Amongst the latter was the *Hartford Courant*, which positioned it across the width of the front page on 31 March 2003. The caption beneath it stated: 'A BRITISH SOLDIER from the Irish Guard orders fleeing Basra residents to get down near the Al Zubayr Bridge leading into the besieged city after their position came under fire from Iraqi forces holding the city Sunday.' A second line added: 'The civilians had gathered at the bridge, hoping to flee the city, when Iraqi paramilitaries opened fire on the British forces manning the bridge checkpoint', before directing the reader to the accompanying story on page A3. 'It was a great image,' the

Courant's assistant managing editor for photography and graphics stated, 'and I missed the manipulation, and I feel bad for everyone involved' (cited in Irby 2003).

It was another *Courant* employee, as it happened, who noticed that something seemed to be wrong with the photograph, namely the apparent duplication of figures in the background. Initial assumptions that there was some sort of technical glitch with the digital transmission via the satellite soon gave way to the painful realization that this was a deliberate attempt to deceive (a 600 per cent magnification in Photoshop helped to reveal the evidence). Walski, still in southern Iraq, was contacted by telephone and asked for an explanation. Evidently he did not hesitate to admit what he had done, and offered to resign. Managers at the *LA Times*, whilst sympathetic to his personal predicament, moved decisively to fire him for what they considered to be a serious breach of trust with the paper's readers. An 'Editor's Note', placed within a box in the bottom right-hand corner of the front page, was published in the next edition. It stated:

> On Monday, March 31, the Los Angeles Times published a front-page photograph that had been altered in violation of Times policy.
>
> The primary subject of the photo was a British soldier directing Iraqi civilians to take cover from Iraqi fire on the outskirts of Basra. After publication, it was noticed that several civilians in the background appear twice. The photographer, Brian Walski, reached by telephone in southern Iraq, acknowledged that he had used his computer to combine elements of two photographs, taken moments apart, in order to improve the composition.
>
> Times policy forbids altering the content of news photographs. Because of the violation, Walski, a Times photographer since 1998, has been dismissed from the staff. The altered photo, along with the two photos that were used to produce it, is published today on A6.
>
> (*Los Angeles Times*, 2 April 2003)

A policy forbidding the alteration of news photographs was also in place at the *Courant*, where staff members were reportedly crestfallen to learn that it had been violated. 'This is a huge embarrassment to the industry', one of its staff photographers stated at the time. 'This sort of thing damages the credibility of all of us', he added. 'Once you've lost your trust, you might as well be selling aluminum siding' (cited in McCarthy 2003a).

Reactions to this 'digital deception' – as it was described in some accounts – received attention in press reports around the globe, and sparked considerable debate within the blogosphere. Further insight into the situation was provided by one of Walski's former colleagues at the *LA Times*, photographer Don

Bartletti, who had seen him shortly after the shots were taken. 'He is my friend and I respect the heroic images that he made and the tremendous effort that he has contributed', he told Poynter Online from Kuwait City. 'When I saw him, I really did not recognize him. He was sunburned, had not eaten in days, nor slept in 36 hours, his clothes were filthy, his beard – all over the place. And he smelled like a goat' (cited in Irby 2003). Other photojournalists weighed in to describe the extent to which the stress of working in a war zone, coupled with sleep deprivation, can lead to a state of mental exhaustion whereby lapses in professionalism become more likely. (Walski, in an apology emailed to the entire photography staff at the *LA Times*, readily acknowledged his 'complete breakdown in judgment'.) Intense competition amongst photojournalists, fuelled by adrenaline and a keen sense of rivalry, was cited as a further contributory factor. 'It's about beating the other guy', stated photo editor Jim Mahoney of the *Boston Herald*. 'But sometimes in an effort to make that moment, you can lose sight of the picture [. . .] the big picture, as well as the one in front of you' (cited in Gelzinis 2003). Still others pointed to the type of temptation engendered by digital technology itself, that is, the ease with which photojournalists in the field can perform 'touch ups' on images to 'clean' away 'noise' or to achieve better 'balance'. Walski's transgression, some suggested, was that he took aesthetic matters too far. His desire to compose an image that was pleasing to the eye meant that he overstepped a boundary, thereby calling into question the integrity of the image itself as an accurate reflection of reality. 'Any time you make up anything at all, you shouldn't be working at a newspaper', *LA Times* managing editor Dean Baquet told *The Washington Post*. 'He made this picture something we're not even sure occurred. He heightened the drama of the picture. It's like changing a quote to make it more dramatic' (cited in Kurtz 2003).

Not everyone agreed, however. Given the technical constraints associated with digital technology, some critics argued, it is necessary to dispel once and for all the illusion that the news photograph can be objective (the promise of the digital image to be more 'truthful' in its representation than its film predecessor being untenable, in their view). Photographer Pedro Meyer, for example, maintained that the *LA Times* lacked a valid reason for dismissing Walski. The content of the composite image, he believed, had not been altered in its essence. In his words:

> . . . they have fired someone for doing a professional job in trying to come up with a better picture, the same way that any of their journalists polish a text so that it reads better and is succinct. (Why should a photographer be deprived of doing exactly the same that other professionals are doing on a daily basis as long as the information is not distorted?). The only

> explanation I can find, is that by accusing the photographer and attempting to portray themselves as publishing 'unmanipulated' news, they are seeking to conceal the factual reality of their biased and one-sided presentation of the overall news. That seems to be the more important issue at hand.
>
> (Meyer 2003)

For Meyer, the more significant concern was the attempt made by the *LA Times* to use this issue as a smokescreen of sorts, one intended to cover up 'the wholesale abdication of their responsibility in bringing to the public any news other than what the Pentagon or the White House wishes them to publish'. This line of defence was quickly challenged by other critics, however, such as Frank Van Riper (2003) writing in *The Washington Post*. In his opinion, Meyer was simply wrong, in his contention, to suggest that a professional journalist would 'polish' a direct quote from a source. 'Remember,' he admonished Meyer, '*news photographs are the equivalent of direct quotations* and therefore are sacrosanct – the situational ethics of Walski's apologists notwithstanding.' A reputable photojournalist will make various technical adjustments to a digital image, but would never alter its 'key elements'. These elements, in his view, 'like the key words in a direct quote, simply are off limits to manipulation'.

The language of radio news

Perhaps the most striking feature of radio as a purveyor of news is the evanescent nature of its language, a quality which arguably accentuates the sense of immediacy already heightened by its mode of address. Radio news is at its best when it is relaying 'breaking stories', that is, news which is 'happening now'. This capacity to 'scoop' or 'first' other news media is one of its primary advantages, while the brevity of its ephemeral reports is a key limitation. In terms of an actual word count, of course, the radio news item typically provides a mere fraction of the information contained, for example, in a newspaper account (see also Crook 1998). Nevertheless, as Crisell (1986) argues, radio provides the listener with an indexical sense of the news, that is, it can provide the voices, sounds, noises and so forth of the 'actuality' of the news event:

> On the radio we hear the noises of the news, or at least the informed view or the eyewitness account 'straight from the horse's mouth' and often on location – outdoors, over the telephone – that newspapers can only *report* in the bland medium of print, a medium bereft of the inflections, hesitations and emphases of the living voice which contribute so largely

> to meaning, and also less able to evoke the location in which the account was given.
>
> (Crisell 1986: 100, original emphasis)

The radio news item, he maintains, declares a direct connection with the listener; it establishes a sense of proximity to the 'world out there' with a degree of vividness impossible to capture in a printed news text.

It is this expressive impact of radio news language which engenders a unique set of issues. Chief among them is the concern that the radio newsworker's choice of descriptive words, together with the use of actuality sounds, will lead to an immoderate degree of persuasive influence being imposed on the listener. The selection and codification of news language, as Leitner (1983: 54) argues, has to be responsive to radio's institutional requirements of 'impartiality' and 'balance': 'Referring to one and the same event with the words *slaughter, murder*, *killing* or *assassination*, or to the same group of persons as *terrorists* or *freedom fighters*, may raise questions both of style (appropriateness) and fact.' In his study of BBC radio (and television) news production, Schlesinger (1987: 229–30) cites a corporation memorandum which defines the proper use of terms such as 'guerrillas', 'terrorists', 'raiders', 'gunmen' and 'commandos', in part by explicitly appealing to the newsworker's 'common sense'. In this context, he contends, the concept of 'impartiality' is 'worked out within a framework of socially endowed assumptions about consensus politics, national community and the parliamentary form of conflict-resolution' (Schlesinger 1987: 205).

Also at issue here is how the authoritativeness of this language is linked to the spoken accent associated with its delivery 'on air'. For many listeners in Britain, for example, 'BBC English' is virtually synonymous with received pronunciation or 'RP'. It has long been argued by corporation executives that the 'neutrality' of the newsreader, and with it the prestige of the newscast, is likely to be reinforced through the use of an RP accent (such is also the case, if arguably to a lesser extent, on National Public Radio in the US). As Crisell (1986) writes:

> On the one hand RP is still commonly regarded as the badge of the well-educated, professionally successful or the socially privileged and therefore as the accent of 'those who know best, the most authoritative'. On the other hand, its universal intelligibility [throughout Britain] accords it the status of a 'non-accent': it minimizes the element of idiosyncrasy and even of 'personality' in the voice, for which reason the BBC has seldom allowed it to be replaced in the delivery of news or official announcements by the regional accents which are widely heard elsewhere on the networks.
>
> (Crisell 1986: 83)

Implicit to this projection of the newsreader's 'personality' at the level of enunciation, according to Crisell, is its indexical function as a purported guarantee of the 'impersonality' of the larger broadcasting institution (see also Lewis and Booth 1989; Bell 1991; Shingler and Wieringa 1998). That is to say, to the extent that 'editorial bias' is held to be embodied, literally, in the voice of the newsreader, the avowed 'objectivity' of the news organization itself will be preserved.

Related studies of radio interviews, whether occurring in newscasts or current affairs programmes, have similarly generated interesting insights into the characteristic rules or conventions of radio discourse (as have analyses of 'talk' and 'call-in' radio formats; see Hutchby 1991, 2005; Scannell 1991; Gibian 1997a, b). Several of these studies have looked beyond the interviewer's posing of questions to examine the communicative strategies she or he is likely to invoke in order to facilitate the interpretation of the interviewee's answers. By keeping the assumed needs of the implied listener in mind at all times, the interviewer manoeuvres to clarify points (often by summarizing, paraphrasing or reinforcing them through repetition) which might otherwise be too complex to be easily grasped. Issues of clarity with regard to style, tone, syntax and diction are directly linked to assumptions about what background knowledge or shared experiences the audience are imagined to possess. Similarly, it is the interviewer who is charged with the responsibility of adjudicating between contending truth-claims, of sorting out 'right' from 'wrong', in broad alignment with the implied listener's 'horizon of expectations' (Bakhtin 1981) *vis-à-vis* the speaking practices deemed appropriate to these factual genres of radio talk.

This line of inquiry is further developed in Fairclough's (1998) analysis of the early weekday morning *Today* programme broadcast on BBC Radio 4, arguably the most influential radio news programme in Britain due to its perceived impact on 'opinion leaders'. He suggests, for example, that interviewers in the course of their interaction with interviewees play a crucial role in rearticulating different discourses together, one implication of which is the reaffirmation of certain protocols of 'conversationalization'. Of particular significance is a 'lifeworld discourse', that is, the presenter's rendition of the 'discourse of ordinary people in ordinary life'. It is this discourse, he argues, which combines with an 'ethos of common sense' to construct, in turn, a basis against which the different viewpoints of the interviewees can be evaluated. This shift away from the 'authority' and 'distance' more traditionally associated with BBC newscasts, Fairclough (1998: 160) maintains, 'appears to be a democratizing move, but it is at the same time an institutionally controlled democratization: the voices of ordinary people are "ventriloquized" rather than directly heard'.

A close reading of radio interview transcripts can help to identify the types of strategies typically employed by interviewers on programmes such as *Today*.

The imposition of orderliness on these interactions, for example, may be shown to be a discursive accomplishment which relies on the cooperation of the interviewee to a remarkable degree. In extending Fairclough's argument concerning this strategic invocation of an ethos of 'common sense' to justify the disciplinary rules regulating these exchanges, it is important to recognize just how fraught these dynamics are with uncertainty, ambiguity and contradiction. Indeed, as Gibian (1997b) observes:

> In the verbal ebb and flow, we're very conscious of who has the floor, who asks the questions, who sets the vocabulary, the tone, the issues; who interrupts, who is silenced or excluded; who gains through the irrational attractions of style, charisma, voice quality, media training; who feels the strong pull of conformity and consensus, the fear of ostracization; and so on.
>
> (Gibian 1997b: 139–40)

These seemingly free-flowing 'exchanges' must be contained within the limits of 'impartiality' if the interviewer's 'neutralistic stance' is to be maintained, a task which requires considerable skill to achieve. Any damage inflicted upon this stance by interviewees, as Greatbatch (1998) contends, would lead to the interviewer being identified with a particular ideological position, a problem which would have to be verbally 'repaired' without delay. In this way, the 'normal bounds of acceptability' which both enable and constrain radio interview interactions are shown to require constant policing to ward off potential threats to their appropriation of 'common sense' (as is similarly the case with televisual interviews; see also Clayman 1991; Harris 1991; Roth 1998; Hutchby 2005; Montgomery 2009).

The textuality of television news

The 'moment' of the broadcast news text is clearly a fluid one; its meanings are dispersed in ways which analyses of actual newscasts as static constructs or artefacts cannot adequately address. Turning now to televisual news, of particular interest are the ways in which it seeks to implicate its audience in a specific relationship of spectatorship, ostensibly that of an unseen onlooker or witness. Televisual news claims to provide an up-to-the-minute (now) narrative which, in turn, projects for the viewers a particular place (here) from which they may 'make sense' of the significance of certain 'newsworthy' events for their daily lives. As Hall *et al.* (1976) point out:

> The facts must be arranged, in the course of programming, so as to present an intelligible 'story': hence the process of presentation will reflect the

> explanations and interpretations which appear most plausible, credible or adequate to the broadcaster, his [or her] editorial team and the expert commentators he [or she] consults. Above all, the known facts of a situation must be translated into intelligible *audio-visual signs, organised as a discourse*. TV cannot transmit 'raw historical' events as such, to its audiences: it can only transmit pictures of, stories, informative talk or discussion about, the events it selectively treats.
>
> (Hall *et al*. 1976: 65)

Accordingly, it is the codified definitions of reality which are regarded as the most 'natural', as the most representative of 'the world out there', that are actually the most ideological.

In order to unpack the conventionalized dynamics of these processes of representation, this section will provide a brief discussion of several pertinent aspects of British televisual newscasts. Specifically, a number of different opening sequences for BBC and ITN newscasts will be examined with an eye to identifying the more pronounced features characteristic of their respective modes of address. This schematic reading is advanced against the current of televisual 'flow' (Williams 1974), so to speak, in order to pinpoint, if in a necessarily partial and highly subjective manner, several conceptual issues for further, more rigorous examination.

Apparent across the range of the different BBC and ITN newscasts under consideration are several shared features:

Interruption: the opening sequence, usually composed of a 15- to 20-second segment of brightly coloured computer-animated graphics, rapidly unfolds to a sharply ascending piece of theme music (the use of trumpets is typical). Its appearance announces the interruption of the flow of entertainment programming by signalling the imminent threat of potentially distressing information (most news, after all, is 'bad news').

Liveness: the opening sequence helps to establish a sense of urgency and, in this way, anchors a declaration of immediacy for the newscast's larger claim to authoritativeness. The news is coming directly to you 'live'; its coverage of 'breaking news' is happening now (even though most of the content to follow will have been pre-recorded).

Time–space: each of these segments privileges specific formulations of temporality (ticking clocks are used by both the BBC and ITN, which signal the up-to-theminuteness of the news coverage) conjoined with those of spatiality (images of revolving globes spin to foreground an image of the British nation as defined by geography, in the case of the BBC; while for ITN's *News at Ten*, a London cityscape at night is slowly panned until the camera rests on a close-up of the clockface of the main parliamentary building, the apparent seat of political power).

Comprehensiveness: implicit to this progressively narrowing focal dynamic around time–space is an assertion of the comprehensiveness of the news coverage. The news, having been monitored from around the world, is being presented to 'us' from 'our' national perspective. That is, 'we' are located as an audience within the 'imagined community' (Anderson 1991) of the British nation.

Professionalism: the final shot in the succession of graphic sequences (ostensibly sounded by the gong of Big Ben in the case of ITN) brings 'us' into the televisual studio, a pristine place of hard, polished surfaces (connotations of efficiency and objectivity) devoid of everyday, human (subjective) features. A central paradox of broadcast news, as Crisell (1986: 90–1) writes, 'is that if there is one thing more vital to it than a sense of authenticity, of proximity to the events themselves, it is a sense of clear-sighted detachment from them – of this authenticity being mediated through the remote, sterile atmosphere of the studio'.

The camera smoothly glides across the studio floor while, in the case of the *ITN Lunchtime News*, a male voice-over sternly intones: 'From the studios of ITN (.) the news (.) with Nicholas Owen and Julia Somerville.' Both newsreaders are situated behind a shared desk, calmly organizing their scripts. Serving as a backdrop for them is what appears to be a dimly lit (in cool blue light) newsroom, empty of people but complete with desks, computer equipment, and so forth. Similarly, for the *News at Ten*, as the male voice-over declares: 'From ITN (.) News at Ten (.) with Trevor McDonald', the newsreader appears in shot seated behind a desk, typing on an invisible keyboard with one hand as he collects a loose sheaf of papers with his other one (which is also holding a pen). Whether it is ITN or the BBC, it is the institution behind the newsreader which is responsible for producing the news; it is the very 'impersonality' of the institution which, in ideological terms, is to be preserved and reaffirmed by the 'personality' of the newsreader.

As a result, the mode of address utilized by the respective newsreaders at the outset of the newscast needs to appear to be 'dialogic' (Bakhtin 1981) in its formal appeal to the viewer's attention. This dialogic strategy of co-presence is to be achieved, in part, through the use of direct eye contact with the camera (and thus with the imagined viewer being discursively inscribed). As Morse (1986: 62) observes, 'the impression of presence is created through the construction of a shared space, the impression of shared time, and signs that the speaking subject is speaking for himself [or herself], sincerely' (see also Hartley and

Montgomery 1985; Marriott 1995; Tolson 1996; Morse 1998; Cottle 2005). The impersonally professional space of the studio is, in this way, personalized in the form of the newsreader who, using a language which establishes these temporal and spatial relations of co-presence with the viewer, reaffirms a sense of shared participation.

Nevertheless, these dialogic relations of co-presence are hierarchically structured. The *direct* address speech of the newsreader (note that the 'accessed voices' will be restricted to *indirect* speech and eye contact) represents the 'news voice' of the network: the newsreader stands in for an institution charged with the responsibility of serving a public interest through the impartiality of its reporting. For this reason, these relations of co-presence need to be organized so as to underwrite the signifiers of facticity and journalistic prestige, as well as those of timeliness and immediacy.

In addition to the steady gaze of expressive eye contact, the visual display of the newsreader's authority is further individualized in terms of 'personality' (white males still predominate), as well as with regard to factors such as clothing (formal) and body language (brisk and measured). This conventionalized appeal to credibility is further enhanced through aural codes of a 'proper' accent (almost always received pronunciation) and tone (solemn and resolute). Such factors, then, not only may help to create the impression of personal integrity and trustworthiness, but also may ratify the authenticity of the newsreader's own commitment to upholding the truth-value of the newscast as being representative of her or his own experience and reliability. Personalized terms of address, such as 'good afternoon' or 'good evening', may similarly work to underscore the human embodiment of news values by newsreaders as they seemingly engage in a conversational discourse with the viewers.

The newsreader or 'news anchor', as Morse (1998: 42) observes, 'is a special kind of star supported by subdued sartorial and acting codes that convey "sincerity" '. Taken to an extreme, this can lead to 'Ken and Barbie journalism' where, as van Zoonen (1998) argues, the charge is made that physical attractiveness of the 'anchor team' is taking precedence over their competence as journalists. Also at issue here is the related trend, particularly pronounced in local news, of 'happy talk'. 'As the name suggests,' van Zoonen (1998: 40) writes, 'these are merry little dialogues between the anchors showing how much they like each other and how much they love their audiences.' The main purpose behind 'happy talk', according to her interviews with newsworkers, is 'to "people-ize" the news, as one news editor has put it, and to suggest that journalists and audiences are one big happy family'.

The immediacy of the implied discursive exchange is thus constrained by the need to project a sense of dialogue where there is only the decisive, if inclusionary, voice of the newsreader. As Stam (1983) writes:

> The newscaster's art consists of evoking the cool authority and faultless articulation of the written or memorised text while simultaneously 'naturalising' the written word to restore the appearance of spontaneous communication. Most of the newscast, in fact, consists of this scripted spontaneity: newscasters reading from teleprompters, correspondents reciting hastily-memorised notes, politicians delivering prepared speeches, commercial actors representing their roles. In each case, the appearance of fluency elicits respect while the trappings of spontaneity generate a feeling of unmediated communication.
>
> (Stam 1983: 28)

In play are a range of deictic features which anchor the articulation of time ('now', 'at this moment', 'currently', 'as we are speaking', 'ongoing' or 'today') to that of space ('here', 'this is where' or 'at Westminster this morning') such that the hierarchical relationship of identification for the intended viewer is further accentuated.

Contingent upon these relations of co-presence is what has been characterized as the regime of the 'fictive We'. That is, the mode of address employed by the newsreader, by emphasizing the individual and the familiar, encourages the viewer's complicity in upholding the hegemonic frame (see Stam 1983; Morse 1986, 1998; Holland 1987; Doane 1990; Wilson 1993). To the extent that the newsreader is seen to speak not only 'to us', but also 'for us' ('we' are all part of the 'consensus'), then 'we' are defined in opposition to 'them', namely those voices which do not share 'our' interests and thus are transgressive of the codified limits of common sense. As Stam (1983: 29) points out, there needs to be a certain 'calculated ambiguity of expression' if a diverse range of viewers are to identify with the truth-claims on offer: 'The rhetoric of network diplomacy, consequently, favours a kind of oracular understatement, cultivating ambiguity, triggering patent but deniable meanings, encouraging the most diverse groups, with contradictory ideologies and aspirations, to believe that the newscasters are not far from their own beliefs.' As a result, in attempting to authorize a preferred reading of the news event for 'us', the newsreader aims to frame the initial terms by which it is to be interpreted.

The rules of the hegemonic frame, while in principle polysemic (open to any possible interpretation), are typically inflected to encourage a relation of reciprocity between the viewers' and the newsreader's 'personal' sense of 'news values'. The voice-over of the newsreader, in seeking to specify 'what is at issue' in each of the headlined news stories, begins the work of organizing the news event into a preferred narrative structure for us, the viewers. Words are thus aligned with images to affirm, and then reinforce, the interpellative appeals of the news voice and the strategy of visualization: viewers can 'see for themselves' a range of the elements constitutive of what journalists often call the five Ws and H (who, what, where, when, why and how) of the news lead. Moreover, as Doane (1990: 229) writes, 'the status of the image as indexical truth is not inconsequential – through it the "story" touches the ground of the real'. The extent to which these news headlines are made to 'touch the ground of the real' is thus dependent upon the degree to which hegemonic relations of reciprocity are established such that it is *obvious* to viewers that these are the most significant news events of the day for them to know about, and that it is *self-evident* how they are to be best understood.

Here it is also important not to overlook the larger performative task of these opening sequences for the newscast. That is to say, attention also needs to be directed to their dramatic role in attracting and maintaining the interest of the viewer and, moreover, the sense of reassurance they offer through their very repetition from one weekday to the next (a sharp contrast is provided by the headline of a news bulletin which suddenly 'interrupts' regular programming; see Doane 1990; Harrington 1998). News headlines seek to incorporate the extraordinary into the ordinary; the strangeness of the social world (and hence its potential newsworthiness) is to be mediated within the terms of the familiar. A news event can make sense to the viewers only if they are able to situate it in relation to a range of pre-existing 'maps of meaning' (Hall *et al.* 1978) or forms of cultural knowledge about the nature of society.

The framework of interpretation set down by the news headline thus not only tends to nominate precisely 'what is at issue' and how its significance is to be defined, but also must reaffirm the viewers' sense of what is consequential, or at least relevant, in the context of their daily lives. The language utilized in these opening sequences, both verbal and visual, may therefore be analysed as one way in which the newscast indicates the normative limits of the sense of newsworthiness it attributes to its audience. Clearly, then, once a mode of inquiry elects to seize upon the embeddedness of the newscast in the now and here by prioritizing for critique precisely those elements which are usually ignored in analyses of this type, new aspects of the political struggle over the social relations of signification will be brought to the fore for further exploration.

'The obvious facts of the matter'

Over the course of this chapter's discussion, an attempt has been made to highlight a basis for future research efforts. It is with this aim in mind that I wish to suggest in this closing section that investigations into news discourse may advantageously extend the theoretical trajectory outlined above in a number of substantive ways. To briefly outline one such possibility, I would argue that the concept of hegemony needs to be elaborated much further than it has been to date in journalism studies. Specifically, in a manner which would better enable researchers to account more rigorously for the complex ways in which the news media, as key terrains of the ongoing political struggle over the right to define the 'reality' of public issues, operate to mediate the risks, threats and dangers engendered across the society they purport to describe.

This aim could be realized, in part, by focusing our analyses more directly on the indeterminacies or contradictions (the exceptions to the conventionalized rules) implicated in news discourse's preferred appropriations of 'the world out there'. Here I am suggesting that we need to be much more sensitive to the contingent nature of the representational strategies being used in news discourse. Attempts to demonstrate how these strategies are organized to disallow or 'rule out' alternative inflections of reality should, at the same time, seek to identify the extent to which the same strategies are being challenged, even transgressed, over time. Given that the *naturalization* of any truth-claim is always a matter of degree, it is crucial that analyses recognize the more subtle devices by which common sense has to be continuously revalidated as part of the reportorial performance, and thereby avoid a reliance upon rigid, zero-sum formulations of hegemony to sustain their theses.

Such an approach may enable us to identify much more precisely the nature of the processes by which this form of media discourse structures the public articulation of truth. Following Williams (1974: 130), who contends that the 'reality of determination is the setting of limits and the exertion of pressures, within which variable social practices are profoundly affected but never necessarily controlled', I would agree with those who argue that a much greater conceptual emphasis needs to be placed on how news conditions what counts as 'truth' in a given instance, and who has the right to define that truth. At the same time, though, equal attention needs to be given to discerning the openings for different audience groups or 'interpretive communities' to potentially recast the terms by which 'truth' is defined in relation to their lived experiences of injustice and inequalities (once again, after Williams, determination is not a single force, but rather an exertion of continuous, but often unpredictable, pressures). Such a shift in focus would mean that research questions posed within a narrowly framed domination–opposition dynamic could be clarified through a much more fundamental interrogation of the very precepts informing the fluid configuration of facticity in the first place.

News discourse could thus be deconstructed not only through a critique of its projection of journalistic distance and 'impartiality', but also by resisting its movement toward closure around common-sense criteria of inclusion and exclusion. It follows that in addition to asking *whose* common sense is being defined by the news account as *factual*, we need to ask: by what representational strategies is the viewer being invited to 'fill in the gaps', or being encouraged to make the *appropriate*, *rational* inferences, in order to reaffirm journalistic procedures for handling contrary facts which are otherwise discrepant to the news frame? In my view, once this 'setting of limits' on the narrativization of meaning has been denaturalized to the point that the politics of its *naturalness* are rendered explicit, analyses may proceed to identify in news discourse the slippages, fissures and silences which together are always threatening to undermine its discursive authority. In other words, this type of research may be able to contribute to the empowerment of those counter-hegemonic voices seeking to contest the truth politics of news discourse, not least by helping to first disrupt and then expand the ideological parameters of 'the obvious facts of the matter'.

6 NEWS, AUDIENCES AND EVERYDAY LIFE

> Serious, careful, honest, journalism is essential, not because it is a guiding light but because it is a form of honourable behavior, involving the reporter and the reader.
>
> (Martha Gellhorn, foreign news correspondent)

> I have to believe that a better informed world is more civilised, more compassionate, more ready to act and to help. But I do not think it is my place to tell the audience what to do.
>
> (Kate Adie, BBC news correspondent)

Pronouncements about how the 'average person' relates to the news media often invoke a continuum of sorts, one where the drowsily indifferent 'couch potatoes' are positioned at one end and the hyperactive 'news junkies' are at the other. Somewhere in between, it follows, is where most news consumers can be situated, particularly where television news is concerned (still the most popular source of news for people in countries such as Britain and the US).

It is surprising to note how few news organizations in either country conduct regular, systematic research into who makes up their audience, a problem which parallels the insufficient number of investigations being undertaken within an academic context. A number of the studies which have been launched do point out, however, that care needs to be taken to avoid thinking of 'the news audience' at too abstract a level. Such a phrase, after all, defines people who may or may not actually choose to define themselves in this way and, in any case, risks transforming them into a fixed, rigid totality of individuals on the basis of only one aspect of their engagement with the media. Accordingly, just as the claim that journalists are participants, knowingly or not, in some sort of wilful conspiracy to encodify the dictates of a 'dominant ideology' in the newsroom may be safely dismissed, so may the corresponding assertion that news viewers, listeners and readers be regarded as passive, alienated dupes indoctrinated into a state of 'false consciousness'.

At issue for this chapter is the need to elucidate how the materiality of news culture is intimately imbricated in the varied realities of everyday experience. With this aim in mind, our attention first turns to a series of issues raised in critical investigations of newspaper readership. In the course of mapping a number of the most salient features of this research terrain, particular attention is given to exploring the ways in which the cultural dynamics of newspaper reading are interwoven throughout the cultural fabric of our everyday realities. Next, analyses of the television news audience are centred for critique, in the first instance by drawing upon Hall's (1980) highly influential encoding–decoding model. This conceptual model is examined with an eye to its importance for investigating how television news discourses encourage the viewer to negotiate or 'decode' the fluidly contradictory dynamics of their 'preferred meanings' as being inferentially consistent with the dictates of 'common sense'. The ensuing discussion focuses on the need to situate the television newscast within the household in order to discern how the profuse flow of its sounds and images are negotiated by the viewer on an ordinary, 'lived' basis.

Mapping the newspaper audience

Attempts to 'measure' the audience for a particular newspaper usually begin with its daily circulation figures. These figures provide an indication of each newspaper's relative share of the market, although distortions can creep in where copies have been given away for free or sold at a reduced price in order to give the numbers an upward boost. In any case, circulation is different from readership as more than one person typically reads a single copy of a given title. As a general rule, it is assumed in most industry calculations that between two and three people may be counted as readers per copy. Precisely how best to quantify a 'reading threshold' for a given newspaper, however, is itself hotly disputed. For some industry studies, 'reading' may simply refer to the availability of a newspaper in a household, for others it means that some of its pages have at least been scanned, while others define reading as a thorough engagement with its contents (the reader's recollection of which may then be assessed the next day).

The most typical methods employed to collect data about newspaper audiences are interviews, conducted either face to face or over the telephone, and opinion surveys, usually involving a questionnaire circulated via the post. In addition, newspapers will often survey their own readers by including a questionnaire for them to fill in and return, possibly in exchange for a chance to win a prize. A range of different groups have a direct interest in knowing more about the characteristics associated with a newspaper's readership. These groups include, in the first instance, the owners of the newspaper, its editors and marketing people. Readership data, as Brown (1994: 106) argues, serve 'as evidence of the success (or otherwise) of attracting the size and profile of audience aimed for via a particular policy on editorial contents and their treatment'. In the second instance, groups which also have a vital stake in acquiring information about a newspaper's readers include advertising agencies, market research organizations and, of course, potential advertisers.

It is almost always the case that the price listed on the front page of a serious, 'quality' newspaper generates only a relatively small share of the revenue necessary for the title to meet the costs of publication. The principal source of revenue is the sale of advertising space; the number of advertisements sold determines the size of the news hole, not the other way around. Journalists are all too aware of the status of the newspaper as a commodity, the financial success of which depends on attracting the type of readers of interest to specific advertisers (several of the titles at the 'popular' end of the spectrum, in contrast, depend primarily on sales revenue because their readers are less 'desirable' in marketing terms). In light of the demands of advertisers, then, it is not surprising that the 'upmarket' newspaper's projection of an 'average' or 'typical' reader is likely to prefigure a middle-class, educated person who is middle-aged and interested in public affairs. It is precisely this type of person whom many advertisers would define as their 'target audience', hence their aspiration to purchase the attention of this reader being sold by the 'serious' press.

Beyond these types of generalized assumptions, however, most newsworkers actually know very little about their readership, and tend to be highly sceptical of claims made on the basis of market research (see also Tunstall 1996; Lewis 2001). After some forty years as a newspaper journalist in Britain, Alastair Hetherington (1985: 37–8) maintains that 'very few journalists have more than a hazy personal view of their public'. He supports his point with quotations from a number of reporters:

> Oh, we're writing for the editor of course. He's the audience.
> My wife, she's the critic.
> Will it get people talking over the breakfast table or in the pub? That's what I ask myself.
> If I like it, that's the only quotient I put on it. I reckon that I'm an average reader.

Analyses based on interviews with newsworkers recurrently suggest that forms of direct audience feedback, such as letters and telephone calls, have only a limited impact on newsworkers' rudimentary impressions of their readers (see also Bell 1991: 87–90). Indeed, these types of respondents evidently tend to be dismissed as being 'atypical' or 'unrepresentative' due to a general conviction among newsworkers that 'the bulk of audience reaction is from cranks, the unstable, the hysterical and the sick' (cited in Schlesinger 1987: 108; see Ericson *et al.* 1987: 193–6; Bromley 1998b).

Nevertheless, there appears to be a growing trend in the British 'quality' press, encouraged by the Press Complaints Commission among others, to regularly print 'corrections' and 'apologies' with 'due prominence' when warranted (a longstanding practice for their US equivalents). For this and related reasons, a number of the national dailies have also taken the further step of appointing a newspaper ombudsperson to investigate readers' concerns on their behalf. Similarly growing in prominence is the practice of ensuring a 'right to reply' to help rectify harmful inaccuracies. Such developments run counter to what the *Guardian*'s ombudsperson, Ian Mayes (1998), calls 'the culture of concealment' slowly changing among newspapers. This culture, he argues, 'urges journalists never to admit mistakes, to dismiss those who complain as cranks, and – however often we call for accountability in others – to remain unaccountable ourselves' (Mayes 1998: S2, 2).

Academic studies of newspaper readerships have been undertaken via an extensive array of conceptual and methodological approaches, some of which entail extremely complex sociopsychological models in their attempts to quantify 'audience behaviour'. Of particular interest in my view, however, are those investigations which have sought to explore the actual ways in which readers engage with their newspapers as an ordinary part of everyday life. Bausinger's (1984) work, for example, attempts to identify several of the rituals associated with newspaper reading in the household (in this case in Germany). This study suggests that these rituals may be rendered more clearly visible when their very 'normality' is disrupted, as in a situation where a newspaper has not been published and therefore not delivered as usual in the morning.

> Under these circumstances the newspaper publishers receive a great number of telephone calls, which they gladly register as proof of the importance of their products. This is certainly not wrong, but is this a question of the missing content of the newspaper, or isn't it rather that one misses the newspaper itself? . . . [R]eading it proves that the breakfast-time world is still in order – hence the newspaper is a mark of confirmation, and that will surely have an effect on both its content and its structure.
>
> (Bausinger 1984: 344)

It follows, he argues, that the day-to-day use of newspapers needs to be set in relation to that of other media (especially radio and television), as well as 'non-media conditions', in order to account for the highly selective ways in which people relate to any one medium.

Bausinger (1984: 349–50) then proceeds to characterize newspaper reading not as an 'isolated, individual process', but rather as a 'collective process' typically transpiring 'in the context of the family, friends, colleagues'. The contents of newspapers, like those of other media, are 'materials for conversation', the precise meaning of which is the subject of discursive interaction among readers (see also Anderson 1991; Hartley 1996). Clearly, then, as he rightly points out: 'A bit of wild thinking is needed to catch and describe this complex world in all its rational irrationality' (Bausinger 1984: 351).

Sceptical laughter? Reading the tabloids

Critical investigations of newspaper audiences typically focus on the 'quality' end of the market, that is, on the 'respectable' daily titles of national prominence. The reason for this tendency, in part, is because these publications are usually deemed to have the greatest impact across society, especially in terms of their influence on the governmental sphere. Studies of the 'tabloid', 'popular' or 'mass consumption' press are growing in prominence, however, as increasing numbers of researchers seek to realign their analyses so as to address journalism as a form of popular culture. In Britain, daily tabloid titles such as the *Sun* (about 3.0 million circulation) or the *Mirror* (about 1.5 million circulation), for example, secure far greater circulation figures than do their elite rivals, such as *The Times* (about 0.6 million circulation) or the *Guardian* (about 0.4 million circulation). Additional points of comparison include differences in their respective size, news values, mode of address, language (both written and visual), readership and price, all of which inform distinct strategies of representation.

If more than one tabloid editor prefers to use the phrase 'un-popular press' to describe the 'quality' titles, for some members of the latter the tabloids symbolize journalism sunk to its lowest depths. To be called 'the greatest tabloid journalist of all time', media commentator Clive James once remarked, is 'tantamount to calling a man the greatest salesman of sticky sweets in the history of dentistry' (cited in Stephens 1988: 113). In any case, there is little dispute that the ways in which the popular newspapers treat matters of public concern stand in marked contrast with the 'serious', 'high-minded' reporting of the 'qualities'. As Sparks (1992) argues:

> the popular press embeds a form of immediacy and totality in its handling of public issues. In particular, this immediacy of explanation is achieved

> by means of a direct appeal to personal experience. The popular conception of the personal becomes the explanatory framework within which the social order is presented as transparent . . . [T]he 'personal' obliterates the 'political' as an explanatory factor for human behaviour.
>
> (Sparks 1992: 39–40)

This overemphasis on the 'personal' as it is defined in relation to the immediate issues of daily life leads Sparks to maintain, in turn, that readers of tabloid newspapers are being denied the means to recognize the structural basis of power relations in society as a totality. News which is highly personalized in its representations of reality makes it that much more difficult for readers to identify means of articulating their resistance to these power relations.

This view is only partly shared by Fiske (1992), who outlines an alternative stance by drawing attention to further distinctions between 'official' and 'tabloid' news as they have developed in the US (examples of the latter he cites include the *Weekly World News* and the *National Enquirer*). 'Official' news, in his view, prefigures a top-down definition of information based on convictions regarding 'what the people ought to know for a liberal democracy to function properly' (Fiske 1992: 49). That is to say, official news promotes a certain form of knowledge, one which is largely defined in relation to public sphere events, by matters of policy, and not by the particularities of everyday life. 'The social reality it produces,' Fiske (1992: 49) contends, 'is the habitat of the masculine, educated middle class, the habitat that is congenial to the various alliances formed by the power-bloc in white patriarchal capitalist societies.' Significantly, this type of knowledge produces what he calls a 'believing subject', that is, a reader who generally accepts its claims as being self-evidently true. It is at this level, then, that its difference from tabloid news is most apparent.

> The last thing that tabloid journalism produces is a believing subject. One of its most characteristic tones of voice is that of a sceptical laughter which offers the pleasures of disbelief, the pleasures of not being taken in. This popular pleasure of 'seeing through' them (whoever constitutes the powerful *them* of the moment) is the historical result of centuries of subordination which the people have not allowed to develop into subjection.
>
> (Fiske 1992: 49)

Where official news accounts normalize rational definitions of reality through appeals to 'objectivity', tabloid journalism subverts the very idea of rationality.

Examples of headlines taken from various weekly US 'supermarket tabloids' included in a study conducted by Hogshire (1997) support this latter point all too clearly:

> SEX-CHANGE WOMAN MAKES SELF PREGNANT! . . . Scientists confirm 'first of a kind' case
>
> (*Sun*)
>
> JOHN LENNON IS ALIVE! Electrifying recent photo
>
> (*Sun*)
>
> FAMILY CLAIMS 500-lb SPACE ALIEN RAIDED THEIR REFRIGERATOR!
>
> (*Weekly World News*)
>
> DOLLY THE CLONED SHEEP KILLS A LAMB – AND EATS IT!
>
> (*Weekly World News*)

Not only is 'objective' journalism's appeal to value-free, neutral information disrupted, but also the very ideological disciplines regulating what counts as 'truth' are being flagrantly transposed. For news to be pleasurable, and thus popular, Fiske (1992: 57) suggests, it needs to provoke conversation: 'It is by taking up and recirculating the issues of news orally that the people construct aspects of the public sphere as relevant to their own.' The apparent irrelevance of much 'official' (or 'top-down') news for many readers is thus directly linked to its repression of alternative or oppositional knowledges. 'Unlike official news,' Fiske (1992: 52) maintains, 'popular news makes no attempt to smooth out contradictions in its discourse; indeed it exploits them, for unresolved contradictions are central to popular culture.' It is this contradictoriness, he argues, which the 'ordinary' reader can identify with as being consistent with their daily experience of trying to cope with inequalities of power: 'Knowing when to dissemble and go along with the system and when not to is a crucial tactic of everyday life' (Fiske 1992: 53; see also Connell 1992; Gripsrud 1992).

In her study *For Enquiring Minds: A Cultural Study of Supermarket Tabloids*, Bird (1992) similarly refuses to dismiss tabloid news as trivial 'trash', arguing instead that researchers need to understand why it is the case that millions of readers across the US 'find a valued place for the papers in their lives' (see also Bird 2009). It was with this end in mind that she arranged to place a notice in the *Examiner* inviting readers to share with her their experience of reading it and other tabloids, such as the *National Enquirer*, the *Weekly World News*, the *Globe*, the *Sun* and the *Star*. Fifteen members of this self-selected group (114 letters were received), as well as one other person, were then interviewed. Bird is quick to acknowledge that her respondents did not constitute a scientifically representative sample, yet believes that they were nevertheless reasonably close to the 'typical buyers' envisaged by the *Examiner*'s staff: that is, 'mostly white, predominantly female, and middle-aged or older' (Bird 1992: 113). Interestingly, few of these respondents use the word 'tabloid' to refer to publications like the *Examiner*, generally preferring terms like 'paper', 'magazine' or an affectionate 'tabs'. The style of the tabloids tends to be described as 'fun', 'exciting', 'newsy', 'interesting' or 'gossipy'.

Although most of Bird's respondents consider the news stories to be well researched and verified, none of them accept everything presented on the pages of their tabloid as being true (Bird 1992: 121–2). That said, some find pleasure in assuming an 'as if' stance, playing along with the item's truth-claims to see how far their own willingness to believe can be stretched. Most readers, however, appear content to 'pick and choose' what they believe according to their existing interests and beliefs, with only a small minority of 'self-conscious' or 'ironic' readers stating that these 'sleazy' and 'vulgar' titles were an enjoyable kind of 'slumming' (Bird 1992: 118). Apparent across the range of responses is a perception that the tabloids provide a means to counter the constant flow of 'bad news' being presented in 'proper' newspapers and television newscasts. As Bird writes:

> [A]n important element in their readings is indeed a form of resistance to dominant values – an awareness, for example, that they 'should' be reading about news and current affairs but find these studies boring and irrelevant. The perception that tabloids offer 'untold stories' about anything from government waste to a movie star's romance is important to them because it suggests some sense of knowing and control over things that are really out of control.
>
> (Bird 1992: 204–5)

Still, as she quickly points out, the sense of pleasure derived from a feeling of control is very different from actually having control and, moreover, 'resistance is not subversion'. Bird suggests that tabloids, as an endless 'source of laughs', help readers 'cope with their lives and feel good about themselves, but they do not give them power to change their lives' (see the following chapters for a discussion of the related gender and racial issues).

The word 'tabloid', as noted previously, signifies a very different meaning in a British context. The vast majority of readers in Britain purchase their newspaper in a tabloid format (the one daily broadsheet yet to adopt a tabloid format is the *Daily Telegraph*). Although these titles share certain characteristics with their weekly US namesakes (including common ownership in the case of those titles controlled by Rupert Murdoch's companies), none would consider regularly publishing the types of stories identified by the headlines listed above. The one national daily publication which might be so inclined, the *Daily Sport*, is not generally regarded to be a newspaper. Instead, these five tabloids provide – to varying degrees of depth – 'straight' news coverage of public affairs, although each arguably places a premium on entertaining, as opposed to informing, the reader. Their preferred modes of address draw on distinctive styles of language (everyday vernacular, direct 'straight talking') and presentation (snappy headlines, provocative photographs, visually compelling forms of layout) so as to enhance their popular appeal. As several analyses have documented, however, their 'light and breezy' news items can often be shown to anchor, in hegemonic terms, an array of prejudices (sexist, racist, homophobic, xenophobic and so forth) as being synonymous with 'public opinion' or 'what our readers think' (see Curran *et al.* 1980; Dahlgren and Sparks 1991, 1992; Engel 1996; Franklin 1997; Stephenson and Bromley 1998; see also Lewis 2001; Lewis *et al.* 2005; Pickering 2008).

Notable among the small number of studies conducted with British tabloid readers to date is Pursehouse's (1991) analysis of interview data gathered with regular readers of the *Sun*. This study, although somewhat preliminary in that it is based on only thirteen in-depth interviews (the people chosen were deemed to fulfil the 'ideal reader role' set down by the title), furnishes a series of intriguing insights into *how* this, the most popular of Britain's dailies, may be typically negotiated by its readers. By encouraging his interviewees to discuss their routine use of the newspaper in the context of their own personal lives, Pursehouse is able to situate the activity of *Sun* reading in relation to work and domestic arrangements. In both spheres, he suggests, the tabloid offers a 'temporary respite' of sorts from the monotony of labour, an important form of distraction from specific tasks requiring concentration. As a resource, the *Sun* can be used as a shared talking point with others or, alternatively, as a site of 'private' leisure space in order to avoid such interactions. One thing it is not, however, is a reliable source of fair or balanced reporting. In the words of three of the interviewees, for example:

> I find a lot of pleasure in the way that a lot of the *Sun* articles are written . . . I read a story like – like the classic 'Freddie Starr Ate My Hamster' and nobody in their right mind is goin' to believe that – but as a piece of journalism to me it's – it's fun.
>
> (Julie)

> I watch the news on telly: so you get it straight.
>
> (Ian)

> I usually see the news once a day . . . it's a truer report.
>
> (Helen)

Far from being 'passively acquiescent' or 'misguided' about the truth-value of the tabloid's news coverage, then, most of these readers simply claim to look to television for their 'real news'.

Important aspects of the *Sun*'s popular appeal identified by this group of interviewees evidently include its humour, 'street credible' sociability and simplifying 'common sense'. As Pursehouse (1991: 121–2) observes: 'It gains credibility, almost becomes friends with readers, through appearing to "talk the same language".' The basis of this 'friendship', he argues, is on the grounds of 'a shared joke', although much of what counts as the *Sun*'s 'fun persona' is gender-specific in that the tabloid typically positions itself as 'one of the lads' (indeed this 'humour', as Holland (1998: 26) writes, can 'all too easily harden into malice and the sexual fun into a leery, sneery soft misogyny'; see also Chapter 7). At the same time, forms of ethnocentrism are recurrently discernible in its projection of whiteness as a norm in its 'humour' (see Chapter 8). Not surprisingly, however, the tabloid claims for itself an apolitical status, one consistent with its appeals to the 'down-to-earth' qualities of its 'fun-loving' readers who take pleasure in photographs of topless female models on 'Page Three', 'saucy' and scandalous tales, the problem pages, and so forth.

According to Pursehouse (1991), the tabloid characteristically rejects 'politics' in favour of 'entertainment', leading him to suggest:

> [In] some ways the horoscopes, crosswords, cartoons, sport pages and television chat say the most about *The Sun*'s politics. It is a world of 'entertainment', consumerism, easy self-pleasure, rather than social concerns or active, productive contributions to society . . . *The Sun* [during the period of the interviews] was able to turn far-reaching 'public', ideological values into accessible personal stories . . . Above all, *The Sun* was involved in the apparent depoliticising of politics itself and public life, turning all into individual issues, personalities and choices . . . as larger senses of social groups were denied or fragmented.
>
> (Pursehouse 1991: 125)

This language of depoliticization was implicitly reaffirmed by many of the interviewees, as indicated in quoted statements such as: 'Oh I don't like politics' (Sam), 'I am not a political animal' (Julie) or '[politics] don't interest me' (Jackie). Comments such as these are evidence for Pursehouse of the success the *Sun* enjoys in making 'ordinary' its most entrenched cultural assumptions in a way which enables them to be taken up and lived by its readers as being consistent with a seemingly apolitical self-identity.

'Decoding' television news

Turning our attention now to the television news audience, it is advantageous to retain this important commitment to investigating the complex ways this medium is actually used by individuals in their day-to-day lives. As has been argued in Chapter 5, the television news account, far from simply 'reflecting' the reality of an event, actually works to construct a codified definition of what should count as the reality of the event. It follows that this dynamic, if inchoate, process of mediation is accomplished in ideological terms, but not simply at the level of television news as a discrete text. By focusing on how this text is consumed or 'decoded', the fluidly contingent conditions under which it is negotiated as 'meaningful' will be centred for analysis.

In seeking to address the moment of viewing or 'decoding' television news, it is crucial to recognize how the production or 'encoding' of the actual news accounts structures the hegemonic rules by which social reality is to be negotiated by the news audience. To clarify how analyses may best discern the extent to which the codes of television news discourse are embedded in relations of hegemony, many researchers have drawn on a conceptual model introduced by Hall (1980) at the Centre for Contemporary Cultural Studies at the University of Birmingham. The encoding–decoding model, as it was quickly dubbed at the time, remains to this day the singularly most influential attempt to come to terms with these issues within cultural and media studies (see Seiter *et al.* 1989; McGuigan 1992; Morley 1992; Ang 1996; Allan 1998a; Langer 1998; Bird 2009; Madianou 2009; Philo 2009; see also Hall 1994). By situating television news discourse in relation to the variable conditions of its encoding and decoding within the continually evolving limits of common sense, these critical modes of inquiry provide us with a far more dynamic understanding of meaning production than those efforts which treat it as an object in isolation, removed from its ideological context.

It follows, according to Hall, that while the encoding and decoding of the television news message are differentiated moments (that is, they are not perfectly symmetrical or transparent), they are related to one another by the social relations of the communicative process as a whole (Hall 1980: 130). Before this form of discourse can have an effect, however, it needs to be appropriated as a personally relevant discourse by the television viewer, that is, it has to be 'meaningfully decoded'. It is this set of decoded meanings which 'influence, entertain, instruct or persuade, with very complex perceptual, cognitive, emotional, ideological or behavioural consequences' (Hall 1980: 130). The ideological form of the message thus occupies a privileged position *vis-à-vis* the determinate moments of encoding and decoding. These moments each possess their own specific modality and 'conditions of existence', for while their respective articulation is necessary to the communicative process, the moment of encoding cannot 'guarantee' that of decoding. That is to say, the moments of encoding and decoding are 'relatively autonomous': they are inextricably bound up with one another, but there will be highly varied degrees of symmetry ('understanding' and 'misunderstanding') between the encoder–producer and the decoder–receiver.

Hall outlines three hypothetical positions (derived, in part, from Parkin 1973) from which decodings may be constructed. These 'ideal-typical' reading positions, all of which are available at the moment of decoding, may be distinguished as follows with regard to television news.

1 When the viewer of a television news account decodes its message in alignment with its encoding, the viewer is occupying the 'dominant-hegemonic position'. From this position, Hall argues, the 'authoritative', 'impartial' and 'professional' signification of the news event is being accepted as perfectly obvious or natural. The compliant viewer, operating inside the dominant subjectivity that the news account confers, thereby reproduces the hegemonic 'definition of the situation' in ideological terms.
2 In what Hall characterizes as the 'negotiated position', the viewer understands the preferred definition being mobilized by the television news account, but does not relate to it as being self-evidently 'obvious' or 'natural'. Although viewers recognize its general legitimacy as a factual report, certain discrepancies, contradictions or 'exceptions to the rule' within their own (personal) situational context are identified. The news account is seen to be encouraging one interpretation over and above other, more appropriate possibilities.
3 The final reading position is that which is consistent with an 'oppositional' code. That is to say, the viewer apprehends the logic of the dominant-hegemonic position in such a manner that the authority of its definition is directly challenged. Hall offers the example of a viewer who follows 'a debate on the need to limit wages but "reads" every mention of the "national interest" as "class interest" ' (1980: 138). In this way, the dominant code has been reinflected within a resistant, counter-hegemonic framework of reference.

Here it is important to note that these 'ideal-typical' reading positions are being marked for purposes of analytical clarity, and that they are not to be conflated with actual empirical or lived positions. In other words, researchers have recognized the need to try to interrogate the precepts underpinning the rather abstract neatness of these decoding positionalities. The viewer's engagement with an actual television newscast is likely to engender a complex range of (often contradictory) positionalities as the activity of negotiating meaning is always contingent upon the particular social relations of signification in operation (see Corner 1980; Wren-Lewis 1983; Philo 1990, 2009; Lewis 1991; Morley 1992; Moores 1993; Silverstone 1994, 2007; Scannell 1996, 1998; Richardson 1998; Madianou 2009).

Despite the rather abstract nature of its postulates, the encoding–decoding model allows for the issue of textual determination to be addressed as a fluidly heterogeneous process without, at the same time, losing sight of the ways in which it is embedded in relations of power. The status of the television news viewer is not reduced to that of a victim of false consciousness (one who passively acquiesces to the dictates of a dominant ideology being imposed via the text), nor is it to be celebrated such that the viewer is to be accorded with an ability to identify freely with multiple interpretations of the text in a wildly immaterial fashion. Instead, by situating this dynamic activity as a negotiated process within certain conditional, but always changing, parameters, the encoding–decoding model succeeds in highlighting a spectrum of potential positions to be occupied, however fleetingly, in a determinant manner.

Central to the encoding–decoding model, then, is a recognition that the codification of meaning in television news discourse is necessarily constitutive of a particular politics of signification. What is at stake is the need to clear the conceptual space necessary for the investigation of the specific cultural relations at work in the discursive legitimation of certain hegemonic definitions of reality. From this vantage point, the communicative strategies utilized in television news to construct a sense of the very taken-for-grantedness of hegemony may be shown to be structuring 'in dominance' what is, at least in principle, a polysemic text. More to the point, once it is acknowledged that the full range of meanings potentially associated with a given message do not exist 'equally' (true polysemy), then new questions arise as to why particular meanings are being preferred over other possibilities. The ideological dynamics of hegemony may therefore be explicated, at least in part, through an examination of the integration of television news into everyday routines within the household. For a news narrative to be 'read' as an impartial reflection of 'the world out there', its explanations of the social world need to be aligned with the lived experiences of its assumed audiences.

Critical efforts to document arguments of this type in relation to the decoding of television news discourse have utilized the research strategies of ethnography to considerable advantage. Evidence drawn from these ethnographic accounts often suggests that how people watch television news is much less determined by the actual content of the newscast than it is conditioned by the social relations of its consumption. In tracing the contours of the social contexts of viewing characteristic of domestic life in the household, the varied social uses to which television news is put have been examined in association with the (usually unspoken) rules by which the very 'normality' of everyday life is defined and reproduced.

The everydayness of news

In attempting to situate television news within the habits, rituals and taken-for-granted routines of everyday life, Silverstone's (1994, 2007) research makes a significant conceptual contribution. In examining the rhythmic ordering of the day's activities, he argues, it is necessary to discern the (often mundane) practices in and through which people sustain a personal sense of continuity from one day to the next. He points out that this feeling of constancy, of confidence in the stability of the world around us, is an important aspect of what Giddens (1990) has described as the project of 'ontological security' (see also McGuigan 1999; Bird 2009).

Shaping a viewer's engagement with television, it follows, may be a deeply felt need for continuity as a kind of defence against the fears, worries or threats typically associated with an increasingly stressful world. Silverstone (1994: 16) suggests that of the various genres of programming on television, it is the news which most clearly demonstrates 'the dialectical articulation of anxiety and security'. It is precisely this dialectical tension between television news's creation of apprehension and its narrative resolution which encourages the viewer to find in the newscast a sense of reassurance. This sense of reassurance, as Silverstone (1994) proceeds to elaborate, is more closely tied to the form of the news programme than to the items within it:

> Reassurance is not provided only, of course, in the content of reporting. On the contrary. Yet the levels of anxiety that could be raised (and of course may well be either inevitably or deliberately raised) are ameliorated both in terms of the structure of the news as a programme (the tidying of papers, mutual smiles and silent chat following a 'human interest' story complete news bulletins, except under exceptional circumstance of crisis or catastrophe, all over the world), and in terms of its reliability and frequency.
>
> (Silverstone 1994: 16–17)

The embeddedness of television news in the cultures of everyday life thus corresponds to the structured regularity of its ritualized 'flow' (Williams 1974) of information (see also Allan 1997b). More than that, however, the daily repetition of its preferred ways of mediating society's risks and dangers generates a comforting sense of familiarity and predictability. Consequently, it is the combination of these factors which, according to Silverstone, underpins the creation and maintenance of the viewer's sense of well-being and trustful attachment to the world beyond the television screen.

To further develop this line of inquiry, the scheduling of newscasts over the course of the day is deserving of critical attention. Several researchers have argued that these structures presuppose a representative domestic pattern within the household (current sub-genres being variations of breakfast news, lunchtime news, early evening news or suppertime news, the evening news, late-night news, and so forth). This inscription of television's institutional basis in its programming protocols is also revealed in the strategies employed to build and hold an audience throughout the day. Paterson's (1990: 31–2) discussion of the scheduler's lexicon identifies several of the key formulations in play, including 'inheritance factor' (a programme which follows a particularly popular one is likely to inherit a proportion of that audience), 'pre-echo' (people tuning into a programme often watch the end of the preceding one, and thus may be encouraged to watch it in future) and 'hammocking' or 'tent-poling' (a less popular programme is placed between two popular ones in order to benefit from inheritance and pre-echo), among others. Newscasts thus provide the scheduler with a means to facilitate the structuration of programming flow, namely by serving as points of transition in the routines of daily life and between different genres of entertainment (see also Williams 1986 [1984]; Scannell 1996; Harrington 1998; Langer 1998).

Morse (1986) illustrates some of the potential implications of these dynamics for those people who work both inside and outside of the household when she writes:

> Morning and prime time news occur at key thresholds in the day between work and leisure. Morning news precedes the transit from the privacy of the home, where one kind of reality prevails, to the realm of work, a reality with entirely different roles, hierarchies and rules. Morning news can be used as an alarm and pacing device to speed the viewer/auditor into the rhythms of the work world; the news, however lightly attended, may also orient her/him in social reality . . . In contrast, the evening news has a more hierarchical 'work' structure in its anchor–reporter relations, and the set, dress and demeanour of the news personalities are from the world of work and its imposed roles . . . The evening news is a mixed form . . . which aids the transition between one reality and another – between the attentiveness demanded by the world of work and the relaxation promoted by the TV fare of prime time drama and entertainment and the exhaustion of work.
>
> (Morse 1986: 74–5)

A number of these themes are echoed in Hjarvard's (1994) account of how news programmes perform a ritual function: by tying together the different elements of the schedule, news 'provides variation as well as continuity'. The privileged status of the news as a 'reality-oriented genre' tends to be exploited by schedulers: 'the openness of the news structure creates the impression that the earlier reported events continue in a parallel time, but "behind" the screen while we watch other programmes' (Hjarvard 1994: 314). This is an illusion, he argues, 'since social reality is not made up by a limited number of events, but by an infinite number of social interactions', and yet it is an illusion which has arisen because 'the reports of events have already been initiated as *continuous stories*' (Hjarvard 1994: 314).

In attempting to understand better the gendered dynamics of decoding, researchers have recognized the necessity of investigating the actual ways in which women and men relate to television news, respectively. In an early study, entitled 'Housewives and the mass media', Hobson (1980) examines how a range of factors inform a sexual division of household labour which, in turn, conditions a gender-specificity with regard to programming preferences. Her female interviewees (young working-class mothers of small children) revealed a tendency to demarcate television news into a 'masculine' domain.

> There is an *active* choice of programmes which are understood to constitute the 'woman's world', coupled with a complete *rejection* of programmes which are presenting the 'man's world' [predominantly news, current affairs, 'scientific' and documentary programmes]. However, there is also an acceptance that the 'real' or 'man's world' is important, and the 'right' of their husbands to watch these programmes is respected: but it is not a world with which the women in this study wanted to concern themselves. In fact, the 'world', in terms of what is constructed as of 'news' value, is seen as both alien and hostile to the values of women.
>
> (Hobson 1980: 109)

The social world, as represented in news discourse, is generally seen by the women in this study to be 'depressing' and 'boring'. Still, Hobson (1980: 111) points out that 'the importance of accepted "news values" is recognised, and although their own world is seen as more interesting and relevant to them, it is also seen as secondary in rank to the "real" or "masculine" world' (see also Feuer 1986; Gray 1992; and also see Fiske's (1987: 308) critique of television news as 'masculine soap opera').

Morley (1986), in his study entitled *Family Television: Cultural Power and Domestic Leisure*, reaffirms the general trajectory of Hobson's findings. Employing a qualitative, interview-based research strategy, Morley collected material from 18 inner London familial ('white', primarily working- and lower middle-class) households. Overall, Morley is able to suggest that once a distinction is made between 'viewing' and 'viewing attentively and with enjoyment', it is possible to discern a marked gendering of people's engagement with television news. Regarding programme type preference, Morley writes:

> My respondents displayed a notable consistency in this area, whereby masculinity was primarily identified with a strong preference for 'factual' programmes . . . and femininity identified with a preference for fictional programmes . . . Moreover the exceptions to this rule (where the wife prefers 'factual programmes', etc.), are themselves systematic. This occurs

> only where the wife, by virtue of educational background, is in the dominant position in terms of cultural capital.
>
> (Morley 1986: 162–3)

By accentuating this sense of the lived nature of the television news experience, Morley demonstrates why this medium needs to be located as an integral part of everyday life in the household and as such acknowledged as one of several sites of contestation. Television news, as his work and that of Hobson illustrates, can be the object of a micropolitics of domestic power, the material nature of which may be shaped by the hierarchical dictates of familial ideology.

'How come they call it news if it's always the same?' is a rather intriguing question posed by a child in a *New Yorker* magazine cartoon (cited in Silverstone 1994: 16). Somewhat curiously given the amount of public debate concerning the possible 'effects' of television on young minds, investigations into children's engagement with television news in the household are few and far between. Much of the available research tends to suggest that television news (and current affairs) programmes are unlikely to be watched by children by choice. That is to say, typically they watch because that is what happens to be on at the time (who holds the 'remote control' or the 'zapper' is a question of power) or because they are under pressure to do so by their parents and teachers (or indirectly by their peer groups). Newscasts are generally seen to be lacking the qualities which those programmes actually popular with children possess to attract and hold their attention. Indeed, some research suggests that children are likely to consider television news to be 'too serious' and 'boring', and that when they do watch it they often find it both difficult to follow and emotionally unsettling (see also Carter and Messenger Davies 2005; Mendes *et al.* 2009; see also Richards 2009).

Several pertinent issues are raised in this regard in a major study conducted by Sheldon (1998) with children between 5 and 12 years of age in Australia. Specifically, her study drew upon findings from both exploratory focus group discussions (29 groups in total, involving 225 children) and a quantitative opinion survey of 1602 children across 54 primary schools. These findings were then set in relation to data derived from interviews with parents (a matched sample of 517 mothers and fathers). It is interesting to note that in this study parents identified news and current affairs as being the types of programmes most likely to upset their children in this 5–12 age range. Responses cited by Sheldon (1998: 82–3) include:

> The news scenes, like the Somalia footage or children starving or if she sees guns on TV she'll cover her eyes – even documentaries with animals dying.
>
> (Mother, 35–44 years)

> Current affairs stuff worries her, when she sees kids being hurt or older people being bashed or robbed – basically any injustices. Most of the stuff that upsets her is seen on the news. Any factual real life stuff.
>
> (Father, 35–44 years)

The majority of the children taking part in the study (92 per cent) indicated that they watch the news, typically citing reasons such as personal interest (36 per cent) and a desire to find out what had happened that day (25 per cent). A common point of concern expressed was the impact of news imagery:

> We usually get our tea when the news is on and therefore I don't like watching it when all the blood and guts and that sort of stuff is on when you are eating.
>
> (Carlo, Grade 3/4)

Still, this study reports that the children generally felt that the news should be telling people what was taking place in the world.

> They need to show it because that is what happened and they are just showing what happened.
>
> (Alicia, Grade 5/6)

Overall, Sheldon (1998: 91) found that representations of violence were a major cause of concern for children, particularly for girls, although 'for both sexes, "real life" television, as it is presented in news and current affairs programmes, was much more disturbing than fictional or fantasy violence'.

The day-to-day negotiation of television news by an older group of young people, mainly in the 14–18 age range, is one aspect of Gillespie's (1995) ethnographic study of media consumption. The subjects of her study are young people of Punjabi family background living in Southall, West London, evidently the largest South Asian community outside the Indian subcontinent. In focusing on how they engage with television as part of their everyday lives, Gillespie pays particular attention to issues of age, ethnicity and identity. An array of rich insights are produced into the domestic rituals of news viewing in families where teenagers often play a vital role in translating newscasts for their parents and grandparents. While most of the teenage informants in this study find it difficult either to understand Punjabi radio broadcasts or to read the Punjabi press (their parents' key points of reference), they are generally much better able to discuss news in English than their older family members.

This competence with television news helps them to acquire status as an adult. 'No matter how boring they find particular bulletins,' writes Gillespie (1995: 109), 'great significance is attached to TV news as a genre, because it is seen as an invitation to the world of adult affairs.' In the words of one of her informants:

Sangita: You feel kind of grown up when you talk about the news, you know, it's serious, and you have to take some things seriously, but a lot of the time we just muck about, laugh and joke so talking about news is a way of growing up.

By assuming this special responsibility as an interpreter, the teenagers are made to engage directly with a form of television discourse they typically regard as being both adult and middle class.

Pervinder: By watching the news, your parents know that you've gone through a stage, that you can talk in an adult way, you watch them talking about the news in an adult way and then you begin to fit in; you don't seem like a child any more . . . they treat you as a *chust* kid, you know, grown up.

Herjinder: . . . when you watch the news you get amazed at all the big words they use but you get a sense of how they are supposed to be used and that gives you another approach; it sort of helps you to express yourself.

In addition to vocabulary, accent and speech patterns, other factors which Gillespie (1995: 111) identifies as impeding the teenagers' comprehension included the newscasts' authoritative mode of address, class-specific assumptions about background knowledge, and the duration and degree of detail used in the reports. Still, she points out that with their growing skills in translation, these teenagers are able to acquire fuller knowledge of the social world beyond certain cultural and linguistic barriers (see also Buckingham 1997; Barnhurst 1998; Barker 1999; Tester 2001; Poole and Richardson 2006; el-Nawawy and Powers 2009; Mendes *et al.* 2009).

A number of the underlying aspects of these approaches to the news audience are clarified through an innovative framework developed in the work of Jensen (1986, 1995). Here data were gathered through interviews with various individuals living in a metropolitan area of the north-eastern United States concerning their negotiation of television news in the household. In taking issue with the claim that the very process of watching television news may be properly conceived of as a politically oppositional activity in and by itself, Jensen argues that counter-hegemonic decodings are not in themselves a concrete materialization of political power. 'Resistance,' he argues, 'is always resistance by someone, to something, for a purpose, and in a context' (Jensen 1995: 76). It follows that in addition to questioning whether or not the 'preferred meanings' of the newscast are accepted (or not) by the viewer, attention needs to turn to consider the designated social uses of this genre of discourse and how they have evolved over time. Equally important are the changing forms of its actual relevance to viewers in terms of their lived experience of the everyday.

Briefly, Jensen (1995) identifies four general types of 'uses' which the viewers in his study ascribed to television news in terms of its significance for their daily lives.

First, television news has *contextual uses*, that is, the (usually gendered) roles and routines of ongoing activities in the household, especially with regard to domestic labour, are often partially structured by news viewing. The daily rhythms associated with news times, he argues, have become *naturalized*: 'There are no arguments [among the respondents], for example, that the evening news might be scheduled differently, fitting news to everyday life rather than vice versa' (Jensen 1995: 81).

Second, there are *informational uses* of television news for the viewers, particularly in their roles as 'consumer, employee, and, above all, as citizen and voter'. Here Jensen (1995: 84–5) discerns a tension in the interview material from his respondents between 'the active and public uses that are associated with the news genre in a political perspective and . . . its more limited practical relevance for audiences in terms of "keeping up" with issues for the purpose of conversation or voting in political elections'. One respondent, identified only as a 'printer', is quoted by Jensen as making a typical statement about the opportunity for political participation:

> Well, I can vote. As far as taking it any further, I don't know. I guess the opportunity will have to arise. Being, you know, I feel I'm just the average person out here.
>
> (Jensen 1995: 84)

Third, the implications of this tension for the social definition of news are even more pronounced with respect to what Jensen calls the *legitimizing uses* of television news. His interview material indicates that the political relevance of news to the viewer may be characterized in terms of the twin concepts of control and distance: 'The news may give its audience a sense of control over events in the world which would otherwise appear as distant . . . it is the *feeling* of control which is crucial, even if "you can't do anything about it" ' (Jensen 1995: 85). To the degree that television news is seen by the viewer to offer a 'generalized sense of community', then, it is equally likely to be considered to be an adequate forum for the articulation of public issues (see also Dahlgren and Sparks 1991, 1992; McLaughlin 1993, 1998; Garnham 1994; Corner 1995; Dahlgren 1995; Hartley 1996; Allan 1997a; Moeller 1999; Philo 1999; Tester 2001).

Finally, Jensen pinpoints the *diversional uses* of television news as discussed by his respondents, namely the variety of its visual pleasures for the viewer. The designated social uses for news, while generally defined by the respondents as distinct from those of entertainment, nevertheless share with them several important features. In particular, the 'holding power' of the visual narrative is deemed to be significant. The respondents attached salience not only to the visuals of the news events, which were seen as communicating 'a sense of experiential immediacy' (words such as 'pleasing', 'enjoyable', 'easy', 'vivid' and 'exciting' are used by the respondents), but also to the actual performance of the news. In the case of newsreaders, for example, both journalistic competence and personal appeal are stressed, while other respondents emphasized the appeal of 'nice, trivial information'.

Together, Jensen's four types of 'uses' suggest that although individuals make their own sense of what the political significance of the news is for them, their perceptions are constrained by the ways in which what counts as 'politics' is being represented.

> The reception of television news, accordingly, can be seen as an agent of *hegemony* which serves to reassert the limits of the political imagination . . . [E]ven though the social production of meaning may be seen as a process in which the prevailing definition of reality can be challenged and revised, the conditions of that process are established within particular historical and institutional frameworks of communication. The polysemy of mass media discourses is only a political potential, and the oppositional decoding of mass communication is not yet a manifestation of political power.
>
> (Jensen 1995: 90)

From this perspective, it follows that new research strategies need to be adopted so as to further explore the extent to which television news discourse operates to 'reassert the limits of the political imagination' through the lived conditions of the everyday (see also Hagen 1994; Tester 1994). After all, as Jensen (1995: 77) contends: 'If audiences do not perceive news as a specific resource for political awareness and action, then, arguably, the legitimacy of the political process and its institutions is called into question.'

'Technology-savvy young people'

These explorations of the everydayness of news culture provide us with a rich starting point for further research. By engaging with the apparent 'normality' of how readers, listeners and viewers 'make sense' of the news, we are better able to look beyond the fixed text–audience dichotomy indicative of so much previous research on news audiences.

Moreover, it has been shown that by situating the lived materiality of news culture within an evaluative context, we can begin to discern a conceptual pathway through, on the one hand, a deterministic model of the audience as passive onlookers whose thinking is controlled by a 'dominant ideology' and, on the other hand, a model which celebrates an active audience free to pick and choose any possible interpretation from a news text in an indeterminate manner. As we have seen, an alternative approach which recognizes the need to investigate people's deeply engrained habits of interacting with news discourses as part of their lived experience of the everyday resists a rigid analytical separation of news discourse from the conditions of its decoding. In its place is a conceptual commitment to interrogating the fluidly contradictory cultural relations of textual negotiation in all of their attendant complexities. The materiality of news discourse, it follows, is made 'real' within certain variable yet determinant limits. That is to say, it is contingent upon the embodied experience of power relations as they traverse the contested terrain of ordinary culture.

In rounding out this chapter's discussion, our attention turns to a speech delivered in the Spring of 2005 by media mogul Rupert Murdoch, chair and chief executive officer of News Corporation, to an audience of newspaper editors. In the view of some who were there, his comments signalled the moment when time was effectively called on the newspaper, at least in its familiar paper and ink format, thereby ushering in a radical rethink of its very future. Murdoch's intervention, the *Economist* magazine predicted, 'may go down in history as the day that the stodgy newspaper business officially woke up to the new realities of the internet age' (*The Economist*, 21 April 2005). Of particular interest, in light of this chapter's focus, is what he had to say about how young people relate the news.

In outlining what he perceived to be the 'fast developing reality' confronting the newspaper industry, and its startling implications for the future, Murdoch offered a blunt assessment. 'Scarcely a day goes by without some claim that new technologies are fast writing newsprint's obituary', he began. 'Yet, as an industry, many of us have been remarkably, unaccountably complacent.' In conceding that he personally had not done as much about it as he should have done 'after all the excitement of the late 1990s', he admitted that he thought of himself as a 'digital immigrant', someone still 'searching for answers to an emerging medium that is not my native language'. As he proceeded to elaborate:

> I wasn't weaned on the web, nor coddled on a computer. Instead, I grew up in a highly centralized world where news and information were tightly controlled by a few editors, who deemed to tell us what we could and should know [. . .] The peculiar challenge then, is for us digital immigrants – many of whom are in positions to determine how news is assembled and disseminated – to apply a digital mindset to a set of challenges that we unfortunately have limited to no first-hand experience dealing with.
>
> (Murdoch, 2005)

Describing his two daughters as 'digital natives', that is, young people who will 'never know a world without ubiquitous broadband internet access', he underscored his contention that a generational shift was under way. 'We need to realize that the next generation of people accessing news and information, whether from newspapers or any other source, have a different set of expectations about the kind of news they will get', he declared. This includes, in turn, 'when and how they will get it, where they will get it from, and who they will get it from'. Ever the businessperson, Murdoch saw in this looming crisis for the newspaper industry a critical set of difficulties, but also an opportunity to 'improve our journalism and expand our reach' in a manner consistent with his larger corporate interests.

From Murdoch's perspective, the 'dramatic revolution taking place in the news industry today' revolves around the fact that 'technology-savvy young people' are becoming increasingly likely to turn to the web as their news medium of choice. Drawing upon audience data from a recent report by Merrill Brown (2005) for the Carnegie Corporation of New York, a philanthropic foundation, he explained why he considered certain 'ominous' findings to be especially 'alarming' for the viability of newspapers. Although local television news may be the most accessed source of news for consumers between the ages of 18 and 34, the study suggests, internet portals (such as 'the Yahoos, Googles and MSNs') are fast becoming their favoured destination for news. '44 per cent of the study's respondents said they use a portal at least once a day for news, as compared to just 19 per cent who use a printed newspaper on a daily basis', he stated. Looking forward over the next three years, the study 'found that 39 per cent expected to use the internet more to learn about the news, versus only 8 per cent who expected to use traditional newspapers more'. Hence, in light of figures such as these, Murdoch believes that a 'revolution' is under way with respect to how young people access their news. Moreover, he is convinced, they also do not 'want to rely on a god-like figure from above to tell them what's important. And to carry the religion analogy a bit further, they certainly don't want news presented as gospel.' Rather, in marked contrast, young people prefer 'news on demand' or, to put it another way, they 'want control over their media, instead of being controlled by it'. Highlighting an array of examples to illustrate his argument, not least the impact of blogs, he contends that young people need news that is continuously updated because they want 'a point of view about not just what happened, but why it happened. They want news that speaks to them personally, that affects their lives.'

Recrafting newspaper journalism in light of these 'revolutionary' factors will entail the disruption of centuries old traditions. Certainly this dynamic conception of young people as digital natives – individuals who actively question, probe and seek out different angles in the news online – throws into sharp relief some of the more familiar assumptions that typically guide industry judgements about how best to extend the reach of newspapers via the internet. In issuing this call for media orthodoxies to be reconsidered, Murdoch is insisting that 'we must challenge – and reformulate – the conventions that so far have driven our online efforts'. In other words, while the speed of technological change is a pressing concern, even more worrisome for Murdoch is 'our ability to make the necessary cultural changes to meet the new demands'. To succeed in effecting a 'complete transformation of the way we think about our product' will entail recognizing, in turn, that 'too many of us editors and reporters are out of touch with our readers'. Rather than asking 'Do we have the story?', the question should be 'Does anyone want the story?' It is in facing certain unpleasant truths, then, that new ways forward can be found. There is much cause for optimism, in Murdoch's view, so long as operations are 'streamlined' and more 'nimble', but also – crucially – by becoming much more responsive to the views of audiences. 'We may never become true digital natives,' he states, 'but we can and must begin to assimilate to their culture and way of thinking.' There is little doubt in his mind that this 'monumental, once-in-a-generation opportunity' cannot be missed; 'if we're successful,' he declared, 'our industry has the potential to reshape itself, and to be healthier than ever before.'

7 THE GENDERED REALITIES OF JOURNALISM

> [T]he hierarchy of newspapers was set in stone in the 19th century and remains the same, despite all the evidence that newspapers have got to change or die. News is still considered the most important department, followed by politics, business, sport – all areas traditionally and, to a large extent, still dominated by men.
>
> (Lynn Barber, UK journalist)

> For the women of my age, it is interesting to us that we now have an accusation that we are only where we are because we are women. For a long time we were told we couldn't be anywhere because we were women.
>
> (Cokie Roberts of ABC News)

Over one hundred years ago, a British trade newspaper published a rather telling news item on the growing prominence of women reporters. This July 1889 account announced the 'invasion of Fleet Street's sanctity [by] journalistic damsels everywhere taking their place at the reporters' table, or hurrying up to the offices about midnight with their "copy" – chiefly Society news' (cited in Hunter 1992: 688). If, from the vantage point of today, the use of this type of language to describe the work of female newsworkers is so anachronistic as to be almost amusing, this is not to deny that many of the gendered inequalities it inadvertently identifies are still with us.

Neatly pinpointed in this quotation are a number of themes that will inform this chapter. In the first instance, for example, there is the notion of female journalists *invading the sanctity* of the newsroom – today it is still a predominantly male domain of work, the dynamics of which are largely shaped by patriarchal norms, values and traditions. Recurrently it is the case, as several of the studies to be discussed document, that women are being denied an equal place at the *reporters' table*. Similarly, the pejorative connotations of the phrase *journalistic damsels*, echoes of which are arguably discernible in the use of quotation marks around the word *copy*, highlight sexist assumptions about women's professional capacities as journalists. These assumptions, moreover, appear to correspond with a hierarchical division between the 'hard' news (serious and important) to be covered by male journalists and, in marked contrast, the *Society* or 'soft' news (trivial and insignificant) reported by female journalists. There is little doubt, of course, which type of news is to be understood as being consistent with the ethos of *Fleet Street*, and which type threatens its proclaimed journalistic integrity.

Turning to the early days of televisual news broadcasting in Britain, the ways in which appeals to 'journalistic integrity' were similarly gendered are all too apparent. The first woman to read the news regularly on national television (as noted in Chapter 3) was Barbara Mandell for Independent Television News, who began presenting the midday bulletin on 23 September 1955. Evidently it was Mandell's 'pleasant good looks, open manner and mellifluous voice' which Aidan Crawley, the first editor of ITN, thought made her particularly suited to newscasting (Purser 1998; see also Crawley 1988; Hayward 1998). Given the small audience that the noon bulletin attracted, however, cost-cutting measures meant that it was the first to be dropped from the news schedule in January 1956. It was not long before Mandell reappeared on the screen, however, this time introducing items as part of a 'domestic segment'. The painted set used as the backdrop for her presentation assumes a particular significance in ideological terms given that it depicted a household kitchen – until, reportedly, viewers complained about the unwashed dishes. As Geoffrey Cox, the next editor of ITN, would later remember: 'Her scripts were always very clear . . . and with a nice touch when that was needed. On screen she was not very assertive . . . nor was she a political person. But she had a very good voice' (cited in Purser 1998). Eventually Mandell returned to newscasting, if only briefly, when she was asked to present the Sunday evening bulletins. According to Cox's recollections: 'To put a woman in charge of a main bulletin in those days, I feared, would be seen as a gimmick.'

It would not be until 1960 before a BBC national televisual newscast regularly featured a female newsreader. Nan Winton briefly assumed this role on Sunday's 9:00 pm programme. As she later stated:

> I didn't realise what a revolutionary thing it was . . . I didn't have any trouble from the press or from the public, it was the editorial staff who were a bit dodgy, men in their middle years who'd come from Fleet Street

> . . . they certainly were a bit ambivalent about me. They were very, very serious about the News. It was a very serious business.
>
> (Cited in Thumim 1998: 97)

These insights find an echo, as Thumim (1998) proceeds to show, in the words of Stuart Hood, a senior member of the BBC's directorate at the time:

> I thought it would be rather nice to have a woman news reader on television. Now this was greeted with alarm and dismay and resistance by my editors. The thought that a woman could be the conveyor of truth and authority on the television screen was something they just couldn't imagine, couldn't accept.
>
> (Cited in Thumim 1998: 97)

This situation would improve only very slowly as the norms of televisual news were being consolidated institutionally (Angela Rippon became the BBC's first regular female newsreader in 1975; Anna Ford joined ITN's *News at Ten* in 1978). Although it is possible to identify several interventions to enhance the profile of women on television, as Thumim (1998: 102) maintains, it was the case that 'more often than not these foundered on the rocks of convention and prejudice, being perceived, in the event, as *unsuitable, distracting*, with insufficient *gravitas*'.

Flash forward to a more recent scene in Washington DC in January 2007, when White House officials invited network and cable anchors, together with the Sunday political show hosts, to a meeting with senior Bush administration officials to discuss the war in Iraq. CBS News's Katie Couric (2007) later recalled feeling that the meeting was 'a little disconcerting' when she realized – looking around the room – that something was wrong.

> I couldn't help but notice, despite how far we've come, that I was still the only woman there. Well, there was some female support staff near the door. But of the people at the table, the 'principals' in the meeting, I was the only one wearing a skirt. Everyone was gracious, though the jocular atmosphere was palpable.
>
> The feminist movement that began in the 1970s helped women make tremendous strides – but there still haven't been enough great leaps for womankind [. . .] That meeting was a reality check for me – and not just about Iraq. It was a reminder that all of us still have an obligation to ask: Don't more women deserve a place at the table too?
>
> (Couric 2007)

Today the day-to-day news culture of most newspaper and broadcast organizations is still being defined in predominantly male terms. While there has been a dramatic increase in the number of women securing jobs in journalism, white middle-class men continue to occupy the vast majority of positions of power throughout the sector. Women are still not being promoted to senior decision-making posts in proportion to the overall role they play in the profession. At a time when news organizations are facing ever more intensive (and increasingly globalized) forms of competition, and when female readers, listeners and viewers remain elusive as ever, the costs of this failure to treat women fairly in the journalistic workplace continue to mount.

Feminist critiques of objectivity

To clarify several of the key issues at stake in this chapter's discussion, our attention turns in the first instance to the gender politics of 'objective' reporting. While critical researchers have succeeded in documenting the means by which journalists reproduce a professionalized news culture in their day-to-day activities, insufficient attention has been granted to the question of how gender relations shape these (largely unspoken) norms of reportage. In what ways, researchers may proceed to ask, do these professional norms centre the predispositions, 'habits of mind' and attitudes of white, middle-class male journalists? In other words, why is it usually the case that these journalists' 'instinctive' judgements about the 'credibility' or 'expertise' of news sources lead, in turn, to such a small portion of the accessed voices being those of women? Moreover, to what extent do male journalists regard their female colleagues as 'deviating' from these norms in their approaches to validating 'objective' truth-claims?

To be an 'impartial' reporter, as has been argued in previous chapters, means being socialized into obeying certain rituals of naming, describing and framing realities, even if 'objectivity' is self-reflexively posited as an ideal never to be entirely realized in practice. Feminist researchers have sought to intervene in the ongoing debates about news 'objectivity' from a variety of different vantage points. A principal point of contention concerns the gendering of the dominant discourses of truth being mobilized by journalists, that is, the extent to which a 'gender bias' is discernible in the ritualized practices of 'objective' news reporting. Here three distinct modes of inquiry may be briefly sketched as follows:

- *Neutrality position*: for some feminists seeking to uphold 'objectivity' as a journalistic ideal, the problem is one of male norms, values and beliefs being allowed to subjectively distort 'what really took place'. Good reporting, they maintain, is gender-neutral reporting. Advocates of this position call for journalists to observe a rigorous adherence to systematized methods of gathering and processing 'concrete facts' dispassionately so as to ensure that news accounts are strictly 'impartial'. The 'truth' of the 'real world' is to be discovered through these facts; 'gender biased' journalism can thus be avoided so long as news accounts accurately reflect reality.

- *Balance position*: other feminists have sought to highlight the gender-specificity of 'objectivity', that is, the essential distinctions between female and male apprehensions of reality derivative of sexual difference. In their view, only women are justified in speaking for women as a social group: personal experience, it follows, stands as the arbiter of 'truth'. Using a language of 'balance', they contend that 'objectivity' is primarily a matter of ensuring that male values are counterpoised by female ones in a given news account (or range thereof). This is to be achieved by news organizations employing equal numbers of male and female journalists, as well as through changes in newswork practices (such as ensuring that a representative selection of female voices are accessed as news sources).
- *Counter position*: a further position adopted by some feminists is marked by a resolve to effectively jettison the concept of 'objectivity' altogether due to its perceived complicity in legitimizing patriarchal hegemony. In their view, this concept prefigures a dichotomy between the knower and the known which is untenable: facts cannot be separated out from their ideological, and hence gendered, conditions of production. Moreover, they argue, the imposition of this false dichotomy is further masculinized to the extent that it obviates the experiences of women as being 'outside' the realm of what are proclaimed to be universally valid standards of reason, logic and rationality. What counts as 'truth' in a given instance is determined by who has the power to define reality.

It is evident from these differing positions, situated as they are among a myriad of alternative ones, that the relationship between discourses of 'objectivity' and gender relations is politically charged. Feminist efforts committed to deconstructing this relationship have sought to render problematic the often subtle, taken-for-granted strategies in and through which journalists, knowingly or not, routinely define 'what counts as reality' in alignment with patriarchal renderings of the social world.

This reference to defining 'reality' resonates with a diverse range of feminist critiques of Enlightenment thought, in general, and masculinist definitions of truth, in particular. The final declaration of truth under relations of patriarchy, many of these critiques contend, is imposed upon women by men as a means to legitimize diverse forms of oppression. The invocation of a monologic truth is masculinized to the extent that (predominantly white, elite) men's orientations to 'the world of facts' are accepted as the most *appropriate* vantage points from which the immutable truth of reality is to be revealed. Taken for granted in this masculinist epistemology is the presupposition that reality may be assumed to be a *given* (it exists 'out there'), and that as such it constitutes the standard by which truth and falsity are to be impartially measured. Once it is resolved that there is one, absolute Truth, then the 'search for objectivity' becomes essential if the ideal of abstract, universal knowledge is to be realized. Male hegemony is thus contingent upon the displacement of counter-hegemonic, namely feminist, discourses as being complicit in the 'distortion' or misrepresentation of reality.

A key point of contention for a range of feminist interventions, therefore, has been the (often tacit) masculine/feminine dichotomy prefigured in androcentric definitions of knowledge. More specifically, the gendered basis of this hierarchical dichotomy has been shown to be dependent upon a separation of the knower (subject) from the known (object). This separation naturalizes, to varying degrees, a series of dualisms whereby 'masculine' discourses about reality (held to be objective, rational, abstract, coherent, unitary and active) are discursively privileged over 'feminine' ones (posited as subjective, irrational, emotional, partial, fragmented and passive). Implied in this dynamic is the precept that 'feminine knowledge' is to be understood as being inferior to 'masculine truth' and, as such, is to be recognized as constituting its Other. This conflation of the masculine with the rational, and the feminine with the irrational, serves to sanction the exclusion of women's truth-claims as falling outside the prescribed parameters of reason (reason is deemed to both represent and embody truth). It is only 'logical', on these grounds, that women are to be denied the authoritative status of 'objective knower'.

Not surprisingly, then, the appeal to 'objectivity' becomes a defensive strategy, one which assists the journalist in countering charges of sexism (as well as those of racism, among others) being levelled at specific instances of reporting. A journalism genuinely committed to impartiality, its adherents insist, cannot be sexist. So long as the appropriate procedural rules are followed, 'tangible facts' will be separated out from the values expressed through partisan argument and opinion; indeed, it is the task of the 'good' reporter to ensure that this segregation is achieved. Consequently, the journalist's invocation of 'objectivity' may be analysed as an androcentric instance of definitional power to the extent that it ex-nominates (places beyond 'common sense') those truth-claims which do not adhere to masculinist assumptions about the social world.

Macho culture of newswork

In attempting to prioritize for discussion the 'objective' journalist's claim of referential transparency, this issue of how relations of patriarchy inform the 'discipline of objectivity' as a seemingly apolitical ('gender-neutral') normative ideal is critical. Such a problematic avoids many of the familiar pitfalls of the 'objectivity' versus 'bias' debate as it has developed in various studies of news discourse. At stake, in my view, is the need to recentre the problem of representation in a way which overcomes the limitations of those approaches which, on the one hand, consider news language to be 'value-neutral', and those approaches which, on the other hand, treat it as being inescapably determined by patriarchal values. Such an approach, I want to suggest, entails a commitment to exploring the multiplicity of (en)gendered orientations *encouraged*, but not compelled, by a news account's inflection of truth.

In order to secure a politicized understanding of news discourse as an (en)gendered construction, then, attention needs to address the newsroom as a site of power. More specifically, the intricate ways in which the ontological hierarchies of gender relations shape the journalist's everyday, routine methods of processing 'reality' need to be unravelled. In attempting to examine the ways in which gender is embedded in the work routines of the newsroom, Steiner (1998) poses a series of vital questions:

> Do reporters' perceptions enter into their work, for example, in their definitions of newsworthiness, choice of assignments, approaches to sources, or ethical decision-making? What have been the power relations operating in the production of news work? Who has helped whom? Who provided encouragement and mentoring? What are the consequences of working with stubborn colleagues or dictatorial editors? What about sexual harassment in the newsroom? Or being underpaid, or underappreciated, or underutilized? Or being positioned as the token woman on staff?
>
> (Steiner 1998: 145–6)

Answers to questions such as these are anything but straightforward, particularly when the 'gender issue' is typically defined in exclusively female terms. That is to say, the dictates of male-centred reporting dynamics are only rarely problematized *vis-à-vis* questions of 'maleness' or 'masculinity'; instead, they are much more likely to be regarded as simply being consistent with institutional norms (see also Croteau and Hoynes 1992; Allan 1998b). In the words of one male journalist writing for the *Independent*: 'The way papers are produced may have changed dramatically in the last decade – green screens replacing eyeshades and metal spikes – but a macho culture still reigns in the nation's newsrooms' (Brown 1997: 3).

In the case of the US, the 1990s saw women's presence in the newsroom increase to about one-third of the journalistic workforce, and yet they are still routinely denied the opportunity to compete fairly for a senior position. Drawing on a range of statistical studies, Lafky (1993: 90) suggested that very little progress had been made since the mid-1980s when 'only 6 per cent of the top newspaper jobs and 25 per cent of the middle management newspaper jobs were held by women' (see also Stewart 1997). Cokie Roberts of ABC News recalled during an interview on CNN's *Larry King Live*:

> Well, pre-affirmative action, when I was looking for jobs early on, people said, out loud and without any hesitation, 'We don't hire women to do that. We will not hire women to deliver the news. Their voices are not authoritative. We don't hire women as writers. Men would have to work for them, and we can't have that.' It was overt, and nobody was even embarrassed about it.
>
> (Transcript in Braver 1997)

Similarly, Jane Pauley, at the time a newscaster with NBC News, had this to say in the same interview:

> [W]hen I got my job at WISH-TV in Indianapolis, the news director interviewed 30, 50, 100, whatever, women, because he had to find a woman. It was FCC [Federal Communications Commission] license renewal time in that newsroom, and there were no women in the newsroom, there were none . . . I don't know whether it was a quota, but that's why they were looking for a [female reporter].
>
> (Transcript in Braver 1997)

Viewed from the vantage point of today, it is apparent that the success of high-profile women journalists such as Roberts and Pauley – and Couric, mentioned above – has gone a considerable distance toward breaking down the barriers to gender equality, but they nonetheless remain largely intact (see also de Bruin and Ross 2004; Chambers *et al.* 2004; Everbach 2006; Chambers and Steiner 2009). A recent survey conducted by the American Society of Newspaper Editors (ASNE), for example, found that men continue to outnumber women in full-time daily newspaper positions by a 63 per cent to 37 per cent margin (ASNE 2008). The same study found that minority women accounted for 17.16 of female newsroom staffers, thereby revealing a further dimension to institutionalized inequalities (see Chapter 8 of this volume).

Studies of British news organizations recurrently show that the vast majority of senior journalists and editorial decision makers are men, with most estimates placing the number at higher than 80 per cent. Recent research conducted by the Sutton Trust (2006), for example, indicates that the 'proportion of women among the top 100 news journalists increased from 10 per cent in 1986 to 18 per cent in 2006' (see also Dougary 1994; Tunstall 1996; Christmas 1997; Women in Journalism 1998). 'White, middle-class males have had it all their own way at the BBC since the days of Lord Reith and it is frankly amazing the extent to which they still have it their own way in the new millennium', former BBC newsreader Anna Ford recently stated (cited in Walker 2008). Journalist Glender Cooper reaffirms this view with reference to her own experience. When she joined the BBC in 2002, she recalls, 'I was taken aside by an editor (another white, middle-class man so ground down by the system that he was promoted soon afterwards) and given advice on how to succeed as a serious news journalist.' He suggested, she adds, 'straightening my naturally curly hair to look more "authoritative". He also expressed regret that my eyes looked too big on screen.' The factors involved are complex, as Aldridge (2001) points out on the basis of her study involving interviews with women working in the UK regional press, but appear to revolve around status hierarchies founded on 'hard news' experience. What may appear to be deep-seated beliefs in a meritocracy based on performance, her findings suggest, would be better explained in terms of structural barriers to advancement:

> In newspapers, it is constantly affirmed, you are only as good as your most recent work, yet this logic of performativity is not followed through. To reach a position of influence you do not only need to demonstrate *current skills and abilities* but *specific past experience*, crucially a senior post related to breaking hard news. Full-time jobs in core news-related functions are almost impossible to combine with primary responsibility for dependants: '. . . in the whole of our newsroom [women] who have children and are still newsgatherers . . . I can't think of any . . .' (Senior reporter, 25, city evening paper). [. . .] When my respondents talked about their own lives and prospects, or recounted the difficulties of women colleagues, the constantly recurring theme was the hours of work – not just long, but unsocial, or unpredictable, or all three – characteristic of a ruthlessly profit-driven enterprise framed around the 'newsday'.
>
> (Aldridge 2001)

Similar patterns are evident in the news organizations of other countries. Robinson (2005) examines the impact of the 'glass ceiling' on women's advancement in Canadian newsrooms, where equity legislation – helpful in securing women employment – has not had the desired effect where promotion is concerned. McGregor (2006) describes what she calls the 'pervasive power of man-made news' in New Zealand's news media. While little progress has been made by women at the editorship level, she argues, matters are improving for senior women just below that level. Djerf-Pierre (2007) points out that in Sweden, even though women were making up 50 per cent of the profession by 2005, journalism remains a 'male-dominated' field. There is a 'gender logic' shaping definitions of status, prestige and power, her research contends, one that works to align masculinity with 'ideas about what constitutes good journalism' (2007: 99).

Van Zoonen (1998: 34), drawing upon her own research into the Dutch news media as well as a survey of an international range of studies conducted since the early 1980s, identifies the following recurrent inequalities:

- daily journalism, whether it is print or broadcasting, is dominated by men
- the higher up the hierarchy or the more prestigious a particular medium or section is, the less likely it is to find women
- women tend to work in areas of journalism that can be considered an extension of their domestic responsibilities and their socially assigned qualities of care, nurturing and humanity
- regardless of difference in years of experience, education level and other socioeconomic factors, women are paid less for the same work.

Underpinning these inequalities, she argues, are discriminatory recruitment procedures stemming from sexist attitudes among key decision makers in the news production process. As Skidmore (1998: 207) suggests in light of the evidence that she has gathered among British newsworkers, 'male dominance in journalism has produced a macho culture of newsgathering – aggressive and domineering but also one of male camaraderie and "bonding" – which excludes women' (see also Sebba 1994; see also Gallagher 2001; Mahtani 2005).

Female journalists working in this predominantly male environment, according to much of the available feminist research in a range of national contexts, are regularly pressured to adopt masculinized forms of reporting which some find to be inconsistent with their own professional identity and thus alienating (there can also be, as Santos (1997: 123) argues, a professionally driven tendency 'to write white'). As would be anticipated given this situation, and as has been documented by feminist researchers, the interests of female journalists as participants in defining the organization's news agenda often encounter considerable resistance from male colleagues. Not only are they likely to find themselves being assigned 'soft' news assignments, customarily deemed by their male colleagues to be of lesser importance, but also they have to live up to what van Zoonen (1998) characterizes as a 'double requirement'. That is to say, women reporters are often compelled to demonstrate that they can be 'good' journalists while still being 'real', 'truly feminine' women. In the Netherlands, van Zoonen maintains:

> [M]any female journalists feel that they are primarily judged as women; they are subject to ongoing comments on their looks and they have to regularly confront friendly heterosexual invitations or unfriendly sexual harassment. Playing the game of heterosexual romance means that women will lose their prestige as professional journalists. But women who ignore it, or worse – criticize it – will not be accepted by their male

> colleagues as real women; instead they are seen as bitches, viragos or – the worst – 'feminists'.
>
> (Van Zoonen 1998: 37)

These kinds of tensions can be particularly evident where 'old boys' networks are in operation within the organization and, as is often the case, at the level of news sources (see also Alwood 1996; Ross 2001, 2005).

Investigations into the gender politics of sourcing information highlight the extent to which news accounts continue to privilege the truth-claims of male sources and spokespersons. Despite the growing numbers of female politicians, public officials and other professionals, van Zoonen (1998: 35) argues, it is overwhelmingly the case that the sources journalists choose to include in their accounts are male. These choices are seen to be 'reflecting the personal networks of male journalists rather than being a representation of actual gender divisions among sources' (van Zoonen 1998: 35–6). This systemic under-representation of women as news actors and as expert sources (as well as their limited appearance as reporters) needs to be contextualized in relation to the patterns of discrimination they encounter across the (mutually determining) 'public' and 'private' spheres (McLaughlin 1993; Fraser 1994; Len-Ríos *et al.* 2005). When women's voices are actualized in news accounts, as Holland (1987) points out:

> it tends to be either as an anonymous example of uninformed public opinion, as housewife, consumer, neighbour, or as mother, sister, wife of the man in the news, or as victim – of crime, disaster, political policy. Thus not only do they speak less frequently, but they tend to speak as passive reactors and witnesses to public events rather than as participants in those events.
>
> (Holland 1987: 138–9)

A further pertinent aspect of this issue, as Kitzinger (1998) argues, concerns how journalists are themselves judged in relation to source dynamics. In her interviews with British journalists, she found that 'although both male and female journalists used their "gut feelings" in judging source credibility, some female journalists claimed that their "gut feelings" were dismissed by male editors as "subjective" or "biased" '. This when, at the same time, 'their male colleagues' "gut feelings" were seen to constitute "common sense" or "professional instinct" ' (Kitzinger 1998: 198).

Research conducted by the Project for Excellence in Journalism (PEW) offers quantitative data to support this line of critique. Drawing on findings from an examination of some 16,800 news stories across 45 different US news outlets (16 newspapers, four nightly newscasts, three network morning shows, nine cable programmes, and nine internet news sites) during 20 randomly selected days over a nine month period in 2004, researchers discovered that men are called upon as news sources more than twice as often as women. 'More than three quarters of all stories contain male sources, while only a third of stories contain even a single female source', the report found, a disparity that was upheld across the different news media under scrutiny (PEW 2005: 2). Further findings included:

- In every topic category, the majority of stories cited at least one male source.
- In contrast, the only topic category where women crossed the 50 per cent threshold was lifestyle stories.
- The subject women were least likely to be cited on was foreign affairs.
- Newspapers were the most likely of the media studied to cite at least one female source in a story (41 per cent of stories). Cable news, despite all the time it has to fill, was the least likely medium to cite a female source (19 per cent of stories), and this held true across all three major cable channels.
- On network TV, the morning news programmes, which often cover lighter fare, relied more on female sources. The evening newscasts were somewhat less likely, but still did so more than cable.
- The sports section of the newspaper stood out in particular as a male bastion. A mere 14 per cent of stories on the front page of the sports section cited a woman, versus 86 per cent that contained at least one male source.

(PEW 2005: 2–3)

When set in relation to US society in general, where women made up 52 per cent of the population (and about 47 per cent of the employed civilian workforce) at the time, this disparity is all the more telling. Here the researchers caution that there is no implied suggestion that journalists should seek to achieve a balance between genders in every news story. That said, their conclusions do lead them to suggest that steps need to be taken to 'create more opportunity for female voices to emerge', and urgently so (PEW 2005: 17; see also Cann and Mohr's (2001) similar findings for television news in Australia).

In light of issues such as these, then, it is apparent that these norms of reportage need to be contextualized in relation to longstanding institutional power differentials within the journalistic workplace (where they tend to be all too readily defended with reference to a work ethos consistent with masculinized 'traditions' and 'customs'). Most newsrooms appear to be characterized by a gendered division between 'hard' news (such as economics, politics, government and crime) reporters, who tend to be men, and 'features' reporters, who are more likely, at least in relative terms, to be women. This division, far from correlating with the 'natural competencies' of individual male and female reporters ('men are better suited for the cut-and-thrust of hard news'), is frequently indicative of a sexual division of labour in the journalist's own household. Female reporters are more likely to experience a 'double-day' of work, one where they perform a disproportionate share of domestic (especially child care) responsibilities, than do their 'more professionally committed' male colleagues (see Lafky 1993; van Zoonen 1994; Lont 1995; see also Adam 1995). These forms of labour are somewhat easier to manage in relation to the more regularized, structured and predictable hours associated with features reporting.

Some feminists make the additional point that sexualized divisions of news-work are also embedded in the reporting process at the level of narrative modes of address. 'Even when women select the same news content as men,' according to Linda Christmas (1997: 3), a journalist with over thirty years of experience in newspaper and television news, 'they write it in a different manner.' In her view:

> Women want news that is 'relevant', news you can 'identify with', news that is explained in terms of their lives. Issues therefore are 'personalised', or 'human-ised' in order that the reader understands the relevance. This move recognises: that women prefer to communicate with the reader; they put readers' needs above those of policy-makers and other providers of news; that women tend to be more 'people' oriented rather than issue orientated; that women place greater importance on seeing news 'in context' rather than in isolation; and that women like to explain the consequences of events.
>
> (Christmas 1997: 3)

Following this line of argument, then, several feminists have called for further research to be undertaken into the means by which news is being distorted by a 'male bias'. That is, they seek to draw attention to how certain masculinized practices of reporting are being mobilized, intentionally or not, to justify the entrenchment of patriarchal news values at the expense of female-centred ones. The androcentric imperatives of journalism are discernible not only in definitions of newsworthiness, they argue, but also in the ruthless competition to be first with the news (so as to 'scoop' rivals), an over-reliance on male sources, and a fetishization of facts for their own sake (typically presented outside of their social, and therefore gendered, context).

At this level, and in light of the developments described above, new investigations are focusing on the changing nature of women's occupational status within news organizations. It is a shared conviction among many female journalists (as well as their academic counterparts) that the increased presence of women in the newsroom will necessarily encourage substantive changes in newswork practices. Women, some feminists argue, are more inclined than men to endorse informal, non-hierarchical management structures and to support collectively based decision-making processes. One example which appears to illustrate this point concerns Karla Garrett Harshaw, one of the very few African American daily newspaper editors in the US. She maintains that she would never have advanced to her current position had she followed the advice of her white male supervisors:

> At the time that I was expressing interest in middle management – I wanted to become an assistant city editor – one upper level manager was pretty candid about telling me that I didn't fit the image of a newsroom manager. One of the things he said was that I laughed a lot, people liked me and that my general personality was very different from people who were in middle management. If you looked around the newsroom at the people who were in middle management, they were young white males . . . I was energized by that conversation.
>
> (Cited in Stewart 1997: 69)

These types of developments need to be set in relation to current trends in the 'downsizing' of news organizations, however, as the number of journalists they employ are often being 'trimmed back' just as women are beginning to make serious inroads into management. 'Many journalists of color,' Stewart (1997: 85–6) observes, 'feel that the shutdowns and cutbacks have a more adverse effect on minorities, especially minority women, because when layoffs occur the most recently hired workers are generally terminated.'

In terms of news content, more female reporters arguably means that the lines between 'hard' and 'soft' news will continue to blur, leading to a news agenda defined more closely with strong 'human interest' angles. At the same time, however, other researchers have questioned the extent to which arguments such as these can be supported as a general rule. Many are sceptical of the claim that there is a 'woman's perspective' which female journalists inevitably bring to their reporting. Many of these feminists have initiated a conceptual shift in order to look beyond notions such as 'male bias', a term they suggest prefigures the possibility of 'non-bias' and with it 'gender-neutrality'. From this vantage point, the notion of 'male bias' is an idealistic formulation and, as such, is untenable from a perspective aiming to explicate the lived negotiation of gender relations within contested matrices of power. In their view, there are no essential categories of 'maleness' and 'femaleness' which male and female journalists (or their readers) occupy, respectively. 'The most difficult question for women,' writes Arthurs (1994: 83), 'is how to transform [media] institutions in a way that will give a voice to their aspirations and experiences without falling back on an unchanging and undifferentiated definition of what it means to be female.'

Critical analyses, I want to propose, may proceed to engage in the difficult task of deconstructing the prevailing norms of newswork so as to pinpoint the ways in which the 'macho culture' of the newsroom (and 'in the field') is reproduced on a day-to-day basis. The enduring salience of discourses of 'objectivity', it follows, needs to be understood within these (sometimes hostile) occupational contexts. For it is at the level of the everyday, in the ordinary and often mundane activities of processing 'raw facts', that certain types of news values, information gathering techniques and styles of presentation inform not only the construction of truth but also its narration in androcentric terms.

Gender politics of representation

Feminist and gender-sensitive forms of textual analysis have long been concerned with how women are portrayed in news media discourses, much of this work employing the notion of 'stereotypes' to advantage. Stereotypes are typically defined in this type of research as consisting of 'standardized mental pictures' which provide sexist judgements about women such that their subordinate status within a male-dominated society is symbolically reinforced. Consequently, a journalist's deployment of these stereotypes, far from being harmless, trivial or 'just a bit of fun', is instead seen to be contributing to the ideological reproduction of patriarchal social relations. Demands to reform these types of stereotypical practices in journalism have tended to centre on the need to make news texts more 'accurate' or 'true to real life' in their depiction of women's experiences. At the same time, other feminists have sought to radically extend this notion of 'stereotyping' so as to highlight the fluidly contradictory, and often contested, cultural dynamics underpinning their ideological purchase. Much of this work has initiated a conceptual shift to elaborate the attendant issues of representation in terms of the hegemonic gendering of news as a masculinized form of discourse.

In Britain, one particularly salient controversy over the representation of women is the case of the 'topless' female models routinely displayed on Page Three of the tabloid newspaper, the *Sun* (easily the best-selling daily title in Britain). The *Sun*'s 'Page Three principle', as Holland (1983, 1998) describes it, is one aspect of the tabloid's relentless pursuit of 'pleasure'. This invitation to the reader to partake in the celebratory enjoyment on offer through its photographs, layout, language and mode of address is all too clearly gendered around heterosexual male privilege. As Holland (1983: 85) writes:

> A purveyor of pleasures, an organiser of your pleasures, my pleasures . . . But are they my pleasures? Am I not, rather, repelled by those pleasures called on by the *Sun*, by its appeal to a trivial sexuality, by its insults to the female body, by its jokes at the expense of women, its flippancy . . . To put it bluntly, I know the *Sun* does not want me. The *Sun* does not want spoilsports, killjoys, those who are not prepared to join in the high jinks, the sauciness, to allow a flirty encounter to brighten their day.
>
> (Holland 1983: 85)

Only true '*Sun*-lovers' can appreciate the Page Three 'girls', 'those luscious ladies you drool over at breakfast' (the use of 'you' here, as Holland suggests, separates out from the audience those 'men who share the joke'). 'Page Three dominates the meaning of "woman" in the *Sun*,' according to Holland (1983: 93), 'and women readers must cope with this meaning.' This type of imagery addresses a female audience, she argues, in part through the *Sun*'s conviction that the Page Three principle is embodied in all women: 'It is part of the *Sun*'s discourse on female sexuality which invites sexual enjoyment, sexual freedom and active participation in heterosexual activity' (1983: 93; see also Stratford 1992; Castanñeda and Campbell 2006; Moritz 2009).

The *Sun*'s construction of a 'willing and eager female sexuality' across its pages, Holland contends, represents a constant struggle to define and contain a cultural politics of sexual identity. To contextualize the ideological appeals mobilized by the *Sun* in historical terms, the tabloid needs to be situated as part of a stridently rightward, pro-Thatcherite movement associated with Kelvin MacKenzie who took over the editorship in 1981. 'The central image of the semi-naked "nice girl" and her welcoming smile,' she writes, 'was developed as a politics of disengagement' (1998: 25). To illustrate this point, Holland (1998: 26) proceeds to quote from an item, captioned 'Page Three is good for you', published alongside a Page Three photograph in 1984:

> P3's titillating tit-bits are just what the doctor ordered – as a tonic against all the world's gloomy news. Research has shown that the *Sun*'s famous glamour pictures are a vital bit of cheer for readers depressed by strikes, deaths and disasters.
>
> (Holland 1998: 26)

Evidence of this 'research' takes the form of this quotation attributed to 'A London psychologist' in the item:

> When you think how gloomy and threatening most of the news has been lately – strikes, assassinations, hijacks, starving millions and the falling pound – you need Page Three as a shot in the arm. I am sure the *Sun*'s

famous beauties are a vital safely valve for the country's men when things in general seem to be getting out of hand.

It is at the level of Page Three that the *Sun* arguably seeks to dictate the terms by which issues of sexuality and lifestyle are to be normalized most clearly. Holland (1998) uses the phrase 'intemperate abuse' to characterize the *Sun*'s language of representation in this regard. 'In the daily mosaic of the newspaper,' she writes, 'the image of the sexy woman continues to be laid against female demons like single mothers, lesbian teachers and ugly women' (1998: 26; here the participation of some female journalists in the apparent 'laddish' culture at the tabloid is similarly relevant. For example, it was the Woman's Editor, Wendy Henry, who reportedly shouted the word 'Gotcha!' when the news came in over the teleprinter that an Argentine warship had been sunk by a British submarine during the Falklands/Malvinas conflict, the word later being used as the infamous headline for the story: Engel 1996: 274; see also Chippendale and Horrie 1992).

In the case of 'supermarket tabloids' in the US, studies suggest that their representations of women almost always reaffirm patriarchal definitions of 'femininity' (needless to say, feminists – or 'women's libbers' as they are invariably called in these titles – are typically portrayed as constituting a threat to 'decent folk'). Still, as Bird (1992) argues, it is important to note that women are at least present in tabloid news to a far greater extent than they are in so-called 'mainstream' news discourse. Although this enhanced degree of presence is understandable given that the readership for these types of tabloids is predominantly female, it is surprising that it has not led to a greater range of representations being mobilized. Instead, the dominant news values in play present what Bird describes as a 'distinctly conservative picture of women', albeit one which leaves at least some space for negotiation around the borders. More specifically, according to her examination of tabloid content, Bird's study contends that:

> marriage and children are of prime importance – tabloid heroines are not successful career women but women who make unusual marriages and succeed as mothers. Villains, on the other hand, are women (and men) who disrupt the family ideal. Celebrities are often seen as hopelessly pursuing the quest for a perfect marriage and family; perennial favorites . . . will never be truly happy until they find the perfect mate.
>
> (Bird 1992: 76–7)

In so doing, the tabloids attribute a positive value to many aspects of daily life, particularly nurturing and personal relationships, typically devalued elsewhere in the news media due to their identification as being 'feminine'.

In seeking to contextualize these insights in relation to the findings gathered via her readership study, Bird maintains that the ways in which her female respondents actively insert tabloid narratives into their lives are directly linked to this affirmation of familial ideology. These respondents evidently place a high value on the tabloids due to the validation they offer for their concerns for family and interpersonal relations. This is the case, she suggests, even though 'many had lived or were living very difficult lives, victims of spouse abuse, lack of money, and the generalized oppression of being an "old-fashioned housewife" ' (Bird 1992: 208). She proceeds to suggest that these tabloids help their female readers to feel better about themselves, to cope more effectively with daily experiences of inequality. This sense of pleasure and comfort is not to be confused, however, with a project of empowerment to actually help readers to change their lives. Rather, this type of publication, in Bird's (1992: 209) words, 'charms its readers and beckons them into a world where life is dangerous and exciting. But when the journey is done, it soothes them with reassurances that, be it ever so humble, there really is no place like home.'

Returning to the so-called 'serious', 'objective' news media in both Britain and the US, it is fair to say that instances of blatantly sexist reporting typically appear far less frequently than they do in places such as the 'scandal sheets'. As some critics have argued, however, the forms of sexism associated with the 'quality end of the market' can be all the more insidious for being communicated inferentially as opposed to explicitly. My reading of British newspaper and broadcast news suggests that invocations of reality asserted by men may be shown consistently, but not exclusively, to command the available discursive terrain over those advanced by women. The boundaries demarcating this terrain are fluid and yet contingent, that is, while they undergo constant changes in alignment with the diverse pressures (hegemonic and counter-hegemonic) brought to bear upon them, they will remain hierarchically grounded in conditions of dominance so long as patriarchal truth-claims are deemed to correspond with 'the real world'.

This patriarchal inflection of truth, far from occurring in a wildly indeterminate manner, takes place within what is a discursive economy of Otherness where women's experiences are recurrently effaced, trivialized or marginalized. This despite the codes of 'objective' reporting which dictate, as noted above, that such evaluations should not take place on the basis of gender; rather, 'the facts must be allowed to speak for themselves'. Significantly, however, the gendered-specificity of these codes is all too often apparent, for example, in the newsworker's use of

- generic pronouns such as 'he' to refer to both male and female news actors, or in phrases where 'public opinion' is reduced to 'the views of the man on the street'

- an explicit marking of gender when the news actor is female (e.g. 'the female judge' as opposed to 'the judge')
- the use of gendered descriptive terms (a woman's age, physical appearance and marital status are much more likely to be seen as relevant than they will be for men)
- male-centred naming strategies ('wife', 'girlfriend', 'mistress').

Due, in part, to these types of codified practices, women are regularly depicted as passive, and sexualized agents to be defined in relation to an active male news actor (see also Rakow and Kranich 1991; Cameron 1992; Clark 1992; Mills 1995; Hartley 1998).

Discursive practices such as these invite, to varying degrees, the reader to adopt a textually preferred, that is, masculinized, reading position as being inferentially consistent with 'objectivity'. The oft-repeated dictum that 'hard news requires hard newsmen' simultaneously prefigures a male reader as the projected norm. Crucial questions may therefore be raised regarding the range of presumptions about 'the audience' being operationalized as 'common sense' in the language of the news account. By asking: 'who is the implied reader of this account?' the subtle (or, for the British tabloid press, often not so subtle) discursive strategies by which the account's assumed audience is situated in gendered (and frequently explicitly racialized) terms may be disrupted. In the case of British newspaper discourse, for example, a reader typified as male is likely to be positioned as being primarily interested in public affairs (the realms of business, government and sport), while the assumed female reader tends to be positioned as being more interested in personally 'private' or domestic concerns, such as health, 'relationships', fashion, 'beauty' and child care. In many ways, then, the news account's ascription of different attributes and interests to its male and female readers, respectively, directly corresponds with the patriarchal (as well as class-specific and ethnocentric) rationales underpinning the 'pursuit of objectivity'.

Still, many newspaper commentators are now pointing to what they claim is a growing 'feminization' of the news. News organizations, they argue, are becoming ever more inclined to attract female readers, often due to the influence of advertisers. While the subject of much debate among journalists, it would appear that the rising importance of women as a distinct audience group in demographic terms is helping to dissolve this 'hard' versus 'soft' news dichotomy. So-called 'women's issues', once almost entirely restricted to the 'women's page' or its equivalent because they were deemed by male newsworkers to be 'trivial', 'lightweight' or, at best, 'human interest' stories, are increasingly finding their way onto the 'hard' news agenda. Whether or not this shift will be sustained, and what long-term impact (if any) it will have on the prevailing 'macho culture' in the newsroom discussed above, remains to be seen. As will become apparent in the next section, researchers committed to investigating news coverage of male acts of violence against women, for example, have every reason to be sceptical.

(En)gendering violence in the news

Reports of male violence being perpetrated against women have appeared in the news on a routine basis since the emergence of popular newspapers in the nineteenth century. In both Britain and the US, as noted in Chapter 1, it was the emergence of a popular press in the nineteenth century which ushered in fresh types of news values. These newspapers placed a particular emphasis on luridly sensational crime stories, frequently attempting to regale their readers with news stories revolving around sex and violence (see Chibnall 1977; Schudson 1978; Carter and Thompson 1997; Carter and Weaver 2003).

In the context of her historical overview of the growth of sex crime coverage in the US, Benedict (1992) examines several instances of pertinent newspaper coverage. Of particular relevance, she observes, are the sexist (and frequently racist) assumptions underpinning the news language typically being used to represent these crimes. More specifically, her evidence indicates that US newspapers, to varying degrees, habitually draw upon two types of narratives which serve to reinforce a certain rape 'mythology' which is highly dangerous. These two narratives, in Benedict's (1992) words, tend to assume the following form:

> The 'Vamp' version: *The woman, by her looks, behavior or generally loose morality, drove the man to such extremes of lust that he was compelled to commit the crime.*
>
> The 'Virgin' version: *The man, a depraved and perverted monster, sullied the innocent victim, who is now a martyr to the flaws of society.*
>
> (Benedict 1992: 23)

Both of these narratives, she argues, are harmful both to the survivors of a rape attack and to public understanding of this type of event. 'The vamp version,' according to Benedict (1992: 24), 'is destructive because it blames the victim of the crime instead of the perpetrator.' The virgin version is similarly destructive in her view because 'it perpetuates the idea that women can be only Madonnas or whores, paints women dishonestly, and relies on portraying the suspects as inhuman monsters' (Benedict 1992: 24).

To the extent that these narratives are imposed (often unconsciously) by journalists on the sex crimes they cover, Benedict contends, certain rape myths will be validated. Examples of these rape myths she identifies include 'rape is sex', 'the assailant is motivated by lust', 'the assailant is perverted or crazy', 'the assailant is usually black or lower class', 'women provoke rape', 'women deserve rape', 'only "loose" women are victimized', 'a sexual attack sullies the victim', 'rape is a punishment for past deeds' and 'women cry rape for revenge'. It is precisely these kinds of rape myths which, in her view, force journalists to represent survivors of sex crimes in accordance with the false images generated by the two news narratives outlined above. 'As long as the rape myths hold sway,' Benedict (1992: 24) writes, 'journalists are going to continue to be faced with the excruciating choice between painting victims as virgins or vamps – a choice between lies.'

Further evidence to support this line of inquiry may be found in Meyers's (1997) examination of how local journalists report male violence against women in Atlanta, Georgia, a city with one of the highest homicide rates in the US. Echoing Benedict's (1992) argument briefly sketched above, she similarly maintains that news representations of female survivors of male violence typically polarize around a culturally defined 'virgin–whore' or 'good girl–bad girl' dichotomy which conceals the gendered patterns of domination and control endemic to social structures. Indeed, on the basis of her textual analysis of the reporting of anti-women violence on the pages of the *Atlanta Journal-Constitution*, as well as the television news coverage aired on the city's network affiliates, Meyers (1997) goes so far as to state:

> By perpetuating male supremacist ideology and the myths, stereotypes, and assumptions that underlie it, the news ultimately encourages violence against women. News reports of women as victims of sexist violence act as both a warning to women and a form of social control that outlines the boundaries of acceptable behavior and the forms of retribution they can expect for transgression . . . [T]he vulnerability of women is a given and, linked to questions of complicity, remains lurking in the shadows of representation. Was she where she shouldn't have been? Did she fail to take precautions – to lock a door, to arrange for security? Did she do something to provoke the attack?
>
> (Meyers 1997: 9)

The findings Meyers draws from her textual analysis of anti-women news coverage lead her to suggest, in turn, that the conventional forms of news presentation associated with these crimes are actually harmful to the interests of all women (see also Weaver 1998). News reports which blame victims instead of treating them with respect contribute to the reinforcement of prejudice at a societal level, she argues, while the humiliation, guilt or anguish they cause to the women involved is almost never acknowledged.

The material Meyers gathers through in-depth interviews held with eight reporters and one editor working in the Atlanta metropolitan area concerning how they go about processing news about sex crimes is similarly illuminating. Given that these journalists are confronted with a relatively large number of acts of violence to potentially cover, Meyers was interested to know about the standards of newsworthiness being applied. Although differences in emphasis are recognizable between the individual interviewees' respective experiences in newspaper, radio and television journalism, it quickly becomes apparent that a 'hierarchy of crime' exists within reporting. At the top of this hierarchy is murder, considered to be the most serious of crimes and, as such, usually generating the largest share of coverage. 'If somebody's shot and they don't die, then it's not a story', explained one of Meyers's (1997: 90) respondents. 'That sounds cold, but that's just the way it works.'

Significantly, however, these interviews also suggest that domestic violence, even when it leads to battering, rape or a murder being committed, is often considered to be non-newsworthy due to its very ordinariness as part of everyday life. In the words of one television reporter: 'If someone gets shot on a street corner and it turns out to be a domestic argument, the chances of that making the air are slim' (Meyers 1997: 90). This reliance on extraordinariness as a guiding principle of newsworthiness, Meyers (1997: 98–9) argues, means that violence against women is likely to be ignored by journalists unless there is something 'quirky' about it or it has an 'unusual twist' (see also Pritchard and Hughes 1997; Carter 1998; Kitzinger 1998, 2004; Macdonald 1998; McLaughlin 1998; Skidmore 1998; Wykes 1998; Carter and Weaver 2003; Mason and Monckton-Smith 2008).

One of the most systemic studies of sex crime reporting conducted in Britain is that of Soothill and Walby (1991), who examined a range of examples over forty years of newspaper coverage. Briefly, this investigation identifies four sets of issues which the authors consider to be particularly salient.

First, *seeking the sensational*: the focus of the popular press on the sensational (as opposed to the ordinary) leads to the construction of the sex beast, the sex fiend or the sex monster as the major theme in the coverage of sex crime. The national press, according to Soothill and Walby (1991: 35), 'will retain interest in a case only if there is scope for the construction of a sex fiend who continues to wreak havoc on a community'. Often the coverage of the police search for the perpetrator is written to generate the excitement of 'the chase', hence the greater likelihood that an attack will be reported where the assailant was not previously known by the victim (1991: 146). For this and related reasons, 'the construction of a sex fiend helps to sell newspapers' (1991: 35).

Second, *producing a cascade effect*: during the trial for a sex offender, the authors argue, the popular press frequently resorts to the deliberate use of distortion and exaggeration in order to maintain the momentum for public attention. This type of coverage can have a particularly harmful 'cascade effect', forcefully overflowing on to all of those people connected with the crime, no matter how remotely. Many of these people may suffer dramatic consequences in their own personal lives due to this kind of publicity. As Soothill and Walby (1991: 148) write: 'There seem to be no limits to the extent that the popular press will seek to provide background material to titillate their readership.'

Third, *embracing a narrow definition of sex crime*: while news reporting of sex crimes is extensive, only a very small number of cases receive sustained coverage. The news media, due to a variety of reasons (not least of which is their conception of their readership's 'boredom threshold' where sex crimes are concerned; on journalists' 'child abuse fatigue', see Kitzinger 1998; Skidmore 1998), place a selective emphasis on 'unconventional' types of attack in preference to the more 'customary' ones. As a result, there is a subsequent narrowing of what counts as a 'legitimate' sex crime worthy of journalistic attention. For example, Soothill and Walby (1991: 148) contend that 'the message consistently comes across that the only "real" rape or "real" sexual assault is committed by a stranger'. News media interest narrows still further after the offender has been convicted and imprisoned, with only the most notorious criminals receiving coverage.

Fourth, *information and explanation*: efforts by journalists at both 'quality' and popular newspapers to look beyond specific events to address the larger social context within which sex crimes take place are, at best, minimal. This study similarly suggests that event-centred news coverage obscures the pervasive nature of sex crimes across society. In the absence of proper analyses of the causes of these crimes, the reader is provided with very little by way of useful information to effect change. 'When law changes on sex crime are being proposed in Parliament,' Soothill and Walby (1991: 149) note as one example, 'the general approach of the media is essentially of two kinds – trivialise or ignore the debate.' They suggest that although better informed accounts are often written by women columnists, much remains to be done to progressively transform those areas of the newspaper which have a greater impact. This study by Soothill and Walby (1991) thus usefully pinpoints a range of issues which challenge the very assumptions underpinning journalistic configurations of 'normality' where the reporting of sex crimes is concerned.

Several of these issues have recently been taken up by researchers similarly committed to examining the ways in which the news media contribute to the ideological normalization of male violence against women. Carter's (1998: 231) study of 850 pertinent news accounts drawn from the British tabloid press, for example, leads her to argue that much of this coverage encourages readers to believe that sexual violence is a 'natural', seemingly inevitable part of ordinary experience in modern society. It is this formulation of ordinariness, she maintains, that prompts journalists to seek out ever more spectacular incidents of 'femicide' to retain their readership. The implications of which, as Carter writes, are profound:

> This daily diet of representations of the most brutal forms of sexual violence constructs the world outside as well as inside the front door as highly dangerous places for women and girls, one in which sex crimes have become an ordinary, taken-for-granted feature of everyday life.
>
> (Carter 1998: 231)

To denaturalize the gender politics of news coverage of male violence, then, is to centre questions of power. Kitzinger's (1998) analysis of news reporting strategies involved in the coverage of 'false memory syndrome' (a medical condition supposed to affect how adults recall memories of abuse as children) highlights, among other concerns, the ways in which anti-feminist discourses shape the gendered criteria of source credibility. A related study by Skidmore (1998), which takes as its focus news coverage of child sex abuse, documents the resistance of male journalists to attend to this issue and the ways in which their female colleagues' attempts to place it on the 'hard' news agenda are routinely undermined as a result (see also Wykes 1998; Critcher 2003).

To further illustrate the need to repoliticize the sense of normality associated with acts of male violence, our attention turns to a specific instance of reporting – a front page story which appeared in the 12 June 1998 edition of the *Daily Mail*, often described as 'mid-market' in its appeal and in its mode of address:

> WIFE WHOSE AFFAIR LED TO PRISON FOR HER HUSBAND
>
> THIS is the woman whose love affair led to a seven-year jail sentence for her husband yesterday.
>
> City broker Julien [B] had come home unexpectedly to find his wife partially clothed on the settee of their living room with her lover, company owner David [N].
>
> As Mr [N] fled, [B] used one of the shoes he left behind to batter his wife Wendy. She was left with a fractured skull and two brain clots and spent ten days in intensive care.
>
> Despite her serious injuries, Mrs [B] pleaded for her husband to be spared prison when he appeared in court yesterday. She said: 'I still love him and I think we have a chance of making a go of it'.
>
> But in a decision which infuriated [B]'s family and left the unfaithful

wife sobbing, Judge [BW] QC said the attack was so serious that it had to be punished by prison.

FULL STORY: PAGE FIVE

Source: Daily Mail, 12 June 1998, page 1; surnames reduced to first letter to conceal identity

This news account provides a startling illustration of how a female victim of a brutal act of male violence can find herself being blamed for the crime (she is pictured to one side of the account). In both its headline and the opening sentence, this account seeks to establish a direct causal linkage between a woman's 'love affair' and a jail sentence imposed on her husband, the attacker. Such a formulation of blame, in my view, serves to implicitly suggest that the perpetrator of the assault, Julien B, is not actually responsible for his actions. Rather, this account appears to encourage the inference that Wendy B is deserving of her injuries because of the hurt the discovery of the affair caused her husband.

Further aspects of the account which also appear to impute guilt for the attack on to its victim include the terms used to describe the news actors themselves. In the course of the narrative, for example, the male news actors are defined in relation to their public identities ('city broker' in the case of Julien B and 'company owner' for David N), while the victim of the assault is described in turn as 'wife', 'woman', 'Wendy', 'Mrs B' and 'unfaithful wife'. This use of terms ensures that Wendy B is identified strictly in terms of her relationship to Julien B. Such a strategy arguably works to reinforce the (unspoken) dictates of familial ideology to the point that their transgression warrants male violence as a legitimate response. These ideological tensions are similarly discernible, at least in my reading, in the final paragraph of the account. Here Wendy B, despite the emphasis on her marital status, is posited as being outside of the familial dynamic: 'decision which infuriated [B's] family and left the unfaithful wife sobbing'. Precisely who constitutes a member of '[B's] family' is not disclosed in the account; instead, it informs the reader (again, implicitly) that Wendy B is to be positioned as a non-family member due to an alleged sexual encounter with someone other than her husband.

It is only possible to speculate, of course, as to why this violent assault received front page treatment in the *Daily Mail*. Part of the reason may have to do with the fact that the survivor of the attack is both white and evidently middle-class, two factors which according to the available research suggest that the crime would be more likely to be considered journalistically important. Moreover, as one of the newsworkers interviewed by Meyers (1997) suggested, albeit in a very different context, violent attacks 'are more common in lower-income strata and I guess you don't expect it in the idyllic suburbs. And so when something like it happens, it's out of place. And things that are out of place, in essence, are news' (Meyers 1997: 96). In any case, however, further research is clearly required in order to better discern the extent to which instances of news coverage such as this one in the *Daily Mail* are shaping the boundaries of the larger discursive field within which public policy-making decisions concerning these issues are being debated. In the absence of adequate legal measures to enhance the protection of women from male violence, particularly in the household, the need for far more responsible forms of reporting grows more urgent every day.

To bring this chapter to a close, then, it is important to recognize that although women have made crucial gains in the field of news reporting which have fundamentally altered the types of sexist dynamics which once characterized the profession, much remains to be done. Journalist Anne Sebba (1994: 10) is not alone when she looks forward to the day when 'women reporters are working in sufficient numbers that they are no longer judged by their looks, their personalities or their private lives and when we, the audience, are able to absorb merely the news they are reporting'. Much hope for the future rests with the significant numbers of women now entering the profession: occupational figures for countries such as Britain and the US show that we are currently witnessing a steady rise in the relative share of positions being secured by young women reporters. Still, it is important to bear in mind a point that Arthurs (1994: 100) makes in her discussion of the British media industry: 'More women in the industry is not enough: there need to be more women with a politicised understanding of the ways in which women's subordination is currently reproduced, and with the will to change it.' And, it goes without saying, male journalists will have to cease being part of the problem in order to join their female colleagues in finding solutions. 'The key workplace issue, with women as with black people and Asians, is that while some have risen high, virtually none have got to the very top', Max Hastings (2008), former editor of the *Telegraph*, recently observed. 'Until they do so the perception, if not the reality, of discrimination will persist.'

It is to this related issue of social exclusion based on discourses of racial difference that our attention turns in the next chapter.

8 RACIAL DIVERSITY IN THE NEWS

> The overarching challenge is to rid our journalism of any vestige of an 'us and them' attitude, of an unspoken regard of any community or group as 'others' . . . The long-hallowed cult of journalistic 'objectivity' has too often been a veneer for what is essentially a predominating white male point of view in our news culture.
>
> (John Phillip Santos, US journalist)

The word 'race' is one of the most politically charged in the journalistic vocabulary. Aptly characterized as one of modern society's 'rawest nerves', race is a cultural construction embedded in hierarchical relations of power. News media representations of race in 'Western' countries, one study after the next suggests, are recurrently framed within the boundaries of dominant white cultural attitudes. Instances where news coverage looks beyond 'blood, bullets and sound-bites', to borrow US journalist Sig Gissler's phrase, are few and far between. 'From birth to death,' Gissler (1997: 105) writes, 'race is with us, defining, dividing, distorting.' Many of these studies suggest that news reporting devoted to race-related issues is more than likely to be as sensational and superficial as it is politically dangerous. This exigency is apparent not only in tabloid news formats, usually the most blatant when it comes to exhibiting racial prejudice, but also in the types of coverage ordinarily situated at the so-called 'quality' end of the news spectrum. As Indarjit Singh (1998), a British journalist, observes:

> What passes for news has to be geared to demand, and sadly the way to profit lies in pandering to baser human instincts and prejudices. It is this that leads newspapers, for example, to carrying banner headlines: 'Asian

> landlord evicts tenant for eating beef' while on an inside page there is a much smaller item reporting an earthquake in which more than 5,000 people have died.
>
> (Singh 1998: 74)

This pandering to prejudice is clearly at odds with any notion of journalistic professionalism, let alone 'impartial', socially responsible reporting. Such forms of discrimination, moreover, obscure the decisive ways in which the news media shape what counts as a community's 'way of life', and with it the inclusionary ('us') and exclusionary ('them') notions of 'belonging' which encourage only some people to feel 'at home' in that community.

It is this cultural division between 'us and them' precisely as it is affirmed, transformed and contested across the terrain of the news media which serves as the point of departure for this chapter's discussion.

Constructing 'us' and 'them'

In attempting to elucidate the extent to which the media construct and reproduce ideologies of racism, Hall (1990) calls attention to the specific practices in and through which certain racist assumptions are reaffirmed in discursive terms as a matter of course. The question of race, he argues, is routinely defined on the basis of what may be described as a racist 'common sense' that is pervasive in British society. It is this taken-for-granted, 'naturalized' world of common sense that makes the ideologies of racism virtually disappear. 'Since (like gender) race appears to be "given" by Nature,' Hall (1990: 9) contends, 'racism is one of the most profoundly "naturalised" of existing ideologies.' In order to denaturalize these discourses of race, it is the largely unspoken – and frequently unconsciously held – images, premises and explanations governing the interpretation of 'reality' which need to be rendered problematic. By drawing upon certain types of strategies to 'make sense' of the social world, Hall (1990: 11) maintains, the media 'construct for us a definition of what *race* is, what meaning the imagery of race carries, and what the "problem of race" is understood to be'. That is to say, they 'help to classify out the world in terms of the categories of race'. It is the ideological limits associated with different discourses of race which Hall insists need to be acknowledged, a recognition which signals a conceptual break from those views which hold that there is a singular, uniformly racist conception of the world in operation across the media. As he writes:

> The media are not only a powerful source of ideas about race. They are also one place where these ideas are articulated, worked on, transformed and elaborated . . . It would be simple and convenient if all the media were

> simply the ventriloquists of a unified and racist 'ruling class' conception of the world. But neither a unifiedly conspiratorial media nor indeed a unified racist 'ruling class' exist in anything like that simple way.
>
> (Hall 1990: 11–12)

In moving beyond notions of conspiracy, Hall is rejecting the idea that the media are racist simply because there are racist people working behind the scenes to present the world in such terms. Even where this is the case, what matters most are the organizational norms, structures and practices which condition what is represented and how. 'What defines how the media function,' Hall (1990: 20) argues, 'is the result of a set of complex, often contradictory, social relations; not the personal inclinations of its members.' To engage with the power of this discourse, it follows, it is necessary to recognize its capacity to constrain what can, and cannot, be said about issues of race and ethnicity.

This naturalization of racism, while fluid and contradictory, is a longstanding feature of cultural modernity. As such, it can be difficult to denaturalize the ideological purchase of its 'common sense'. In order to better distinguish the 'vocabulary', 'syntax' and 'grammar' of race on which the media draw, then, Hall proceeds to make a crucial distinction between two types of racism:

- *'Overt' racism*: Hall uses this term to refer to those occasions where favourable media coverage is granted to what are explicitly or openly racist positions and arguments. Such coverage is more likely to appear in the right-wing newspaper press than on televisual news, he argues, in part because of the regulative requirement to be 'impartial' imposed on the latter institutions.
- *'Inferential' racism*: here Hall is referring to those seemingly naturalized representations of situations where racist premises or propositions are being inscribed in the media coverage as a set of unquestioned assumptions. These representations 'enable racist statements to be formulated without ever bringing into awareness the racist predicates on which the statements are grounded' (Hall 1990: 13).

Open or overt racism, as Hall argues, consistently finds expression on the pages of the popular or tabloid press, among other places. Not only do these newspapers, to varying degrees, circulate and popularize openly racist ideas, but also they actively legitimize their public expression via a populist mode of address. 'Racism,' he writes, 'becomes "acceptable" – and thus, not too longer after, "true" – just common sense: what everyone knows and is openly saying' (1990: 13). Inferential racism, in contrast, is even more widespread in the British media. Indeed, according to Hall, it may be regarded as being 'in many ways more insidious because it is largely *invisible* even to those who formulate the world in its terms' (Hall 1990: 13; see also Hartmann and Husband 1974; Braham 1982; Gordon and Rosenberg 1989; Searle 1989; Jordan and Weedon 1995; Mullan 1996; Ferguson 1998; Gabriel 1998; Ross 1998; Mahtani 2005; Sonwalkar 2005; Pickering 2008).

Examples of how this formulation of the social world can invoke a cultural division between 'us and them' continue to be all too abundant on the pages of British newspapers. Although some commentators argue that instances of overt racism are declining in number as titles such as the *Sun* and the *Mirror* slowly move 'upmarket', others suggest that the imperatives of inferential racism continue to be a salient feature of much reporting. The editorial leader associated with the main front page item on the 25 May 1998 edition of the *Sun* might be seen as an example:

> THIS LITTLE PIGGY IS A RACIST
> Cops seize mum's display for upsetting Muslims

As the item unfolds, it becomes apparent that the news event centres around a woman, Nancy B, whose collection of porcelain pigs (which she had displayed in a window facing the street) has been seized by the police following formal complaints ostensibly lodged by some of her Muslim neighbours, who deemed the display to be racially offensive. A number of discursive strategies are employed throughout the item, which seem to leave little doubt that the reader is being invited to identify with the 'ANGRY mum', also described as 'Patriotic Nancy'. Still, the reporting at least makes an attempt at journalistic balance when towards the end of the item it shifts perspective to include a hint of diversity in opinion among 'local Muslims'. That is, following several quotations attributed to angry neighbours, it is reported that 'one Muslim said: "Although I found it offensive, it was not obvious racism. She does not deserve all this abuse".'

It is left to the *Sun*'s editorial page for what could be seen as a more explicitly discriminatory rendering of the event to be heard:

> THE SUN SAYS
> *Pig headed*
> *WATCH out, bigots about.*
> That's the sign that should go up in Leicester.
> Racial and religious intolerance are rearing their ugly heads.
> *Not among the whites – among the local Asian Muslims.*
>
> They complain that a collection of ceramic pigs in a house window is racially offensive.
>
> That's daft. But not as ridiculous as the police going round to the house and seizing the pottery pigs as 'evidence'.

Culture

What will the Pig Squad do next: shut down Tescos for selling bacon?
The unbending attitude of militant Muslims who think they have a right to to [sic] *impose their culture in a Christian country is frightening.*

There has to be give and take if we are all to get on together. But it seems WE give and THEY take.

This does nothing for racial harmony. It just makes Muslims look mean-minded – which the vast majority are not.

This country is very easy-going and accepting of its new citizens.
But pigs will fly before we put up with this kind of nonsense.

Source: Sun, 25 May 1998, p. 8; original emphasis

It seems that the implied reader of this editorial, in my view, is clearly being invited to infer that to be of 'this country' is to be a white Christian. The 'we' versus 'they' dichotomy it constructs is evidently consistent with a racialized rendering of cultural identity, one which might be seen to hold the following organizing oppositions in ideological tension:

'the whites'	v	'local Asian Muslims'
'we'	v	'pig headed', 'bigots'
tolerant	v	'racial and religious intolerance'
reasonable	v	'daft'
'give and take'	v	'unbending attitude'
'Christian country'	v	'impose their culture'
'racial harmony'	v	'Militant Muslims'
'WE give'	v	'THEY take'
'very easy-going and accepting'	v	'frightening'
sense	v	'nonsense'

Further oppositions are similarly apparent, of course, but this short list pinpoints some of the ways in which they can reinforce one another so as to discursively anchor a preferred inflection of Muslim identity as a foreign 'Other' (see also Hafez 2000; Karim 2000). The 'we' projected by the editorial's mode of address finds its racialized definition in opposition to a 'they' positioned as being 'outside' of the imagined community of *Sun* readers.

Overt instances of racism do not appear frequently on the pages of the so-called 'serious', 'quality' broadsheet newspapers in Britain, particularly so in a politically centre-left title like the *Guardian*. Nevertheless, a brief comparison of two news headlines concerned with racial discrimination in the realm of sport, published almost thirty years apart, is telling:

> MAY A CLUB REFUSE NEGRO?
> The Supreme Court (USA) has reserved its decision whether a swimming and tennis club . . . was entitled to discriminate against Negro members.
>
> (*Guardian*, 15 October 1969)

This news headline appears strangely anachronistic from the vantage point of today due to its use of the term 'Negro' (the news item is cited in Hartmann and Husband 1974: 135). The extent to which this term was ideologically naturalized for *Guardian* readers in 1969 is open to question, of course, but it is certainly doubtful that it could appear in a current edition of the newspaper without sparking a surprised reaction by today's reader. Compare it, then, with an item which appeared in 1998:

> WHITE CLUBS FEAR ETHNIC CRICKETERS
> A cricketing apartheid is being created with black and Asian cricketers being ostracised by white clubs because they are perceived as too competitive and aggressive.
>
> (*Guardian*, 8 May 1998)

This news headline, in contrast with the first one, may appear to some readers as being harmless enough, avoiding as it does the use of a term as powerfully resonant as 'Negro'. Similarly, it identifies the cricket clubs in question as being 'white', something which is simply taken for granted in the first news item's account of the swimming and tennis club. Nevertheless, neatly encapsulated in this headline is the racist presupposition that to be 'white' is not to be 'ethnic'. That is to say, it is being inferentially assumed in the headline that ethnicity does not encompass whiteness: only other, non-white people can be members of an ethnic group. Whiteness thus becomes naturalized as a non-raced norm against which ethnicity is measured.

A further illustration of several of these dynamics may be found in Hartley's (1992) discussion of 'Wedom' and 'Theydom' as they pertain to news representations of Aboriginal communities in Australia (see also Hartley 1996). In describing the ways in which news discourse is organized around strategies of inclusion and exclusion, he proceeds to show how the 'we' of Australian citizenship typically mobilized in news items rules out as 'foreign' those who are deemed not to belong. Journalists, he argues, routinely categorize Aboriginal people and their actions as being constitutive of a 'they', a process realized in and through a number of different reporting practices. Here it is possible to draw out from Hartley's discussion five particularly salient issues associated with these practices:

- *Balance*: Aboriginal people, according to Hartley (1992: 207), tend to be exempted from the conventionalized notions of journalistic balance which would otherwise apply: 'There are not "two sides" to an Aboriginal story – not two *Aboriginal* sides, that is, only an Aboriginal side and a "balance" supplied by, for instance, police, welfare, legal or governmental authorities.'
- *Naming*: news photographs of Aboriginal people 'are routinely printed without name captions; they are representative of their race, not of their persons, even in so-called positive human interest stories' (1992: 207, 209). In sharp contrast, Hartley argues, scrupulous care is taken to identify those people who are located from within what he refers to as the domain of 'Wedom'.
- *Identity*: journalists habitually situate Aboriginal people within the confines of a Theydom where their personal identities are exclusively defined as consisting in being 'unlike us' in Wedom. By this negative logic, Aborigines are characterized as a unified group whose individual members are 'all the same'. Attendant difficulties include 'recognizing internal differences in the overall Aboriginal community, not distinguishing between traditional and urban Aborigines, or between different geographical, political and other positions among them' (1992: 209).
- *Citizenship*: 'Aborigines who are stereotyped as outsiders or as tribal,' Hartley (1992: 209) writes, 'cannot be seen as citizens with rights.' It is much more likely for Aboriginal people to appear in news accounts as welfare recipients or criminals. Consequently, 'a spokesperson who insists on the citizenship or the rights of Aborigines, as opposed to conforming to welfare or corrective stereotypes, is likely to be represented in the news as an extremist' (1992: 209).
- *Access*: only rarely is it the case, Hartley contends, that Aboriginal people are asked for their opinion by journalists, or provided with the opportunity 'to represent themselves in the media with their own agenda of newsworthy issues or their own debates about possible solutions to problems they can identify for themselves' (1992: 209). Exceptions to the routine restrictions placed on news access typically occur where verisimilitude is required to support the predetermined 'line' of the news story.

These types of reporting practices, with the strategies of inclusion and exclusion which they entail, have in Hartley's view become naturalized to the point of virtually being 'common sense' among many Australian journalists. To the extent that a potential news story concerning Aboriginal people can be made to conform to existing 'definitions of the situation', he argues, its chances of receiving coverage improve significantly. That is to say, he writes, 'if the story represents Aborigines as "they" rather than as "we", and makes sense of them as in need of protection, correction or welfare, and not in terms of what they may wish to say and do for themselves' (Hartley 1992: 210).

Turning to the United States, Entman's (1997: 29) research into television news production suggests that despite the efforts of journalists to portray the news 'objectively', the choices they make when reporting the day's events appear to 'feed racial stereotypes' (see also Entman 1990, 1992). The rise of entertainment values, he contends, is leading to sensationalist forms of news coverage which have the effect of encouraging white hostility toward minority groups such as African Americans. Local televisual news, in particular, 'paints a picture of blacks as violent and threatening toward whites, self-interested and demanding toward the body politic – continually causing problems for the law-abiding, tax-paying majority' (Entman 1997: 29). Far from informing their audiences about the realities of racial discrimination, televisual newscasts are contributing to a climate of fear between the dominant 'ingroup' (whites) and the 'outgroup' (blacks) across society. Pressures to make the news entertaining are making it even more difficult for social issues, such as urban poverty and its causes, to be covered in sufficient depth. Indeed, Entman (1997: 29) is of the view that what is increasingly superficial reporting 'may also be making urban America less governable, deepening the chasm of misunderstanding and distrust between blacks and whites' (see also Reeves and Campbell 1994; Campbell 1995; Gandy 1998; Jacobs 2000; Newkirk 2000).

African Americans, according to Les Payne of *Newsday* magazine, are 'disproportionately included in negative coverage – as prostitutes, drug dealers, welfare recipients, second-story men, unwed mothers'. As he observes: 'It's a strange place, this black world the media project' (cited in Dates and Pease 1997: 79). The cultural politics of 'us and them' suffuse the construction of news discourse in ways which help to create and reinforce the fears of what are predominantly white audiences toward other ethnic groups. In order to render problematic the narrative conventions which sustain different forms of racism, it is necessary to disrupt the taken-for-granted assumptions about 'race' which inform what counts as journalistic 'common sense'. As an editor of the *Times-Picayune* in Louisiana points out: 'We don't realize how much our newspapers reflect one point of view – the white point of view' (cited in Gissler 1997: 111). Meanwhile, at the *Sun* in Baltimore, one white reporter comments: 'Minority reporters call our news meetings the "Pale Male Club" ' (cited in Shipler 1998). The intricate, often subtle ways in which white perspectives shape the framing of news reports concerning race-related issues can have a profound effect on public attitudes to racial discrimination (as well as on those of government policy makers), an effect which an otherwise conscientious white newsworker might never have intended.

Wilson and Gutiérrez (1995) highlight the importance of placing these changing dynamics within a historical perspective. Specifically, they identify five developmental phases, the first four of which they suggest have been commonly experienced by people of colour confronted with white news organizations in the course of US history:

- *Exclusionary phase*: a sustained refusal to acknowledge the initial social presence of people of colour in news media reports contributed to their exclusion from the outset as visible members of 'mainstream' society. 'For that reason,' Wilson and Gutiérrez (1995: 153) write, 'racial exclusion in news set the course followed by the other phases of non-Whites' treatment in the news. It was a course of alienation between Whites and non-Whites.'
- *Threatening-issue phase*: recurrently it is the case that the first appearances of non-white cultural groups in news media reports are directly linked to a perception of the group as posing a threat to the established social order. Beginning with the characterization of Native American Indians in the colonial and early national press as 'savages' endangering 'civilized' whites, successive minority groups have been transformed into objects of fear.
- *Confrontation phase*: almost always following closely behind the above phase is a social confrontation between the non-white group and the white population, the news coverage of which is typically framed within an 'us versus them' perspective. The response may be violent in nature, examples of which cited by Wilson and Gutiérrez (1995: 155) are 'the Indian wars of the westward expansion, the Mexican War, or the lynchings of Blacks in the South, Mexicans in the Southwest and Asians in the West', or it may culminate in legislative action (segregation laws, peace treaties, immigration laws, and so forth). Further outcomes include the race riots which 'dominate the news with a historical consistency that has involved virtually every non-White racial group' (1995: 155).
- *Stereotypical selection phase*: the need to restore social order in the aftermath of these types of confrontation entails a shift in news coverage so as to facilitate the transition into a post-conflict period. News reportage, according to Wilson and Gutiérrez, necessarily adapts so as to ensure that white people's apprehensions where people of colour are concerned can be effectively 'neutralized'. Journalists, by selectively drawing on stereotypical images in their news stories, accomplish two objectives: '(a) The general audience is reassured that non-Whites are still "in their place" (i.e., the reservation, ghetto, etc.) and (b) those who escape their designated place are not a threat to society because they manifest the same values and ambitions as the dominant culture and overcome the deficits of their home communities' (1995: 157).

- *Multiracial coverage phase*: the antithesis of the exclusionary phase, multiracial news coverage promotes social understanding. 'At present this phase is still largely a vision,' Wilson and Gutiérrez (1995: 158) maintain, 'but it is within the grasp of a society determined to include all Americans in the quest for social and economic equality' (1995: 158). This type of news will be reported from a perspective where the 'us' being invoked is made to represent all citizens, thereby ensuring that people of colour are represented on equal terms with white people. Unwarranted fears based on prejudices will be alleviated, the authors suggest, as the last vestiges of racism are finally removed from the 'gatekeeper ranks'.

These different phases, while usefully differentiated in this way, are necessarily interconnected. It is similarly important to note that the boundaries between them are relatively fluid and, moreover, inevitably contested as the ideological struggles transpiring over the news media unfold in complex, and contradictory, ways.

Reporting law and order

Questions of 'law and order' are central to many of the news media discourses in circulation around issues of 'race'. Many of these issues were thrown into sharp relief in the US when a number of cities witnessed social upheaval in the form of 'race riots' during the 1960s. One of the first to take place occurred in Harlem, New York, during the summer of 1964, followed by another in the 'black ghetto' of Watts in Los Angeles during August 1965 (34 people died and almost 1000 were injured). Further racial conflicts erupted over the next two summers, eventually leading President Lyndon B. Johnson to launch a National Advisory Commission on Civil Disorders to investigate the causes of the tensions in 1967. Released in March 1968, the Kerner Commission report, as it was called after Governor Otto Kerner of Illinois who headed the inquiry, declared that the country was effectively dividing into two societies, 'one black, one white, separate and unequal'. The report expressed its indictment of the news media's complicity in exacerbating racial conflicts in clear language:

> Our fundamental criticism is that the news media have failed to analyze and report adequately on racial problems in the United States and, as a related matter, to meet the Negro's legitimate expectations of journalism . . . The media write and report from the standpoint of a white man's world . . . Slights and indignities are part of the Negro's daily life, and many of them come from what he now calls the 'white press' – a press that repeatedly, if unconsciously, reflects the biases, the paternalism, the indifference of white

> America. This may be understandable, but it is not excusable in an institution that has the mission to inform and educate the whole of our society.
> (Cited in Dennis 1997: xix)

On 4 April, just weeks after the Kerner Commission report was published, the main leader of the civil rights movement, Martin Luther King Jr, was assassinated in Memphis, Tennessee. News coverage of the assassination, like that of the racial conflicts which ensued, powerfully underscored the extent to which the bigotry of segregationists was being processed within the 'commonsense' frameworks of news narratives.

Many of the points raised in the Kerner Commission's appraisal of the news media continue to be all too relevant today. This is not to deny that genuine progress has been made, rather it is to acknowledge that much more remains to be done. Standing in the way of the kinds of reforms which might have otherwise been achievable over these past decades, many researchers argue, have been the discourses on 'race' being articulated by politically right-wing voices. The Reagan and Bush administrations, like the Thatcher and Major governments in Britain, consistently played the 'race card' to electoral advantage at a number of different levels. At stake was the mobilization of a hegemonic project whereby a racist 'common sense' could be developed and sustained in the interests of white privilege. Tenets of what Hall (1988) cogently characterized as 'authoritarian populism' with regard to Thatcherism were being actively reinscribed as part of the reactionary rhetoric of the New and Religious Right from the early days of Reaganism (both of which continue to wield significant influence today). The 'quality of American life' as previously enjoyed by white, middle-class and upper-class males was under threat, according to this rhetoric, and those deserving of the blame included, among others, ethnic minority (especially black and Latino) groups, feminists, gays and lesbians, single mothers, poor people and 'illegal immigrants' (Gray 1995; see also Rakow and Kranich 1991; Reeves and Campbell 1994; Shah and Thornton 1994; Kellner 1995; Fiske 1996; Rodriguez 1999; Chavez 2001).

Televisual news, in particular, played a central role in what Herman Gray (1995) describes as the consolidation of a 'conservative cultural and political hegemonic bloc'. The types of images being inflected from one newscast to the next, he argues, routinely depicted blackness as a sign of otherness to 'the very idea of America':

> As a sign of this otherness, blackness was constructed along a continuum ranging from menace on one end to immorality on the other, with irresponsibility located somewhere in the middle. Only through such appeals to menace and irresponsibility, framed and presented in television news through figures of black male gang members, black male criminality,

> crumbling black families, black welfare cheats, black female crack users, and black teen pregnancy, could such claims on America (and its image of middle-class, heterosexual, masculine whiteness) find resonance within the discourse of traditional values.
>
> (Gray 1995: 17)

Televisual news, which throughout this period became increasingly reliant on factors such as immediacy, brevity, drama and conceptual simplicity, made a decisive contribution to an ideological shift around discourses of 'race' and 'morality'. The limits of 'popular common sense' were being redrawn in ways which consistently defined members of ethnic minorities as deviants, dependants and threats. 'If television news was to be believed,' Gray (1995: 34) writes, 'these mostly black and brown people seemed to commit more crime, have more babies, use more drugs, and be more incompetent with respect to individual and civic responsibility and indifferent with respect to their obligations.' This discursive construction of a black/white dualism as a threat to social stability and public morality is most readily discernible in news coverage of crime-related incidents. A number of studies have been conducted which document the degree to which crimes committed by African Americans, particularly those including a sexual element, receive a disproportionate amount of coverage than would otherwise be expected were the suspect in question white. Underlying much of this reporting, Fiske (1996: 80) argues, is an entrenched white hysteria about 'the power of the black male body', a body which by its very presence is depicted as constituting a sexualized racial danger to the 'fragility of the white social order' (see also Benedict 1992; Jordan and Weedon 1995; Rhodes 2005). Controversies in the 1990s which highlighted these white fears about black male bodies being 'out of control' include:

- Allegations of sexual harassment against Supreme Court Justice Clarence Thomas by former colleague Anita Hill during his televised Senate confirmation hearings in 1991 (see Garber 1993; Fiske 1996).
- The conviction of heavyweight boxer Mike Tyson for the 'date rape' of a young woman, at the time a beauty pageant contestant, in 1992 (see Lule 1995; Rowe 2004).
- The 'riots' which erupted in Los Angeles in 1992 following the announcement of the 'not guilty' verdicts in the court case of the white police officers videotaped brutally beating the black motorist Rodney King (see Nichols 1994; Swenson 1995; Hunt 1997; van Loon 1997; Alexander and Jacobs 1998; Gray 1998).
- A police investigation into allegations of child sexual abuse against pop singer Michael Jackson in 1993 (see Hinerman 1998).
- The televised murder trial of former athlete, televisual sports commentator

and film actor Orenthal James ('OJ') Simpson following the June 1994 fatal stabbing of his ex-partner Nicole Brown Simpson and her friend Ronald Goldman (see Shipp 1994; McKay and Smith 1995; Morrison and Lacour 1997; McLaughlin 1998).

In the case of these and other such media figures of the 1990s, it is possible to identify, after Fiske (1996: 256), the ways in which the mediated identity of black men is racialized, sexualized and, whether found guilty or not, criminalized (see also Campbell 1995; Pritchard and Hughes 1997). Typically suffusing this kind of news coverage is what Fiske calls 'dislocated racism'; that is to say, racism may be considered to be dislocated 'when it is apparently to be found only in the behaviors of a racial minority and never in those of the white power structure' (Fiske 1996: 272; see also Dyer 1997; Jacobs 2000). To the extent that so-called 'race neutral' news reporting naturalizes the racelessness of whiteness in hegemonic terms, then, it is actually working to reproduce the dominant position of the white majority within a racially divided society.

In order for this racial hierarchy to be reaffirmed as 'common sense', however, the hegemonic construction of whiteness must undergo constant renewal lest its ideological premises lose their popular saliency. It is this insight into the partial, contingent nature of such forms of hegemony that informs the collective project behind Hall *et al.*'s (1978) ground-breaking book *Policing the Crisis*. Briefly, their investigation documents how 'mugging' was 'discovered' by the British news media in the early 1970s as 'a frightening new strain of crime', one to be blamed primarily on young, black West Indian males living in the inner city. In the course of mapping the part played by the news media in the ensuing ideological rupture, a rupture which led to severe state interventions 'in the interests of law and order', the appearance of a *crisis of hegemony* is identified. In their words:

> A crisis of hegemony marks a moment of profound rupture in the political and economic life of a society, an accumulation of contradictions. If in moments of 'hegemony' everything works spontaneously so as to sustain and enforce a particular form of class domination while rendering the basis of that social authority invisible through the mechanisms of the production of consent, then moments when the equilibrium of consent is disturbed, or where the contending class forces are so nearly balanced that neither can achieve that sway from which a resolution to the crisis can be promulgated, are moments *when the whole basis of political leadership and cultural authority becomes exposed and contested.*
>
> (Hall *et al.* 1978: 217, original emphasis)

The subsequent creation of a 'moral panic' across the field of the news media, in particular the daily press, contributed to a reconfiguration of 'the public consensus about crime' along far more authoritarian, and explicitly racist, lines (see also Critcher 2005; Guedes Bailey and Harindranath 2005). A recurrent feature of the news reports examined is that 'mugging' is unquestioningly identified with black youth living in 'crime prone' urban 'trouble spots', and that this is a 'new problem' requiring 'proper policing'.

Crime control agencies, in seeking to secure popular approval amongst the white majority for more coercive 'get tough' measures (for example, the length of sentences for 'petty street crime' rose dramatically), had much to gain by having the news media accept their definition of a 'mugging epidemic'. Hall *et al.* (1978) examine a variety of the strategies employed, to varying degrees, by the daily press to reinflect the language of crisis being generated by these agencies. This focus on how certain frameworks of interpretation were set in motion allows them to show, in turn, how the racialized limits for much of the political debate about what constituted this 'breakdown of public morality' and who was to blame for it (and, moreover, which measures would be necessary to end the crisis) were established. Particular attention is thus given to the means by which news organizations routinely reproduce the social definitions of the powerful largely – but not entirely – at the expense of those definitions advanced by oppositional or counter-hegemonic voices. In practice, this meant that the resultant news coverage consistently failed to contextualize 'mugging' in relation to conditions of economic deprivation, out of which crime arises, electing instead to promote 'the all too intelligible syntax of race [so as to affix] a false enemy: the black mugger' (Hall *et al.* 1978: 395).

The news media's stigmatization of young black people living in economically depressed areas became even more pronounced over the course of the 1980s. Daily press representations of the 'riots' which took place in Britain in the summer of 1981, beginning in Southall in West London before moving on to other cities, form the basis of a study by Hansen and Murdock (1985). Their conception of news as a 'field of continual conflict in which competing discourses struggle for publicity and legitimacy' leads them to draw attention to the ideological conflicts, such as those over 'English-ness', played out in the press. More specifically, it is shown that Britain's indigenous black population is defined by right-wing voices in politics, such as that of then Prime Minister Margaret Thatcher, as well as in the press coverage, 'as an inherently alien presence which threatens "our" national culture and traditional way of life' (Hansen and Murdock 1985: 233). Moreover, this study documents how 'racist stereotypes of blacks as "naturally" less rational and controlled than whites have fused with older images of the inner city as an "internal colony" to produce a particularly potent image of threat' (1985: 233). Much of this news coverage, the authors contend, exhibited a mode of address structured around interlocked oppositions between 'us' (decent citizens, the police, and the voices of the newspapers) against 'them' ('thieves', 'looters', 'thugs', 'yobs', 'madmen', 'hooligans', 'wild mob of youths', 'demons' and 'ghouls'). In this way, not only were the 'rioters' separated out from the community as an external enemy, but also the social factors underlying their actions were ostensibly depoliticized by being attributed to 'natural' forces or to the 'nature' of the people involved (Hansen and Murdock 1985: 248–9; see also Fowler 1991; Pickering 2008).

Cottle (1993, 1994), in his investigation of televisual news coverage of the 'Handsworth riots' of 1985, identifies the 'competing repertoires of preferred terms' used by journalists and their sources to define the contested realities of inner city disorder. Even the term 'riot' itself, he points out, tends to position the event in question as a problem of criminality to be confronted by the 'forces of law and order'. In sharp contrast, the use of terms such as 'rebellion' or 'uprising' shift the semantic field, according to Cottle (1993: 164), 'to that of the purposeful action of a united group, who, reacting against an oppressive social order, collectively react against the problem which is now perceived to be an illegitimate state of social exclusion and oppression'. Accordingly, the interpretative frameworks being mobilized in and through journalistic vocabulary (words and images) may be read as encouraging certain definitions of the situation over alternative ones. In his analysis of representations of 'race' in relation to the explanations being advanced for the disturbances, Cottle shows how references to the structural causes of the conflicts (including social deprivation and the acute levels of inner city unemployment) found only limited expression in the news coverage. 'What is worse,' he argues, 'when issues of racism have been raised these have centred on the minority ethnic communities themselves – once again localizing the problem to a question of intra-community rivalry' (Cottle 1993: 184; see also van Dijk 1991; Jacobs 2000; Wykes 2001; Law 2002).

Building on these insights, Cottle (2004) turns his attention in a later study to the news reporting of the murder of Stephen Lawrence, an 18-year-old black student killed in an unprovoked racist attack as he was waiting for a bus to take him to his London home in April 1993. In exploring the reasons why this murder generated an unprecedented degree of press attention at the time – and, even more remarkably, over the next ten years – he identifies a number of contributory factors. The image of Stephen Lawrence gained an iconic status, he argues, primarily because of the way audiences were encouraged to relate to him, and the tragedy that befell him, via intensely emotional, personalized forms of reporting. In effect, Cottle contends, the news media – especially newspapers – played an integral role in 'performing' the ensuing criminal case through a complex, uneven and frequently contradictory process of cultural mediation unfolding over this ten-year period. That is to say, in transforming the murder into a 'mediatised public crisis' demanding governmental, police and legal responses, the media invoked appeals to moral solidarities intended to 'touch' – in highly affective ways – the social conscience of diverse publics. The *Daily Mail*, for example, took the extraordinary step of publishing photographs of the five white men suspected of committing the hate crime on its front page beneath the headline: 'MURDERERS: The Mail accuses these men of killing. If we are wrong, let them sue us' (14 February 1997; see also McLaughlin 2005). To the extent Lawrence became a powerful symbol, he was also a catalyst for change, prompting over the years – as Cottle documents in his analysis of the news reporting – widespread discussion and debate about the relative extent to which racism is, in effect, institutionalized throughout British society. 'The media performance summoned a subjunctive view of how society should be,' he writes, 'which mandated the flows of moral opprobrium and approbation that penetrated both culture and polity with affect' (2004: 191). The Lawrence case thus represents an all too rare occasion, Cottle adds, when news reporting contributed to the positive renewal of civic life, having 'served to progressively reconfigure the contested terrain of "race", racism and British identity' (2004: 195).

While there are grounds for cautious optimism that matters are improving, much work remains to be done. A report commissioned by the Greater London Authority (GLA) to investigate British print media coverage of Muslims and Islam from mid-2006 to mid-2007 makes this point all too apparent. While some examples of good practice were in evidence (such as 'one-off news items, features, projects and investigative articles'), they were found to be exceptions to the general rule. Much more typical were news reports depicting a basic antagonism between the West and Islam, with Muslims portrayed as 'a threat to traditional British customs, values and ways of life' (GLA 2007: xiii). Distortions, exaggerations and oversimplifications regularly crept into the coverage, often expressed in a tone of language that was emotive, even alarmist. Amongst the report's recommendations for change were the following:

- News organisations should review their coverage of issues and events involving Muslims and Islam, and should consider drawing up codes of professional conduct and style guides about use of terminology. Such codes of professional conduct should be based on their own best practice.
- News organisations should take measures, perhaps within the framework of positive action in equalities legislation, to recruit more journalists of Muslim heritage who can more accurately reflect the views and experiences of Muslim communities.

- News organisations should also consider how best to give Muslim staff appropriate professional support and to prevent them being pigeon-holed as specialists in minority issues rather than concerned with the full spectrum of an organisation's output.
- News organisations should treat seriously complaints relating to distorted coverage of Islam and Muslims in the media.

(GLA 2007: xiv–xv)

Underpinning each of these recommendations is a shared acknowledgment that anti-Muslim prejudice needs to be recognized and treated as a form of discrimination. Its harmful effects work in both directions. That is to say, prejudicial reporting is likely to 'produce, provoke and increase feelings of insecurity, suspicion and anxiety amongst non-Muslims', while, at the same time, being 'likely to provoke feelings of insecurity, vulnerability and alienation amongst Muslims' (GLA 2007; see also Poole and Richardson 2006; Harker 2009).

Laura Smith (2007), a *Guardian* journalist and one of the researchers for the report (alongside her colleague Hugh Muir), found in the course of conducting her enquiry that basic journalistic standards were routinely compromised where news stories could be given a 'Muslim slant'. Regarding the difficulties of effecting change, however, she provides the following insight:

> Journalists, myself included, always get a bit snippy when they are criticised. Having worked for newspapers whose editorial line I might not have agreed with, I know the pressures journalists can be under to make a story work, regardless of the facts. But we as a profession need to take more responsibility for the stories we put into the public domain and the effect they have on wider society. True or not, these stories sink deep into public consciousness and can't help but influence the way people perceive each other. When, as in the case of stories involving Muslims, and before them black people and Jewish people, they are not balanced by more rounded coverage, the results can be deeply damaging.
>
> (Smith 2007)

Journalist Angela Phillips (2007), commenting on the report's findings and also her own related research, points out that 'journalists right across the press, whether on liberal newspapers or more conservative ones, have a lot of thinking to do about issues of representation'. New ways must be found to move beyond the discourse of 'tolerance' typically professed by newspapers in order to actually stop representing Muslims as 'visitors' in 'our' country, and thereby properly recognize everyone as fellow citizens with equal rights.

'Writing white': ethnic minorities and newswork

One of the many features currently shared by both British and US news organizations is that the newsworkers they employ are predominantly white and male. In the case of British newspaper organizations, one attempt to produce statistics suggests that reporters from ethnic minorities make up a mere fraction of 1 per cent of the journalistic workforce (Ainley 1998; see also Gordon and Rosenberg 1989). The need for far greater diversity is apparent in the televisual newsroom as well, where evidence indicates that the growing presence of ethnic minority reporters in front of the camera does not correspond, in relative terms, with the situation behind the scenes. Recommendations for improving news organizations' sensitivity to race-related matters advanced by parliamentary committees and reports (such as the last Royal Commission on the Press), like the guidelines set down by bodies such as the Press Complaints Commission or the National Union of Journalists, are laudable in intent but inadequate in practice (see Ross 1998). BBC director-general Greg Dyke's comment in 2001 that the Corporation was 'hideously white' (albeit not racist, in his view) still resonates today.

It is an uncomfortable fact, former head of Sky News Nick Pollard (2007) argues, that little has changed in broadcasting newsrooms. 'That goes for pretty much every facet of operations – presenters, reporters, producers, camera crews and certainly for newsroom executives', he points out. In considering why this is the case, Pollard underscores a further dimension:

> It's partly a matter of class too – not something as immediately visible as race, of course, but just as entrenched. Newsrooms, with some notable exceptions, are pretty middle-class places, and that's not going to change anytime soon. Recruitment is, more than ever, from the ranks of graduates and postgraduates. With university fees rising, that implies well-off, supportive parents and ambitious, focused offspring. It also seems to be true that for many of the ethnic middle class, journalism is still not seen as something worth striving for, certainly not something on a par with say medicine or the law.
>
> (Pollard 2007)

Mehdi Hasan, editor in the news and current affairs department at Channel 4, describes how he copes with these tensions on a daily basis. 'Over the years, at the BBC, ITV and Sky, I have worked with countless producers and reporters who had never met a Muslim before they met me,' he states, 'or if they had, it was invariably an unrepresentative and loony extremist who they were interviewing or profiling for a story' (cited in the *Independent*, 23 July 2007). False and simplistic assumptions continue to permeate news organizations, he argues, having become deeply entrenched over time. Max Hastings (2008), in recalling his days as editor of the *Daily Telegraph* in the 1990s, describes how he gradually became 'very conscious of the embarrassing whiteness of the newspaper offices over which I myself presided'. It was not the case that the *Telegraph* discriminated against ethnic minority candidates applying for positions, he insists, but rather that there were few applicants in the first place. 'In a very modest fashion,' he adds, 'I set about recruiting some black and Asian journalists, because it was plain that unless we took the initiative, nothing would happen.' There is little doubt that in the years since, challenges to the status quo have proved to be remarkably ineffective in bringing about substantial change. 'It is not embarrassing but shaming,' Brian Cathcart (2008) points out, 'because of the complacency it reveals in an industry of cultural and political importance that remains a stranger to diversity and likes it that way.'

The situation in the US is only marginally more encouraging. In 1968, when the aforementioned report of the Kerner Commission was being released, fewer than 1 per cent of US journalists were African American (de Uriarte 1997: 146). Not surprisingly, the report demanded that news organizations 'bring more Black people into journalism' in order to improve the quality of reporting. Since the mid-1960s, some progress has been made, although not nearly enough. As former *New York Times* correspondent and Pulitzer Prize winner David K. Shipler (1998) observes, the rate of change has not been sufficient and, even worse, appears to be slowing down. Using statistics from the American Society of Newspaper Editors (ASNE), he points out that 'the representation of blacks on news staffs has stagnated at a low plateau of under 6 percent [and] blacks moving into managerial ranks remain too scarce to be counted as a reform completed'. He maintains that ASNE's data, which were collected in 1996, also show that only 11.5 per cent of newsroom staff are members of an ethnic minority (primarily defined as African Americans, Hispanics, Asian Americans, and Native Americans) at a time when they make up 26 per cent of the US population (see also Lafky 1993; Stewart 1997). 'Newsrooms,' Shipler writes, 'are not hermetically sealed against the prejudices that play perniciously just beneath the surface of American life.' More recent ASNE statistics – discussed below – reaffirm this point, even though some improvement has been made.

As a number of researchers are quick to point out, however, greater diversity in the news organization does not automatically translate into more diverse forms of news coverage. 'Instead,' de Uriarte (1997: 146) argues, 'minorities in the newsroom still find themselves confronting the bulwark of objectivity that excluded minority perception shaped by minority realities.' That is to say, when the news media view the social world they do so through a 'prism of hegemony', one guided by the notion of journalistic 'objectivity' which 'has long been white and largely remains so today' (de Uriarte 1997: 144). Accordingly, to achieve the aim of a truly integrated newsroom will require a far more profound change than that associated with affirmative action initiatives alone. If it is the case, as she suggests, that it is in 'the contemporary newsroom where "qualified" minorities almost uniformly are perceived to be those who are least disruptive to the newsroom culture, including its ideology of objectivity', then the whiteness of objectivity must be fundamentally recast if a greater diversity of voices are to be heard (see also Santos 1997).

Journalist Ellis Cose (1997: 3) reaffirms this point from a different angle when he poses the question: 'Is objectivity (or even fairness) possible when dealing with people from different racial groups and cultural backgrounds?' Moreover, he asks: 'Does "getting it right" mean anything more virtuous than conforming to prevailing prejudice?' The ways in which racist presuppositions are implicated in the routinized practices of news production, from the news values in operation to 'gut instincts' about source credibility, are often difficult to identify, let alone reverse. Efforts intended to disrupt the ideological purchase of 'objective' reporting practices are likely to meet considerable resistance in the white dominated newsroom. 'Operating under the strictures of "objectivity" and facing conflicting expectations and uncertainties,' Entman (1990: 343) contends, 'journalists are neither authorized nor eager to engage in such exercises.' Important insights in this regard are also provided by Sig Gissler, a former editor of the *Milwaukee Journal*, who observes:

> It's easier to cover racial stories in the conventional superficial manner and keep a lid on feelings. In newsrooms, race is usually discussed warily. Black reporters, for example, are often reluctant to speak up for fear of being tagged whiners. Meanwhile, white reporters bite their tongues for fear of being labeled racists, the most scalding epithet in the news business today.
> (Gissler 1997: 110–11)

For minority journalists struggling to adopt to what de Uriarte (1997: 147) aptly describes as 'the hegemonic newsroom culture', the pressures to conform are considerable. It is a 'sad fact', she writes, that 'minorities are often hired for their ability to fit in rather than for their ability to provide new or diverse voices' (see also Quiroga 1997; Wong 1997; Pritchard and Stonbely 2007; Harker 2009).

This pressure to 'fit in' is nowhere more pronounced than at the level of the news organization's economic imperatives. 'Minority staff,' according to Gandy (1997: 42), 'may challenge the selection and framing of stories about race in ways that conflict with market-oriented strategies suggested by a newspaper's consultants.' It is this market orientation which explains, in part, why journalists continue to devote a disproportionate degree of attention to the lives of the white and the wealthy. All of the major news organizations, as Hacker (1997: 74) points out, have predominantly white audiences, a 'bottom line' which 'black employees are expected to understand and appreciate'. Regardless of the type of news event being processed, it follows, news accounts 'must be pitched to white readers, in ways whites can square with their preconceptions and perceptions' (Hacker 1997: 72; see also Newkirk 2000). These types of tensions indicative of the drive to make the news palatable to white readers and viewers need to be denaturalized at every level. 'For journalists of color,' argues journalist John Phillip Santos (1997: 123), 'it means resisting the professionally driven tendency, as one *Seattle Times* reporter termed it, "to write white", which he described as employing "a certain language, a certain code".'

It is precisely this kind of resistance which is at the heart of Hall's (1990) call for the development of an 'anti-racist common sense'. In seeking to intervene in the realm of news culture with the aim of closing the painful gap between 'us and them', every effort must be made to take up his challenge 'to undermine, deconstruct and question the unquestioned racist assumptions on which so much of media practice is grounded' (Hall 1990: 8). At stake is the urgent task of identifying and then subverting the prejudicial, discriminatory logics which together are blocking the emergence of the forms of 'multiracial coverage' envisaged by Wilson and Gutiérrez (1995) above. In contributing to the perpetuation of this language of 'us and them', the news media, as Gandy (1997: 37) writes, 'have made us see the world as a mean and dangerous place,' and thereby 'diminished the quality of our lives.' Moreover, he continues, 'to the extent that they have emphasized the ways in which the distribution of social and economic risks breaks down along racial lines, they have helped to tear us apart'.

Denaturalizing racism

In the days leading up to the inauguration of Barack Obama as President of the United States, the issue of racism was generating considerable attention in press commentary for obvious reasons. Few news organizations were attending to their own shortcomings over the years, however, preferring to focus on examples of racial discrimination evidenced in other social institutions instead. One exception was the *Meridian Star*, a Mississippi newspaper, which published an apology for its past reporting of civil rights issues. In an editorial, 'We honor and we apologize', it described the efforts of those in East Mississippi who played an integral role in the movement for equality. Its closing paragraphs read:

> There was a time when this newspaper – and many others across the south – acted with gross neglect by largely ignoring the unfairness of

> segregated schools, buses, restaurants, washrooms, theaters and other public places.
>
> We did it through omission, by not recording for our readers many of the most important civil rights activities that happened in our midst, including protests and sit-ins. That was wrong. We should have loudly protested segregation and the efforts to block voter registration of black East Mississippians.
>
> Current management understands while we can't go back and undo some past wrongs, we can offer our sincere apology – and promise never again to neglect our responsibility to inform you, our readers, about the human rights and dignity every individual is entitled to in America – no matter their religion, their ethnic background or the color of their skin.
>
> (Editorial, *Meridian Star*, 18 January 2009)

This apology for 'gross neglect' attracted headlines in its own right, quite possibly – one hopes – encouraging other news organizations to revisit their own past coverage with a critical eye to their complicity in normalizing prejudice. If for some African American observers in the blogosphere the *Meridian Star* apology was a matter of 'better late than never', for others it represented merely a first step that needed to be followed up swiftly with concrete action.

Statistics produced by the American Society of Newspaper Editors (ASNE) underline the significance of this point. Its most recent census of the industry (initiated as an annual exercise following the Kerner Commission report mentioned above) found that the percentage of ethnic minority journalists working at daily newspapers in the US grew minimally in 2007 – specifically, from 13.43 per cent of all such journalists to 13.52 per cent of 52,600 full-time journalists. ASNE President Gilbert Bailon contextualized these data:

> The numbers represent a dual reality: It's mildly encouraging that the minority percentage held steady despite difficult economic times that are causing many cutbacks. On the other hand, the total number of minority journalists employed at daily newspapers declined by nearly 300 people, which follows the pattern for the overall newsroom workforce. Such a trend will not help newspapers in their quest to reach parity with the minority population by 2025.
>
> (ASNE 2008)

Here it is worth noting that 423 of the newspapers responding to the ASNE survey recorded that they had no minorities on their full-time staff (the majority of these papers having circulations of 10,000 copies or less). This when 'a generic, monochromatic newsroom' – to use Bailon's phrase – will be unable to adequately serve its community of readers. To the extent this problem is being further exacerbated by the financial crises, it becomes all the more important to urge managers not to relinquish their commitment to improvements. 'Diversity is not a luxury or a fad', the National Association of Black Journalists (NABJ) observes. 'It is a necessity for telling balanced news stories about America and for putting a fresh story perspective before the readers through the lens of minority journalists' (NABJ 2008).

One example of the form such action can take is described by Harker (2009) with respect to changes under way at some British newspapers. Progress in improving the numbers of ethnic minority reporters employed has been slow, he points out, but is gradually getting better due to a number of strategies. He describes an initiative under way at the *Guardian* newspaper in London where a positive-action work placement programme – intended to attract racial minorities – is in operation. 'The large numbers of intelligent, enthusiastic, hardworking and motivated young men and women we've been able to bring into our office (and, yes, Muslim women too),' he observes, 'have given lie to that old media mantra, "but they don't apply" ' (2009: 313). Further aspects of the plan of action to redress inequality include 'interview, recruitment and management training for editors and section heads; consultations with minority staff; advertising all entry-level jobs externally; and alerting minority journalists on our database when vacancies arise' (2009: 313). A crucial dimension to these efforts, he believes, is ethnic monitoring in order to measure relative progress. This commitment challenges the more typical view expressed by editors, namely that ethnicity is irrelevant in a performance-driven newsroom. In response, Harker asks:

> [W]ithout any supporting information, can newspapers really be sure that their recruitment is unbiased and that their editors see beyond the indeterminate cultural factors that so often lie behind selection decisions, such as: 'Do I feel comfortable with him?' 'Would she be a good laugh down the pub?' 'Would they fit in with our reporting team?' Journalists I contacted who work in some of these newsrooms reported that they are very white places indeed.
>
> (Harker 2009: 314)

Enriching the diversity of the 'internal culture' of a news organization, it follows, is vitally important, and long overdue. 'One may find the occasional black or Asian journalist in a junior role on the commissioning desk, but rarely, if ever, in a position where they can make a decision on what goes into the next day's paper, let alone have any major long-term impact', he adds. The fair treatment of employees within the organization is certain to translate into improvements in the quality of reporting (a further dimension requiring close monitoring), which will be of considerable social benefit to everyone.

Nevertheless, at a time when so many news organizations are struggling to weather the global financial crisis, fears are growing that some will be forced to abandon their commitments to diversity. Editor Mark Fitzgerald believes that there is a 'pervasive feeling that the economy has pushed diversity goals not just to the back burner, but off the stove altogether' (*Editor & Publisher*, 25 July 2008). This retrenchment is being felt in the newsroom, but also in the failure to seize this moment as an opportunity to look beyond traditional (white) conceptions of the news consumer to engage a much wider audience in the community. 'If we don't think about these diverse audiences now, and work hard to get them, we may risk losing them forever,' executive editor Wanda Lloyd contends, before adding that 'diversity staffing and content go hand in hand. It you are committed to one, you are probably committed to both' (cited in Anderson 2008).

9 WAR REPORTING

> Actually too tired, scared and burnt-out to write anything. Yes, we did go out again to see what was hit. Yes, everything just hurts . . . I can't stand the TV or the lies on the news any more. No good news wherever you look.
>
> (Salman Pax, the Baghdad Blogger)

Walter Lippmann's classic text *Public Opinion*, first published in 1922, opens with an intriguing tale. He sets the scene by describing a remote island where British, French and German expatriates live together in a harmonious community. In the absence of telegraphic cables connecting them with the outside world, the islanders rely on a mail steamer to visit every sixty days with the latest newspaper. In September of 1914, however, the steamer is delayed, making everyone even more anxious for news than usual, not least because coverage of a celebrated court trial is the talk of the island. 'It was, therefore, with more than usual eagerness that the whole colony assembled at the quay on a day in mid-September to hear from the captain what the verdict had been', Lippmann (1922) writes. Instead, what they learn comes as a shock. Britain and France, they discover, are waging war against Germany. What were the islanders to think? 'For six strange weeks they had acted as if they were friends,' Lippmann observes, 'when in fact they were enemies' (1922: 3).

This tale highlights a number of issues concerning the mediation of distant conflict. Images of war, conflict and crisis are a routine, everyday feature of our news media. From the morning newspaper's depiction of the tragedies of a 'suicide bombing' in Iraq, to online news reports of crisis in Darfur, to the evening television newscast's coverage of the latest turn in the

Israeli–Palestinian conflict, these images have a profound impact on our perceptions of the human condition. 'Being a spectator of calamities taking place in another country is a quintessential modern experience,' the late Susan Sontag (2003) observed, 'the cumulative offering by more than a century and a half's worth of those professional, specialized tourists known as journalists' (2003: 16). This flow of news stories from distant places amounts to a torrent, featuring turmoil, violence and suffering at a seemingly ever-increasing rate – to which the response, Sontag adds, 'is compassion, or indignation, or titillation, or approval, as each misery heaves into view'. For the journalist, confronted with the challenge of bearing witness to these horrors on our behalf, the effort to document their human consequences entails subtly complex negotiations of significance, of assigning apposite meaning and relevance. The representation of disturbing events is partly constitutive of their reality, which makes this process of mediation acutely political (see also Cottle 2006, 2009). Important questions thus arise regarding the exercise of communicative power and influence, in particular the pivotal role of the news media in identifying, defining and framing certain situations as crises demanding concerted action.

This chapter examines the evolving forms and practices of war correspondence, briefly touching upon a range of examples from recent decades. In tracing what I would term the 'ecology' of its evolving forms and practices, it devotes particular attention to the forms of social exclusion endemic to the 'us' and 'them' dichotomies permeating mainstream war reporting.

Vietnam, the Falklands and the Gulf War

The complex ways in which the news media recurrently project a sense of 'us', a collective 'we' which is explicitly or tacitly mobilized in opposition to a 'them', find daily expression in news accounts concerned with 'the nation'. There can be no 'national we', as Billig (1995) points out, without a 'foreign other', a dynamic which in his view prefigures an 'ideological consciousness of nationhood'. Widely diffused as simply a matter of common sense, this 'nationalized syntax of hegemony' is evoked by newsworkers claiming to speak to and for the nation as a homeland or 'imagined community' (B. Anderson 1991) made up of 'people like us'. Billig observes that the appearance of such representations of 'the nation', for example in the 'Home News', 'European News' and 'Foreign News' divisions mapped by a newspaper, is so pervasive as to be almost banal. And yet, the effectivity of these routine, everyday representations can be deadly, especially at times of state crises leading to war. 'At regular, but intermittent intervals,' he writes, 'the crisis occurs, and the moral aura of nationalism is invoked: heads will be nodded, flags waved and tanks will roll' (Billig 1995: 4;

see also Wallis and Baran 1990; Reeves 1993; Herman and McChesney 1997; van Ginneken 1998; Hoskins 2004; Montgomery 2005; Sonwalkar 2005).

This process of journalistic 'Othering' is frequently reinflected via a language of 'national pride, honour and duty' with its corresponding appeals to loyalty and allegiance. A number of studies concerned with news media coverage of the Vietnam War, for example, document how the familiar tenets of 'objectivity' were recurrently recast in favour of a 'patriotic' reportorial stance. In this way, for example, 'our peace offensive' could be effectively counterpoised against the barbarous hostility of a primitive, dehumanized enemy whose activities needed to be 'neutralized'. Racism, journalist Phillip Knightley (1982: 354) observes, 'became a patriotic virtue. All Vietnamese became "dinks", "slopes", "slants", or "gooks", and the only good one was a dead one. So the Americans killed them when it was clear that they were Vietcong.' And, he adds, 'they killed them when it was clear they were not Vietcong'. In 1967, recalling his time spent reporting on the conflict, journalist James Cameron similarly spoke to these racist precepts in a forceful way:

> I had been to Hanoi, and returned obsessed with the notion that I had no professional justification left if I did not at least try to make the point that North VietNam, despite all Washington arguments to the contrary, was inhabited by human beings . . . and that to destroy their country and their lives with high explosives and petroleum jelly was no way to cure them of their defects . . . This conclusion, when expressed in printed or television journalism, was generally held to be, if not downright mischievous, then certainly non-objective, within the terms of reference of a newspaper man, on the grounds that it was proclaimed as a point of view . . . To this of course there could be no answer whatsoever, except that objectivity in some circumstances is both meaningless and impossible.
>
> (Cameron 1997 [1967]: 172)

And, he might have added, often lethal for those people who fall outside the ideological limits legitimized by its reportorial norms and conventions during wartime. 'Objective' accounts, like carefully edited televisual images, tended to – in the words of another military correspondent – 'make acceptable something which in reality was quite unacceptable' (cited in Royle 1987: 209; see also Chouliaraki 2009).

This point is similarly taken up by journalist John Pilger (1998) in his assessment of newswork in Vietnam, in particular how reporters failed to accurately depict the racist nature of the conflict as he witnessed it. At the same time, he contends that those commentators who claim that journalists were to blame for 'losing the war' because of their criticisms of the military's treatment of the Vietnamese (television reporters are usually cited as the principal culprits) are subscribing to a myth. In Pilger's words:

> In my experience, most journalists had no objection to the 'noble crusade', only to the wisdom of its tactics and the competence of its executors. The war was almost never reported as an all-out American assault on the Vietnamese people, regardless of whether they were communist or non-communist, northerners or southerners; for that was the truth. Instead the war was represented as a gladiators' contest between 'good' teams and 'bad' teams . . . Not surprisingly, this version excluded the fact that the Americans had killed tens of thousands of their South Vietnamese 'allies' and had levelled about half their forests, poisoned their environment and forced millions of them to leave their homes.
>
> (Pilger 1998: 560)

It was only as the points of disagreement between members of the US political and military elite became more publicly salient, often characterized as a battle of opinion between pro-war 'hawks' and anti-war 'doves', that more critical forms of reporting began to emerge to test the limits of the slowly fragmenting elite consensus (see also Gitlin 1980; Hallin 1986, 1994; Royle 1987; Herman and Chomsky 1988; Cumings 1992; Young and Jesser 1997; Lynch 2009; Tulloch and Blood 2009). Nevertheless, the key militarist imperatives shaping the racialized projection of the Vietnamese people as a less than human enemy were still largely intact even after the last of the US ground troops had been withdrawn by the spring of 1973.

Rhetorical appeals to a national identity under threat from an enemy Other evidently informed the decision made by Argentine General Leopoldo Galtieri to order an invasion of the British dependencies of South Georgia and the Falkland Islands, or the Islas Malvinas as they are known in Argentina, through the use of armed force on 2 April 1982. The response in Britain by politicians such as then Prime Minister Margaret Thatcher similarly evoked a principle of nationhood portrayed as being in grave danger. Having 'learned the lessons of Vietnam' where the news media purportedly encouraged opposition to the war to ferment, British officials wasted no time in mobilizing a propaganda campaign designed to ensure that the 'true nature' of the otherwise faceless Argentine enemy would be sympathetically relayed via the news coverage. The types of strategies they employed included the following:

- The selection of 'accredited' British journalists (all male) covering the conflict was limited to 28, all of whom were transported to the area by the navy so that their activities could be monitored by military 'minders'.
- Journalists relied almost entirely on officials for their information, their

access to the fighting being strictly controlled both formally and informally. They were also forced to 'pool' their copy and photographs in order to facilitate military censorship. Any effort to include the word 'censored' on filmed reports was itself censored.
- Satellite facilities were denied, thereby making it impossible for journalists to transmit filmed images of the conflict for television and newspapers except via returning ships (a delay of at least three weeks given the distance of 8000 miles, which meant that much of what was still heavily censored coverage did not appear in Britain until well after the final ceasefire).
- Journalists were routinely given false statements or 'disinformation' to report by their 'handlers', allegedly in the hope of confusing the enemy. Ministry of Defence press officers sought to ensure priority was given to 'good news' so as to 'help morale at home'; the British public, many of them argued, are interested only in 'victories'.
- The constant threat of being removed from the 'pool' system for engaging in any form of critical reporting (deemed 'unco-operative' and therefore contrary to the 'national interest') led to severe forms of self-censorship being practised by the journalists.

Strategies such as these helped to anchor, in ideological terms, the larger public opinion offensive being orchestrated by the British government which characterized the conflict as a decisive battle between good ('us') and evil ('them'). 'The patriotic imperative so deeply rooted in the dominant political and media culture,' writes Keeble (1997: 30), 'together with journalistic self-censorship and the hyper-jingoism and crude enemy baiting of the pops [popular press], all served to transform new militarism into spectator sport.' The effect of which, he adds, was that what was being packaged as a 'largely bloodless' war could be 'consumed as a form of entertainment' (see also Barnett 1984; Glasgow University Media Group 1985; Aulich 1992; Hoskins 2004).

In order to lend legitimacy to the British intervention, the neo-imperialistic configuration of the 'Argies' (a term popularized by the *Sun*) as a new enemy was crucial. For *The Times*, the Argentine invasion was 'an incontrovertibly evil act', hence its declaration that 'we' were 'All Falklanders Now'. Across the spectrum of the newspaper press, although to a lesser extent on the pages of the *Daily Mirror* and the *Guardian*, the Argentine people were depicted in savage terms. Front page headlines published by the *Sun* included 'STICK IT UP YOUR JUNTA' and, perhaps most infamous of all, 'GOTCHA!' on 4 May 1982. The latter account detailed in triumphal terms how the Argentine cruiser *General Belgrano* had been torpedoed and sunk with more than 1200 sailors on board. The tabloid's editor at the time, Kelvin MacKenzie, fearful that he had gone too far as early reports of the casualties began to appear, elected to change the headline after the first edition to 'DID 1,200 ARGIES DROWN?' This sentiment was evidently not shared by the *Sun*'s proprietor, Rupert Murdoch, who reportedly said to MacKenzie about the 'GOTCHA!' headline: 'I wouldn't have pulled it if I were you. Seemed like a bloody good headline to me' (cited in Engel 1996: 274). Critics of this kind of belligerence, including Labour leader Michael Foot, who called on the Prime Minister to end 'the hysterical bloodlust' disgracing British journalism, were routinely labelled as 'appeasers', 'fainthearts' and 'traitors' (even the 'patriotism' of the BBC was called into question by critics angry that its current affairs coverage was in their view 'defeatist' and 'pro-enemy': Harris 1983; Royle 1987; Young and Jesser 1997).

In October of the following year the US invasion of the small Caribbean island of Grenada took place, an opportunity for its military to put into practice several of the 'media management strategies' (exclusion, containment and manipulation) enforced by British officials in the Falklands. There followed throughout the rest of the 1980s and into the 1990s an extensive array of enemy Others who were held by the US news media to personify a pernicious threat to 'our interests'. Included among those being demonized were 'mad dog' Mu'amar Gadaffi of Libya (US warplanes began bombing 'military installations' in April 1986), 'evil, drug-running dictator' General Manuel Noriega of Panama (President George Bush ordered troops in 'Operation Just Cause' to overthrow Noriega's government in December 1989) and, most powerfully of all, the 'new Hitler', Saddam Hussein of Iraq. If among some British politicians the Falklands War had 'laid to rest the ghost of Suez', for President Bush the Persian Gulf War had 'freed America from the memory of Vietnam'. The 'Vietnam syndrome', he claimed, had been 'kicked once and for all' (see Taylor 1992; Jeffords and Rabinovitz 1994; Keeble 1997; Wolfsfeld 1997; Carruthers 2000; McLaughlin 2002).

Numerous studies of the news coverage of the Persian Gulf War have scrutinized, among other things, the military jargon reinflected by many of the journalists involved ('surgical strikes', 'smart bombs', 'friendly fire', 'acceptable losses' and so forth). One of the possible effects of this apparent willingness to reprocess the military's preferred definitions of the situation, it has been argued, is that the reality of the conflict was effectively 'sanitized' for news audiences. Cumings (1992), in his book *War and Television*, makes the point succinctly:

> Remember the Gulf War? Or was that last season's hit show? The Gulf War was a war fought to demolish a memory, but it was also a war that produced no memory. It was our first 'television war': not blood and guts spilled in living color on the living room rug, not the transparent, objective immediacy of the all-seeing eye . . . but a radically distanced, technically

> controlled, eminently 'cool' postmodern optic which, in the doing, became an instrument of the war itself.
>
> (Cumings 1992: 103)

Evidently displaced from this postmodern optic is the loss of human life. Drawing on different sources, Taylor (1998: 160) suggests that current estimates are that 'there were 266 American dead (105 before the war began); forty-seven British dead (the single largest group being killed by US "friendly" fire); two French dead; one Italian dead; twenty-nine Saudis dead; nine Egyptians dead; six United Arab Emirates dead'. Several Israeli civilians were also killed by Iraqi missile attacks (as well as by US military attempts to shoot them down).

In sharp contrast with these estimates, however, is the absence of comprehensive figures for the number of Iraqi people who perished. In part due to the refusal of the US Defense Intelligence Agency, among others, to fully divulge its calculations, precise figures have not been made public. US General Norman Schwarzkopf, leader of the UN alliance, has been quoted as stating: 'We must have killed 100,000', while French officials have placed their estimate at 200,000 Iraqi troops killed (Taylor 1998; see also Jeffords and Rabinovitz 1994). Civilian casualties, due to factors such as the aerial bombardments and the collapse of the urban infrastructure (and with it the spread of disease), as well as the UN economic embargo, have been placed at well over the one million mark by different international research surveys. Perhaps as many as twice that number were turned into refugees, of whom tens of thousands are thought to have died. Consistent with a military language where cities are called 'soft targets' and dead civilians 'collateral damage', the Iraqi people being slaughtered were recurrently described using terms such as 'animals' and 'beasts'. News management in the Gulf War, as Knightley (1991: 5) argues, had at its core 'a deliberate attempt by the authorities to alter public perception of the nature of war itself, particularly the fact that civilians die in war'. This depersonalization of the Iraqi victims of the war (one Harvard University study, according to Keeble (1997: 153), 'estimated that 46,900 children under five died in Iraq between January and August 1991') was made possible in part through a willingness on the part of most journalists to follow a news agenda set down for them by military officials. An overview of the types of terms used by the British press to report on the war, as compiled by the *Guardian Weekly* (Figure 9.1), pinpoints how a racialized 'us and them' frequently underpinned some journalists' choice of descriptive terms.

The ideological tensions discernible in these discursive oppositions indicate the limits of identity formation as it pertains to 'us and them'. The cultural dynamics of racism, intertwined as they are with those of class and patriarchy, assume a *naturalness* which is contingent upon ruling out counter-hegemonic

Figure 9.1 Mad dogs and Englishmen

The following terms have all been used by the British press to report on the war in the Persian Gulf

They have	**We have**
A war machine	Army, Navy and Air Force
Censorship	Reporting guidelines
Propaganda	Press briefings
They	**We**
Destroy	Take out
Destroy	Suppress
Kill	Eliminate
Kill	Neutralise
Kill	Decapitate
Cower in their foxholes	Dig in
They launch	**We launch**
Sneak missiles attacks	First strikes
Without provocation	Pre-emptively
Their men are . . .	**Our men are . . .**
Troops	Boys
Hordes	Lads
They are . . .	**Our boys are . . .**
Brainwashed	Professional
Paper tigers	Lionhearted
Cowardly	Cautious
Desperate	Confident
Cornered	Heroes
Cannon fodder	Dare devils
Bastards of Baghdad	Young knights of the skies
Blindly obedient	Loyal
Mad dogs	Desert rats
Ruthless	Resolute
Fanatical	Brave
Their boys are motivated by	**Our boys are motivated by**
Fear of Saddam	Old-fashioned sense of duty

Figure 9.1 *Continued*

Their boys	**Our boys**
Cower in concrete bunkers	Fly into the jaws of hell
Iraq ships are	**Our ships are**
A navy	An armada
Iraqi non-retaliation is	**Israeli non-retaliation is**
Blundering/Cowardly	An act of great statesmanship
Their missiles are . . .	**Our missiles are . . .**
Aging duds (rhymes with Scuds)	Like Luke Skywalker zapping Darth Vader
Their missiles cause . . .	**Our missiles cause . . .**
Civilian casualties	Collateral damage
They . . .	**We . . .**
Fire wildly at anything	Precision bomb
Their PoWs are . . .	**Our PoWs are . . .**
Overgrown schoolchildren	Gallant boys
Saddam Hussein is . . .	**George Bush is . . .**
Demented Defiant An evil tyrant A crackpot monster	At peace with himself Resolute Statesmanlike Assured
Their planes . . .	**Our planes . . .**
Are shot out of the sky Are zapped	Suffer a high rate of attrition Fail to return from missions

Source: Guardian Weekly reprinted in *Globe and Mail*, 23 February 1991: D5

voices (such as anti-war protest groups, but also those of Arab women and men seeking to resist racist stereotypes) as illegitimate. 'We can kill thousands,' wrote the British historian E.P. Thompson (1980: 51), 'because we have first learned to call them "enemy". Wars commence in the culture first of all and we kill each other in euphemisms and abstractions long before the first missiles have been launched' (see also M. Bell (1995, 1998) on the distinction he makes between 'bystanders' journalism' and a 'journalism of attachment').

The military–media relationship

Military officials, who strive to learn the lessons from one war when planning the next, had much to gain by examining what transpired during the Gulf War of 1991. The advent of rolling 24-hour 'real-time' global television news services, with CNN leading the way, had helped to transform the conflict into a media spectacle akin to a video game. Largely displaced by this 'Nintendo effect', critics pointed out, were the consequences of war, that is, the horrific loss of human life. In the words of veteran war correspondent Chris Hedges (2002):

> The Gulf War made war fashionable again. It was a cause the nation willingly embraced. It gave us media-manufactured heroes and a heady pride in our military superiority and technology. It made war fun.
>
> (Hedges 2002: 142–3)

The blame for this type of reporting, he argues, rests on the shoulders of the press for co-operating so closely with the military:

> Television reporters happily disseminated the spoon-fed images that served the propaganda effort of the military and the state. These images did little to convey the reality of war. Pool reporters, those guided around in groups by the military, wrote about 'our boys' eating packaged army food, practicing for chemical weapons attacks, and bathing out of buckets in the desert. It was war as spectacle, war as entertainment. The images and stories were designed to make us feel good about our nation, about ourselves. The Iraqi families and soldiers being blown to bits by huge iron fragmentation bombs just over the border in Iraq were faceless and nameless phantoms.
>
> (Hedges 2002: 143)

There is little doubt that the ensuing 'sanitized' news coverage succeeded in shaping how media audiences perceived the nature of a 'clean war' waged with 'pinpoint accuracy' in profound ways. News management in the Gulf War, Phillip Knightley (1991) concurs, had at its core 'a deliberate attempt by the authorities to alter public perception of the nature of war itself, particularly the fact that civilians die in war' (1991: 5; see also Cumings 1992; Keeble 1997; Taylor 1998; Hoskins 2004; Kellner 2004; Reese 2004).

Sanitized news coverage, critics pointed out, was certain to produce desensitized audiences, passively observing each development in the 'video game war' with little regard to its implications (the contrast with Vietnam, the 'living room war', being all too telling). Journalistic efforts to enhance public understanding, to counter this obsession with immediacy with rigorous, in-depth reports offering interpretation and context, were being increasingly frustrated.

Throughout the 1990s, Western news organizations were rationalized in the name of cost savings, their budgets for international newsgathering slashed dramatically as economic pressures were brought to bear. The gradual thawing of the Cold War was a further factor, seemingly providing justification for what became a dramatic reallocation of resources away from specialized military reporting (freelancers became the norm as travel budgets were cut and foreign bureaux closed) in favour of more 'popular' (and 'efficient' – i.e. inexpensive) news stories. Some news executives insisted this was simply giving the public what it wanted, pointing to declining viewing (and newspaper circulation) figures as evidence that international news could not attract the necessary advertising revenues to satisfy 'bottom-line' calculations. Less debatable was the fact that owners were increasingly seeing news as a commodity, with some forms of it more profitable than others regardless of accompanying claims made about public service.

Peter Arnett, a household name for his reports for CNN during the Gulf War (he was the only Western correspondent in Baghdad for much of the conflict), was one of several leading journalists to publicly express his discontent at the time. International news coverage in the mainstream US press, he argued, had 'almost reached the vanishing point' since the conflict in the Gulf earlier in the decade:

> Today, a foreign story that doesn't involve bombs, natural disasters or financial calamity has little chance of entering the American consciousness. This at a time when the United States has become the world's lone superpower and 'news' has so many venues – papers, magazines, broadcast and cable TV, radio, newsletters, the Internet – that it seems inescapable. So how is it that Americans have never been less informed about what's going on in the rest of the world? Because we, the media, have stopped telling them.
>
> (Arnett 1998)

Far too many editors had simply embraced 'the canard that readers don't want foreign news', he maintained, even though contrary evidence was available, not least public opinion surveys. Meanwhile more upbeat assessments pointed to how CNN, in pioneering the concept of 'news on demand', had demonstrated that there was public enthusiasm for such stories so long as they were presented in ways that heightened liveness and immediacy. The trick, advocates of the emergent digital technologies believed, was to make the most of the 'new generation' of news gathering strategies promising to revolutionize war reporting.

From the vantage point of the 2003 war in Iraq, one would be forgiven for thinking that the news technologies employed during the first Gulf War seemed strangely antiquated. 'The big difference is that in '91 everything was analog and now everything is digital', stated Dick Tauber, vice president of satellites and circuits for CNN. 'Back then, a satellite transponder could send a single video and audio channel to a satellite and back to headquarters. Now we can send half a dozen channels in the same amount of space.' Moreover, equipment had become smaller, lighter and more robust. Journalists wanting to do a stand-up report to camera, but unable to use a videophone, were able to press mini-portable television stations, called 'fly-aways', into service. 'In the first Gulf War, the fly-away was stowed in 30 cases, the size of luggage, and weighed a ton', Tauber recalled. 'Now it's in 10 or 12 cases the size of a laptop and weighs much less' (cited in Megna 2003). In 1991 the prominent role played by technology in war reporting – which also included email, facsimile or fax machines, night vision equipment, satellite imagery, computer graphics and even remotely operated vehicles for photography – was sufficiently novel to warrant press coverage in its own right. At the same time, journalists were discovering that this technology afforded their editors a greater capacity to monitor their movements, and to make near-constant requests for fresh reports in order to meet the demands of around-the-clock reportage. Similarly attracting attention in this regard was CNN's influential role in tele-diplomacy, with the US and Iraqi presidents both using the network to communicate with one another, as well as with their country's citizens.

Current references to the 'CNN effect' on the conduct of foreign policy can be traced back to these early efforts to come to terms with the news cycle of real-time media. Likely to be seen as a more pressing concern than CNN's influence (now one of several such 24/7 networks), however, is the role of new media forms in reconfiguring the geometry of communicative power (see also Cottle 2009; Matheson and Allan 2009). Howard Tumber and Frank Webster's (2006) examination of the journalistic practices of frontline correspondents has led them to elaborate a conception of 'information wars' to address this transformation. Efforts to understand the use of 'virtuoso technologies' to deliver 'astonishing pictures and sounds from the theatre of war' to audiences in distant places, they argue, must not overlook the wider information environment shaping the interpretation of unpredictable events and their significance:

> First of all, frontline journalists are not easily controlled or manipulated to act as conduits for combatants and their leaders. They have a strong disposition towards 'telling it like it is', they cling to notions of 'objectivity' and they have access to versatile equipment that allows them to report quickly and immediately back to their news organizations. Furthermore, the boundaries between fighting forces are often confused and, perhaps more important, journalists are such a diverse group that once-powerful appeals to support 'our boys' have weakened. Moreover, while embeds are severely constrained by virtue of their locations, news organisations now

> receive an enormous volume and variety of information. What gets into a finished programme or news report may be quite at odds with any single journalist's report.
>
> (Tumber and Webster 2006: 172)

While military weaponry may reflect a massive asymmetry between combatants, it follows, there can be no corresponding assumption that it will engender long-term success in the waging of information war. In the age of the digital camera and the website, Tumber and Webster point out, weaker forces ('who are acutely conscious that the media are globalised phenomena') can disrupt, challenge and often counter the imposition of truth claims by the powerful (see also Tumber 2005, 2009; Moeller 2009).

Our attention turns to Al-Jazeera, the Arabic news network, in the next section. In the course of challenging the more 'sanitized' representations of the conflict prevailing on television newscasts in the West, the network simultaneously recast several assumptions underpinning certain familiar conventions of war reporting.

Al-Jazeera and the sanitization of war

Often described as the 'CNN of the Arab World', Al-Jazeera (which means 'an island' in Arabic) is arguably the region's most influential news organization (see El-Nawawy and Iskandar 2003). Launched in the Qatari capital, Doha, in 1996, the 24-hour satellite television network attracts an audience currently estimated to be about 35 million regular viewers, making it the most widely watched Arab news channel.

Available free of charge throughout much of the Arab world, it is typically a pay-television channel in Europe and North America. Although backed financially by the government of Qatar, Al-Jazeera's journalists consistently maintain that their editorial freedom is not compromised as a result. That said, the network's status as an independent voice in the Arab world, encapsulated in its slogan 'The opinion and the other opinion', is frequently called into question by its many critics. For some, the network's commitment to providing news coverage from an Arab perspective means that it is ideologically compromised, and as such biased against the US and Israel. Other critics, in contrast, have denounced Al-Jazeera for being a Zionist tool, while still others insist that it is little more than a front for the Central Intelligence Agency (CIA). In any case, above dispute is the fact that its news coverage has recurrently placed a considerable strain on Qatar's relations with other countries in the region, including Bahrain, Jordan and Saudi Arabia, where the network's offices have been closed on different occasions.

No stranger to controversy, Al-Jazeera came to prominence across the global media-scape in the aftermath of the dreadful events of 11 September 2001, due to its decision to broadcast taped messages attributed to Osama bin Laden (see also Zelizer and Allan 2002; el-Nawawy and Iskandar 2003; Thussu and Freedman 2003). News organizations around the world paid considerable sums to air edited excerpts, much to the consternation of US officials – not least National Security Advisor Condoleezza Rice, who demanded of television network executives that they 'exercise judgment' (i.e., censorship) in rebroadcasting the messages. Interestingly, most of the considerable traffic to the network's site (www.aljazeera.net) at the time was from the US, despite the fact that its content was entirely in Arabic. During the subsequent 'War on Terror' in Afghanistan, attention was once again directed at Al-Jazeera's role in making available reports of the conflict that challenged the preferred definitions of reality set down by military officials. For this reason alone, further controversy erupted in November 2001 when a US 'smart' bomb destroyed the network's Kabul offices. Intense speculation ensued that the offices had been deliberately destroyed. For example, Nik Gowing, a presenter on BBC World, stated afterwards that Al-Jazeera's only crime was 'bearing witness' to events that the US officials would prefer it did not see. In demanding that the Pentagon be called to account, he pointed out that when the presence of journalists is 'inconvenient' they risk becoming 'legitimate targets' in the eyes of the military – a charge promptly denied, as one would expect, by a Pentagon spokesperson (see Wells 2001).

Following the start of 'Operation Iraqi Freedom', subscriber numbers surged dramatically in response to the intense demand for alternative insights into the conflict. The number of subscribers to the channel in Europe, it was claimed at the time, effectively doubled once the war was under way. The depth of its reporting was recurrently singled out for praise – or condemnation – depending on conflicting perceptions of the relative legitimacy of the war. In addition to reporting from Central Command in Qatar, four of Al-Jazeera's reporters were 'embedded' with the US and British military forces. In the main, however, the network ensured that most of its journalists roamed more freely. Together they covered the breadth of Iraq, including areas where Western journalists did not venture. The Al-Jazeera television crews remained in Baghdad throughout the conflict, as well as in other major battlegrounds such as Basra and Mosul and in Kurdish-controlled northern Iraq.

Not surprisingly, a very different kind of coverage ensued. Tarik Kafala (2003), a BBC News Online reporter, identified a case in point. 'When Western journalists outside Basra were speculating about an uprising on the basis of coalition briefings,' he observed, 'Al-Jazeera's correspondent inside the city was reporting firsthand that "the streets are very calm and there are no indications of violence or riots".' This type of disjuncture between the network's reporting and that of its Western rivals attracted considerable comment. US Secretary of State Colin Powell, for example, criticized the coverage, contending that it 'magnifies the minor successes of the (Iraqi) regime and tends to portray our efforts in a negative light' (cited in Delio 2003). For others, however, it was the very extent to which Al-Jazeera's reporting called into question the more 'sanitized' representations of the conflict that made its presence so important – both on their television screens and, increasingly, on their personal computers (see Gubash 2003).

By including in its reports what were frequently horrific images of civilian casualties, Al-Jazeera reinflected familiar notions of 'balanced' reporting. It was precisely these images, in the view of Faisal Bodi (2003), a senior editor for aljazeera.net, that made Al-Jazeera 'the most sought-after news resource in the world'. In his words:

> I do not mean to brag – people are turning to us simply because the Western media coverage has been so poor. For although Doha is just a 15-minute drive from central command, the view of events from here could not be more different. Of all the major global networks, al-Jazeera has been alone in proceeding from the premise that this war should be viewed as an illegal enterprise. It has broadcast the horror of the bombing campaign, the blown-out brains, the blood-spattered pavements, the screaming infants and the corpses. Its team of on-the-ground, unembedded correspondents has provided a corrective to the official line that the campaign is, barring occasional resistance, going to plan.
>
> (Bodi 2003)

At no time was this difference in news values cast in sharper relief than on 23 March, the night Al-Jazeera broadcast footage of US casualties, as well as Iraqi television's interviews with five US prisoners of war. Al-Jazeera's decision to air the interviews was promptly denounced by US Defence Secretary, Donald Rumsfeld, who alleged that it was a violation of the Geneva Convention protecting prisoners of war. In reply, the network's London bureau chief, Yosri Fouda, argued that Western news reports were being constrained to the extent that they failed to provide accurate coverage. Regarding the Geneva Convention, he insisted that a double standard was being invoked. 'We and other broadcasters were not criticised for showing pictures of Iraqi dead and captured,' he stated, 'or those famous pictures from Guantanamo Bay' (cited in Kafala 2003).

The more heated the ensuing furore became, of course, the more news headlines it generated around the world. The very images deemed by Western news organizations to be too disturbing to screen were being actively sought out by vast numbers of people via online news sites. According to figures compiled by popular search engines, such as Google, Lycos and AltaVista, the term 'Al-Jazeera' was quickly becoming one of the most searched-for topics on the Web. Figures for the week in question indicated that the term 'Al-Jazeera' (and variant spellings) was the term that showed the greatest increase on Google, while Lycos reported that it was the top search term, with three times more searches than 'sex' (a perennial favourite with Web surfers). For Karl Gregory of AltaVista, the popularity of Al-Jazeera's online sites was clear evidence of 'people branching out beyond their normal sources of news' (BBC News Online, 1 April 2003). The decision taken at Al-Jazeera to broadcast the images, as well as to display them online, was justified by its spokesperson, Jihad Ballout, as being consistent with its journalistic ethos of reporting the war as it was being fought on the ground. In his words: 'We didn't make the pictures – the pictures are there. It's a facet of the war. Our duty is to show the war from all angles' (cited in Whitaker 2003; see also Seib 2004; el-Nawawy and Powers 2009).

Blogging the war in Iraq

For many internet commentators, the US-led attack on Iraq represented the 'coming of age' of the internet as a news medium. Regularly singled out for attention was the role of high-speed, broadband internet access, not least its capacity to enable news sites to offer users live video and audio reports, multimedia slideshows, animated graphics, interactive maps and so forth. The rapid rise in the number of users availing themselves of the technology – over 70 million people in the US at the time – meant that providers could further enhance existing types of digital reportage accordingly (Kirkpatrick 2003). Moreover, other commentators pointed to the ways in which online news was consolidating its position as a primary news source. Of significance here, for example, was the extent to which users, especially office workers unable to watch television in the workplace, were relying on the internet for up-to-the-minute news of breaking developments. Research conducted during the first six days of the war by the Pew Internet & American Life Project (2003) indicated that 56 per cent of online users in the US had turned to news sites for reports about the conflict. 'More than half the people who are online are getting their news online – that's never happened before', Lee Rainie, the project's director, maintained. 'It's another milestone moment for online news' (cited in Weaver 2003).

So-called 'Operation Iraqi Freedom' began on 19 March 2003 as the US-led military forces initiated air strikes on leadership 'targets of opportunity' in Baghdad. From the moment news of the first attacks broke, internet traffic to online news services surged dramatically. More people than ever, according to companies monitoring internet traffic such as Hitwise, Nielsen Net Ratings, and the like, were surfing the internet for news and information. In Britain, that day saw the level of traffic to the *Guardian* newspaper's website soar by nearly 30 per cent to around 4.5 million impressions. According to Hitwise research, the *Guardian*'s site was the leading online newspaper service with a 7.26 per cent share of the market, followed by *FT.com* (5.17 per cent), the *Sun* (3.05 per cent), *The Times* (2.86 per cent), the *Telegraph* (2.24 per cent) and the *Independent* (1.51 per cent). Of the non-print sites, the British Broadcasting Corporation's stand-alone news site was ranked highest with a 4.69 per cent share. Evidently traffic to this BBC site was up by 30 to 40 per cent for the day, a level of demand which appeared to have caused the service to repeatedly 'crash' in the early hours (see Timms 2003). Over the course of the days to follow, people going online during office hours appeared to be largely responsible for the surge in traffic to news sites. Many were seeking out alternative news sources, as well as wanting particular types of perspectives about the factors underpinning the conflict. 'These figures show the desire of British surfers to get a real range of informed opinion on the war', argued Tom Ewing, a Nielsen Net Ratings analyst. 'This shows where the internet comes into its own when fast-moving news stories are involved' (cited by *BBC Online*, 15 April 2003).

In the US, Yahoo.com reported that in the first hour following President George W. Bush's announcement that the conflict had started, traffic levels to its site were three times higher. The volume of traffic to its news section jumped 600 per cent the next day (Thursday, 20 March) and again the day after. The sites associated with different television networks proved particularly popular. On the Thursday, CNN.com evidently secured the highest figures for all news sites with 9 million visitors, followed by MSNBC with 6.8 million (about half of the visitors for both sites were accessing them from their workplaces). Other news sites witnessing a significant rise in demand that day included Foxnews.com (77 per cent increase), Washingtonpost.com (29 per cent increase) and USToday.com (17 per cent). 'Without a doubt,' stated Daniel E. Hess of ComScore, 'people are glued to their Web browsers for virtually minute-by-minute updates of the war as it unfolds' (cited in Walker 2003; see also Richtel 2003). Evidently ComScore's measurement of traffic patterns for that Thursday suggested that worldwide traffic to major news sites was 70 per cent higher than the daily average over the previous four weeks. Several news sites responded to the sudden influx of demand by temporarily removing advertising from their home pages so as to improve download times. All in all, most news sites in the US were able to bear the strain of sharp 'spikes' in activity, showing little by way of the 'performance degradation' that was all too typical for the same sites on 11 September 2001 (see Allan 2006).

For many members of the public concerned enough about the crisis to look beyond the confines of the mainstream reporting on offer (see Allan and Zelizer 2004), online news sites were providing vitally important alternative sources of news. Evidence garnered from some internet track monitoring companies suggests that there was a dramatic increase in the numbers of users turning to international news sites around the globe. 'The new war in Iraq has made world news sources far more important', online writer Stephen Gilliard argued. 'While not all news sources are reliable, there is such a gap between the way Americans see the world and the way other people do that it is invaluable to use these resources' (cited in Kahney 2003). If it was frequently difficult for users to judge whether any given source was sufficiently trustworthy, the sheer diversity of the perspectives available online enabled people to supplement their understanding of alternative, even opposing points of view. In addition to international sites, however, an altogether different type of site has similarly attracted a remarkable degree of attention. Specifically, news-oriented Weblogs were rapidly achieving widespread public salience, being heralded as a new interactive form of participatory reporting, commentary and analysis of breaking news. Indeed, by the time of the formal declaration of the invasion, the term 'blog' was rapidly being appropriated into the everyday language of journalism.

Weblogs (blogs for short), as noted above, may be characterized as diaries or journals written by individuals with internet access who are in possession of the necessary software publishing tools (such as those provided by sites such as Blogger.com) to establish an online presence. Most bloggers pull together their resources from a diverse array of other sites, thereby situating a given news event within a larger context, and illuminating multiple dimensions of its elements. The apparent facts or claims being collected are usually time-stamped and placed in reverse-chronological order as the blog is updated, making it easier for readers to follow its ongoing narrative. Customarily the sources of the blogger's information are acknowledged explicitly, with the accompanying hyperlink enabling the user to negotiate a network of cross-references from one blog to the next, or to other types of sites altogether. In principle, the facts or claims presented in any one blog can be subjected to the relentless double-checking of users, some of whom may be even better informed about the events in question than the initial blogger. Any attempt by a blogger to present a partisan assertion as an impartial statement of fact is likely to be promptly recognized as such by other users.

Many news bloggers – a small minority compared to the number of ordinary netizens involved overall – consider themselves to be 'personal' journalists, intent on transgressing the border between 'professional' and 'amateur' reporting. By acting as 'unofficial' news sources on the Web, these blogs link together information and opinion which supplements – or, in the eyes of some advocates, supplants – the coverage provided by 'official' news outlets. The potential of blogs in this regard was widely recognized during the tragic events of 11 September 2001, as discussed above. 'The Weblog world before September 11 was mostly inward-looking – mostly tech people talking about tech things', Glenn Harlan Reynolds of the blog InstaPundit.com observed. 'After 9/11, we got a whole generation of Weblogs that were outward looking' (cited in Gallagher 2002).

Significantly, in the weeks following the atrocity, a new type of blog began to emerge, described by its proponents as a 'warblog'. Taking as their focus the proclaimed 'War on Terror', these blogs devoted particular attention to the perceived shortcomings of the mainstream news media with regard to their responsibility to inform the public about possible risks, threats and dangers. Warbloggers were divided, as one might expect, between those who favoured US and UK military intervention in the Middle East and those who did not. In both cases, however, an emphasis was placed on documenting sufficient evidence to demonstrate the basis for their dissatisfaction with what they deemed to be the apparent biases of the mainstream news coverage of the ensuing conflict in Afghanistan. For pro-warbloggers, a 'liberal bias' was detectable in much mainstream journalism, leading them to call into question the patriotism of well-known reporters and news organizations. In sharp contrast, bloggers opposed to the war were equally convinced that mainstream journalism, with its over-reliance on sources from the Bush administration, the Pentagon and other military sources, pro-war think tanks, and so forth, was failing to provide fair and balanced coverage. Many were able to show, with little difficulty, how voices of dissent were being routinely marginalized, when they were even acknowledged at all. For warbloggers of either persuasion, then, it was desperately important to seek out alternative sources of information from across the Web in order to buttress their preferred perspective.

Few of these online sources originated in Afghanistan, however, due to the severity of the official restrictions imposed on journalists, as well as the limited availability of telecommunications services (an average of two telephones per 1000 people). Accordingly, for many in the blogging communities, it was the US-led invasion of Iraq that proved to be the 'breakthrough' for this grassroots movement. Steven Levy (2003), writing in a *Newsweek* Web exclusive, suggested that blogs 'finally found their moment' as bombs were dropped on the city of Baghdad. The formal initiation of hostilities, he maintained, and 'the frustratingly variegated nature of this particular conflict, called for two things: an easy-to-parse overview for news junkies who wanted information from all sides, and a personal insight that bypassed the sanitizing Cuisinart of big-media news editing'. In Levy's view, blogs were able to 'deliver on both counts'. Adopting a similar line of argument were those who pointed to the success of blogs in attracting attention, especially that of individuals largely indifferent to mainstream reporting (here young people are frequently mentioned), by virtue of their shared intimacy. 'I think that sort of clarity of voice and immediacy is more possible on Weblogs than in any print media', argued Dean Allen of textism.com. 'I can't think of another broadcast medium that has such a potential for directness. Someone reporting live from the battlefield for CNN can't come close' (cited in Allemang 2003). Commenting on this type of 'horizontal' communication, Glenn Harlan Reynolds (2003) of Instapundit.com noted wryly that 'the term "correspondent" is reverting to its original meaning of "one who corresponds," rather than the more recent one of "well-paid microphone-holder with good hair" '.

While it is difficult to generalize, most warbloggers posting from Iraq seemed motivated to share their eyewitness experiences of the conflict so as to counterbalance mainstream news media coverage. The work of CNN correspondent Kevin Sites was a case in point. In addition to filing his television reports, Sites wrote 'behind the scenes' features for CNN.com, all the while maintaining a multimedia blog. Published on his own site, Sites's blog provided his personal commentary about the events he was witnessing from one day to the next, along with various photographs and audio reports that he prepared. Perhaps in light of the media attention Sites's blog received, however, CNN asked him to suspend it on Friday, 21 March 2003. A spokesperson for the network stated at the time that covering war 'is a full-time job and we've asked Kevin to concentrate only on that for the time being' (cited in Kurtz 2003). Sites agreed to stop blogging, later explaining that 'CNN was signing my checks at the time and sent me to Iraq. Although I felt the blog was a separate and independent journalistic enterprise, they did not' (www.kevinsites.net). Reactions from other bloggers were swift. CNN's response, according to Steven Levy (2003) of *Newsweek*, 'was seen in the Blogosphere as one more sign that the media dinosaurs are determined to stamp out this subversive new form of reporting'.

In contrast, MSNBC's support for blogging meant that three warblogs were focused on war coverage at the height of the conflict. 'Weblogs are journalism', argued Joan Connell, one of the site's executive producers. 'They can be used to great effect in reporting an unfolding story and keeping readers informed' (cited in Mernit 2003). Nevertheless, while she does not share CNN's stance that blogs lack a sufficiently 'structured approach to presenting the news', she does believe that there is a necessary role for an editor in the process. In her words: 'Unlike many Weblogs, whose posts go from the mind of the writer straight into the "blogosphere", MSNBC's Weblogs are edited. Our editors scrutinize our Weblogs for accuracy, fairness and balance, just as they would any news story' (cited in Mernit 2003). Not all bloggers on the front lines were associated with a major news organization, however. Many worked as a 'sojo' or 'solo journalist', writing and editing their own copy for both online and print or broadcast media. Being almost constantly on the move meant relying on mobile technologies, such as a notebook computer and digital camera, or even a videophone and mini-satellite dish. Still, for these bloggers, their relative freedom of movement enabled them to pursue the stories which mattered most to them – and the readers of their warblog. Herein lay the popularity of the warblogs amongst users, which in the opinion of journalist Bryony Gordon (2003) was hardly surprising: '[If] a television reporter's movements aren't subject to Iraqi restrictions, then his [or her] report is likely to be monitored by the Allied Forces. Devoid of such regulations, the internet is thriving.'

Freelancer Christopher Allbritton had announced his intention to be the Web's first independent war correspondent in the months leading up to the invasion. His blog, titled Back to Iraq. 2.0 (www.back-to-iraq.com), called upon readers to help contribute to the financial support necessary to fund his travel and expenses in Iraqi Kurdistan. 'It's a marketplace of ideas,' he maintained, 'and those who are awarded credibility by their readers will prosper' (cited in Warner 2003). Support was such that his expenses were met by some 320 donors, allowing him to file daily stories from the country using a borrowed notebook computer and a rented satellite phone. As his blog's daily readership grew to upwards of 25,000, he became accustomed to receiving emails which posed questions and suggested story leads, while others provided useful links to online materials. 'My reporting created a connection between the readers and me,' Allbritton (2003) later observed, 'and they trusted me to bring them an unfettered view of what I was seeing and hearing.' This involvement on the part of his readers in shaping his reporting worked to improve its quality, in his view, each one of them effectively serving as an editor. 'One of the great things about the blogosphere,' he maintained, 'is that there's built-in fact-checking.' Given that so many people will 'swarm' over posts, 'generally the truth of the matter will come out' (cited in Glaser 2003).

Precisely what counts as truth in a war zone, of course, is very much in the eye of the beholder. Above dispute, in the view of many commentators, was that some of the best eyewitness reporting being conducted was that attributed to the warblog of 'Salam Pax' (a playful pseudonym derived from the Arabic and Latin words for peace), a 29-year-old architect living in middle-class suburban Baghdad. Indeed, of the various English-language warblogs posted by Iraqis, none attracted a greater following than Salam's *Where is Raed?* (dear_raed.blogspot.com), which had begun to appear in September 2002. His motivation for blogging was later explained as a desire to keep in touch with his friend Raed, who had moved to study in Jordan. In the months leading up to the initial 'decapitation attack', to use his turn of phrase, the blog contained material ranging from personal – and frequently humorous – descriptions of everyday life, to angry criticisms of the events around him. It was to his astonishment, however, that he discovered that the international blogging community had attracted such intense attention to his site. As word about *Where is Raed?* spread via other blogs, email, online discussion groups and mainstream news media accounts, it began to regularly top the lists of popular blogs as the conflict unfolded. For Salam, this attention brought with it the danger that he would be identified – a risk likely to lead to his arrest, possibly followed by a death sentence. At the same time, speculation over the identity of the Baghdad Blogger – and whether or not *Dear Raed* was actually authentic – was intensifying. Some critics claimed that it was an elaborate hoax, others insisted it was the work of Iraqi officials, while still others maintained that a sinister CIA disinformation campaign was behind it. Salam responded to sceptics on 21 March, writing: '[P]lease stop sending emails asking if I were for real, don't belive [sic] it? then don't read it.' Moreover, he added, 'I am not anybody's propaganda ploy, well except my own' (cited in BBC News Online, 25 March 2003).

Enraged by both Saddam Hussein's Baathist dictatorship and George W. Bush's motivations for the invasion, Salam documented life on the ground in Baghdad before and after the bombs began to drop. This was 'embedded' reporting of a very different order, effectively demonstrating the potential of blogging as an alternative means of war reporting. His warblog entry for 23 March, 8:30 pm, was typically vivid:

> Today's (and last night's) shock attacks didn't come from airplanes but rather from the airwaves. The images al-Jazeera are broadcasting are beyond any description. [. . .] This war is starting to show its ugly face to the world. [. . .] People (and I bet 'allied forces') were expecting things to be much easier. There are no waving masses of people welcoming the Americans, nor are they surrendering by the thousands. People are doing what all of us are doing – sitting in their homes hoping that a bomb doesn't fall on them and keeping their doors shut.
>
> Salam (Pax), dear_raed.blogspot.com

Salam's posts offered readers a stronger sense of immediacy, an emotional feel for life on the ground, than more traditional news sites. For John Allemang (2003), writing in *The Globe and Mail*, 'what makes his diary so affecting is the way it achieves an easy intimacy that eludes the one-size-fits-all coverage of Baghdad's besieged residents'. As Salam himself would later reflect, 'I was telling everybody who was reading the weblog where the bombs fell, what happened [. . .] what the streets looked like.' While acknowledging that the risks involved meant that he considered his actions to be somewhat 'foolish' in retrospect, nevertheless he added: '[It] felt for me important. It is just somebody should be telling this because journalists weren't' (cited in Church 2003).

Bearing witness

Any bold declaration that online journalism will abolish once and for all what Raymond Williams (1982) aptly called the 'culture of distance' will invite a more considered response, once it is situated in relation to the sorts of developments discussed above. As has been made apparent, however, these emergent forms of journalism have the capacity to bring to bear alternative perspectives, contexts and ideological diversity to war reporting, providing users with the means to connect with distant voices otherwise being marginalized, if not silenced altogether, from across the globe. In the words of US journalist Paul Andrews (2003), 'media coverage of the war that most Americans saw was so jingoistic and administration-friendly as to proscribe any sense of impartiality or balance,' hence the importance of the insights provided by the likes of Salam Pax. This 'pseudonymous blogger's reports from Iraq,' Andrews believed, 'took on more credibility than established media institutions.' This point is echoed by Toby Dodge (2003), who argued that Salam managed to post far more perceptive dispatches than those written by 'the crowds of well-resourced international journalists sitting in the air-conditioned comfort of five star hotels'. Communicating to the world using a personal computer with unreliable internet access, he reported 'the traumas and more importantly the opinions of Iraqis as they faced the uncertainty of violent regime change' (see also Seib 2004; Matheson and Allan 2009; Wall 2009).

To close, this chapter has taken as its focus some of the ways in which evolving forms and practices of war reporting afford – and constrain – spaces for acts of witnessing. Alternative approaches – ranging from Al-Jazeera to citizen blogging – have been shown to possess the potential to throw into sharp relief the narrow ideological parameters within which mainstream news media typically operate. Journalists' routine, everyday choices about what to report – how best to do it, and why – necessarily implicate them in a discursive politics of mediation. Before war reporting can become more socially responsible, however, it will have to counter the forms of social exclusion endemic to the culture of distance. A first step in this direction, as this chapter has sought to demonstrate, is to recognize that the culture of distance is, simultaneously, a culture of othering. At stake, in my view, is the need to deconstruct journalism's 'us and them' dichotomies precisely as they are taken up and reinflected in news accounts where the structural interests of 'people like us' are counterpoised against the suffering of strangers. To recast the imperatives of 'here' and 'there', and thereby resist the familiar pull of the culture of distance, it is the corresponding gap between knowledge and action that will have to be overcome.

10 CITIZEN JOURNALISM IN TIMES OF CRISIS

> To practice random acts of journalism, you don't need a big-league publication with a slick Website behind you. All you need is a computer, an Internet connection, and an ability to perform some of the tricks of the trade: report what you observe, analyze events in a meaningful way, but most of all, just be fair and tell the truth, as you and your sources see it.
>
> (J.D. Lasica, online journalist)

The English word 'journalist' can be traced back at least as far as the end of the seventeenth century, with its broad inflection as 'one whose work is to write or edit public journals or newspapers' being widely attested. Matters quickly become rather complicated, however, when one seeks to determine what sort of professional role has been implicitly prescribed by the use of this term in everyday parlance over the years since.

More than a question of semantics, the nature of the proper identity to be affirmed by the journalist within a democracy continues to be hotly contested. Indeed, in recent years, nowhere have the tacit assumptions informing a collective sense of identity been more openly challenged than by the emergence of the 'citizen journalism' movement. In championing the virtues of 'amateur' reporters – especially their freedom from 'professional' complicity in the gatekeeping machinations of Big Media – citizen journalism has succeeded in rattling the foundations of the craft. Reactions to it, from within journalism's inner circles as well as from a wide range of journalism educators, have tended to range from the condemnatory to the dismissive. One such commentator is Samuel Freedman (2006), Professor of Journalism at Columbia University as well as an education columnist for *The New York Times*. Expressing his 'despair over the movement's current cachet', he has argued that despite its wrapping in idealism, 'citizen journalism forms part of a larger attempt to degrade, even to disfranchise journalism as practiced by trained professionals'. At a time when, in his view, 'traditional, reportorial journalism seems so besieged', the threat posed by citizen journalism deserves much wider recognition:

> To treat an amateur as equally credible as a professional, to congratulate the wannabe with the title 'journalist,' is only to further erode the line between raw material and finished product. For those people who believe that editorial gate-keeping is a form of censorship, if not mind control, then I suppose the absence of any mediating intelligence is considered a good thing.
>
> (Freedman 2006)

For critics like Freedman, an appreciation of the differing capacities of 'the amateur, however well-meaning, and the pro' is in serious danger of being lost. The implications for traditional journalism, they fear, may well prove detrimental, hence their calls to shore up the crumbling defences of journalistic identity accordingly (see also Lemann 2006; Allan 2009a, 2009b; Allan and Thorsen 2009).

This chapter's exploration of what constitutes citizen journalism will endeavour to examine the spontaneous actions of ordinary people – more often than not in the wrong place at the wrong time – compelled to adopt the role of reporter. Time and again, their motivation is to bear witness to crisis events unfolding around them. In taking this crisis dimension as our point of departure, we shall investigate the emergent ecology of citizen journalism.

First, though, we need to ask: what is citizen journalism? While there is little danger that consensus is about to emerge any time soon regarding what this term entails, it is nonetheless important to recognize the extent to which competing conceptions of it revolve around crisis reporting. More often than not, commentators will point to the gradual unfolding of an overarching narrative that began to consolidate in the immediate aftermath of the South Asian tsunami of December 2004. This was the decisive moment, they contend, when citizen journalism became a prominent feature on the journalistic landscape. The remarkable range of first-person accounts, camcorder video footage, mobile and digital camera snapshots – many of which were posted online through blogs and personal webpages – being generated by ordinary citizens on the scene (holidaymakers, in many instances) was widely heralded for making a unique contribution to mainstream journalism's coverage. One newspaper headline after the next declared citizen journalism to be yet another startling upheaval, if not outright revolution, being ushered in by internet technology.

News organizations, it was readily conceded, were in the awkward position of being dependent on this 'amateur' material in order to tell the story of what was transpiring on the ground. 'Never before has there been a major international story where television news crews have been so emphatically trounced in their coverage by amateurs wielding their own cameras', observed one British newspaper. 'Producers and professional news cameramen often found themselves being sent not to the scenes of disaster to capture footage of its aftermath, but to the airports where holidaymakers were returning home with footage of the catastrophe as it happened' (*Independent*, 3 January 2005).

Despite its ambiguities, the term 'citizen journalism' appeared to capture something of the countervailing ethos of the ordinary person's capacity to bear witness, thereby providing commentators with a useful label to characterize an ostensibly new genre of reporting. In the years since the tsunami, it has secured its place in journalism's vocabulary (for better or otherwise in the view of many news organizations), more often than not associated with a particular crisis event. It is described variously as 'grassroots journalism', 'open source journalism', 'participatory journalism', 'hyperlocal journalism', 'distributed journalism', or 'networked journalism' (as well as 'user-generated content'), among other terms, but there is little doubt that it is recasting crisis reporting's priorities and protocols in profound ways.

Breaking news

In recognizing that the notion of 'citizen journalism' is a relatively recent innovation, we need to acknowledge that an array of precedents of form and practice emerged long before the actual term was coined. Widely discussed examples include the silent, 8mm 'home movie' recording of John F. Kennedy's assassination in 1963 (see Zelizer 1992) or the camcorder videotape of Rodney King being beaten by Los Angeles police officers in 1991 (see Jacobs 2000). That said, one could go back in time further still, examining deliberations over the status of the 'amateur' in relation to that of the 'professional' – some of which, of course, go back to the earliest days of something recognizable as 'journalism' in the first place.

In internet terms, of course, this is ancient history. Journalist and academic John Naughton (1999), describing his personal recollections about the arrival of the internet in the newsroom, makes a number of perceptive observations. 'For decades,' he writes, 'the Net was below the radar of mainstream journalism – its practitioners didn't even know of its existence. When I used to tell newspaper colleagues that I'd been using email from home since 1975, they would make placatory noises and check the route to the nearest exit' (1999: 30).

It was around 1995, he recalls, that the situation began to change, when 'the conventional media realised something was up'. Precisely what was up, of course, was anything but clear. He observes:

> At first the Net was treated as a kind of low-status weirdo craze, akin perhaps to CB radio and the use of metal-detectors. Then it became the agent of Satan, a conduit for pornography, political extremism and subversion. Next it was the Great White Hope of Western capitalism, a magical combination of shopping mall and superhighway which would enable us to make purchases without leaving our recliners. Then it was the cosmic failure because it turned out that Internet commerce was – shock! horror! – insecure. And so it went, and goes, on, an endless recycling of myths from newspaper clippings, ignorance, prejudice, fear, intellectual sloth and plain, ornery malice.
>
> (Naughton 1999: 30)

Naughton proceeds to note the irony that the hostility some print journalists have directed toward the internet is very similar to that which their 1950s counterparts aimed at early television newscasts. 'Then, as now, the first instinct was to rubbish and undermine the intruder', he comments. 'Television news, said the newspapers, would be vulgar and sensational. There would be fewer words in an entire thirty minute news bulletin than in half a page of *The Times*. And so on' (1999: 31). A further line of attack was to challenge the credibility of the internet as a news provider, typically by characterizing online sites as being inherently untrustworthy – and lacking in the objectivity, professionalism and independence members of the public expected. It was only when it became apparent that people were turning to the internet for their 'hot' or 'breaking' news, despite such dire warnings, that newspapers began, ever so reluctantly, to rethink their relationship to their internet rivals.

Given the significance of breaking news in this regard, it is not surprising that so many of the early indications of citizen journalism's potential – long before the term itself was employed – emerged during crisis events. News flashes about earthquakes in California, home of the fledgling software industry, were a case in point. First in 1989 in San Francisco, but more substantively in Northridge (20 miles west-northwest of Los Angeles) on 17 January 1994, 'the global computer network buzzed into action', to quote from an Associated Press wire service report (AP, 18 January 1994). One early user, evidently a Prodigy subscriber with a wireless modem, alerted the world about the predawn earthquake before mainstream media broke the news. Within twenty minutes of the incident, users began offering first-hand accounts of their experiences, including descriptions of the destruction they had personally witnessed. Others relayed information updates gleaned from the television and radio news coverage to hastily configured newsgroups. While distant users sent emails inquiring about the well-being of relatives, local people with long-distance telephone connections offered to make calls on behalf of those temporarily denied the service in the quake area. Some even offered to help organize rescue operations. For journalist Jon Katz (1994), this electronic response suggested that 'a new news medium' had been born. 'No information structure has ever been able to do anything remotely like it', he argued, seeing in this activity a basis to project an optimistic appraisal of what he termed 'the new information culture'.

Other commentators, as one would expect, were less convinced by this 'network of computer networks' increasingly being called 'the internet' in news reports. Paul Andrews, writing in the *Seattle Times*, argued that when 'the traditional information infrastructure is disrupted – jammed phone lines, power outages, wrecked highways in the case of the quakes and government censorship in the [then-Soviet Union] coup – the Internet shines'. On such occasions, when the internet is 'the only game in town', it acquires 'far more legitimacy, substance and credibility' than would be the case otherwise. Indeed, in Andrews's view, when the internet competes with other media, it is promptly revealed to be 'a noisy and cumbersome sideshow', effectively little more than 'the haunt of amateurs, poseurs and incompetents' (*Seattle Times*, 30 April 1995). For those sharing this line of argument, real journalism did not take place on the internet.

And yet, as Naughton observed above, it was in 1995 that the situation began to change. Indeed, historical accounts often state that this was the year when users in the West 'fell in love' with the internet. If the web was in effect three years old by then, its presence was slowly becoming a reality for increasing numbers of people due to the popular take-up of online services using Netscape's refashioned browser software. (In the United States, for example, the Microsoft Network, or MSN, was launched in July and had acquired over 500,000 subscribers by the end of the year.) Now it was possible to click a mouse to access information on a computer database directly on the Web, as opposed to typing addresses such as 'Telnet 192.101.82.300' to retrieve it. The release of Microsoft's Windows 95 operating system in August was front-page news around the world, a clear sign that personal computing was becoming increasingly mainstream. It would be some time, however, before the internet would be widely regarded as a news source in its own right, a transformation brought about in large part by its capacity for crisis reporting.

Crisis reporting

Historical assessments of online news in its infancy often underscore the significance of crisis events in the latter half of the 1990s – precedents of form and practice, including the reporting of the Oklahoma City bombing, the crash of TWA flight 800, the Heaven's Gate mass suicide, and the death of Princess Diana – with respect to their contribution to the growing status of the internet as a news source. Each of these and related instances help to pinpoint the emergent ecology of online news, that is, the ways in which its rudimentary reportorial conventions were undergoing a socially contingent process of appropriation, consolidation and reinflection (see also Allan 2006).

It is against this backdrop of shifting priorities between 'old' and 'new' media that the crisis sparked by a 'renegade cyber-journalist', Matt Drudge, needs to be situated. On 17 January 1998, Drudge posted a 'world exclusive' on his fledgling website, the Drudge Report, alleging that President Bill Clinton had conducted a sexual affair with White House intern Monica Lewinsky. The ensuing scandal engulfed the Clinton administration while, at the same time, making Drudge a household name. His website had been set up years earlier, when he worked in the gift shop at CBS television, to share 'little morsels of studio rumors' (his words) that he happened to overhear from time to time. Working from his apartment in Los Angeles, he rapidly established an online following for his postings, despite making no pretence of being a journalist. Described in a newspaper profile as a 'cheerful 29-year-old, looking out of place on the Boulevard of Broken Dreams', he explained how the site operated. 'I use a beat-up Packard Bell 486 desktop running Windows 3.1, with a 28.8 modem. And Netscape Navigator 1.1. I keep going back to earlier versions because they're easier to use.' In the same interview, he expressed his surprise about the growing interest in his site generated by the mainstream media. 'Here I am, I write this thing out in my boxer shorts with my cat, as if I'm passing notes in high school', he stated. Then, suddenly, 'I'm getting mentioned on Rush Limbaugh's radio show – that's 20 million listeners – and the *New York Times* are giving out my address too' (cited in the *Independent*, 29 July 1996).

In the immediate aftermath of the Lewinsky revelations, Drudge's personal philosophy – 'anyone can report anything' – was subjected to intense scrutiny in the press, with much of the commentary scathing in its critique. Drudge himself was well aware that his relaxed attitude to fact-checking invited scorn, but he saw much of the criticism as being elitist in nature, steadfastly refusing to take the blame for an erosion of journalism's standards. 'I'm a citizen first and a reporter second', he insisted. 'The people have a right to know, not the editors who think they know better. You should let people know as much as you know when you know' (cited in AP, 1 February 1998).

This familiar argument, well rehearsed over the course of journalism's history, was suddenly striking a different chord – in the view of some, a deeply disturbing one – in the era of 'instant news' on the internet. The following year, a crisis of an entirely different order would throw into sharp relief the contours of a related set of imperatives shaping the emergence of what would be called 'citizen journalism' in the years to follow.

'The first internet war', as it was widely dubbed by journalists and press commentators, was being waged over the reporting of Kosovo in 1999. 'The battle for hearts and minds is being fought on the net', declared newspaper reporter Simon Rogers, an observation that underscored the rapidly growing significance of web-based journalism (*Guardian*, 26 March 1999). Deserving of particular attention, other observers agreed, was the way these new forms of reporting afforded members of the public in distant places an unprecedented degree of access and immediacy to breaking news in the war zone. This emergent genre of digital war coverage was attracting attention in its own right, including the extent to which it invited a self-reflexive critique among journalists about the relative challenges these technologies posed for the integrity of reportorial practice.

Those welcoming the arrival of digital technologies – the internet, but also satellite dishes, laptops, cell or mobile telephones, audio and video recorders, and the like – encountered the reservations of critics, many of whom were sceptical about the relative advantages to be gained by 'cyber-journalism' where improving war reporting was concerned. In retracing the contours of this debate today, it is remarkable to observe how novel the idea seemed to be that the internet could be used as an alternative platform for the eyewitness accounts of ordinary citizens. First-person accounts of those caught up in the conflict included those of a 'cyber-monk' offering eyewitness reports from a 12th-century monastery, a young Albanian teenager's emails describing daily life sent to her 'electronic pen pal' in the United States (who shared them with news organizations), as well as bulletin-board postings relaying, in horrific detail, what NATO's definition of 'collateral damage' following a bombing raid looked like up close. Time and again, press reports acknowledged how the inclusion of such accounts shaped public perceptions of what was actually happening on the ground (see also Matheson and Allan 2009). In so doing, this 'underground', 'populist', or 'amateur' journalism (as it was variously labelled in the press), performed by ordinary citizens using the Web, fostered a heightened sense of personal engagement for 'us' with the distant suffering of 'them'.

This sense of connection afforded by citizen reporting during a crisis proved to be one of the few bright spots on 11 September 2001. Less than ten minutes after the first passenger jet struck the World Trade Center, eyewitness accounts began to appear on the Web. People were desperate to put into words what they had seen, to share their experiences, even when they defied comprehension. 'This unfathomable tragedy,' online writer Rogers Cadenhead observed, 'reminds me of the original reason the internet was invented in 1969 – to serve as a decentralized network that couldn't be brought down by a military attack.'

Cadenhead's comment was made to newspaper reporter Amy Harmon, who interviewed him on 11 September about the way his WTC attack email discussion list was circulating news about what was happening. 'Amateur news reporters on weblogs are functioning as their own decentralized media today,' Cadenhead pointed out, 'and it's one of the only heartening things about this stomach-turning day' (cited in *The New York Times*, 12 September 2001). The major news sites, typically associated with broadcasters and newspapers, were so overwhelmed by user demand that they could be reached only sporadically as efforts mounted to ward off the danger of complete 'congestion collapse'. The home page of the popular Google.com search engine posted an advisory message that made the point bluntly:

> If you are looking for news, you will find the most current information on TV or radio. Many online news services are not available, because of extremely high demand. Below are links to news sites, including cached copies as they appeared earlier today.
>
> (Google.com, 11 September 2001)

Elsewhere on the Web, however, hundreds of refashioned personal websites began to appear over the course of the day, making available eyewitness accounts, personal photographs and, in some cases, video footage of the unfolding crisis.

Taken together, these websites resembled something of a first-person news network, a collective form of collaborative news-gathering. Ordinary people were transforming into 'amateur newsies', to use a term frequently heard at the time, or instant reporters, photojournalists and opinion columnists. Many of them were hardly amateurs in the strict sense of the word, however, as they were otherwise employed as professional writers, photographers, or designers. 'Anyone who had access to a digital camera and a web site suddenly was a guerrilla journalist posting these things', said one graphic-designer-turned-photojournalist. 'When you're viewing an experience through a viewfinder, you become bolder' (cited in CNET News, 12 October 2001). The contributions to so-called 'personal journalism', or what some described as 'DIY [Do-It-Yourself] reporting' or 'citizen-produced coverage', appeared from diverse locations, so diverse as to make judgements about their relative accuracy difficult, if not impossible. This type of first-person news item was typically being forwarded via email many times over, almost always by people who did not actually know the original writer or photographer. Presumably for those 'personal journalists' giving sincere, unapologetically subjective expression to their experiences, though, the sending of such messages had something of a cathartic effect. In any case, the contrast with mainstream reporting was stark. These first-hand accounts and survivor stories, in the words of reporter Pamela

LiCalzi O'Connell, were 'social history in its rawest, tear-stained form' (*The New York Times*, 20 September 2001).

Alternative truths

The vital contribution made by citizen photographers to enhancing 'our camera mediated knowledge of war', to use Susan Sontag's (2003) evocative phrase, is being increasingly recognized. One especially noteworthy instance, which helped to crystallize both public and journalistic concerns about the imagery of the Iraq war, occurred in April 2004. The *Seattle Times* was able to print a photograph of military coffins being transported back from Iraq – the type of image the Pentagon had banned from media publication, ostensibly out of respect for the privacy of dead soldiers' families – because a civilian working in Kuwait International Airport, Tami Silicio, had emailed a shot taken on her digital Nikon Coolpix (3.2 megapixel) camera to a friend back in the United States. The shot in question showed rows of flag-draped coffins being secured into place on an Air Force cargo plane. Her friend, Amy Katz, forwarded it to Barry Fitzsimmons, photo editor at the *Seattle Times* (Silicio's hometown newspaper).

When the photograph arrived, 'I just said wow', Fitzsimmons recalled. 'The picture was something we don't have access to as the media' (cited in *Seattle Times*, 18 April 2004). In recognizing its extraordinary news value, he also knew that it was 'too powerful an image just to drop into the newspaper' without first establishing the story behind it. Following several emails and telephone calls between Silicio and Fitzsimmons (and, later, staff reporter Hal Bernton), the decision was made to publish one of the images on the front page of the Sunday edition under the headline: 'The somber task of honoring the fallen.' In electing to run the photograph, news editors at the *Seattle Times* were aware that they would be contravening a policy adopted by the Pentagon in 1991, during the first Gulf War, to prohibit news organizations from photographing coffins at military bases. They similarly knew that the photograph was likely to spark strong reactions from readers, not all of whom would agree with the newspaper's position. 'We're not making a statement about the course of the war', Fitzsimmons stated at the time. 'Readers will make their own sense of the picture, their own judgment' (cited in *Seattle Times*, 18 April 2004).

The magnitude of the ensuing controversy caught everyone by surprise, it seemed, with the image promptly reproduced across the mediascape, including on the front pages of several other newspapers around the country. Matters intensified even further when Silicio was abruptly fired from her job in the cargo terminal two days later. Press accounts pointed to 'avalanching public opinion' when describing the 'onslaught of media requests for the photo' and the 'blizzard of media inquiries' into what had happened. (*Seattle Times* editors found themselves being interviewed extensively, from Good Morning America to NBC Nightly News, over several days.) Maytag Aircraft Corporation, Silicio's and her husband's employer, claimed that her action was in breach of both company and base disclosure rules. (Its president was widely quoted as stating that the military had identified 'very specific concerns'.) The *Seattle Times* expressed its regret about her dismissal. 'I'm happy the picture is out,' Fitzsimmons stated, 'but it broke my heart when I found out she lost her job' (cited in *Editor & Publisher*, 22 April 2004). The paper had alerted Silicio about possible risks when obtaining her permission to use the image, having rightly anticipated that there might be repercussions, but remained steadfast in the face of criticism. Managing editor David Boardman insisted that his paper's motives – like those of Silicio herself – were honourable, and there was no anti-war agenda at work. '[We] weren't attempting to convey any sort of political message', he explained, before expressing his disagreement with the military ban. 'The Administration cannot tell us what we can and cannot publish' (cited in *Sydney Morning Herald*, 23 April 2004). Jim Vesely, the paper's editorial page director, described how 'dumbfounded' staffers were by the public response from around the world – 'at one point the emails were coming at one per second' – and how much they appreciated what were 'overwhelmingly positive' reactions on the whole (cited in *Seattle Times*, 2 May 2004).

Although photographs of war and its aftermath have been taken by amateurs since the earliest days of the medium, suddenly it seemed that digitally generated imagery was being heralded – as well as criticized – for its transformative potential. 'In an era when pictures and video can be captured and distributed across the world with a few clicks,' Amy Harmon observed, 'the traditional establishment – the military, the government, the mainstream media – appears to be losing control of the images of war.' Digital technology, she pointed out, 'is forcing a major shift in the expectation of what can be kept private, and it may ultimately hold everyone more accountable for their actions' (*New York Times*, 14 May 2004). In addition to the Silicio case, the examples she cites include a website, TheMemoryHole.org, that posted further images of military coffins being shipped from Iraq (obtained through a Freedom of Information request), the grisly video of Nicholas Berg being decapitated by extremists, and various social networking sites where war images circulate. Most important in this regard, however, were the photographs of Iraqi prisoners being tortured by their American captors in the notorious Abu Ghraib prison 20 miles outside Baghdad. Despite the concerted efforts of human rights groups to draw news media attention to the disturbing allegations being made regarding the US military's mistreatment of Iraqi prisoners, their information was all but ignored by journalists for several months. The story finally broke when digital images casually snapped by soldiers inside Abu Ghraib, effectively documenting the maltreatment on an unimagined scale, found their way into the hands of the mainstream media. The ensuing scandal, according to the official line, revolved around the actions of some 'bad apples' and was not indicative of systemic policies and procedures. Evidence to the contrary was readily available elsewhere on the internet.

Indeed, the disjuncture between official assertions about what was transpiring on the ground in Iraq and what was really happening there was a matter of intense dispute at a number of levels. As noted in the previous chapter, the warblog of 'Salam Pax' was widely heralded by news organizations for the perceptive quality of its insights into life on the ground in Baghdad at a time when few Western correspondents could secure safe access. Since the invasion, the number of warblogs appearing in occupied Iraq has multiplied at a remarkable rate. Such blogs provide web users from around the globe with viewpoints about what life is like for ordinary Iraqis, viewpoints otherwise likely to be routinely ignored or trivialized in their country's mainstream news media (see also Wall 2009). The blog 'Baghdadee' has as its tagline 'An opportunity to hear from witnesses inside Iraq.' 'A Family in Baghdad' posts the online 'diaries' of mother Faiza and sons Raed, Khaled, and Majid. This excerpt, written by Faiza, is indicative of its content:

> Wednesday, 21st, May 2003
>
> Electricity is on at the hours: 6–8 p.m., 2–4 a.m., the Americans are spreading news about achievements they have accomplished . . . but on actual grounds we see nothing . . . we don't know whether they are truthful or not. . . . The schools are open, they are teaching whatever, the importance being for the children to finish their school year. Some schools were destroyed during the war, so, they merged the students with others from another school, and made the school day in two shifts, morning and afternoon . . .
>
> (afamilyinbaghdad.blogspot.com/)

'Baghdad Burning', posted under the name 'Riverbend' (a 'Girl Blog from Iraq'), posted this entry on 7 August 2004:

> 300+ dead in a matter of days in Najaf and Al Sadir City. Of course, they are all being called 'insurgents.' The woman on tv wrapped in the abaya, lying sprawled in the middle of the street must have been one of them too. Several explosions rocked Baghdad today – some government employees were told not to go to work tomorrow.
>
> So is this a part of the reconstruction effort promised to the Shi'a in the

> south of the country? Najaf is considered the holiest city in Iraq. It is visited by Shi'a from all over the world, and yet, during the last two days, it has seen a rain of bombs and shells from none other than the 'saviors' of the oppressed Shi'a – the Americans. So is this the 'Sunni Triangle' too? It's déjà vu – corpses in the streets, people mourning their dead and dying and buildings up in flames. The images flash by on the television screen and it's Falluja all over again. Twenty years from now who will be blamed for the mass graves being dug today?
>
> (riverbendblog.blogspot.com/)

Words from blogs such as these speak for themselves, their importance all too apparent for users looking beyond the narrow ideological parameters of much Western news coverage.

In the next section, our attention turns to three distinctive citizen-led initiatives to recast mainstream reporting, each of them representing 'bottom-up' projects intended to reverse the preoccupations of 'top-down' traditional media. In the first instance, we turn to the Independent Media Center (IMC or IndyMedia for short), a grassroots forum of news reporting about social and political issues. The mission statement posted on its home page describes it as 'a democratic media outlet for the creation of radical, accurate, and passionate tellings of truth', before explaining that it is a collective made up of a diverse range of independent media organizations and hundreds of journalists – professional and amateur alike – committed to social change. 'We work out of a love and inspiration for people who continue to work for a better world,' the statement elaborates, 'despite corporate media's distortions and unwillingness to cover the efforts to free humanity.'

Indymedia, OhmyNews, Wikinews

IndyMedia

The origins of IndyMedia may be traced back to what became known as the 'battle of Seattle' in November 1999, when thousands of people took to the streets of the city to protest against the impact of global free trade relations. News of the events unfolding on the streets of Seattle made headlines around the world. Playing a vital role in this regard was the Independent Media Center with its all-volunteer team of journalists and alternative media activists – including independent video makers, radio producers and web techies – dispersed across Seattle. 'If the mainstream media are like elephants,' observed newspaper reporter Dean Paton (1999), 'then these eclectic independents are mosquitoes, buzzing their messages through cracks and virtual crannies too small and insignificant for CBS or *The New York Times*.' Moreover, he pointed out that the type of reporting being performed by these individuals – whom he describes as 'part-activist, part-journalist' – represents a 'role model for a kind of democratic reporting made possible by new and emerging technologies'. Indeed, he saw in their presence on the scene a 'prototype for the vast democratic media of the future'. The relative advantages of 'open source' reporting became ever more pronounced as the protests intensified. 'Don't hate the media; be the media' quickly proved to be an effective rallying cry for the rapidly fashioned Seattle IMC.

Today there are currently over 150 independent media centres situated in about 45 countries across six continents. While each local IMC admitted into the network shares the aspirations of the collective, each is also relatively autonomous, defining the details of its mission statement, finances and logistical approach on its own terms. Accordingly, although there is a degree of co-ordination from the centre with respect to technical decisions and editorial policy, each of the IMCs associated with the network enjoys sufficient freedom to pursue its own agendas. In refusing to be 'a conscious mouthpiece of any particular point of view', IndyMedia itself avoids any direct association with a partisan position or stance while, at the same time, furnishing the conditions for those who seek to post non-corporate news, information or analysis to be heard. Its aim in encouraging people to 'present their own account of what is happening in the world' on its newswires revolves around a desire to empower individuals to effectively 'become the media' themselves. As such, it is intended to be a 'safe place' for dissent to be articulated, given that no formal prohibition is placed on the points of view expressed, other than that they are respectful of the editorial policy. On those occasions when offensive outbursts of hate occur (sexist, racist, homophobic, and so forth), the discussion can be temporarily blighted until the item in question is 'hidden' from sight – even then, in the case of most centres, it will remain viewable behind the main pages. Ever sensitive to questions of censorship, activists seek to ensure as open a dialogue as possible.

Taken together, editorial rules of inclusion – and, more to the point, exclusion – constitute a political statement. Principled commitments to a collaborative, non-hierarchical mode of operation, based on group consensus, can be sorely tested. Various instances of hate speech – as well as certain libellous allegations – have sparked controversy over the years, earning IndyMedia a certain notoriety in the view of some critics (at one time, Google News moved to suspend IMCs from its searches). Lapses in accuracy, unintentional and otherwise, as well as overly zealous opinions – not to mention occasional acts of deliberate vandalism or sabotage – similarly pose serious problems for 'admins' (trusted to hold the passwords) responsible for maintaining the site's journalistic integrity. Advocates contend that this is the price to be paid for upholding the principle of open publishing, where anyone with an internet connection may publish to the newswire simply by clicking on the 'publish' link. Posts are typically anonymous, which poses questions about accountability. IndyMedia relies on those who are contributing posts to do so in accordance with its editorial guidelines, namely to be thorough, honest and accurate in their reporting, on the understanding that the actual post will not be edited by a designated editorial collective. Those posts that violate the guidelines will be promptly cleared from the front page of the newswire. At the same time, IndyMedia does not seek to set an overall news agenda, choosing to depend instead on its reporters – and readers – to determine what should be covered, how and why. Each of these users, it goes without saying, will exhibit their own biases, so the site advises everyone to read its contents with a critical eye (just as they should do with corporate news, it hastens to add). Anyone objecting to the content of what is posted can express their alternative view by using the 'add your own comments' link situated beneath each post. This strategy, while sound in principle, can be ineffectual at times, as reasoned critique is sometimes lost in a flurry of heated rants and diatribes.

The thorny question of whether or not an individual contributor posting a news item qualifies as a 'journalist' is left by IndyMedia for each person involved to decide for themselves. In the early days, much of the news coverage focused on up-to-the-minute reporting of various demonstrations following in the wake of Seattle around the world. What the activists-turned-DIY reporters lacked in journalistic experience, they typically made up for with enthusiasm and commitment. Gradually, as the network grew and its resources improved, the range of news items expanded to encompass a much wider array of stories and reporting styles. In the case of New York IndyMedia, for example, the collective teaches people how to become good journalists. 'We've had lots of community reporting workshops', states John Tarleton, which have proved worthwhile. He adds:

> [. . .] people have come in off the street with little or no experience, but burning with a story they want to tell. Sometimes it takes them several months to write their first story, but they stick it out. We do a lot of skill sharing – people who want to communicate their ideas can get better at it. Anyone who sticks it out for six months or so can be writing regular news stories. The bottom line is that articles have to be well-written, accurate, fairly non-rhetorical, and convey radical ideas through quality writing and research.
>
> (Cited in Whitney 2005)

There is always the danger, he points out, that good reporting will be discredited by weaker efforts, so certain standards need to be maintained. At the same time, however, questions of quality are unlikely to be answered in strict journalistic terms when for many of the reporters involved what matters most is the message being communicated (see also Salter 2009). Informing their efforts is a keen desire to make available news that can be used to effect social justice, a commitment that will necessarily fashion IndyMedia first and foremost into an alternative, non-commercial resource for citizen power.

OhmyNews

South Korea is frequently described as 'the most wired country in the world', and as such one of the world's leading 'webocracies'. Typically described as an 'online newspaper', its OhmyNews shares some features with IndyMedia, but is organized in accordance with different imperatives – not least its aim to call upon ordinary people to provide a form of reporting that serves as an alternative to the mainstream, conservative media while, at the same time, striving to ensure that the news site generates a financial profit. 'My goal was to say farewell to 20th-century Korean journalism, with the concept that every citizen is a reporter', declared Oh Yeon Ho, the site's founder. 'The professional news culture has eroded our journalism', he adds, 'and I have always wanted to revitalize it. Since I had no money, I decided to use the Internet, which has made this guerrilla strategy possible' (cited in French 2003). This 'guerrilla strategy', as Oh describes it, has indeed proved to be remarkably successful, not only financially – rather unusually for an online news organization – but also in journalistic terms within Korean society.

The shoestring operation behind OhmyNews was set in motion by Oh, a 'lifelong journalistic rabble rouser' (to borrow an apt phrase from *The New York Times*), working with four students who were attending a journalism school where he was employed at the time. Its formal launch on 22 February 2000 at 2:22 pm represented the first major step in the fulfilment of his impassioned belief that all citizens can be paid reporters with the help of the internet. In striving to realize its aim of being 'the people's news source', OhmyNews very quickly established itself as an ambitious challenge to conventional journalism. An initial staff of four (since grown to over 50) were confronted with a range of logistical difficulties in coping with the demands placed upon them by a rapidly growing community of citizen reporters (from an initial 700 to over fifty thousand involved today). The vast majority of stories appearing on the site – some 80 per cent – are written by ordinary citizens keen to try their hand at journalism. The content for the remaining 20 per cent of the newspaper is prepared by staff journalists, some of whom cover major stories, while others assume responsibility for editing and fact-checking the material sent in by 'amateurs', such as students, office workers, police officers and shopkeepers.

'Reporters are not some exotic species,' Oh observes, 'they are everyone who has news stories and shares them with others' (cited in *Financial Times*, 6 November 2004). The site's founding principle is that everyone is invited to participate, once they have registered, by emailing a news or opinion item (or blending of both therein) regarding whatever topic interests them, from highly personal musings about everyday life, to a sports report about a local team's triumph, to a fresh angle on the most pressing international issues of the day. As Oh himself elaborates:

> I think citizens like to write their own articles, but simultaneously, they like to be edited by professional reporters [. . .]. OhmyNews is a kind of combination of the merits of the blog and the merits of the newspaper. We know what the netizen wants: at the end of every article we have a comment area, and one issue had 85,000 comments. That story began with a suggestion from a citizen reporter, and citizens commented, so it's a unique way to generate a lot of content [. . .] Our main concept is the citizen reporter. Our second concept is: demolish the news-writing formula. We say: 'Please communicate in your style: if it is convenient for you, that's fine. Don't just follow the professional reporters.'
>
> (Cited in Schofield 2004)

The overall editorial policy is fashioned to a significant extent by the emphases discernible in the collective response, which means in a practical sense that diverse publics are shaping the agenda. Citizen reporters are openly encouraged to identify stories that the mainstream media are not pursuing. The site's editors sift through the flow of items arriving each day (about 200 on average) to rank them on the basis of their relative newsworthiness, before making a judgement about where to place them in the hierarchy on the site. Those items deemed to warrant priority are positioned on the top of the most prominent pages, while those considered to be of a more specialized interest are relegated to back pages (distinctions are made between 'basic', 'bonus' and 'special' items). Such decisions determine, in turn, the relative size of the payment awarded to the citizen reporter for his or her story. A highly valued item can earn as much as £12 or so (about $20 US), although a more typical sum would be a small fraction of that amount. Even for those employed as editors by OhmyNews (the majority having been drawn from the ranks of citizen reporters), the sense of reward is greater than the monies involved. 'We are becoming very powerful', Bae Eul-sun, a member of the editorial team, comments. 'The pay is lousy, but it is very satisfying to work here because I really feel like I can change the world little by little' (*Guardian*, 24 February 2003; see also Woo Young 2009).

The news site's reputation for investigative reporting is hard-won. Editors interact with citizen reporters on discussion forums, answering questions but also negotiating story ideas, angles and possible sources to approach. 'When the contributors send us stories,' Jean K. Min states, 'we often send them back and ask them not to try to imitate the official news writing style but be themselves instead' (cited in *Helsingin Sanomat*, 8 January 2005). Some critics have noted that certain imbalances exist in this regard, not least with respect to gender and age, which impact on the nature of the items. Statistics gathered by the site indicate that about three-quarters of citizen reporters are male, and that the largest age group is made up of people in their twenties. Other critics complain that little pretence is made of objectivity; rather, citizen reporters typically make their personal point of view explicit, thereby inviting a more dynamic relationship with the reader than that derived from dispassionate forms of journalism. In the eyes of critics, this makes OhmyNews appear less professional than it should be, but its advocates consider this departure from the bland strictures of impartiality to be a virtue. In any case, no formal responsibility is assumed by OhmyNews for the accuracy of the content provided by its reporters, who post using their real identities and in accordance with an agreed code of ethics (copyright for what they write is shared between them and the site). To date, only a handful of stories have sparked legal repercussions – four retractions published in the first four years, none of them serious enough to test this policy. The site has also fallen victim to hoaxes (news that Microsoft's Bill Gates had been assassinated was reported using a source that turned out to be a fake CNN news site), and must always guard against public relations or marketing people posing as citizen reporters so as to try to pass off advertisements for a commercial product or service as a legitimate news item. 'We put everything out there,' states Oh, 'and people judge the truth for themselves' (cited in AP, 12 May 2003).

Now firmly ensconced as a household name in Korea, OhmyNews averages about two million page views each day, with major stories sending those figures skyrocketing. After a slow start, the site has been financially profitable since the autumn of 2003. It relies on advertising revenue in the main, but also sells content licences (such as to the portal Naver as well as to Yahoo Korea) and receives voluntary donations from supporters. 'Making money is important, but more important is maintaining our identity', Oh states. 'The importance of advertisers must not grow too big' (cited in *Helsingin Sanomat*, 8 January 2005). Profits continue to be modest. Song Sung-young, a farmer living in a mountain village southwest of Seoul, has contributed over 200 articles about rural life. 'I earn a little, eat a little and spend a little', he comments. 'I make just a little for each story. That's why OhmyNews is the perfect fit for me' (cited in *LA Times*, 19 June 2007). Matters have improved markedly for some of its citizen reporters, however, due to a recent innovation best described as a tipping service. Readers can now express their appreciation of a particular reporter's story by contributing a small fee directly to him or her on the site. OhmyNews receives a small commission as well, which has proven to be surprisingly lucrative on occasion. Meanwhile, the drive for financial security has seen the site's multimedia presence continue to expand, with new initiatives such as OhmyTV and Web radio under way, and an ever greater emphasis being placed on news photographs in recognition that the majority of Korea's young people carry a camera-equipped mobile telephone with them.

OhmyNews's pioneering efforts to reconcile citizen journalism with the dictates of the financial balance sheet has hardly gone unnoticed, of course. The site, as *Newsweek* magazine has observed, has 'attracted the attention of media giants around the world who wonder: is this Korean start-up the future of journalism?' (*Newsweek*, 18 June 2004). Certainly, Oh and his team took an important step in this direction with the launch of OhmyNews International, an English-language site, in February 2004. It has already gone some distance towards realizing its declared aim of drawing upon 'world citizen reporters' for its content, with some 300 citizen journalists already signed up – and plans for several thousand more to be added over the next few years. It is Oh's ambition to make OhmyNews the 'epicentre of world opinion'. Each country importing its business model enhances the main site's profitability, but he insists that his primary motivation is to see the OhmyNews philosophy, namely 'citizen participatory journalism', spread around the globe. In so doing, it simultaneously extends a political project. 'OhmyNews is a kind of public square in which the reform minded generation meet and talk with each other and find confidence', Oh contends. 'The message they find here: we are not alone. We can change this society' (cited in *Newsweek*, 18 June 2004).

Wikinews

Wikinews – 'the free news source you can write' according to its main page – represents a similarly bold venture launched under the rippling banner of citizen journalism. The site's principal aim, as detailed in its mission statement, is to 'create a diverse environment where citizen journalists can independently report the news on a wide variety of current events'. Computer programmer Ward Cunningham is widely credited with creating the first wiki-software in 1995. Evidently his 'writeable web page' program acquired the term 'wiki' from the Hawaiian phrase 'wiki wiki' (meaning 'quick') which he had happened to notice was being used by a bus service on the islands during his honeymoon visit. Several years later he was contacted by internet entrepreneur Jimbo Wales, who was curious to know whether the 'wiki' concept could be applied to an online encyclopaedia he was planning to develop. In essence, a wiki is an editable page that enables any user to post an item or, alternatively, edit or correct anyone else's item (or even vote for it to be removed) within a wider social network. Any changes made will be recorded for viewing, and can be easily reversed – or further improved upon – by the next person. What would soon prove to work for Wales's multilingual encyclopaedia, Wikipedia, would be pressed into service to create the nascent news service Wikinews soon after.

Wikinews is an initiative of the non-profit Wikimedia Foundation, its parent organization, based in St Petersburg, Florida. Founded by Wales, the Foundation oversees its extraordinarily popular Wikipedia, launched online in January 2001. Wikipedia operates by drawing upon the energies of dedicated volunteers, being financed on the basis of donations from its community of supporters (no online advertising is allowed to appear). The Wiki commitment to developing free, open content for the public in a manner that is ideologically 'neutral' is intended to overcome the digital divide of information inequality. The Wikipedia project is guided by transparent decision-making, where posted entries are never complete, being open to revision and elaboration by anyone at any time. For better or for worse, there is no 'deference to experts' – everyone enjoys equal status within a larger process of 'collective intelligence'. 'Imagine a world in which every single person on the planet is given free access to the sum of all human knowledge. That's what we're doing', states Wales with reference to Wikipedia. In the case of Wikinews, however, a related point is made. 'If the mainstream media can't do good, unbiased journalism,' he adds, 'then we'll have to do it for them' (cited in Ulmanu 2005).

Ideas about how best to establish a collaborative system of news-gathering and reporting continue to evolve. Evidently, the inspiration for Wikinews can be traced back to a two-sentence proposal contained in an anonymous post to the Meta-Wiki community. Writing under the name 'Fonzy' on 5 January 2003, Daniel Alston stated: 'I thought of another brilliant sister project idea: Wiki + news = Wikews. The point of this project is to have the news on a wide variety of subjects, unbiased and in detail.' Intrigued by this suggestion, Erik Möller (using the name Eloquence) drafted the original project proposal. In the months to follow, the idea gradually took shape – initially in the face of opposition expressed by some Wikipedians – with an eye to creating a rudimentary prototype for testing in 2004. A demonstration wiki was introduced by November, which led to a beta version being made operational on 3 December (a German edition was launched at the same time). This decision to proceed had been taken following an online vote, where it received widespread support. In the words of its mission statement:

> We seek to promote the idea of the citizen journalist, because we believe that everyone can make a useful contribution to painting the big picture of

> what is happening in the world around us. The time has come to create a free news source, by the people and for the people. We invite you to join us in this effort which has the potential to change the world forever.

By March 2005, the English version of Wikinews had reached 1000 pages, a remarkable achievement by any measure, albeit one that is easily overshadowed by the spectacular success of Wikipedia, with its millions of entries in over 200 languages. The wiki ethic at the heart of Wikinews invites a particular type of relationship with its volunteer journalists, or 'wikinewsies' as they are sometimes called, that revolves around their continued good will, reliability and – even though the vast majority of them post anonymously – shared accountability (see also Thorsen 2008; Bradshaw 2009).

Mutual trust and co-operation are the key 'checks and balances' guiding the conduct of Wikinews. Given that it is impossible to determine who has posted a particular entry, or altered someone else's, the site is always vulnerable to those seeking to deliberately compromise its integrity as an alternative news source. 'We live in a universe of new media with phenomenal opportunities for world-wide communications and research', remarked one individual claiming to have been defamed in a Wikipedia entry, 'but populated by volunteer vandals with poison-pen intellects' (cited in Seelye 2005). Of particular import for Wikinews in this regard is the policy to be followed by users when referring to points of fact. Specifically, all such sources used for information must be cited, and they must be verifiable, at least in principle, by someone else. In the case of original reporting, field notes must be presented on the article's discussion (Talk) page. 'In Wikipedia, the writing style of an encyclopedia is more timeless', Wales explains. 'You can get it right eventually. It's going to be the same article for many years. With a news story, the actual story has a limited lifespan. If it's not neutral, you've got to fix it quickly' (cited in Glasner 2004b). Disputes over points of fact and interpretation are inevitable, of course, as the site's policy guidelines readily concede: 'None of us are mind-readers, and as nifty as Wikinews is, even this is not a perfect communication medium.' In encouraging users to be patient and polite with one another, it also offers specific tips for resolving problems. Criticisms, as one might expect for a fledgling site, are not in short supply. Some point to gaps in the coverage – identifying important stories that escaped the attention of Wikinews – while others highlight the scoops achieved by the network of volunteer reporters. Still others complain that too large a percentage of the items are rewritten news stories from elsewhere, when what the site needs is more original reporting (a criticism also directed at IndyMedia, as noted above).

Easily the most contentious policy adopted by Wikinews is its insistence that a 'neutral point of view' (NPOV) be upheld by its citizen journalists. For Wales,

NPOV is 'absolute and non-negotiable' for several reasons, the most important of which is that it is the only way to prevent bias ('If you want to tell the world what you think,' he argues, 'try blogging'; cited in Mandel 2005). The incentive for users to avoid exhibiting bias in their writing is readily apparent – failure to do so will mean that your words will be promptly rewritten by someone else. 'The only way it can survive,' he points out, 'is if your writing is acceptable to an extremely wide audience' (cited in Glasner 2004b). In maintaining that news items should be written without bias, the policy revolves around the belief that it is possible to ensure that differing views can be represented fairly. Rather than suggesting that a single, 'objective' point of view is advanced, each item should avoid advocating (explicitly or implicitly) a particular position at the expense of alternative ones. In Wales's original formulation, the NPOV clause states:

> The neutral point of view attempts to present ideas and facts in such a fashion that both supporters and opponents can agree. Of course, 100% agreement is not possible; there are ideologues in the world who will not concede to any presentation other than a forceful statement of their own point of view. We can only seek a type of writing that is agreeable to essentially rational people who may differ on particular points.

Given the site's acknowledgement that 'people are inherently biased', an emphasis is placed on encouraging 'intellectual independence' by presenting multiple viewpoints as fairly as possible so that users can make up their own minds about what to accept as true. 'Neutrality subverts dogmatism' is a key philosophical tenet, one to be rendered in practice as: 'presenting conflicting views without asserting them'. In other words, the prevailing understanding of NPOV is that it is not actually a point of view at all, but rather the conviction that 'when one writes neutrally, one is very careful not to state (or imply or insinuate or subtly massage the reader into believing) that any particular view at all is correct'. The belief that 'fact' can be separated out from 'opinion' – a longstanding, if in my view highly problematic, principle of impartial journalism – is in this way given a novel reinflection to the extent that it is made possible by collaborative contributions from across the community of users.

Accordingly, in contrast with IndyMedia's political agenda, on the one hand, and OhmyNews, where users are free to express a subjective opinion, on the other, Wikinews occupies a more traditional journalistic realm. Not surprisingly, the experiment in reader-written news had been watched closely by commentators – as well as by rival news organizations – from around the world. Enthusiastic speculation about other possible applications of the idea, including its potential to facilitate reader involvement in a news organization's investigations (although user statistics show that it is a tiny fraction of the total users who actually involve themselves in the writing and editing), encountered its opposite in the form of scepticism about its viability as a business model. Some considered the wiki format to be irreconcilable, by definition, with the 'brand' of a news organization based on accuracy, amongst other criticisms. Amongst those at least willing to applaud the spirit of the wiki initiative is Jan Schaffer of J-Lab: The Institute for Interactive Journalism. 'There is an enormous capacity for citizens to want to be able to participate in news and information in various ways,' she contends, by 'interacting with it, questioning it, truth-squaring it and creating it. And now that they have the tech tools and the tech skills to do that, the appetite has only increased' (transcript, The NewsHour with Jim Lehrer, 16 November 2005).

Above dispute, in any case, is the way in which Wikinews allows its users endless scope to pursue stories that matter to them. No undue influence is exercised by corporate proprietors, nor are market forces brought to bear, when determining what counts as a newsworthy event deserving of coverage. Still, it is worth noting the extent to which the types of news items they produce tend to reproduce, to varying degrees, journalistic features broadly consistent with mainstream reporting. David Speakman, a Wikinews administrator (whose username is Davod), underlines this point. 'I don't think we at Wikinews have tapped the full capabilities of collaborative journalism for original reporting', he stated. 'Many of the writers are new to news, and try to model themselves after what they are familiar with – newspaper reporting' (cited in Glasner 2004b). There can be little doubt, however, that the potential of Wikinews to contribute to the slow dismantling of several of the more restrictive of these conventions is coming into clearer focus as it evolves. 'We invite you to join us in this effort,' the site's mission statement declares, 'which has the potential to change the world forever.'

'The real reality news'

Efforts to trace the moment 'citizen journalism' entered the journalism lexicon, I noted above, recurrently begin in the aftermath of the South Asian tsunami, when the term itself was appropriated into the journalistic lexicon. With the benefit of hindsight, the significance of the tsunami reporting for what was being increasingly described as a 'citizen journalism movement' in the press became more apparent throughout 2005. The summer of that year, in particular, saw two crises unfold that appeared to consolidate its imperatives, effectively dispensing with claims that it was a passing 'fad' or 'gimmick' for all but its fiercest critics. The bombs that exploded in London on 7 July, like the devastation wreaked by Hurricane Katrina the following month, necessarily figure in any evaluative assessment of how citizen journalism has rewritten certain longstanding reportorial principles.

Particularly vexing for any journalist during a crisis is the need to secure access to the scene. On 7 July, it was impossible to gain entry to London Underground stations because of tight security, which meant that the aftermath of the explosions was beyond reach and out of sight. On the other side of the emergency services' cordons, however, were ordinary Londoners, some of whom were in possession of mobile telephones equipped with digital cameras. These tiny lenses captured the scene of fellow commuters trapped underground, with many of the resultant images resonating with what some aptly described as an eerie, even claustrophobic quality. Video clips taken with cameras were judged to be all the more compelling because they were dim, grainy and shaky, and – even more important – because they were documenting an angle to an event as it was actually happening. 'Those pictures captured the horror of what it was like to be trapped underground', Sky News executive editor John Ryley suggested (cited in *Press Gazette*, 14 July 2005). 'We very quickly received a video shot by a viewer on a train near King's Cross through a mobile', he further recalled. 'And we had some heart-rending, grim stories sent by mobile. It's a real example of how news has changed as technology has changed' (cited in *Independent on Sunday*, 10 July 2005).

Many of these photographs, some breathtaking in their poignancy, were viewed thousands of times within hours of their posting on sites such as Flickr.com or Moblog.co.uk. It was precisely this quality that journalists and editors at major news sites were looking for when quickly sifting through the vast array of images emailed to them. 'Within minutes of the first blast,' Helen Boaden, BBC director of news, affirmed, 'we had received images from the public and we had 50 images within an hour' (cited in the *Guardian*, 8 July 2005). 'This is the first time mobile phone images have been used in such large numbers to cover an event like this', *Evening Standard* production editor Richard Oliver declared. It shows 'how this technology can transform the newsgathering process. It provides access to eyewitness images at the touch of a button, speeding up our reaction time to major breaking stories.' Local news organizations, in his view, were 'bound to tap into this resource more and more in future' (cited in *National Geographic News*, 11 July 2005).

Later the same summer, as Hurricane Katrina caused severe destruction along the Gulf Coast in the United States, citizen journalism was once again at the fore. Voices from within major organizations were quick to concede that it was augmenting their news coverage in important ways. 'I think Katrina was the highest profile story in which news sites were able to fill in the gaps where government wasn't able to provide information, where people were unable to communicate with each other', observed Manuel Perez, supervising producer of

CNN.com. 'A lot of the most compelling info we got was from citizen journalism' (cited in Online News Association, 28 October 2005; see also Vis 2009). Lewis D'Vorkin, editor in chief of AOL News, in reflecting on the ways in which source material was generated by ordinary people, described the site as 'the people's platform'. The interactive nature of the online news experience, he believed, meant that it could offer 'real-time dialogue' between users joining in to shape the news. In D'Vorkin's words:

> While citizen journalism has existed in forms through letters to the editor, 'man on the street' interviews and call-in radio or television shows, the widespread penetration of the Web has promoted the citizen journalist to a new stature. With new technology tools in hand, individuals are blogging, sharing photos, uploading videos and podcasting to tell their firsthand accounts of breaking news so that others can better understand. What we did is the future of news, except it's happening now.
>
> (Cited in WebProNews, 6 September 2005)

The significance of participatory journalism, where 'everyday people' are able to 'take charge of their stories', has taken this long to be properly acknowledged, in his view. 'Can't do it in TV, can't do it in newspapers. That personal involvement is what the whole online news space is all about' (cited in *Los Angeles Times*, 10 September 2005). Michael Tippett, founder of NowPublic.com, concurred. In underscoring the extent to which journalism is being effectively democratized, he contended that perceptions of the journalist as an impersonal, detached observer were being swept away. 'This is the real reality news', Tippett insisted. 'People are uploading videos and publishing blog entries, saying, "Let me tell you about my husband who just died." It's a very powerful thing to have that emotional depth and first-hand experience, rather than the formulaic, distancing approach of the mainstream media' (cited in Lasica 2005).

In the years since, there has been no shortage of crisis events that have similarly figured in appraisals of the changing nature of the relationship between 'professional' journalism and its 'amateur' alternatives. Examples are numerous, but any attempt to list them would likely include the citizen reporting of the Buncefield oil depot explosion in the United Kingdom, the Mumbai train bombings, the protesting monks of Myanmar, the execution of Saddam Hussein, the shootings at Virginia Tech University, and the Wenchuan earthquake (Allan 2006; Allan and Thorsen 2009; Nip 2009; Zelizer 2009), amongst others. More recently, the hostage crisis in Mumbai in November 2008 effectively underscored the role played by citizen journalists using the microblogging service Twitter feeds to relay vital insights warranting much comment in press accounts. Time and again, Twitter was singled out for praise as the best source for real-time citizen news. 'Last night,' Claudine Beaumont of the *Daily Telegraph* pointed out, 'the social web came of age' (*Daily Telegraph*, 27 November 2008). Stephanie Busari (2008) of CNN agreed: 'It was the day social media appeared to come of age and signaled itself as a news-gathering force to be reckoned with.' Still, if Twitter deserved praise as 'a useful tool for mobilizing efforts and gaining eyewitness accounts during a disaster', she cautioned, doubts remained about its status as a trustworthy news source in its own right.

Redefining journalism

It is readily apparent that what counts as journalism in the 'network society' (Castells 2000) is in a state of flux. Familiar reportorial principles are being recast anew by competing imperatives of convergence in the mainstream media – and by those of divergence being played out in the margins by 'the people formerly known as the audience', to use blogger Jay Rosen's (2006) apt turn of phrase.

Not surprisingly, given the bold – even, at times, apocalyptic – pronouncements being made regarding the very future of journalism in this regard, there is little sign that differences in fervently held opinions will be resolved any time soon. Even where there is a shared sense that major news organizations – struggling to cope with slashed budgets in recessionary times – will be increasingly relying upon the appropriation of first-person news reporting, views differ markedly over who should be held responsible for any lapses in quality. While some believe that the occasional mishap should not be allowed to undermine a news organization's commitment to empowering citizens to be reporters, a praiseworthy form of democratization in their eyes, others discern in such incidents a portent of crisis that threatens to unravel the very integrity of the journalistic craft itself.

Citizen journalism is helping to reorganize the communicative networks in ways that have profound implications for the geo-politics of informational power and control. In those countries where the state equates dissent with criminality, where the basic principles of press freedom cannot be taken for granted, the indefatigable determination of ordinary citizens to speak truth to power is remarkable. In seeking to make their claim for such principles, citizen journalists have often paid a very high personal price for challenging the interests of the powerful and the privileged with alternative forms of news reporting. Repressive governments around the world have sought to place strict limits on the blogosphere, refusing to recognize the right of the citizen – let alone the citizen journalist – to express himself or herself freely, without prior restraint or censorship.

In civil-war-torn Liberia, for example, Alfred Sirleaf's efforts to perform a role akin to the citizen journalist are a case in point. As the managing editor of the *Daily Talk*, he writes up news and editorials on a chalkboard positioned on the street outside his 'newsroom' hut every day, thereby providing passersby with important insights into what is happening in Monrovia. Equipped with his 'nose for a good scoop', this 'self-taught newshound' scours newspapers – and calls on an informal network of friends acting as correspondents – for the information necessary to keep everyone 'in the know'. News stories – three or four of which are displayed each morning – are concisely written, relying on street words that people actually use themselves (thus 'big stealing' rather than 'embezzlement', for example). 'I like to write the way people talk so they can understand it well', he told *The New York Times*. 'You got to reach the common [person]' (cited in Polgreen 2006). Crucially, Pru Clarke (2008) points out, Sirleaf has recognized two significant points:

> First, that the war continued because the young soldiers and their supporters didn't have access to any information. [Warlord Charles Taylor] brainwashed them into believing that fighting for him would bring them riches and power. They believed Taylor's fraudulent claims to be the rightful leader, and that Taylor's enemies would subjugate them if they won. They needed to hear the truth if they were to see Taylor for what he was, and to stop fighting. Sirleaf also realized that after a decade of war more than half the Liberian people were illiterate. Those who could read couldn't understand the flowery, overblown prose of the government-sanctioned newspapers. (I still struggle to understand them!) Neither could they afford to pay for them.
>
> (Clarke 2008)

For those unable to read words on a chalkboard, there are symbols: a blue helmet hanging beside the board means that the story involves the United Nations peacekeeping force, while a chrome hubcap represents the president (the 'iron lady' of Liberian politics). In previous years Sirleaf's dedication to citizen reporting has met resistance from those in power during the Taylor regime; he was arrested and spent a brief spell in prison, then went into exile while his newsstand was torn down. Today, with his plywood hut rebuilt, he remains steadfast in his belief that what he is doing matters for the country's emergent democracy. '*Daily Talk*'s objective is that everybody should absorb the news', he maintains. 'Because when a few people out there make decisions on behalf of the masses that do not go down with them, we are all going to be victims' (cited in Polgreen 2006).

To close, the examples of citizen journalism briefly touched upon in this chapter highlight a number of pressing issues. Taken together, they are indicative of a communication continuum that stretches from the BBC, to the Drudge Report to OhmyNews, but also encompasses the lone voices of individuals – such as Alfred Sirleaf above – struggling to be heard against dauntingly formidable odds. Celebratory proclamations about the 'global village' engendered by Web 2.0 ring hollow when we are reminded, in turn, that the majority of the world's population has never made a telephone call, let alone logged on to a computer (see also Bosch 2009; Sonwalkar 2009; Waisbord 2009).

This chapter has sought to assess some of the reasons why new forms of dialogue need to be encouraged regarding citizen journalism today, as well as about where it may be heading tomorrow. In drawing attention to how crisis events in particular throw into sharp relief the imperatives underpinning this debate, the importance of this dialogue becomes all the more apparent. At stake is nothing less than the future of journalism itself. 'We used to call mainstream journalism the "first draft of history" ', Dan Gillmor (2005) has observed. 'Now, I'd argue, much of that first draft is being written by citizen journalists. And what they're telling us is powerful indeed' (see also Deuze 2009; Fiedler 2009; Singer and Ashman 2009). In agreeing with this view, I would add that it signals a further challenge, namely for all of us to discover new ways to recast the rigid, zero-sum dichotomies of the 'professional versus amateur' debate. This will necessarily entail thinking anew about the social responsibilities of the citizen as journalist while, at the same time, reconsidering those of the journalist as citizen.

11 'GOOD JOURNALISM IS POPULAR CULTURE'

> Good journalism *is* popular culture, but popular culture that stretches and informs its consumers rather than that which appeals to the ever descending lowest common denominator. If, by popular culture, we mean expressions of thought or feeling that require no work of those who consume them, then decent popular journalism is finished. What is happening today, unfortunately, is that the lowest form of popular culture – lack of information, misinformation, disinformation, and a contempt for the truth or the reality of most people's lives – has overrun real journalism.
>
> (Carl Bernstein, investigative journalist)

> Our media, which should be informing us, are instead turning out the light and joining the stampede from reality in the blind and mad pursuit of commercial advantage, of profit without honour. The culture of celebrity, like an army of ants, has colonized the news pages both tabloid and broadsheet. That raises the question: when Armageddon threatens, isn't it time – even past time – to work out what, in the sum of things, is the relative news value of a weather person's love life or a footballer's grazed eyebrow?
>
> (Martin Bell, former BBC correspondent)

Bold declarations about the importance of journalism for modern democracy, typically expressed with the sorts of rhetorical flourishes first heard in the early days of the newspaper, are sounding increasingly problematic. Familiar appeals to journalism's traditional role or mission, its social responsibilities *vis-à-vis* a citizenry actively engaging with the pressing issues of the day, appear to have lost much of their purchase. Public criticism – if not outright cynicism – about the quality of the news reporting provided by mainstream media institutions is widespread. Journalists themselves are more often than not seen to be troubled, some quietly lamenting the lost traditions of a once-proud profession, others loudly resisting market-driven obsessions with 'bottom line' profitability. Journalism's commitment to championing the public interest, many of them fear, is being replaced with a cheap and tawdry celebration of what interests the public. It almost goes without saying, of course, that these types of concerns about reportorial integrity are as old as journalism itself, but in these tumultuous times seem to be resonating in new ways.

As will be apparent from the first of the two quotations above, this concluding chapter takes its title from a highly controversial intervention into debates about journalistic practice initiated by one of the most famous reporters in the world, Carl Bernstein. His name, along with that of his former colleague Bob Woodward, is for many people synonymous with the phrase 'investigative reporting'. These were the two reporters who broke the 'Watergate' story on the pages of the *Washington Post*, thereby sparking an investigation into one of the most significant political scandals in United States history. Together with their sources, one of the most important of which was identified only as 'deep throat', they exposed a range of illegal activities being conducted in the highest echelons of the US government. Their news reports, produced under extremely difficult circumstances, set in motion a chain of events which eventually led to the resignation of a disgraced President Richard Nixon under threat of imminent impeachment on 9 August 1974. Bernstein and Woodward proceeded to write a book about their experiences, entitled *All the President's Men*, which was subsequently turned into a critically acclaimed Hollywood film of the same title.

Almost two decades after these momentous events, Bernstein (1992) offered several reflections on post-Watergate journalism to the readers of *The New Republic* magazine in an essay entitled 'The idiot culture'. In sharp, incisive terms, he pinpoints a series of ongoing developments which together appear to be threatening the integrity of what he calls 'real journalism'. Where principled reporting typically relies on 'shoe leather', 'common sense' and a 'respect for the truth', he argues, what currently passes as journalism is regularly failing its audience in many crucial respects. In Bernstein's words:

> increasingly the America rendered today in the American media is illusionary and delusionary – disfigured, unreal, disconnected from the true context of our lives. In covering actually existing American life, the media – weekly, daily, hourly – break new ground in getting it wrong. The coverage is distorted by celebrity and the worship of celebrity; by the reduction of news to gossip, which is the lowest form of news; by

> sensationalism, which is always a turning away from a society's real condition; and by a political and social discourse that we – the press, the media, the politicians, *and* the people – are turning into a sewer.
>
> (Bernstein 1992: 22)

It is Bernstein's perception that there is an alarming degree of arrogance among journalism's practitioners, attributable in part to a persistent failure to engage in self-reflexive scrutiny where their social obligations are concerned. Particularly troubling are the implications of what is a growing emphasis on 'speed and quantity' at the expense of 'thoroughness and quality', let alone 'accuracy and context'. 'The pressure to compete, the fear that somebody else will make the splash first,' he observes, 'creates a frenzied environment in which a blizzard of information is presented and serious questions may not be raised' (Bernstein 1992: 24). Even in those rare instances where such questions are posed, he argues, only seldomly do they engender the considered, thoughtful reporting they deserve.

Accordingly, as the types of reporting Bernstein holds to be indicative of 'real journalism' recede, a 'sleazoid infotainment culture' is slowly becoming entrenched as the norm. The once clear division between the 'serious' and the 'popular' newspaper press, for example, is now increasingly being blurred. Such is also the case between talk show programmes, such as the *Oprah Winfrey Show, Donahue* or *Geraldo*, and news programmes, such as *60 Minutes* or *Nightline*, where differences in their news values are often virtually indistinguishable (see also Sholle 1993; Lull and Hinerman 1997; Shattuc 1997; Langer 1998; Dovey 2000; Ellis 2000; Glynn 2000; Kellner 2003). To the extent that it is possible to speak of news agendas when using a language of 'infotainment', he suggests that there is a direct correlation between the rise of these 'Donahue–Geraldo–Oprah freak shows' and the more recently emergent forms of 'trash journalism'. As Bernstein (1992) declares:

> In this new culture of journalistic titillation, we teach our readers and our viewers that the trivial is significant, that the lurid and the loopy are more important than real news. We do not serve our readers and viewers, we pander to them. And we condescend to them, giving them what we think they want and what we calculate will sell and boost ratings and readership. Many of them, sadly, seem to justify our condescension, and to kindle at the trash. Still, it is the role of journalists to challenge people, not merely to amuse them.
>
> (Bernstein 1992: 24–5)

Hence the fear expressed by Bernstein that journalists are contributing to the formation of an 'idiot culture', one which is rendered distinct from popular culture by its obsession with 'the weird and the stupid and the coarse'. The

US, it follows, is gradually being transformed into a 'talk-show nation', where 'public discourse is reduced to ranting and raving and posturing'. At a time when 'good journalism' is 'the exception and not the rule', he contends, searching questions need to be asked about the responsibilities of the news media *vis-à-vis* the public interest (see also Charity 1995; Merritt 1995; Rosen 1999 on one response, namely 'public journalism').

Many of these points strike an equally powerful resonance in other national contexts. In France, for example, the highly influential sociologist Pierre Bourdieu recently found himself at the centre of a heated public controversy following two lectures he delivered concerning the current state of journalism via the television station of the Collège de France (chosen so as to bypass network control). The lectures were subsequently developed into a short book which became a surprise best-seller in France. Publicity for Bourdieu's intervention was provided, if not with that precise intention in mind, by several journalists furious with his characterization of their profession and its alleged failings. There followed a series of (often acrimonious) exchanges between Bourdieu and his critics which appeared, among other places, on the pages of the monthly journal *Le Monde diplomatique* (see also Marlière 1998). Several interesting insights into the nature of the dispute are provided in the 'Prologue' to the English language edition of the book, published as *On Television and Journalism* (Bourdieu 1998).

Over the course of these lectures, Bourdieu (1998: 2) sought to show how what he terms the 'journalistic field', for him a 'microcosm with its own laws', 'produces and imposes on the public a very particular vision of the political field, a vision that is grounded in the very structure of the journalistic field and in journalists' specific interests produced in and by that field.' Any form of serious political commentary, he argues, is consistently losing out to those forms of news discourse which give priority to simply entertaining the viewer, listener or reader. In-depth current affairs interviews on television, for example, are routinely being transformed into 'mindless talk show chatter' between 'approved' (that is to say, 'safe') speakers willing to participate in what are largely staged 'exchanges'. This relentless search for the sensational and the spectacular, he argues, ensures that an undue emphasis is placed on certain types of dramatic events which are simple to cover. As Bourdieu (1998) elaborates:

> To justify this policy of demagogic simplification (which is absolutely and utterly contrary to the democratic goal of informing or educating people by interesting them), journalists point to the public's expectations. But in fact they are projecting onto the public their own inclinations and their own views. Because they're so afraid of being boring, they opt for

> confrontations over debates, prefer polemics over rigorous argument, and in general, do whatever they can to promote conflict.
>
> (Bourdieu 1998: 3–4)

It follows that individuals seeking to secure access to what he terms 'public space', particularly politicians, have little choice but to adapt to the demands of the journalistic field. Journalists effectively control who can be recognized as a public figure, a process shaped by their perception of who or what is 'interesting', 'exceptional' or 'catchy' *for them*, that is, from the position they occupy in this space. 'In short,' Bourdieu (1998: 51) argues, 'the focus is on those things which are apt to arouse curiosity but require no analysis, especially in the political sphere.'

In suggesting that the journalistic field possesses a relative degree of autonomy from other fields of cultural production, such as the juridical, literary, artistic or scientific fields, Bourdieu is attempting to move beyond any explanation of its characteristics which points exclusively to economic factors. As important as these factors are in shaping what is reported and how, he is aiming to identify the social conditions underpinning journalism as a collective activity which 'smoothes over things, brings them into line, and depoliticizes them' to the 'level of anecdote and scandal'. If sensational news equals market success, then professional standards cannot help but be influenced by audience ratings in a detrimental way. 'Everybody knows the "law" that if a newspaper or other news vehicle wants to reach a broad public,' he writes, 'it has to dispense with sharp edges and anything that might divide or exclude readers.' In other words, he adds: 'It must attempt to be inoffensive, not to "offend anyone", and it must never bring up problems – or, if it does, problems that don't pose any problems' (Bourdieu 1998: 44). Hence despite the fierce relations of competition which exist between different news organizations, the quest for exclusivity (or 'scoops') recurrently yields coverage which is as uniform as it is banal. Consequently, he argues, once the decisive impact of the journalistic field upon other fields is taken into consideration, the current extent of public disenchantment with politics is hardly surprising.

In Britain, it is similarly possible to map the growing prominence of these types of arguments across the public sphere, not least in the forums of debate created by journalists who are more often than not finding themselves on the defensive. One need not agree with every aspect of the arguments advanced above to recognize, as of course many journalists do, that the types of news values once associated with 'serious reporting' are being dramatically recast (see MacGregor 1997; Petley 1997; Aldridge 1998; Bromley 1998a; Curran and Park 2000; McNair 2000; Barnett and Gaber 2001; Keeble 2001; Allan 2002; Cottle 2003a, 2003b; Corner and Pels 2003; Hargreaves 2003; Campbell 2004;

Rowe 2009). In the words of an editorial leader in *The Economist*, the features of a 'modern paradox' are becoming ever more pronounced:

> [I]n this age of globalisation, news is much more parochial than in the days when communications from abroad ticked slowly across the world by telegraph. And here is another [paradox]: that in this information age, newspapers which used to be full of politics and economics are thick with stars and sport.
>
> (*The Economist*, 4 July 1998: 13)

Recent trends in journalism, at least from the vantage point of *The Economist*, suggest that news is 'moving away from foreign affairs towards domestic concerns; away from politics towards human-interest stories; away from issues to people'. The principal explanation cited for these trends is the rapidly growing array of specialist information sources (as 'rolling' news on television, such as BBC News 24 and Sky News, proliferate, publishing costs drop, and the internet expands) becoming available as competition between increasingly market-sensitive news organizations accelerates. It is significant, however, that the editorial leader goes on to reassure its readers that at the end of the day there is little cause for concern: 'People absorb what interests them: if news is too worthy, it goes in one ear and out the other.'

Curiously enough, a 2008 report published by a House of Lords (2008) select committee revealed that during its investigation into news media ownership, the editors interviewed were unwilling to concede that 'hard' news was being abandoned in favour of more entertaining, market-driven alternatives. The report states:

> None of the Editors we talked to were willing to admit to a shift towards a softer news agenda. When asked what type of story was most likely to boost sales they cited strong news stories such as terrorist atrocities. Rebekah Wade [editor of the *Sun*] explained 'there is still a critical place for newspapers' in explaining very big stories. Nevertheless we note that Ms Wade did admit that even her own proprietor [Rupert Murdoch] was 'dismayed by the amount of celebrity coverage' in the *Sun*.
>
> (House of Lords 2008: 18)

Evidence to the contrary was presented by others, however. Ofcom, the independent regulator and competition authority for the UK communications industries, stated that where commercial radio news agendas were concerned, the 'balance between "soft" and "hard" news has, however, swung towards softer news, exposing a clear correlation with pressures on revenue and subsequent reduction in news staff at individual radio stations' (House of Lords 2008: 29). A further insight into 'soft vs hard news' tensions was presented to the committee by Roger Ailes, Chair and CEO of Fox News in the US. In the words of the report:

> Mr Ailes explained that Fox News balance what the audience is looking for with what it is important for them to know 'the appeal of the story plays some role in its prominence'. The emphasis is on domestic news and not on foreign coverage. Fox News is not interested in 'the failure of the Russian wheat harvest'. They have experimented with limiting their coverage of soft news stories. A case in point was the death of Anna Nicole Smith (Smith was a page three model who married a very elderly oil baron). Fox News experimented by not running this story hour-after-hour like the other channels. However, each time they took it off air CNN beat them in the ratings. Mr Ailes explained that sometimes they would like to walk away from a story, but it is difficult to do so. He was clear that he has to respond to market pressures and that the channel exists 'in a ratings society'.
>
> (Minutes of the Meeting with Roger Ailes, in House of Lords 2008: 116)

This testimony is as disingenuous as it is self-serving, in my view, but it does usefully underscore how certain constraints attributed to 'market pressures' in a 'ratings society' translate into justifications for softer, shallower – and more profitable – types of reporting.

Ratings, profits and relevance

Howard Beale, sometimes described as 'the grand old man of news', was the UBS television network's lead anchor for the evening newscast. He often spoke of his commitment to journalistic integrity, and how he had learned his craft in the company of such luminaries as Edward R. Murrow in the early days of broadcasting. Times were changing, however, and the audience ratings for his newscast had started to slip. A once healthy 28 per cent share of the audience declined to a 22 per cent share over recent years, before slowly spiralling downwards to a 12 per cent share. The network's executives, all too aware of the implications for advertising revenue, made the decision that changes would have to be introduced. The president of the News Division dutifully informed Beale that he was fired, effective in two weeks' time.

During the evening newscast the next day, Beale turned to the camera and made the following announcement:

> Ladies and gentlemen, I would like at this moment to announce that I will be retiring from this program in two weeks' time because of poor ratings.

> Since this show was the only thing I had going for me in my life, I have decided to kill myself. I'm gonna blow my brains out right on this program a week from today. Tune in next Tuesday. That should give the public relations people a week to promote the show. We ought to get a hell of a rating out of that – a fifty share, easy.

Chaos broke loose, beginning in the television studio (where Beale was literally removed from his newsdesk), but soon spreading across the country as viewers reacted. Beale found himself at the centre of a media storm, while the network's switchboard was deluged with angry calls. The ensuing crisis was compounded for network executives, however, by the fact that with the prospect of watching an on-air suicide in the offing, the newscast's audience share had surged upwards. Beale's request to be allowed back on the air, so as to bid farewell to the viewers in a more dignified manner, was granted. He quickly seized the opportunity, however, to unleash a furious tirade. Speaking to reporters afterwards, he declared: 'Every day, five days a week, for fifteen years, I've been sitting behind the desk, the dispassionate pundit, reporting with seemly detachment the daily parade of lunacies that constitute the news and just once I wanted to say what I really felt.'

For network executives struggling to justify the continued existence of a news division to shareholders upset about the annual $33 million deficit it incurred (evidently the division produced 'the lowest rate of return' on their investment), the dramatic increase in ratings generated by Beale's newfound notoriety had to be maintained. In order to capitalize on it, they offered him his own show, where he could speak his mind freely. Beale accepted, promptly becoming 'the mad prophet of the airwaves' for the network. Infuriated by the state of current affairs, such as the economy, inflation and the oil crisis, he challenged and provoked his viewers in equal measure. During one show, he issued them a command: 'I want you to get up right now, sit up, go to your windows, open them and stick your head out and yell – "I'm as mad as hell and I'm not going to take this anymore!" ' Over the course of the shows that followed, he targeted a wide range of social concerns, not least the influence of television itself. 'Television is not the truth,' he declared, '[it is an] amusement park. Television is a circus, a carnival, a travelling troupe of acrobats, storytellers, dancers, singers, jugglers, side-show freaks, lion tamers and football players. We're in the boredom-killing business.' Unfortunately, if all too predictably, Beale himself eventually became boring to viewers, whose attention drifted away in favour of more entertaining distractions on the rival networks. The steady decline in ratings forced the hand of anxious executives, who arranged to have Beale assassinated – during a live broadcast, naturally enough – in a desperate effort to preserve the network's profitability.

The story of Howard Beale is a fictional one, fortunately enough, having been memorably depicted in the film *Network* (1976). Nominated for ten Academy Awards, winning four of them, writer Paddy Chayefsky's treatment of 'the hollow, lurid wasteland of television journalism' (to borrow one film reviewer's apt turn of phrase) attracted considerable public interest at the time. Watching it today, however, its critique resonates even more deeply. *Network*, as the discussion above suggests, is remarkably prescient in its anticipation of the problems that currently beset television journalism. In the US – the film is set in New York – the main three television networks are owned by multinational corporations, all of which have their primary interests invested in areas outside of journalism. ABC News is owned by the Walt Disney Company, CBS News is part of Viacom, and NBC News is controlled by General Electric. In the mid-1970s, when *Network* appeared in cinemas, these three networks' newscasts reached more than 70 per cent of the audience. Today, it frequently falls below 30 per cent – indeed, as Barkin (2003) points out, 'it is not at all unusual for the combined network rating for the three newscasts to be less than that of the 1970s CBS by itself' (2003: 4). This state of decline is attributable to a number of different factors, each of which – to varying degrees – has undermined the traditional conceptions of prestige and public service once associated with national newscasts. 'In the golden age – the 1970s – the network really regarded the news division as the jewels in the crown', Av Westin, a former vice president of ABC news, has observed. 'Now all of that is gone. The bottom line has become the paramount consideration, not the editorial line' (cited in *Boston Globe*, 2 March 2002; see also Compton 2009; Gans 2009; Petley 2009).

The logic of the corporate balance sheet dictates that a television network can make significantly more money by trimming news budgets, even eliminating them altogether wherever possible. It is precisely this bottom-line-driven logic which recently threatened one of the most distinguished newscasts in the US, namely ABC News's programme 'Nightline', anchored by Ted Koppel. In March of 2002, rumours emerged that ABC had made a strong bid to lure David Letterman, the host of the rival CBS network's 'Late Show', to occupy the 'Nightline' timeslot. It was envisaged that 'Late Show', with its frantic mix of Letterman's celebrity interviews with comedic material, including 'stupid pet tricks' and 'top-10 lists', would prove to be much more popular with the right sort of viewers. That is to say, while both 'Nightline' and 'Late Show' garnered about four million viewers a night, respectively, the latter programme secured a younger audience profile, which tends to be more attractive to advertisers. Of particular interest to advertisers are people of ages 18 to 34, who are judged to be much more likely to be seeking out entertainment, as opposed to news and information, especially at that time of day. More to the point, however, because these younger viewers have yet to make their 'brand choices', to use the language of product marketing, their 'eyeballs' are more lucrative than those of older viewers (who are less open to persuasion where advertised brands are concerned).

Evidently, the death knell for 'Nightline', one of the most celebrated news programmes in US broadcast history, had been sounded. News staffers expressed their outrage. 'People are enormously upset', stated one ABC News employee. 'This just came out of the blue. We're stunned' (*Washington Post*, 2 March 2002). In the absence of an official announcement from ABC News, much was made in press reports of various anonymous statements attributed to the network's executives. At stake for the network, it seemed, were the usual concerns about ratings and profits. Moreover, though, one executive had been widely quoted as stating: 'The relevancy of *Nightline* just is not there anymore.' Koppel (2002), in a response published in the *New York Times*, refuted these claims. 'Conservatively speaking,' he wrote, ' "Nightline" has earned well over half a billion dollars for a succession of corporate owners over the years. The program continues to be profitable to this day.' Regarding the allegation about relevancy, Koppel was blunt. '[I]n these times,' he argued, 'the regular and thoughtful analysis of national and foreign policy is more essential than ever.' Clearly angered, he added that 'it is, at best, inappropriate and, at worst, malicious to describe what my colleagues and I are doing as lacking relevance.' In the days to follow, claims and counter-claims continued to circulate, until Letterman announced on 11 March 2002 that he would be keeping his talk show at CBS, at least for the time being.

The thorny issue of 'relevancy' continues to linger, however. This controversy over the future of 'Nightline' had transpired some six months after the September 11 atrocities, the very time when national news organizations were insisting that significant changes were under way to enhance and reinvigorate national and international news coverage (see Zelizer and Allan 2002). The fact that ABC was 'even considering taking aim at "Nightline" was seen as an ominous sign inside the news division', as Rutenberg and Carter (2002) observed at the time. Indeed, they contend, it was perceived to be 'the latest of a number of slights and the most striking indication yet that the network's parent, the Walt Disney Company, would not hesitate to cut back on news to improve its balance sheet'. In the aftermath of the 'Nightline' crisis, many news commentators were wondering aloud whether television news on the national networks was on the verge of extinction. Several pointed to the overall decline of audience trends for network news programmes (especially, as noted above, in the case of younger viewers), suggesting that the 'writing was on the wall'. Others in a similar vein cited the proliferation of 24-hour cable and satellite news channels – namely CNN, Fox News, and MSNBC, respectively – for their impact on ratings. Still others maintained that the expansion of Web-based news sites was to blame for drawing potential viewers away from the networks. In any case, 'Nightline' was judged to be in a precarious situation – in the words of *New York Times* columnist Maureen Dowd (2002), it remained 'a lonely holdout with a strong commitment to journalistic principles'.

Nowhere are the journalistic principles of television news thrown into sharper relief than where the interests of public service collide with the private ones of shareholders. To the extent that the news agenda is determined by its potential for generating advertising revenue, newscasts will consistently prioritize stories revolving around crime, celebrity and 'lifestyle issues' over and above (expensive, less 'ratings-efficient') international stories. Martin Bell (2003), recently retired from the BBC after more than thirty years in journalism, is in little doubt that television news is on a downward trajectory. He contends that all too frequently it 'serves us less as a window on the world than as a barrier to it. Its screen is only a screen in the original sense – something that blocks our view of what lies on the other side of it' (2003: 6). Deserving of being singled out for particular criticism, Bell believes, are the rolling, 24-hour news services. They have special responsibilities, he writes, which are defined by F-words:

> They aim to be first and fastest with the news. Their nature, too often, is to be fearful, feverish, frenzied, frantic, frail, false and fallible. Some mistakes are bound to be made, as they always have been, by journalists seeking to discover the truth in the fog of breaking news; but those mistakes do not have to be as *systemic* as they have become in the rolling news business, when rumour masquerades as fact, and networks compete wildly with each other to get their speculation in first.
>
> (Bell 2003: 71; emphasis in original)

Bell is particularly troubled where the reporting of terrorism is concerned, but believes the point can be made more widely. In calling for a measure of self-criticism amongst journalists, as well as a code of practice (long overdue, in his opinion), he proceeds to issue an appeal for a return to first principles. The test of excellence, he argues, is not 'We got it first!' but rather 'We got it right!' (2003: 71; see also Robinson 2002; Dickinson 2009; Jacquette 2009; Thussu 2009).

More often than not, this incessant drive to be the first to break the story can mean that due care and accuracy are sacrificed in the heat of the moment. Turning to the ongoing crisis in Iraq, for example, a wide array of commentators have expressed their alarm about this drive for immediacy for its own sake, not least with regard to the implications for reportorial standards. Former BBC director general Greg Dyke effectively focused public attention on this problem in April 2003. Speaking at a journalism conference in London, he addressed the challenges confronting television news. 'We must temper the drama and competition of live, rolling news with the considered journalism and analysis people need to make sense of events', he argued (BBC News Online, 24 April 2003). More than that, however, Dyke added: 'Commercial pressures may tempt others to follow the Fox News formula of gung-ho patriotism but for the BBC this would be a terrible mistake.' In acknowledging that Fox News's partisan pro-Bush stance had helped it to overtake CNN in average daily viewer ratings, he insisted that such 'unquestioning' support for the White House was typical of the other US broadcast news media during the conflict. In a fragmented marketplace, he argued, no news operation was sufficiently strong or brave enough to stand up to government or military officials. Attempts to mix flag-waving patriotism with journalism, he feared, would inevitably undermine television news's credibility in the eyes of the public. 'Essential to the success of any news organisation,' he stated, 'is holding the trust of its audiences' (see also Preston 2008; McNair 2009; Meikle 2009; Owen and Purdey 2009; Rantanen 2009; Wahl-Jorgensen and Hanitzsch 2009).

Celebrities, tabloidization and infotainment

'If it bleeds,' the old saying goes, 'it leads.' This succinct – and, it has to be said, rather tactless – declaration of news values has long been associated with certain disreputable practices held to be characteristic of 'tabloid' journalism. Today, increasing numbers of critics believe that a process of convergence is under way, one where certain 'populist' preoccupations – by definition, vulgar, trivial, and 'downmarket' in style and (lack of) substance – can be blamed for blurring the once distinctive standards of 'quality' reporting. Many of these critics contend that this process will necessarily lead to 'bite-size McNugget journalism', to use the BBC's Andrew Marr's apt turn of phrase, and with it a 'dumbing down' effect. Some go even further, arguing that it is intensifying to the point that journalism's traditional social responsibilities are looking increasingly anachronistic in a world of 'reality-based' infotainment.

Several pressing concerns raised by this apparent convergence are pinpointed in Franklin's (1997) use of the term 'newszak' (a term which underpins his related notion of 'McJournalism': see Franklin 2005). Specifically, newszak is intended to characterize what he considers to be a growing tendency in British journalism to retreat from investigative, 'hard' news reporting in favour of ever 'softer', 'lighter' stories. The editorial priorities of journalism, he maintains, are being fundamentally realigned in accordance with the dictates of the marketplace:

> Entertainment has superseded the provision of information; human interest has supplanted the public interest; measured judgement has succumbed to sensationalism; the trivial has triumphed over the weighty; the intimate relationships of celebrities from soap operas, the world of sport or the royal family are judged more 'newsworthy' than the reporting of significant issues and events of international consequence. Traditional news values have been undermined by new values; 'infotainment' is rampant.
>
> (Franklin 1997: 4)

For Franklin, this transformation has profound implications for public information and democracy. 'Newszak', he writes, 'understands news as a product designed and "processed" for a particular market and delivered in increasingly homogenous "snippets" which make only modest demands on the audience' (1997: 4–5). Given the intensification of market pressures to compete over these audiences – as well as to attract advertisers interested in reaching them – the increasing prevalence of tabloid journalism, Franklin maintains, is hardly surprising. Moreover, to the extent that 'news is converted into entertainment', it follows that there will be a corresponding decline in the availability of other kinds of news, not least foreign, parliamentary and investigative reporting. In a regulatory climate where market-driven journalism is fast becoming the norm, he adds, newszak 'will flourish without restraint' (1997: 231; see also Dahlgren and Sparks 1992; Bird 1997; Lull and Hinerman 1997; Krajicek 1998; Stephenson and Bromley 1998; Berry 2000; Thompson 2000; Turner *et al.* 2000; Barnett and Gaber 2001; Bird 2002; Gitlin 2002; Corner and Pels 2003; Couldry 2003; Schudson 2003; Franklin 2005; Baym 2009; Rowe 2009; Thussu 2009).

Of the various 'populist' preoccupations informing tabloid news values, the growing influence of 'human-interest journalism' about celebrities is easily one of the most conspicuous. The origins of this form of news coverage can be traced at least as far back as the mid-nineteenth century, although arguably today's 'culture of celebrity' consolidated its more rudimentary features in journalistic terms shortly after the arrival of television (see Marshall 1997, 2005; Gabler 1998; Rojek 2001; Ponce de Leon 2002). In this regard, the perceptive insights of historian Daniel J. Boorstin's (1961) classic study, *The Image: A Guide to Pseudo-Events in America*, continue to warrant close attention. Written at a time when social critics were raising the alarm about what they perceived to be a crisis in standards and values in public life, Boorstin's commentary struck a chord across the political spectrum. Then, as now, fears were being expressed about the seemingly fabricated, inauthentic, frequently alienating nature of modern societies – or, in Boorstin's words, 'the thicket of unreality which stands between us and the facts of life' (1961: 3). Journalism, together with political rhetoric, advertising, public relations and the like, deserved to be criticized in his view for being complicit in the 'making of illusions which flood our experience'. More and more of this experience, he argues, actually consists of what he terms 'pseudo-events', that is, highly contrived occurrences taking place to satisfy the public demand for startling, vividly intriguing news. In a world where 'the shadow has become the substance', media celebrations of 'celebrity news', in particular, were figuring all too prominently.

'The celebrity,' Boorstin observes, 'is a person who is known for his [or her] well-knownness' (1961: 57). In order to unravel this apparent tautology, he suggests that the celebrity needs to be recognized as being, in effect, a human pseudo-event, someone whose persona is 'fabricated on purpose to satisfy our exaggerated expectations of human greatness' (1961: 58). To clarify what is at stake here, it is necessary to define what constitutes a pseudo-event in more detail. For Boorstin, it is a happening that possesses the following characteristics:

1 It is not spontaneous, but comes about because someone has planned, planted or incited it. Typically, it is not a train wreck or an earthquake, but an interview.
2 It is planted primarily (not always exclusively) for the immediate purpose of being reported or reproduced. Therefore, its occurrence is arranged for the convenience of the reporting or reproducing media. Its success is measured by how widely it is reported. Time relations in it are commonly fictitious or factitious; the announcement is given out in advance 'for future release' and written as if the event has occurred in the past. The question, 'Is it real?' is less important than, 'Is it newsworthy?'
3 Its relation to the underlying reality of the situation is ambiguous. Its interest arises largely from this very ambiguity. Concerning a pseudo-event the question, 'What does it mean?' has a new dimension. While the news interest in a train wreck is in *what* happened and in the real consequences, the interest in an interview is always, in a sense, in *whether* it really happened and in what might have been the motives. Did the statement really mean what it said? Without some of this ambiguity a pseudo-event cannot be very interesting.
4 Usually it is intended to be a self-fulfilling prophecy. The hotel's thirtieth anniversary celebration, by saying that the hotel is a distinguished institution, actually makes it one.

(Boorstin 1961: 11–12)

Once the 'machinery of information' has clicked into gear (reporters, like press agents, being vital cogs), the celebrity – in all likelihood 'notorious for [his or her] notoriety' – becomes an entertaining distraction for audiences. The public lives of individual celebrities may transpire in the blink of an eye, but journalism's penchant for the 'packaged' news of pseudo-events is ceaseless. 'In the democracy of pseudo-events,' he writes, 'anyone can become a celebrity, if only he [or she] can get into the news and stay there' (1961: 60).

The 'rising tide of pseudo-events', it follows, washes away the traditional distinction between 'hard' and 'soft' news. News events become little more than 'dramatic performances' (from interviews to news conferences, 'leaks' and self-promoting stunts) where everyone aims to follow their 'prepared script'. For journalists struggling to 'manufacture' news, the 'geometric progression' of one pseudo-event to the next is welcome, their very ritualization making reportorial tasks easier to handle. In other words, and here Boorstin makes one of his most biting remarks, 'Freedom of the Press' is often 'a euphemism for the prerogative of reporters to produce their synthetic commodity' (1961: 29). Amongst the few exceptions to this general rule, he maintains, is the reporting of crime. 'The world of crime,' he writes, 'is a last refuge of the authentic, uncorrupted spontaneous event' (1961: 254). Crimes, in the main, are not pseudo-events, given that they are only rarely committed for the purpose of being reported. Accordingly, in a society where the 'degradation of public tastes to the trivial and the unserious' is everywhere to see, he believes that this quest for spontaneity is vital. It is this same quest which partly explains, in his view, 'our morbid interest in the private lives, in personal gossip, and in the sexual indiscretions of public figures' (1961: 255). While most of the public actions of celebrities (including, of course, certain 'star' journalists) are contrived, occasionally there are moments where something happens that has not been prepared in advance for public display. Such moments are eagerly seized upon, Boorstin suggests, because of 'our desperate hunger for the spontaneous, for the non-pseudo-event' (1961: 254).

Boorstin's study has been largely neglected in news and journalism research to date, which is one of the reasons I have dwelt upon it here. While some of its more philosophical propositions have informed the work of cultural theorists, not least that of Marshall McLuhan and Jean Baudrillard, respectively, much more could be done to elaborate further upon its insights. Several researchers have taken some important steps in this direction, however, engaging with what they call the 'tabloidization' of journalism. While few of them acknowledge Boorstin's work directly, it is often possible to discern in the course of their analyses a complementary mode of enquiry.

In using the term 'tabloidization', attention is typically drawn to a perceived realignment of 'serious' (factual, worthy, respectable, upmarket) conceptions of news values with those associated with the 'tabloid' (sensational, superficial, prurient, downmarket) press. This shift in priorities, and its negative impact on informed coverage of public affairs, is said to be most readily discernible at the level of content, format and design in newspapers, but also – even more worryingly in the eyes of some – news broadcasting. Moreover, while this apparent trend is arguably most pronounced in the US news media (Alger 1998; Schechter 1999; Glynn 2000; Bird 2002; Grochowski 2002), critical research suggests that it can be shown to be gaining momentum as it circulates around the globe. Studies of tabloidization have also focused on the news media in Australia (Langer 1998; Turner 1999); Britain (Bromley and Tumber 1997; Barnett 1998; Bromley 1998a; McNair 1998, 2000; Dovey 2000; Winston 2002); China (Huang 2001); Germany (Esser 1999); Scandinavia (Djupsund and Carlson 1998); and southern Europe (Machin and Papatheoderou 2002), amongst other national contexts (see also Sparks and Tulloch (2000) for pertinent essays on Germany, Hungary, Japan, and Mexico, in addition to the US and UK).

Critics contend that processes of 'tabloidization', to the extent that they erode 'serious', 'principled' journalistic criteria of newsworthiness, threaten to undermine the integrity of the 'quality' end of the news reporting spectrum. In addition to the conflation of 'hard' and 'soft' news agendas, and with it the privileging of scandal, gossip, celebrity and sports over and above politics and economics, 'information' is said to be merging with 'entertainment' into an 'infotainment' muddle. Much is made, therefore, of how editorial commentary (features and opinion columns) appears to be flourishing at the expense of 'proper' reporting. These critics observe that it is evidently much more 'cost effective' to hire someone to sit at a desk and wax philosophical about the pressing issues of the day than to employ journalists to actually investigate what is happening. Quality reporting requires sufficient financial investment, but also time, effort and specialized knowledge, amongst other human resources. Comment may not be free, but facts are without doubt much more expensive – to reinflect C.P. Scott's well-known declaration (see p. 27 this volume). Simon Hoggart (2003), who writes for Scott's *Guardian* today, is scathing in his criticism. 'The point about the tabs,' he argues, 'is that they don't regard facts as having their own integrity. Instead they are treated like grains of wheat, puffed full of air, coated with sugar, and served up for breakfast in a brightly coloured box.' Moreover, in his view, the 'tabloids have, deep down, a serious contempt for their readers, who are seen as simple souls, ready to believe what they are told'.

Hoggart is one of many critics from within journalistic circles who take strong exception with this tendency to embrace a tabloid-driven ethos – one where truth, he adds, tends to be reduced to 'what you can get away with' (see also Hoggart 1995). Interestingly, however, where some academic critics adopt a similar position, even using a language of 'moral panic' to describe the dangers of tabloidization, others are more inclined to be circumspect. Tabloidization, as

Gripsrud (2000) points out, is something of a tabloid term itself, being more akin to a journalistic buzzword than a scholarly concept (2000: 285). In calling for a more nuanced understanding of the forms and processes in question, he argues that a 'degree of "tabloidization" is not always a bad thing. It takes, if not all sorts, then at least many sorts of journalism to make a democratic media system work as it should' (2000: 299). Arguing in a similar vein is Langer (1998), who affirms the general line of criticism outlined above while, at the same time, making a case for the 'other news' (tabloid journalism's so-called 'trivialities') to be given careful scrutiny on their own terms. Turner (1999) adopts a related stance, but wishes to 'jettison the category of tabloidization as too baggy, imprecise and value-laden to be of any use' (1999: 70). In acknowledging that many of the fears expressed about 'tabloidization' are grounded in an elitist hostility toward popular culture itself, he nevertheless believes that more specialized forms of critique are required to engage with the attendant complexities (see also Barnett 1998; Glynn 2000; Holland 2001; Sonwalkar 2002; McGuigan 2004). Still, it is in the course of his analysis of the ways in which 'tabloidization' pinpoints how the personal and the private are emphasized over and above the public and the structural that Sparks (2000) makes the case for its heuristic value. '[F]or all its faults and imprecisions,' he remarks, 'tabloidization [is] a category that, properly used, catches some of the key elements of that reformulation' (2000: 36).

To situate the processes frequently attributed to 'tabloidization' within the larger imperatives shaping journalism today, it is useful to consider the media owner's perspective. In the case of Rupert Murdoch, whose News Corp. is widely perceived to be a champion – or perpetrator in the eyes of critics – of tabloid values, his views help to further illuminate the issues at stake. Evidently, Murdoch considers the word 'tabloid' to be largely misunderstood, according to his biographer Michael Wolff (2008). 'Tabloid' in the Murdoch context is an idea of immediacy, sharpness, efficiency and emotion – 'it's news at its most visceral and powerful and entertaining', he writes. 'The craft, and it is a high craft, is compression. Necessary and vital compression' (2008: 210). The 'tabloid model' underpins what Murdoch regards as the successful transformation of newspapers such as *The Times* of London, a process which as Wolff points out is 'still bitterly contested':

> The anti-Murdoch argument is that he took an upmarket paper famous for its probity, detail, and specialized focus on matters of policy and government, with long-practiced standards and traditions of fairness, restraint, expertise, and impartiality, and transformed it into a middle-market paper expedient about its coverage and its quality controls, casual about its areas of expertise, and willing to sacrifice the attention to detail sought by a

limited group for the general-interest superficiality sought by a larger audience.

(Wolff 2008: 230)

From Murdoch's vantage point, however, a different set of criteria should be brought to bear when making judgements. His purchase of a 'money-losing paper of record for the establishment' has been turned into a newspaper responsive to the changing dictates of the marketplace. 'General-interest news outlets that once maintained a strict, hierarchical sense of news have – in the face of competition from speciality outlets and in an effort to attract a wider, often younger or more female demographic – embraced a softer, more feature-oriented idea of what's important', Wolff adds (2008: 230–1). Liberal sentiments about journalistic quality, as Murdoch would be inclined to perceive them, fail to register where it matters most, namely where readers decide which newspaper to purchase. Indeed, it is the extraordinary success of the unapologetically tabloid titles – such as the *Sun* and the *News of the World* – which makes a 'flagship' newspaper like *The Times* viable ('synergies' between Murdoch's *New York Post* and *Wall Street Journal* being a further case in point).

Strategies for change

To declare that journalism is in a state of crisis, some commentators maintain, risks overstating the severity of these developments. Frequently taking a broad historical perspective, they make the argument that these types of debates about reportorial integrity are as old as journalism itself. Even if it is true that the gap between news and entertainment is narrowing (which they dispute), it does not necessarily follow in their view that there is a corresponding 'dumbing-down' of news content. Rather, they insist, the criteria being used to judge standards of 'quality' are quickly becoming out of date. Where some critics hold journalists responsible for pandering to populist prejudices, a number of these commentators are of the view that news values are undergoing a process of democratization. They believe that people want 'news you can use', that is, news which speaks directly to their personal experiences of daily life, as opposed to news content driven by the interests of politicians and other 'talking heads'. The resultant 'tabloidization' of international news coverage, they suggest, thus has as much to do with an enhanced concern with local issues as it does with ever sharper 'efficiency cuts' in the financial budgets of news organizations.

A further type of response, as journalist Ian Hargreaves (2003) points out, is that which enquires, typically with a world-weary expression: 'crisis, what crisis?' Shortly thereafter the assertion is usually made that journalism's standards have always been under attack and, moreover, that the fiercer the attacks, the healthier journalism must be. However, this kind of insouciance, Hargreaves believes, cannot deny that 'the public has a right to expect that journalists will take seriously the responsibilities that come with their privileges' (2003: 17). Accordingly, in his view, journalists should welcome 'the new mood of interrogation about their values, standards and professional practices', for they have much to gain. At stake, of course, is public trust in journalism itself, something that requires constant reaffirmation. While Hargreaves – rather optimistically in my opinion – largely puts his faith in 'market mechanisms' to do 'the job of sorting out the trustworthy from the unreliable', nevertheless he does acknowledge that journalists have to be honest, accountable and willing to submit themselves to public scrutiny. The alternative, he warns, is all too dangerous. Should the 'time-constrained citizen' proceed to 'note the unreliability of much news and switch off, settling for a quiet life, away from the information storm', then the very freedom of the press will be called into question (2003: 266; see also Stevenson 2003; Zelizer 2004; Atton 2009; Glaser 2009; Hampton 2009; Örnebring 2009). There is little doubt in his mind that journalism will have to 'reabsorb the values of democracy into its own self-conduct' so as to ensure a more adequately informed, and thus empowered, citizenry.

Precisely what role can journalism play, then, in efforts to establish a citizen's democracy? It is precisely this question which is at the heart of Herbert J. Gans's (2003) *Democracy and the News*. Building on his evaluative assessment of current debates about the news media's social responsibilities, he proceeds to outline the basis for a 'blueprint for action' to bring about a revival of democracy. For Gans, a citizen's democracy is that 'form of representative government that maximizes the political responsibilities, rights, and, most important, the public decision making of citizens without impairing the function of the economic and political system' (2003: 113). It follows, then, that to help bring about an enlarged role for the citizenry in its own governance, journalists must be better attuned to the needs of their audience in how they report the news. Accordingly, Gans makes several suggestions – some of which, he readily admits, are more feasible than others – to begin the work of figuring out how best to effect change:

- *User-friendly news*: journalists, in Gans's view, must find new ways to persuade audiences to take an active interest in the news, especially where the reporting of political and economic issues is concerned. Journalists need to make the news more user-friendly while, at the same time, expanding their definitions of what counts as news so as to create space for types of coverage that audiences consider to be significant.

- *Localizing national and international news*: working on the assumption that most people are more interested in local rather than national or international news (except where events of major significance are concerned), Gans suggests that journalists 'localize' their reporting. To clarify, he is proposing that distant news events be turned 'into local stories by reporting the effects, implications, and impacts of what happens in the larger world for the local community' (2003: 94).
- *Participatory news*: conventional forms of news coverage, Gans believes, tend to be top-down in perspective, with the viewpoints of ordinary citizens seldom represented. In the interest of balance, then, Gans argues that space be made for 'participatory news' as well, by which he means 'news designed to provide direct or indirect aid to citizens who wish to participate or know how others are participating' in politics (2003: 95). Journalists, it follows, must make a greater effort to encourage members of the public to become involved.
- *Explanatory journalism*: in contrast with traditional forms of journalism, which typically focus on the 'who', 'what', 'where', 'when' and 'how' of a news story, explanatory journalism places a priority on 'why' questions. It does so for two purposes: first to help people understand the deeper causes underlying what is happening and, secondly, to assist them in doing something about it.
- *Opinions and 'news opinions'*: in contrast to the view that journalism should 'stick to the facts', Gans maintains that the news media should include more opinions, for two reasons. First, where journalists have developed informed opinions through investigative work, they can alert audiences to personal views in their reportage – judgements otherwise obscured by the dictates of objectivity. Second, this will help to turn implicit views and opinions – which, to some extent, are inescapable anyway – into explicit ones, which is more honest.
- *Multi-perspectival news*: in an ideal situation, Gans contends, news would make available all possible perspectives on a given phenomenon. In practice, however, multi-perspectival 'means making a place in the news for presently unrepresented viewpoints, unreported facts, and unrepresented, or rarely reported, parts of the population' (2003: 103). Journalism from below, so to speak, is a corrective for the top-down perspectives noted above. As such, it speaks to the interests of those who face prejudice from powerful elites, whether on the basis of their class, gender, ethnicity, sexuality or other, related factors.
- *Other news formats*: conventional formats for 'straight' news, whether those associated with newspapers or broadcast journalism, have proved remarkably stable over time – too stable, in the opinion of Gans. He welcomes the

prospect of change, especially if experimentation in different formats helps to enable different kinds of coverage, including more unusual types of stories. Incorporating elements of humour, satire and commentary alongside the 'straight' news, for example, might have a particular appeal for younger audiences, he suggests.

Two further proposals, already hinted at above, round out Gans's agenda for change. *New tasks and new journalists* revolves around his conviction that new forms of journalistic expertise need to be generated. Most news, he points out, is gathered by 'generalists'. These 'all-purpose reporters' cover 'so many different topics that they often lack the background knowledge – or the time to acquire it – to ask the most significant or telling questions of their sources' (2003: 108). Such expertise comes at a price, of course, which leads to Gans's final proposal, *Paying for better news*. 'If the news is as central to democracy as journalists argue,' he writes, 'then more needs to be spent so that its impact is maximized' (2003: 109). Not surprisingly, Gans is sceptical about the likelihood of capitalist owners and shareholders accepting lower profits, just as he is doubtful that governmental regulatory bodies will intervene to advance the public interest in this regard. Alternative possibilities, however, might include the use of tax incentives, or other forms of public subsidy, to encourage the necessary investment in improving the news. Even direct government funding, heresy in places like the US, deserves to be considered, in Gans's view. Even more radically, national news media might be created as utilities – either on a non-profit or limited-profit basis – so as to reach audiences currently all but ignored by other news media (see also Gans 2009).

Each one of these proposals speaks to a pressing concern that demands precisely this type of imaginative engagement. Gans is to be commended, in my opinion, for thinking outside the box. While some of these proposals are clearly more practicable than others, there can be little doubt that their active consideration will help to reinvigorate familiar debates about how best to improve the quality of journalism today. Here it is important to bear in mind, though, the extent to which the news media will resist any form of change which calls into question their influence. An analysis of the structural factors which constrain, even preclude, certain kinds of innovation will promptly discern how the exercise of corporate power places severe limits on what can be achieved at any given juncture. While Gans signals his awareness of these limits, especially where he addresses the imperatives of profit maximization directly, he nevertheless remains optimistic about the opportunities for reform. And it is 'reform' of the current system, in his view, which is at stake. His conception of citizen's democracy, as noted above, is one which will not 'impair' the 'function of the economic and political system'.

Therein lies the rub, however, for those who are committed to a progressive politic that seeks to do more than curb the ideological excesses of the current system. Reform is insufficient in and by itself, they would contend, when the sort of democratic ideal envisaged by Gans actually demands a far more fundamental restructuring of the distribution of economic, political and cultural power within society. Where journalism possesses the potential to help facilitate processes of democratic governance, not least with respect to holding those in positions of power publicly accountable for their actions, more typically it serves to lend legitimacy to the inequalities endemic to modern societies. Democracy requires a far more robust exchange of viewpoints, and a journalism up to the challenge of giving them vigorous expression. As this chapter has shown, new forms of dialogue about journalism's future need to be fostered, particularly where the decline in public trust is concerned. Perfunctory prescriptions for reform, for tinkering with the existing system of checks and balances, are not enough; for journalism to be democratized in ways consistent with the public interest, structural change is required. 'The creation of an independent press,' as Carey (2002) argues, 'will require both judicial and legislative action so that journalism can earn enough profit to make it attractive but release it as well from slavish dependence on the laws of the market' (2002: 89). Journalism's commitment to public service, in other words, must take priority over profits. This means, he adds, that 'the press may have to rely on a democratic state to create the conditions necessary for a democratic press to flourish and for journalists to be restored to their proper role as orchestrators of the conversation of a democratic culture'.

In the meantime, the prospects for the reinvention of journalism remain uncertain, at best, and bleak, at worst. The 2009 *State of the News Media Report*, produced by the Project for Excellence in Journalism (PEJ), offers little comfort – indeed, quite the opposite – in its examination of the US news industry. Some of its findings, in its own words, were 'chilling':

> Newspaper ad revenues have fallen 23% in the last two years. Some papers are in bankruptcy, and others have lost three-quarters of their value. By our calculations, nearly one out of every five journalists working for newspapers in 2001 is now gone, and 2009 may be the worst year yet.
>
> In local television, news staffs, already too small to adequately cover their communities, are being cut at unprecedented rates; revenues fell by 7% in an election year – something unheard of – and ratings are now falling or are flat across the schedule. In network news, even the rare programs increasing their ratings are seeing revenues fall.
>
> Now the ethnic [minority] press is also troubled and in many ways is the most vulnerable because so many operations are small.

> Only cable news really flourished in 2008, thanks to an Ahab-like focus on the election, although some of the ratings gains were erased after the election.
>
> Perhaps least noticed yet most important, the audience migration to the Internet is now accelerating. The number of Americans who regularly go online for news, by one survey, jumped 19% in the last two years; in 2008 alone traffic to the top 50 news sites rose 27%. Yet it is now all but settled that advertising revenue – the model that financed journalism for the last century – will be inadequate to do so in this one. Growing by a third annually just two years ago, online ad revenue to news websites now appears to be flattening; in newspapers it is declining.
>
> (PEJ 2009)

The 'fundamental question facing journalism,' the report's authors suggest, is whether the news industry can 'win a race against the clock for survival,' that is, can it 'find new ways to underwrite the gathering of news online, while using the declining revenue of the old platforms to finance the transition?' Whatever time is left on the clock, it adds, two developments are reducing it still further. First, the speed by which audiences are migrating to the Web makes apparent the need for the news industry to 'reinvent itself sooner than it thought'. Second, the economic recession becomes a determinant factor, dramatically curtailing the ability of the news industry to find new sources of revenue. 'Journalism, deluded by its profitability and fearful of technology, let others outside the industry steal chance after chance online', a key consequence being that advertising has effectively become 'decoupled' from news. It is the absence of any understanding of how to 'convert this more active online audience into revenue' which goes some distance to explain why, in the report's assessment, the prospects for improvement are so grim.

There seems little doubt that the decline of 'old' news media, not least the newspaper, corresponds directly to the rise of 'new' forms of journalism on the internet, a trend the economic recession has exacerbated (see also Compton 2009; Deuze 2009; Fenton 2009). The impact registers most visibly in plummeting revenues, business closures and job losses, but is also being increasingly felt in ways which are less perceptible at first. Where the decline – or even demise, some fear – of newspapers is concerned, for example, Joe Matthews (2009) points out:

> This is the daily tragedy of all the layoffs and buyouts and departures at U. S. newspapers and magazines. You can count up the journalists who have left the profession and are out of work, but much of the carnage of the ongoing media industry can't be measured or seen: corruption undiscovered, events not witnessed, tips about problems that never reach anyone's ears because those ears have left the newsroom. With fewer

> watchdogs, you get less barking. How can we know what we'll never know?
>
> (Matthews 2009)

In saying 'goodbye' to the 'age of newspapers,' Paul Starr (2009) contends that we are saying 'hello' to a 'new era of corruption.' He writes:

> News coverage is not all that newspapers have given us. They have lent the public a powerful means of leverage over the state, and this leverage is now at risk. If we take seriously the notion of newspapers as a fourth estate or a fourth branch of government, the end of the age of newspapers implies a change in our political system itself. Newspapers have helped to control corrupt tendencies in both government and business. If we are to avoid a new era of corruption, we are going to have to summon that power in other ways. Our new technologies do not retire our old responsibilities.
>
> (Starr 2009)

This question of social responsibility would appear to have eluded the degree of attention it deserves. For the editors of *The New Republic*, the crisis in journalism runs deeper than the crisis in its business model – journalism, they contend, is suffering a crisis of legitimacy. They believe that an anti-media backlash is under way, one directed from both the political right and left, which has engendered a 'poisonous atmosphere'. Rhetorical assaults on the credibility of the press, they write, 'destroys its authority in the culture, giving cover to politicians who would rather avoid dealing with reporters in the first place' (*The New Republic*, 4 March 2009). Recognizing that many venerable newspapers and magazines will close their doors in the days ahead, they add that 'the old ideals embodied in these institutions must not be permitted to join the carnage'.

The desperate situation in the US is being watched closely around the world, not least in Britain. 'Look across the Atlantic and shudder as great names fall like tombstones', observes Polly Toynbee (2009) of the *Guardian*. Writing in early 2009, in the immediate aftermath of the *Los Angeles Times* declared bankrupt, the Chicago *Tribune* and the Philadelphia *Inquirer* in administration (with the San Francisco *Chronicle* on the verge), and the Seattle *Post-Intelligencer* following the *Christian Science Monitor* 'to the newsprint graveyard', she declared a state of emergency. British newspapers are certain to collapse as well, unless – she argues – the government steps in to help for the sake of democracy. 'Serious journalism never paid its way', she maintains, and now that the business model that used to sustain it has 'crashed' because of the internet, government initiatives must be introduced to create the conditions for alternative types of subsidy (echoing Carey's and Gans's points, respectively, made above). Concerns about press freedom need to be reconsidered when 'suddenly the end looks perilously nigh', just as government talk about 'community engagement' could be recast to recognize a role for local trusts to support journalism otherwise unsustainable in market terms. New solutions need to be found now, which necessarily entails acting before a way to monetize the internet is found. The national press 'risks following American newspapers to the great spike in the sky', she points out. 'Britain without the *Mail* or the *Sun* would be a happier place, less biliously nihilist, less miserable, angry and afraid. But democracy without the scrutiny of good journalism is unthinkable.'

Points of departure

In bringing this discussion to a close, I wish to highlight a set of pressing issues which in my view deserve much more critical attention than they have typically received to date. Accordingly, briefly outlined below is a range of questions revolving around a specific aspect of the changing nature of news culture, each of which is intended to bring to the fore conceptual concerns for further discussion and debate.

What does 'freedom of the press' mean today? Given that most definitions focus on the constraints placed by governments on the right to express ideas, opinions and information, what impact are the changing dynamics of news media ownership (particularly with respect to the growing degree of concentration, conglomeration and globalization) having on these same 'freedoms'? Is news slowly turning into a commodity like any other, its value to be measured primarily in terms of 'bottom-line' profitability? If so, would it be practicable, or even desirable, to regulate news content (for example, by imposing on newspapers the same 'impartiality' constraints placed on broadcasters)?

Is the notion of a 'public sphere' still viable and, if so, how can journalism best fulfil its social responsibilities? Is it the case that only 'free markets' (and 'market-friendly' regulatory regimes) ensure diversity of expression and open public debate? Or, alternatively, are critics such as Habermas (1989) correct to argue that the commercialization of mass communication networks has virtually displaced 'rational-critical debate' into the realm of cultural consumption, thereby transforming active citizens into indifferent consumers? In what ways will journalism have to change in order to enhance civic participation in government, and thereby help to close what is clearly a widening gap between those with 'information capital' and those without it?

If, by definition, it is impossible for journalists to be completely 'objective', then should they not abandon the pretence of being 'unbiased' altogether? If so, what sort of normative language should replace these familiar concepts? Is it enough for journalists to try to be 'balanced' and 'fair', or should they adopt new approaches to writing news which explicitly mark the constructed nature of each account's codes and conventions? How might a collective decision to relinquish the language of 'objectivity' empower, or possibly disempower, various social groups attempting to contest certain forms of news coverage?

How does 'truth' relate to 'fact'? Do journalists, as some of them argue, have a fundamental obligation to determining 'the truth' of any given situation? Or is it their task to secure the best available definition of the truth, thereby conceding that absolute truth does not exist? Then again, would it be advantageous for journalists to dispense with the notion of truth altogether in favour of concentrating strictly on matters of fact? In any case, how best to lay bare the gendered (male), racialized (white) and class-specific (middle- and upper-class) conventions underpinning many of the more entrenched journalistic discourses of truth?

In what ways should journalism seek to refashion its relationship with its communities, and thereby enhance public trust? Given that citizen journalism is here to stay, how can journalists embrace – and see their reporting enriched by – the contributions made by ordinary citizens intent on storming the ramparts of the journalistic profession? If 'everyone can be a journalist', then how might journalism education best reinvent itself accordingly? What strategies can be developed to eliminate the forms of social exclusion – based on class, gender, ethnic and sexual discrimination – which so often inhibit equal participation in journalism?

In what ways must journalistic institutions change to first arrest and then reverse the current decline of audience figures for 'serious' news, especially with respect to young people? While some journalists and critics are charging that the division between 'news' and 'entertainment' is becoming dangerously blurred, what form should a truly popular journalism take for individuals otherwise disinclined to follow news and current affairs? If the familiar conventions associated with 'objectivity' and 'impartiality' are seen to be off-putting – contrived, even insincere – then how best to recast such conventions to encourage public engagement? By what criteria should the 'quality' of news provision be judged?

Is journalism a fully-fledged profession and, if so, does it need a formal code of ethics? In what ways do the current practices broadly regarded as being constitutive of 'professional' reporting serve to include certain voices and exclude alternative ones? How do these (often tacit) judgements about 'professionalism' inform the hiring and promotion of men and women within news organizations? Moreover, how do they shape the routine strategies by which journalists handle different sources when processing news accounts? Might professional status unduly restrict or even control how journalists go about their work, or would it enhance their relative autonomy from managerial influence within a news organization?

How best to safeguard investigative reporting in an age of 'churnalism'? – to use journalist Nick Davies' (2008a, 2008b) term. Reporters working with scant resources under intense time pressure are increasingly being forced to abandon their active, independent role in news gathering in order to meet story quotas, thereby becoming 'passive processors of unchecked, second-hand material, much of it contrived by PR [Public Relations] to serve some political or commercial interest. Not journalists, but churnalists' (2008a: see also Davies 2008b; Franklin *et al.* 2009). How, then, to halt the further erosion of what used to be regarded as 'shoe leather' reporting, where news judgement was based on a double-, even triple-checking of facts and a close, methodical interrogation of sources?

When some news organizations find themselves without a sufficiently robust business model to underpin the costs of quality reporting, where can alternative sources of revenue be secured? Some prefer to live in denial, others call on government to relax already weakened rules on media ownership (the hope being that competition can be eliminated by acquisition), while still others wait patiently for the Web to be 'monetized' to their advantage. Meanwhile, even the likes of Paul Dacre (2008), editor of London's *Daily Mail* tabloid ('dull doesn't sell newspapers. Boring doesn't pay the mortgage'), is concerned about the impact on the press's social responsibilities: 'If the local press fails to survive,' he asks, 'who is going to cover the magistrates' and coroners' courts and the local council meetings that are the corner stones of local democracy?'

How best to realize the potential of the internet as a news source? In what ways will the forms and practices of online journalism have to develop in order to further enhance its reportorial integrity? How to overcome the obstacles in the path of this kind of development, such as corporate ownership of major news sites, the growing standardization of online formats, the influence of advertising on content, and the ideologically narrow (if all too familiar) conceptions of news values and source credibility in operation, amongst others? Moreover, how might online journalism help to counter the forms of social exclusion endemic to the global network society? That is to say, how might it contribute to the creation of progressive forms of citizenship across the digital divide?

Overall, then, this brief sketch of several particularly salient issues (located, as they are, among an array of others) illuminates some of the key features of the ongoing debates I have considered to be central to this book's analytical and strategic agendas. In electing to conclude by outlining them in this rather provocative fashion, it has been my intention to help establish several possible points of departure for future critical explorations of news culture. It goes without saying, of course, that I hope this book will prove to be of some use in these explorations.

REFERENCES

Adam, B. (1995) *Timewatch: The Social Analysis of Time*. Cambridge: Polity Press.

Adam, B. (1998) *Timescapes of Modernity: The Environment and Invisible Hazards*. London: Routledge.

Adam, G.S. (2001) The education of journalists, *Journalism: Theory, Practice, and Criticism*, 2(3): 315–39.

Ainley, B. (1998) *Black Journalists, White Media*. Stoke-on-Trent: Trentham.

Aldridge, M. (1998) The tentative hell-raisers: identity and mythology in contemporary UK press journalism, *Media, Culture and Society*, 20(1): 109–27.

Aldridge, M. (2001) The Paradigm Contingent Career? Women in Regional Newspaper Journalism, *Sociological Research Online*, 6(3). www.socresonline.org.uk/6/3/aldridge.html

Alexander, J.C. and Jacobs, R.N. (1998) Mass communication, ritual and civil society, in T. Liebes and J. Curran (eds) *Media, Ritual and Identity*. London: Routledge.

Alger, D. (1998) Megamedia, the state of journalism, and democracy, *Press/Politics*, 3(1): 126–33.

Allan, S. (1997a) News and the public sphere: towards a history of objectivity and impartiality, in M. Bromley and T. O'Malley (eds) *A Journalism Reader*. London: Routledge.

Allan, S. (1997b) Raymond Williams and the culture of televisual flow, in J. Wallace, R. Jones and S. Nield (eds) *Raymond Williams Now: Knowledge, Limits and the Future*. London: Macmillan.

Allan, S. (1998a) News from NowHere: televisual news discourse and the construction of hegemony, in A. Bell and P. Garrett (eds) *Approaches to Media Discourse*. Oxford: Blackwell.

Allan, S. (1998b) (En)gendering the truth politics of news discourse, in C. Carter, G. Branston and S. Allan (eds) *News, Gender and Power*. London: Routledge.

Allan, S. (2002) *Media, Risk and Science*. Buckingham and Philadelphia, PA: Open University Press.

Allan, S. (2005) Hidden in plain sight: journalism's critical issues, in S. Allan (ed.) *Journalism: Critical Issues*. Maidenhead and New York: Open University Press.

Allan, S. (2006) *Online News: Journalism and the Internet*. Maidenhead and New York: Open University Press.

Allan, S. (2009a) Histories of citizen journalism, in S. Allan and E. Thorsen (eds) *Citizen Journalism: Global Perspectives*. New York: Peter Lang.

Allan, S. (2009b) Introduction: recrafting news and journalism, in S. Allan (ed.) *The Routledge Companion to News and Journalism*. London and New York: Routledge.

Allan, S. and Thorsen, E. (eds) (2009) *Citizen Journalism: Global Perspectives*. New York: Peter Lang.

Allan, S. and Zelizer, B. (eds) (2004) *Reporting War: Journalism in Wartime*. London and New York: Routledge.

Allan, S., Adam, B. and Carter, C. (eds) (2000) *Environmental Risks and the Media*. London and New York: Routledge.

Allbritton, C. (2003) Blogging from Iraq, *Nieman Reports*, Fall, 82–5.

Allemang, J. (2003) Where everybody is a war reporter, *The Globe and Mail*, www.globeandmail.com, 29 March.

Altschull, J.H. (1995) *Agents of Power: The Media and Public Policy*, 2nd edn. White Plains, NY: Longman.

Alwood, E. (1996) *Strait News: Gays, Lesbians and the News Media*. New York: Columbia University Press.

Anderson, A. (1997) *Media, Culture and the Environment*. London: UCL Press.

Anderson, A., Petersen, A. and David, M. (2005) Communication or spin? Source – media relations in science journalism, in S. Allan (ed.) *Journalism: Critical Issues*. Maidenhead and New York: Open University Press.

Anderson, A., Petersen, A., Wilkinson, C. and Allan, S. (2009) *Nanotechnology, Risk and Communication*. London and New York: Palgrave.

Anderson, B. (1991) *Imagined Communities*, 2nd edn. London: Verso.

Anderson, M.D. (2008) Minority journalists push media to maintain diversity commitment, *Issues in Higher Education*, 24 July.

Andrews, P. (2003) Is blogging journalism?, *Nieman Reports*, Fall, 57(3): 63–4.

Ang, I. (1996) *Living Room Wars: Rethinking Audiences for a Postmodern World*. London: Routledge.

Arnett, P. (1998) 'Goodbye, world', *American Journalism Review*, November.

Arthurs, J. (1994) Women and television, in S. Hood (ed.) *Behind the Screens*. London: Lawrence and Wishart.

ASNE (American Society of Newspaper Editors) (2008) Newsroom Employment Census. www.asne.org/index.cfm?id=1138

Asquith, I. (1978) The structure, ownership and control of the press, 1780–1855, in G. Boyce, J. Curran and P. Wingate (eds) *Newspaper History*. London: Constable.

Atton, C. (2002) *Alternative Media*. London: Sage Publications.

Atton, C. (2009) Alternative journalism: challenging media power, in S. Allan (ed.)

The Routledge Companion to News and Journalism. London and New York: Routledge.

Aulich, J. (1992) Wildlife in the South Atlantic: graphic satire, patriotism and the Fourth Estate, in J. Aulich (ed.) *Framing the Falklands War*. Buckingham: Open University Press.

Bagdikian, B.H. (1997) *The Media Monopoly*, 5th edn. Boston, MA: Beacon.

Bakhtin, M. (1981) *The Dialogic Imagination*. Austin, TX: University of Texas Press.

Banks, A. (1994) Images trapped in two discourses: photojournalism codes and the international news flow, *Journal of Communication Inquiry*, 18(1): 118–34.

Barker, C. (1999) *Television, Globalization and Cultural Identities*. Buckingham: Open University Press.

Barker, S.M. (2003) *American Television News*. Armonk, NY: M.E. Sharpe.

Barker-Plummer, B. (1995) News as a political resource: media strategies and political identity in the US women's movement, 1966–1975, *Critical Studies in Mass Communication*, 12(3): 306–24.

Barkin, S.M. (2003) *American Television News: The Media Marketplace and the Public Interest*. Armonk, NY and London: M.E. Sharpe.

Barnett, A. (1984) Some notes on media coverage of the Falklands, in F. Barker, P. Hulme, M. Iversen and D. Loxley (eds) *Confronting the Crisis*. Colchester: University of Essex.

Barnett, S. (1998) Dumbing down or reaching out: is it tabloidisation wot done it?, in J. Seaton (ed.) *Politics and the Media*. Oxford: Blackwell.

Barnett, S. (2005) Opportunity or threat? The BBC, investigative journalism and the Hutton Report, in S. Allan (ed.) *Journalism: Critical Issues*. Maidenhead and New York: Open University Press.

Barnett, S. and Gaber, I. (2001) *Westminster Tales: The Twenty-first-century Crisis in Political Journalism*. London: Continuum.

Barnhurst, K.G. (1998) Politics in the fine meshes: young citizens, power and media, *Media, Culture and Society*, 20(2): 201–18.

Barnhurst, K.G. and Nerone, J. (2001) *The Form of News: A History*. New York: Guilford.

Barnouw, E. (1990) *Tube of Plenty*, 2nd edn. New York: Oxford University Press.

Barthes, R. (1973) *Mythologies*. London: Paladin.

Bateson, G. (1972) *Steps to an Ecology of Mind*. New York: Ballantine.

Bausinger, H. (1984) Media, technology and daily life, *Media, Culture and Society*, 6(4): 343–51.

Baym, G. (2009) Real news/fake news: beyond the news/entertainment divide, in S. Allan (ed.) *The Routledge Companion to News and Journalism*. London and New York: Routledge.

Becker, H.S. (1967) Whose side are we on? *Social Problems*, 14(3): 239–47.

Becker, K. (1992) Photojournalism and the tabloid press, in P. Dahlgren and C. Sparks (eds) *Journalism and Popular Culture*. London: Sage Publications.

Becker, K. (1995) Media and the ritual process, *Media, Culture and Society*, 17(4): 629–46.

Bekken, J. (1995) Newsboys: the exploitation of 'Little Merchants' by the newspaper industry, in H. Hardt and B. Brennen (eds) *Newsworkers: Toward a History of the Rank and File*. Minneapolis, MN: University of Minnesota Press.

Bell, A. (1991) *The Language of News Media*. Oxford: Blackwell.

Bell, A. (1998) The discourse structure of news stories, in A. Bell and P. Garrett (eds) *Approaches to Media Discourse*. Oxford: Blackwell.

Bell, A. and Garrett, P. (eds) (1998) *Approaches to Media Discourse*. Oxford: Blackwell.

Bell, M. (1995) *In Harm's Way*. Harmondsworth: Penguin.

Bell, M. (1998) The journalism of attachment, in M. Kieran (ed.) *Media Ethics*. London: Routledge.

Bell, M. (2003) *Through Gates of Fire*. London: Weidenfeld and Nicolson.

Belsey, A. and Chadwick, R. (eds) (1992) *Ethical Issues in Journalism and the Media*. London: Routledge.

Benedict, H. (1992) *Virgin or Vamp: How the Press Covers Sex Crimes*. New York: Oxford University Press.

Bennett, L.W., Lawrence, R.G. and Livingston, S. (2007) *When the Press Fails: Political Power and the News Media from Iraq to Katrina*. Chicago, IL: University of Chicago Press.

Bennett, T. (1982) Theories of the media, theories of society, in M. Gurevitch, T. Bennett, J. Curran and J. Woollacott (eds) *Culture, Society and the Media*. London: Methuen.

Berkowitz, D. (ed.) (1997) *Social Meanings of News*. Thousand Oaks, CA: Sage Publications.

Bernstein, C. (1992) The idiot culture, *The New Republic*, 8 June: 22–8.

Berry, D. (ed.) (2000) *Ethics and Media Culture: Practices and Representations*. Oxford: Focal Press.

Bianculli, D. (1992) *Taking Television Seriously: Teleliteracy*. New York: Touchstone.

Billig, M. (1995) *Banal Nationalism*. London: Sage Publications.

Bird, R. (1997) *The End of News*. Toronto: Irwin.

Bird, S.E. (1992) *For Enquiring Minds: A Cultural Study of Supermarket Tabloids*. Knoxville, TN: University of Tennessee Press.

Bird, S.E. (2002) Taking it personally: supermarket tabloids after September 11, in B. Zelizer and S. Allan (eds) *Journalism After September 11*. London and New York: Routledge.

Bird, S.E. (2009) News practices in everyday life: beyond audience response, in S. Allan (ed.) *The Routledge Companion to News and Journalism*. London and New York: Routledge.

Bliss, Jr, E. (1991) *Now the News*. New York: Columbia University Press.

Bodi, F. (2003) Al-Jazeera tells the truth about war, *Guardian*, 28 March.

Boorstin, D.J. (1961) *The Image: A Guide to Pseudo-Events in America*. New York: Vintage.

Bosch, T. (2009) Radio news: re-imagining the community, in S. Allan (ed.) *The Routledge Companion to News and Journalism*. London and New York: Routledge.

Bourdieu, P. (1998) *On Television and Journalism*, translation by P.P. Ferguson. London: Pluto.

Boyce, G., Curran, J. and Wingate, P. (eds) (1978) *Newspaper History*. London: Constable.

Boyd-Barrett, O. (1978) Market control and wholesale news: the case of Reuters, in G. Boyce, J. Curran and P. Wingate (eds) *Newspaper History*. London: Constable.

Boyd-Barrett, O. (2005) Journalism, media conglomerates and the Federal Communications Commission, in S. Allan (ed.) *Journalism: Critical Issues*. Maidenhead and New York: Open University Press.

Boyd-Barrett, O. and Rantanen, T. (eds) (1998) *The Globalization of News*. London: Sage Publications.

Boyle, R., Rowe, D. and Whannel, G. (2009) Delight in trivial controversy? Questions for sports journalism, in S. Allan (ed.) *The Routledge Companion to News and Journalism*. London and New York: Routledge.

Bradley, P. (1998) Mass communication and the shaping of US feminism, in C. Carter, G. Branston and S. Allan (eds) *News, Gender and Power*. London: Routledge.

Bradshaw, P. (2009) 'Wiki journalism', in S. Allan and E. Thorsen (eds) *Citizen Journalism: Global Perspectives*. New York: Peter Lang.

Braham, P. (1982) How the media report race, in M. Gurevitch, T. Bennett, J. Curran and J. Woollacott (eds) *Culture, Society and the Media*. London: Methuen.

Brants, K., Hermes, J. and van Zonnen, L. (eds) (1998) *The Media in Question: Popular Cultures and Public Interests*. London: Sage Publications.

Braver, R. (1997) Show and tell: reporters meet politicians on *Larry King Live*, in S. Iyengar and R. Reeves (eds) *Do the Media Govern?* Thousand Oaks, CA: Sage Publications.

Brennen, B. (2009) Photojournalism: historical dimensions to contemporary debates, in S. Allan (ed.) *The Routledge Companion to News and Journalism*. London and New York: Routledge.

Briggs, A. (1961–95) *The History of Broadcasting in the United Kingdom*, Vols 1–5, *The Birth of Broadcasting*. London: Oxford University Press.

Briggs, A. (1970) *The War of Words*, Vol. III, *The History of Broadcasting in the United Kingdom*. London: Oxford University Press.

Brighton, P. and Foy, D. (2007) *News Values*. London: Sage Publications.

Bromley, M. (1997) The end of journalism? Changes in workplace practices in the press and broadcasting in the 1990s, in M. Bromley and T. O'Malley (eds) *A Journalism Reader*. London: Routledge.

Bromley, M. (1998a) The 'tabloiding' of Britain: 'quality' newspapers in the 1990s, in H. Stephenson and M. Bromley (eds) *Sex, Lies and Democracy*. London: Longman.

Bromley, M. (1998b) 'Watching the watchdogs?' The role of readers' letters in calling the press to account, in H. Stephenson and M. Bromley (eds) *Sex, Lies and Democracy*. London: Longman.

Bromley, M. (2005) Subterfuge as public service: investigative journalism as idealised journalism, in S. Allan (ed.) *Journalism: Critical Issues*. Maidenhead and New York: Open University Press.

Bromley, M. and O'Malley, T. (eds) (1997) *A Journalism Reader*. London: Routledge.

Bromley, M. and Tumber, H. (1997) From Fleet Street to cyberspace: the British 'popular' press in the late twentieth century, *European Journal of Communication Research*, 22(3): 365–78.

Brooker-Gross, S.R. (1985) The changing concept of place in the news, in J. Burgess and J.R. Gold (eds) *Geography, the Media and Popular Culture*. London: Croom Helm.

Brookes, R. (1990) 'Everything in the garden is lovely': the representation of national identity in Sidney Strube's *Daily Express* cartoons in the 1930s, *Oxford Art Journal*, 13(2): 31–43.

Brookes, R. (2002) *Representing Sport*. London: Arnold.

Brookes, R. and Holbrook, B. (1998) 'Mad cows and Englishmen': gender implications of news reporting on the British beef crisis, in C. Carter, G. Branston and S. Allan (eds) *News, Gender and Power*. London: Routledge.

Brown, M. (1994) Estimating newspaper and magazine readership, in R. Kent (ed.) *Measuring Media Audiences*. London: Routledge.

Brown, M. (2005) Abandoning the news, Carnegie Corporation of New York, 3(2): Spring. www.carnegie.org/reporter/10/news/

Brown, R. (1997) Untitled opinion column, *Independent*, 6 October.

Buckingham, D. (1997) News media, political socialization and popular citizenship: towards a new agenda, *Critical Studies in Mass Communication*, 14(4): 344–66.

Burns, T. (1977) *The BBC: Public Institution and Private World*. London: Macmillan.

Busari, S. (2008) Tweeting the terror: how social media reacted to Mumbai, CNN, 27 November.

Cameron, D. (1992) *Feminism and Linguistic Theory*, 2nd edn. London: Macmillan.

Cameron, D. (1996) Style policy and style politics: a neglected aspect of the language of the news, *Media, Culture and Society*, 18(2): 315–33.

Cameron, J. (1967) Journalism: a trade, in M. Bromley and T. O'Malley (eds) (1997) *A Journalism Reader*. London: Routledge.

Campbell, C.P. (1995) *Race, Myth and the News*. London: Sage Publications.

Campbell, F. (1999) *The Construction of Environmental News*. Aldershot: Ashgate.

Campbell, V. (2004) *Information Age Journalism: Journalism in an International Context*. London: Arnold.

Camporesi, V. (1994) The BBC and American broadcasting, 1922–55, *Media, Culture and Society*, 16(4): 625–39.

Cann, D.J. and Mohr, P.B. (2001) Journalist and source gender in Australian television news, *Journal of Broadcasting & Electronic Media*, 45(1): 162–74.

Carey, J.W. (1986) The dark continent of American journalism, in R.K. Manoff and M. Schudson (eds) *Reading the News*. New York: Pantheon.

Carey, J.W. (2002) American journalism on, before, and after September 11, in B. Zelizer and S. Allan (eds) *Journalism After September 11*. London and New York: Routledge.

Carlson, P. (2003) In the line of fire, *The Washington Post*, 3 April.

Carper, A. (1997) Marketing news, in P. Norris (ed.) *Politics and the Press*. Boulder, CO: Lynne Rienner.

Carruthers, S.L. (2000) *The Media at War*. London: Macmillan.

Carter, C. (1998) When the 'extraordinary' becomes 'ordinary': everyday news of sexual violence, in C. Carter, G. Branston and S. Allan (eds) *News, Gender and Power*. London: Routledge.

Carter, C. and Messenger Davies, M. (2005) 'A fresh peach is easier to bruise': children and traumatic news, in S. Allan (ed.) *Journalism: Critical Issues*. Maidenhead and New York: Open University Press.

Carter, C. and Thompson, A. (1997) Negotiating the 'crisis' around masculinity: an historical analysis of discourses of patriarchal violence in the *Western Mail*, 1896, in M. Bromley and T. O'Malley (eds) *A Journalism Reader*. London: Routledge.

Carter, C. and Weaver, C.K. (2003) *Violence and the Media*. Buckingham and Philadelphia, PA: Open University Press.

Carter, C., Branston, G. and Allan, S. (eds) (1998) *News, Gender and Power*. London and New York: Routledge.

Castanñeda, L. and Campbell, S. (eds) (2006) *News and Sexuality: Media Portraits of Diversity*. Thousand Oaks, CA: Sage Publications.

Castells, M. (2000) *The Rise of the Network Society*, 2nd edn. Oxford: Blackwell.

Cathcart, B. (2008) News hit by whiteout, *New Statesman*, 13 October.

Chalaby, J.K. (1996) Journalism as an Anglo-American invention, *European Journal of Communication*, 11(3): 303–26.

Chambers, D. and Steiner, L. (2009) The changing status of women journalists, in S. Allan (ed.) *The Routledge Companion to News and Journalism*. London and New York: Routledge.

Chambers, D., Steiner, L. and Fleming, C. (2004) *Women and Journalism*. London and New York: Routledge.

Chaney, D. (1994) *The Cultural Turn*. London: Routledge.

Chapman, G., Kumar, K., Fraser, C. and Gaber, I. (1997) *Environmentalism and the Mass Media: The North–South Divide*. London: Routledge.

Charity, A. (1995) *Doing Public Journalism*. New York: Guilford.

Chavez, L.R. (2001) *Covering Immigration: Popular Images and the Politics of the Nation*. Berkeley, CA: University of California Press.

Chibnall, S. (1977) *Law and Order News: An Analysis of Crime Reporting in the British Press*. London: Tavistock.

Chippendale, P. and Horrie, C. (1992) *Stick it Up Your Punter: The Rise and Fall of* The Sun. London: Mandarin.

Chouliaraki, L. (2009) Journalism and the visual politics of war and conflict, in S. Allan (ed.) *The Routledge Companion to News and Journalism*. London and New York: Routledge.

Christmas, L. (1997) *Chaps of Both Sexes? Women Decision-makers in Newspapers: Do They Make a Difference?* Wiltshire: Women in Journalism in association with *The BT Forum*.

Church, R. (2003) Interview with Salman Pax, CNN International, Transcript Number 100302 cb. K18, 3 October.

Clark, K. (1992) The linguistics of blame: representations of women in *The Sun*'s reporting of crimes of sexual violence, in M. Toolan (ed.) *Language, Text and Context*. London: Routledge.

Clarke, P. (2008) The Daily News: Liberia, *World Vision Report*, 28 September.

Clayman, S.E. (1991) News interview openings: aspects of sequential organization, in P. Scannell (ed.) *Broadcast Talk*. London: Sage Publications.

Clayton, A. (2003) *London's Coffee Houses*. London: Historical Publications.

Coleridge, N. (1993) *Paper Tigers*. London: Heinemann.

Compton, J.R. (2009) Newspapers, labor and the flux of economic uncertainty, in S. Allan (ed.) *The Routledge Companion to News and Journalism*. London and New York: Routledge.

Connell, I. (1992) Personalities in the popular media, in P. Dahlgren and C. Sparks (eds) *Journalism and Popular Culture*. London: Sage Publications.

Cooper, G. (2008) The hell of being white, middle-class and male, *Telegraph*, 22 December.

Corner, J. (1980) Codes and cultural analysis, *Media, Culture and Society*, 2: 73–86.

Corner, J. (1995) *Television Form and Public Address*. London: Arnold.

Corner, J. and Pels, D. (eds) (2003) *Media and the Restyling of Politics*. London: Sage Publications.

Cose, E. (1997) Seething in silence: the news in black and white, in E.E. Dennis and E.C. Pease (eds) *The Media in Black and White*. New Brunswick, NJ and London: Transaction.

Cottle, S. (1993) *TV News, Urban Conflict and the Inner City*. Leicester: Leicester University Press.

Cottle, S. (1994) Stigmatizing Handsworth: notes on reporting soiled space, *Critical Studies in Mass Communication*, 11(3): 231–56.

Cottle, S. (1995) The production of news formats: determinants of mediated public contestation, *Media, Culture and Society*, 17(2): 275–91.

Cottle, S. (ed.) (2003a) *Media Organization and Production*. London: Sage Publications.

Cottle, S. (ed.) (2003b) *News, Public Relations and Power*. London: Sage Publications.

Cottle, S. (2004) *The Racist Murder of Stephen Lawrence: Media Performance and Public Transformation*. Westport, CT: Praeger.

Cottle, S. (2005) In defence of 'thick' journalism: or how television journalism can be good for us, in S. Allan (ed.) *Journalism: Critical Issues*. Maidenhead and New York: Open University Press.

Cottle, S. (2006) *Mediatized Conflict*. Maidenhead: Open University Press.

Cottle, S. (2009) *Global Crisis Reporting: Journalism in the Global Age*. Maidenhead: Open University Press.

Couldry, N. (2003) *Media Rituals: A Critical Approach*. London: Routledge.

Couric, K. (2007) A woman at the table, *CBS Blogs*, CouricandCo., 17 January.

Cowan, B. (2005) *The Social Life of Coffee*. New Haven, CT: Yale University Press.

Coward, R. (2009) Me, me, me: the rise and rise of autobiographical journalism, in S. Allan (ed.) *The Routledge Companion to News and Journalism*. London and New York: Routledge.

Cox, G. (1995) *Pioneering Television News*. London: John Libbey.

Craven, L. (1992) The early newspaper press in England, in D. Griffiths (ed.) *The Encyclopedia of the British Press*. London: Macmillan.

Crawley, A. (1988) *Leap Before You Look*. London: Collins.

Crisell, A. (1986) *Understanding Radio*. London: Methuen.

Crisell, A. (1997) *An Introductory History of British Broadcasting*. London: Routledge.

Critcher, C. (2003) *Moral Panics and the Media*. Buckingham and Philadelphia, PA: Open University Press.

Critcher, C. (2005) Mighty dread: journalism and moral panics, in S. Allan (ed.) *Journalism: Critical Issues*. Maidenhead and New York: Open University Press.

Crook, T. (1998) *International Radio Journalism*. London: Routledge.

Croteau, D. and Hoynes, W. (1992) Men and the news media: the male presence and its effect, in S. Craig (ed.) *Men, Masculinity and the Media*. London: Sage Publications.

Cumberlege, G. (1946) *War Report*. London: Oxford University Press.

Cumings, B. (1992) *War and Television*. London: Verso.

Curran, J. (1978) The press as an agency of social control: an historical perspective, in G. Boyce, J. Curran and P. Wingate (eds) *Newspaper History*. London: Constable.

Curran, J. (1990) Culturalist perspectives of news organisations: a reappraisal and a case study, in M. Ferguson (ed.) *Public Communication: The New Imperatives*. London: Sage Publications.

Curran, J. (2002) *Media and Power*. London and New York: Routledge.

Curran, J. and Couldry, N. (eds) (2003) *Contesting Media Power: Alternative Media in a Networked World*. Lanham, MD: Rowman and Littlefield.

Curran, J. and Park, M.-J. (eds) (2000) *De-Westernizing Media Studies*. London and New York: Routledge.

Curran, J. and Seaton, J. (1997) *Power Without Responsibility: The Press and Broadcasting in Britain*, 5th edn. London: Routledge.

Curran, J. and Seaton, J. (2003) *Power Without Responsibility: The Press and Broadcasting in Britain*, 6th edn. London: Routledge.

Curran, J., Douglas, A. and Whannel, G. (1980) The political economy of the human interest story, in A. Smith (ed.) *Newspapers and Democracy*. Cambridge, MA: MIT Press.

Curran, J., Ecclestone, J., Oakley, G. and Richardson, A. (eds) (1986) *Bending Reality: The State of the Media*. London: Comedia.

Czitrom, D.J. (1982) *Media and the American Mind: From Morse to McLuhan*. Chapel Hill, NC: University of North Carolina Press.

Dacre, P. (2008) Speech to Society of Editors, 9 November. http://www.pressgazette.co.uk/story.asp?storyCode=42394§ioncode=1

Dahlgren, P. (1995) *Television and the Public Sphere*. London: Sage Publications.

Dahlgren, P. and Sparks, C. (eds) (1991) *Communication and Citizenship*. London: Routledge.

Dahlgren, P. and Sparks, C. (eds) (1992) *Journalism and Popular Culture*. London: Sage Publications.

Danna, S.R. (1975a) The rise of radio news, in L.W. Lichty and M.C. Topping (eds) *American Broadcasting: A Source Book*. New York: Hastings House.

Danna, S.R. (1975b) The press–radio war, in L.W. Lichty and M.C. Topping (eds) *American Broadcasting: A Source Book*. New York: Hastings House.

Dates, J.L. and Pease, E.C. (1997) Warping the world – media's mangled images of race, in E.E. Dennis and E.C. Pease (eds) *The Media in Black and White*. New Brunswick, NJ and London: Transaction.

Davies, J. (1994) *Broadcasting and the BBC in Wales*. Cardiff: University of Wales Press.

Davies, N. (2008a) Introducing *Flat Earth News*, *Guardian*, 4 February.

Davies, N. (2008b) *Flat Earth News*. London: Chatto and Windus.

Davis, A. (1976) *Television: Here is the News*. London: Severn.

Day, R. (1989) *Grand Inquisitor*. London: Pan.

Day, R. (1995) Foreword, in G. Cox, *Pioneering Television News*. London: John Libbey.

Dayan, D. and Katz, E. (1992) *Media Events*. Cambridge, MA: Harvard University Press.

Deacon, D. and Golding, P. (1994) *Taxation and Representation: The Media, Political Communication and the Poll Tax*. London: John Libbey.

De Bruin, M. and Ross, K. (2004) *Gender and Newsroom Cultures*. Crestkill, NJ: Hampton Press.

De Burg, H. (2008) *Investigative Journalism*, 2nd edn. London and New York: Routledge.

Delio, M. (2003) US tries e-mail to charm Iraqis, *Wired News*, 13 February.

Dennis, E.E. (1997) Preface, in E.E. Dennis and E.C. Pease (eds) *The Media in Black and White*. New Brunswick, NJ and London: Transaction.

Dennis, E.E. and Pease, E.C. (eds) (1997) *The Media in Black and White*. New Brunswick, NJ and London: Transaction.

De Uriarte, M.L. (1997) Exploring (and exploding) the US media prism, in E.E. Dennis and E.C. Pease (eds) *The Media in Black and White*. New Brunswick, NJ and London: Transaction.

Deuze, M. (2009) The future of citizen journalism, in S. Allan and E. Thorsen (eds) *Citizen Journalism: Global Perspectives*. New York: Peter Lang.

Devereux, E. (1998) *Devils and Angels: Television, Ideology and the Coverage of Poverty*. Luton: University of Luton Press.

Dicey, E. (1997 [1905]) Journalism old and new, in M. Bromley and T. O'Malley (eds) *A Journalism Reader*. London: Routledge.

Dickey, J. (1987) Heterosexism and the lesbian image in the press, in K. Davies, J. Dickey and T. Stratford (eds) *Out of Focus: Writings on Women and the Media*. London: The Women's Press.

Dickinson, R. (2009) Making up the news: journalists, deviance and social control in news production, in S. Allan (ed.) *The Routledge Companion to News and Journalism*. London and New York: Routledge.

Djerf-Pierre, M. (2007) The gender of journalism, *Nordicom Review*, Jubilee Issue 2007, 81–104.

Djupsund, G. and Carlson, T. (1998) Trivial stories and fancy pictures?, *Nordicom Review*, 19(1): 101–14.

Doane, M.A. (1990) Information, crisis, catastrophe, in P. Mellencamp (ed.) *Logics of Television: Essays in Cultural Criticism*. London: British Film Institute.

Dodge, T. (2003) An Iraqi in cyberspace, *The Times Literary Supplement*, 24 October.

Donsbach, W. (2009) Journalists and their professional identities, in S. Allan (ed.) *The*

Routledge Companion to News and Journalism. London and New York: Routledge.
Dougary, G. (1994) *The Executive Tart and Other Myths: Media Women Talk Back*. London: Virago.
Dovey, J. (2000) *Freakshow: First Person Media and Factual Television*. London: Pluto.
Dowd, M. (2002) Render unto Eisner . . . , *The New York Times*, 13 March.
Downie, Jr, L. and Kaiser, R.G. (2002) *The News About the News: American Journalism in Peril*. New York: Alfred A. Knopf.
Dyer, R. (1997) *White*. London: Routledge.
Ecclestone, J. (1992) National Union of Journalists, in D. Griffiths (ed.) *The Encyclopedia of the British Press*. London: Macmillan.
Eldridge, J. (ed.) (1993) *Getting the Message: News, Truth and Power*. London: Routledge.
Eldridge, J. (ed.) (1995) *Glasgow University Media Group*, Vol. 1. London: Routledge.
Elliott, P. (1978) Professional ideology and organisational change: the journalist since 1800, in G. Boyce, J. Curran and P. Wingate (eds) *Newspaper History*. London: Constable.
Ellis, J. (2000) *Seeing Things: Television in the Age of Uncertainty*. London: I.B. Tauris.
El-Nawawy, M. and Iskandar, A. (2003) *Al-Jazeera: The Story of the Network that is Rattling Governments and Redefining Modern Journalism*. Cambridge, MA: Westview.
El-Nawawy, M. and Powers, S. (2009) News influence and the global mediasphere: a case study of Al-Jazeera English, in S. Allan (ed.) *The Routledge Companion to News and Journalism*. London and New York: Routledge.
Emmison, M. and McHoul, A. (1987) Drawing on the economy: cartoon discourse and the production of a category, *Cultural Studies*, 1(1): 93–112.
Engel, M. (1996) *Tickle the Public: One Hundred Years of the Popular Press*. London: Victor Gollancz.
Engelman, R. (1996) *Public Radio and Television in America*. Thousand Oaks, CA: Sage Publications.
Entman, R.M. (1990) Modern racism and the images of Blacks in local television news, *Critical Studies in Mass Communication*, 7(4): 332–45.
Entman, R.M. (1992) Blacks in the news: television, modern racism and cultural change, *Journalism Quarterly*, 69(2): 341–61.
Entman, R.M. (1993) Framing: towards clarification of a fractured paradigm, *Journal of Communication*, 43(4): 51–8.
Entman, R.M. (1997) African Americans according to TV news, in E.E. Dennis and E.C. Pease (eds) *The Media in Black and White*. New Brunswick, NJ and London: Transaction.
Entman, R.M. (2004) *Projections of Power: Framing News, Public Opinion, and US Foreign Policy*. Chicago, IL: University of Chicago Press.
Epstein, E. (1973) *News from Nowhere*. New York: Random House.
Ericson, R.V., Baranek, P.M. and Chan, J.B.L. (1987) *Visualising Deviance: A Study of News Organisations*. Toronto: University of Toronto Press.

Ericson, R.V., Baranek, P.M. and Chan, J.B.L. (1989) *Negotiating Control: A Study of News Sources*. Toronto: University of Toronto Press.

Ericson, R.V., Baranek, P.M. and Chan, J.B.L. (1991) *Representing Order: Crime, Law, and Justice in the News Media*. Toronto: University of Toronto Press.

Esser, F. (1999) 'Tabloidization' of news, *European Journal of Communication*, 14(3): 291–324.

Everbach, T. (2006) The culture of a women-led newspaper, *Journalism and Mass Communication Quarterly*, 83(3): 477–93.

Fairclough, N. (1989) *Language and Power*. London: Longman.

Fairclough, N. (1995) *Critical Discourse Analysis*. London: Longman.

Fairclough, N. (1998) Political discourse in the media: an analytical framework, in A. Bell and P. Garrett (eds) *Approaches to Media Discourse*. Oxford: Blackwell.

Fang, I. (1997) *A History of Mass Communication: Six Information Revolutions*. Boston, MA: Focal Press.

Fejes, F. and Petrich, K. (1993) Invisibility, homophobia and heterosexism: lesbians, gays and the media, *Critical Studies in Mass Communication*, 10(4): 396–422.

Fenton, N. (2009) News in the digital age, in S. Allan (ed.) *The Routledge Companion to News and Journalism*. London and New York: Routledge.

Ferguson, R. (1998) *Representing 'Race': Ideology, Identity and the Media*. London: Arnold.

Feuer, J. (1986) Narrative form in American network television, in C. MacCabe (ed.) *High Theory/Low Culture: Analysing Popular Television and Film*. New York: St Martin's Press.

Fiedler, T. (2009) Crisis alert: Barack Obama meets a citizen journalist, in S. Allan and E. Thorsen (eds) *Citizen Journalism: Global Perspectives*. New York: Peter Lang.

Fishman, M. (1980) *Manufacturing the News*. Austin, TX: University of Texas Press.

Fiske, J. (1987) *Television Culture*. London: Routledge.

Fiske, J. (1992) Popularity and the politics of information, in P. Dahlgren and C. Sparks (eds) *Journalism and Popular Culture*. London: Sage Publications.

Fiske, J. (1996) *Media Matters: Race and Gender in US Politics*, revised edn. Minneapolis, MN: University of Minnesota Press.

Fleming, D. (1993) *Media Teaching*. Oxford: Blackwell.

Foote, J.S. (1992) Women correspondents' visibility on the network evening news, *Mass Communication Review*, 19(1–2): 36–40.

Fowler, R. (1991) *Language in the News*. London: Routledge.

Fowler, R., Hodge, B., Kress, G. and Trew, T. (1979) *Language and Control*. London: Routledge and Kegan Paul.

Franklin, B. (1997) *Newszak and News Media*. London: Arnold.

Franklin, B. (2005) McJournalism: the local press and the McDonaldization thesis, in S. Allan (ed.) *Journalism: Critical Issues*. Maidenhead and New York: Open University Press.

Franklin, B. (ed.) (2008) *Pulling Newspapers Apart: Analysing Print Journalism*. London: Routledge.

Franklin, B. and Murphy, D. (eds) (1998) *Making the Local News*. London: Routledge.

Franklin, B., Lewis, J. and Williams, A. (2009) Journalism, news sources and public relations, in S. Allan (ed.) *The Routledge Companion to News and Journalism*. London and New York: Routledge.

Fraser, N. (1994) Rethinking the public sphere: a contribution to the critique of actually existing democracy, in C. Calhoun (ed.) *Habermas and the Public Sphere*. Cambridge, MA: MIT Press.

Freedman, S. (2006) Outside voices, *Public Eye*, CBSNews.com, 31 March.

French, H.W. (2003) Online newspaper shakes up Korean politics, *The New York Times*, 6 March.

Gabler, N. (1998) *Life: The Movie*. New York: Vantage.

Gabriel, J. (1998) *Whitewash: Racialized Politics and the Media*. London: Routledge.

Gallagher, D.F. (2002) A rift among bloggers, *The New York Times*, 10 June.

Gallagher, M. (2001) *Gender Setting: New Agendas for Media Monitoring and Advocacy*. London: Zed Books.

Galtung, J. and Ruge, M. (1981) Structuring and selecting news, in S. Cohen and J. Young (eds) *The Manufacture of News*, revised edn. London: Constable.

Gandy, Jr, O.H. (1997) From bad to worse: the media's framing of race and risk, in E.E. Dennis and E.C. Pease (eds) *The Media in Black and White*. New Brunswick, NJ and London: Transaction.

Gandy, Jr, O.H. (1998) *Communication and Race*. London: Arnold.

Gans, H. (1979) *Deciding What's News*. New York: Vintage.

Gans, H.J. (2003) *Democracy and the News*. Oxford and New York: Oxford University Press.

Gans, H.J. (2009) News and democracy in the United States: current problems, future possibilities, in S. Allan (ed.) *The Routledge Companion to News and Journalism*. London and New York: Routledge.

Garber, M. (1993) Character assassination: Shakespeare, Anita Hill, and JFK, in M. Garber, J. Matlock and R.L. Walkowitz (eds) *Media Spectacles*. New York: Routledge.

Garnham, N. (1994) The media and the public sphere, in C. Calhoun (ed.) *Habermas and the Public Sphere*. Cambridge, MA: MIT Press.

Gavin, N.T. and Goddard, P. (1998) Television news and the economy: inflation in Britain, *Media, Culture and Society*, 20(3): 451–70.

Gelzinis, P. (2003) Trying to understand a former colleague's lapse in judgment, *The Boston Herald*, 3 April.

Gibian, P. (ed.) (1997a) *Mass Culture and Everyday Life*. New York: Routledge.

Gibian, P. (ed.) (1997b) Newspeak meets newstalk, in P. Gibian (ed.) *Mass Culture and Everyday Life*. New York: Routledge.

Giddens, A. (1990) *The Consequences of Modernity*. Cambridge: Polity.

Gillespie, M. (1995) *Television, Ethnicity and Cultural Change*. London: Routledge.

Gillmor, D. (2005) Tsunami and citizen journalism's first draft, *Dan Gillmor on Grassroots Journalism, Etc.*, 6 January.

Gissler, S. (1997) Newspapers' quest for racial candor, in E.E. Dennis and E.C. Pease

(eds) *The Media in Black and White*. New Brunswick, NJ and London: Transaction.
Gitlin, T. (1980) *The Whole World is Watching: Mass Media in the Making and Unmaking of the New Left*. Berkeley, CA: University of California Press.
Gitlin, T. (2002) *Media Unlimited*. New York: Henry Holt.
GLA (Greater London Authority) (2007) The search for common ground: Muslims, non-Muslims and the UK media, www.london.gov.uk
Glaser, M. (2003) For bloggers, NYT story was fit to print, *Online Journalism Review*, 10 June.
Glaser, M. (2004) To their surprise, bloggers are force for change in big media, GlobalEcho.org, 7 June.
Glaser, M. (2009) Citizen journalism: widening world views, extending democracy, in S. Allan (ed.) *The Routledge Companion to News and Journalism*. London and New York: Routledge.
Glasgow University Media Group (1985) *War and Peace News*. Milton Keynes: Open University Press.
Glasner, J. (2004) All the news that's fit to Wiki, *Wired*, 22 April.
Glover, S. (1999) *The Penguin Book of Journalism: Secrets of the Press*. London: Penguin.
Glynn, K. (2000) *Tabloid Culture*. Durham, NC: Duke University Press.
Goffman, E. (1974) *Frame Analysis*. New York: Harper and Row.
Goldie, G.W. (1977) *Facing the Nation: Television and Politics, 1936–1976*. London: Bodley Head.
Golding, P. and Murdock, G. (1996) Culture, communications and political economy, in J. Curran and M. Gurevitch (eds) *Mass Media and Society*. London: Arnold.
Gordon, B. (2003) The internet is having a field day – war 'blogs' are everywhere, *Telegraph*, 2 April.
Gordon, P. and Rosenberg, D. (1989) *Daily Racism: The Press and Black People in Britain*. London: Runnymede Trust.
Gramsci, A. (1971) *Selections from the Prison Notebooks*. New York: International.
Gray, A. (1992) *Video Playtime: The Gendering of a Leisure Technology*. London: Routledge.
Gray, H. (1995) *Watching Race: Television and the Struggle for 'Blackness'*. Minneapolis, MN and London: University of Minnesota Press.
Gray, H. (1998) Anxiety, desire and conflict in the American racial imagination, in J. Lull and S. Hinerman (eds) *Media Scandals*. Cambridge: Polity.
Greatbatch, D. (1998) Conversation analysis: neutralism in British news interviews, in A. Bell and P. Garrett (eds) *Approaches to Media Discourse*. Oxford: Blackwell.
Greenslade, R. (2003) *Press Gang: How Newspapers Make Profits from Propaganda*. London: Macmillan.
Griffiths, D. (ed.) (1992) *The Encyclopedia of the British Press*. London: Macmillan.
Gripsrud, J. (1992) The aesthetics and politics of melodrama, in P. Dahlgren and C. Sparks (eds) *Journalism and Popular Culture*. London: Sage Publications.
Gripsrud, J. (2000) Tabloidization, popular journalism, and democracy, in C. Sparks

and J. Tulloch (eds) *Tabloid Tales: Global Debates over Media Standards*. Lanham, MD: Rowman and Littlefield.

Grochowski, T. (2002) The 'tabloid effect' in the O.J. Simpson case, *International Journal of Cultural Studies*, 5(3): 336–56.

Gross, L. (1989) Out of the mainstream: sexual minorities and the mass media, in E. Seiter, H. Borchers, G. Kreutzner and E. Warth (eds) *Remote Control*. London: Routledge.

Gubash, C. (2003) New Arab TV channels show clout, MSNBC.com, 31 March.

Guedes Bailey, O. and Harindranath, R. (2005) Racialised 'othering': the representation of asylum seekers in the news media, in S. Allan (ed.) *Journalism: Critical Issues*. Maidenhead and New York: Open University Press.

Habermas, J. (1989) *The Structural Transformation of the Public Sphere*. Translated by T. Burger with F. Lawrence. Cambridge, MA: MIT Press.

Habermas, J. (1992) Further reflections on the public sphere, in C. Calhoun (ed.) *Habermas and the Public Sphere*. Cambridge, MA: MIT Press.

Hacker, A. (1997) Are the media really 'White'?, in E.E. Dennis and E.C. Pease (eds) *The Media in Black and White*. New Brunswick, NJ and London: Transaction.

Hackett, R. (2005) Is there a democratic deficit in US and UK journalism?, in S. Allan (ed.) *Journalism: Critical Issues*. Maidenhead and New York: Open University Press.

Hackett, R.A. (1991) *News and Dissent: The Press and the Politics of Peace in Canada*. Norwood, NJ: Ablex.

Hackett, R.A. and Zhao, Y. (1998) *Sustaining Democracy? Journalism and the Politics of Objectivity*. Toronto: Garamond.

Hafez, K. (ed.) (2000) *Islam and the West in the Mass Media*. Cresskill, NJ: Hampton.

Hagen, I. (1994) Expectations and consumption patterns in TV news viewing, *Media, Culture and Society*, 16(3): 415–28.

Hall, S. (1977) Culture, the media and the 'ideological effect', in J. Curran, M. Gurevitch and J. Woollacott (eds) *Mass Communication and Society*. London: Arnold.

Hall, S. (1980) Encoding/decoding, in S. Hall, D. Hobson, A. Lowe and P. Willis (eds) *Culture, Media, Language*. London: Hutchinson.

Hall, S. (1981) The determinations of news photographs, in S. Cohen and J. Young (eds) *The Manufacture of News*, revised edn. London: Constable.

Hall, S. (1988) *The Hard Road to Renewal*. London: Verso.

Hall, S. (1990) The whites of their eyes: racist ideologies and the media, in M. Alvarado and J.O. Thompson (eds) *The Media Reader*. London: British Film Institute.

Hall, S. (1994) Reflections upon the encoding/decoding model: an interview with Stuart Hall, in J. Cruz and J. Lewis (eds) *Viewing, Reading, Listening: Audiences and Cultural Reception*. Boulder, CO: Westview.

Hall, S., Connell, I. and Curti, L. (1976) *The 'Unity' of Current Affairs Television*, Working Papers in Cultural Studies. Birmingham: Centre for Contemporary Cultural Studies.

Hall, S., Critcher, C., Jefferson, T., Clarke, J. and Roberts, B. (1978) *Policing the Crisis: Mugging, the State, and Law and Order*. London: Macmillan.

Hallin, D.C. (1984) Cartography, community, and the Cold War, in R.K. Manoff and M. Schudson (eds) *Reading the News*. New York: Pantheon.

Hallin, D.C. (1986) *The 'Uncensored War': The Media and Vietnam*. New York: Oxford University Press.

Hallin, D.C. (1994) *We Keep America on Top of the World: Television Journalism and the Public Sphere*. New York: Routledge.

Halloran, J.D., Elliott, P. and Murdock, G. (1970) *Demonstrations and Communication: A Case Study*. Harmondsworth: Penguin.

Hamilton, J.T. (2004) *All the News That's Fit to Sell: How the Market Transforms Information into News*. Princeton, NJ: Princeton University Press.

Hampton, M. (2009) The Fourth Estate ideal in journalism history, in S. Allan (ed.) *The Routledge Companion to News and Journalism*. London and New York: Routledge.

Hansen, A. (ed.) (1993a) *The Mass Media and Environmental Issues*. Leicester: Leicester University Press.

Hansen, A. (1993b) Greenpeace and press coverage of environmental issues, in A. Hansen (ed.) *The Mass Media and Environmental Issues*. Leicester: Leicester University Press.

Hansen, A. and Murdock, G. (1985) Constructing the crowd: populist discourse and press presentation, in V. Mosco and J. Wasko (eds) *The Critical Communications Review*. Norwood, NJ: Ablex.

Harcup, T. (2007) *The Ethical Journalist*. London: Sage Publications.

Hardt, H. and Brennen, B. (eds) (1995) *Newsworkers: Toward a History of the Rank and File*. Minneapolis, MN: University of Minnesota Press.

Hargreaves, I. (2003) *Journalism: Truth or Dare?* Oxford: Oxford University Press.

Harker, J. (2009) Race and diversity in the news, in S. Allan (ed.) *The Routledge Companion to News and Journalism*. London and New York: Routledge.

Harrington, C.L. (1998) 'Is anyone else out there sick of the news?': TV viewers' responses to non-routine news coverage, *Media, Culture and Society*, 20(3): 471–94.

Harris, M. (1978) The structure, ownership and control of the press, 1620–1780, in G. Boyce, J. Curran and P. Wingate (eds) *Newspaper History*. London: Constable.

Harris, M. (1997) Farewell to Fleet Street?, in M. Bromley and T. O'Malley (eds) *A Journalism Reader*. London: Routledge.

Harris, R. (1983) *GOTCHA! The Media, the Government and the Falklands Crisis*. London: Faber and Faber.

Harris, S. (1991) Evasive action: how politicians respond to questions in political interviews, in P. Scannell (ed.) *Broadcast Talk*. London: Sage Publications.

Harrison, J. (2006) *News*. London: Routledge.

Hartley, J. (1982) *Understanding News*. London: Methuen.

Hartley, J. (1992) *The Politics of Pictures: The Creation of the Public in the Age of Popular Media*. London: Routledge.

Hartley, J. (1996) *Popular Reality: Journalism, Modernity, Popular Culture*. London: Arnold.

Hartley, J. (1998) Juvenation: news, girls and power, in C. Carter, G. Branston and S. Allan (eds) *News, Gender and Power*. London: Routledge.

Hartley, J. and Montgomery, M. (1985) Representations and relations: ideology and power in press and TV news, in T.A. van Dijk (ed.) *Discourse and Communication*. New York: Walter de Gruyter.

Hartmann, P. and Husband, C. (1974) *Racism and the Mass Media*. London: Davis-Poynter.

Hastings, M. (2008) The Ghaffur case exposes how weak attempts at fairness can be, *Guardian*, 1 September.

Hayward, A. (1998) Obituary: Barbara Mandell, *Independent*, 5 September.

Hedges, C. (2002) *War Is a Force That Gives Us Meaning*. New York: PublicAffairs.

Herd, H. (1952) *The March of Journalism*. London: Allen and Unwin.

Herman, E.S. and Chomsky, N. (1988) *Manufacturing Consent: The Political Economy of the Mass Media*. New York: Pantheon.

Herman, E.S. and McChesney, R.W. (1997) *The Global Media*. London: Cassell.

Hetherington, A. (1985) *News, Newspapers and Television*. London: Macmillan.

Hibberd, S. (1950) '*This – Is London . . .*'. London: Macdonald and Evans.

Hinerman, S. (1998) (Don't) leave me alone: tabloid narrative and the Michael Jackson child-abuse scandal, in J. Lull and S. Hinerman (eds) *Media Scandals*. Cambridge: Polity.

Hjarvard, S. (1994) TV news: from discrete items to continuous narrative? The social meaning of changing temporal structures, *Cultural Studies*, 8(2): 306–20.

Hobson, D. (1980) Housewives and the mass media, in S. Hall, D. Hobson, A. Lowe and P. Willis (eds) *Culture, Media, Language*. London: Hutchinson.

Hoggart, S. (1995) Filleted fish, *New Statesman & Society*, 24 March: 20–1.

Hoggart, S. (2003) From lack of irony to lack of a decent breakfast, *Guardian*, 6 September.

Hogshire, J. (1997) *Grossed-Out Surgeon Vomits Inside Patient: An Insider's Look at Supermarket Tabloids*. Venice, CA: Feral House.

Holland, P. (1983) The page three girl speaks to women, too, *Screen*, 24(3): 84–102.

Holland, P. (1987) When a woman reads the news, in H. Baehr and G. Dyer (eds) *Boxed In: Women and Television*. London: Pandora.

Holland, P. (1998) The politics of the smile: 'soft news' and the sexualisation of the popular press, in C. Carter, G. Branston and S. Allan (eds) *News, Gender and Power*. London: Routledge.

Holland, P. (2001) Authority and authenticity: redefining television current affairs, in M. Bromley (ed.) *No News is Bad News*. London: Longman.

Hollingsworth, M. (1986) *The Press and Political Dissent*. London: Pluto.

Horrie, C. (2003) *Tabloid Nation: From the Birth of the Daily Mirror to the Death of the Tabloid*. London: André Deutsch.

Hoskins, A. (2004) *Televising War: From Vietnam to Iraq*. London: Continuum.

House of Lords (2008) *The Ownership of the News*, HL Paper 122–I. London: The Stationery Office.

Howard, S. (ed.) (1998) *Wired-Up: Young People and the Electronic Media*. London: UCL Press.

Huang, C. (2001) China's state-run tabloids, *Gazette*, 63(5): 435–50.

Hudson, M. and Stanier, J. (1997) *War and the Media*. Phoenix Mill: Sutton Publishing.

Hunt, D.M. (1997) *Screening the Los Angeles 'Riots'*. Cambridge: Cambridge University Press.

Hunter, F. (1992) Women in British journalism, in D. Griffiths (ed.) *The Encyclopedia of the British Press*. London: Macmillan.

Hutchby, I. (1991) The organization of talk on talk radio, in P. Scannell (ed.) *Broadcast Talk*. London: Sage Publications.

Hutchby, I. (2005) News talk: interaction in the broadcast news interview, in S. Allan (ed.) *Journalism: Critical Issues*. Maidenhead and New York: Open University Press.

Inglis, F. (2002) *People's Witness: The Journalist in Modern Politics*. New Haven, CT and London: Yale University Press.

Innis, H.A. (1986) *Empire and Communications*. Victoria, BC: Press Porcépic.

Irby, K. (2003) L.A. Times photographer fired over altered image, PoynterOnline, 2 April.

Jacobs, R.N. (1996) Producing the news, producing the crisis: narrativity, television and news work, *Media, Culture and Society*, 18(3): 373–97.

Jacobs, R.N. (2000) *Race, Media and the Crisis of Civil Society: From Watts to Rodney King*. Cambridge: Cambridge University Press.

Jacquette, D. (2009) Journalism ethics as truth-telling in the public interest, in S. Allan (ed.) *The Routledge Companion to News and Journalism*. London and New York: Routledge.

Jeffords, S. and Rabinovitz, L. (eds) (1994) *Seeing Through the Media: The Persian Gulf War*. New Brunswick, NJ: Rutgers University Press.

Jensen, K.B. (1986) *Making Sense of the News*. Aarhus: Aarhus University Press.

Jensen, K.B. (1995) *The Social Semiotics of Mass Communication*. London: Sage Publications.

Jones, A. (1993) *Press, Politics and Society: A History of Journalism in Wales*. Cardiff: University of Wales Press.

Jordan, G. and Weedon, C. (1995) *Cultural Politics: Class, Gender, Race and the Post-modern World*. Oxford: Blackwell.

Kafala, T. (2003) Al-Jazeera: news channel in the news, BBC News Online, 29 March.

Kahney, L. (2003) Media watchdogs caught napping. *Wired News*, 17 March.

Kaplan, R. (2009) The origins of objectivity in American journalism, in S. Allan (ed.) *The Routledge Companion to News and Journalism*. London and New York: Routledge.

Karim, K.H. (2000) *Islamic Peril: Media and Global Violence*. Montreal: Black Rose.

Katz, J. (1994) Online or not, newspapers suck, *Wired, 2.09*, September.

Keane, F. (1998) The first casualty of television's ratings war is too often the truth, *Independent*, 25 July.

Keeble, R. (1994) *The Newspapers Handbook*. London: Routledge.

Keeble, R. (1997) *Secret State, Silent Press*. Luton: University of Luton Press.

Keeble, R. (2001) *Ethics for Journalists*. London: Routledge.

Keeble, R. (2005) Journalism ethics: towards an Orwellian critique?, in S. Allan (ed.) *Journalism: Critical Issues*. Maidenhead and New York: Open University Press.

Kellner, D. (1995) *Media Culture*. London: Routledge.

Kellner, D. (2003) *Media Spectacle*. London and New York: Routledge.

Kellner, D. (2004) The Persian Gulf TV war revisited, in S. Allan and B. Zelizer (eds) *Reporting War: Journalism in Wartime*. London and New York: Routledge.

Kellner, D. (2005) *Media Spectacle and the Crisis of Democracy: Terrorism, War, and Election Battles*. Boulder, CO: Paradigm.

Kieran, M. (ed.) (1998) *Media Ethics*. London: Routledge.

Kirkpatrick, D.D. (2003) War is test of high-speed web, *The New York Times*, 24 March.

Kitzinger, J. (1998) The gender-politics of news production: silenced voices and false memories, in C. Carter, G. Branston and S. Allan (eds) *News, Gender and Power*. London: Routledge.

Kitzinger, J. (2004) *Framing Abuse: Media Influence and Public Understandings of Sexual Violence against Children*. London: Pluto.

Klaehn, J. (ed.) (2005) *Filtering the News: Essays on Herman and Chomsky's Propaganda Model*. Montreal: Black Rose Books.

Knight, G. (2001) Perspective news: press pre-framing of the 1996 Ontario public service strike, *Journalism Studies*, 2(1): 73–88.

Knightley, P. (1982) *The First Casualty*. London: Quartet.

Knightley, P. (1991) Here is the patriotically censored news, *Index on Censorship*, 20(4/5): 4–5.

Koppel, T. (2002) Network news is still serious business, *The New York Times*, 5 March.

Koss, S. (1984) *The Rise and Fall of the Political Press in Britain*. London: Fontana.

Kovach, B. and Rosenstiel, T. (2001) *The Elements of Journalism*. London: Atlantic Books.

Krajicek, D.J. (1998) *Scooped!* New York: Columbia University Press.

Kress, G. and van Leeuwen, T. (1998) Front pages: (the critical) analysis of newspaper layout, in A. Bell and P. Garrett (eds) *Approaches to Media Discourse*. Oxford: Blackwell.

Kurtz, H. (2003) Altered picture costs LA Times photographer his job, *Washington Post*, 3 April.

Lafky, S.A. (1993) The progress of women and people of color in the US journalistic workforce, in P.J. Creedon (ed.) *Women in Mass Communication*, 2nd edn. Newbury Park, CA: Sage Publications.

Langer, J. (1998) *Tabloid Television: Popular Journalism and the 'Other News'*. London: Routledge.

Lasica, J.D. (2005) Citizens' media gets richer, *Online Journalism Review*, 7 September.

Law, I. (2002) *Race in the News*. London: Palgrave.

Lee, A.J. (1976) *The Origins of the Popular Press in England, 1855–1914*. London: Croom Helm.

Leitner, G. (1983) The social background of the language of radio, in H. Davis and P. Walton (eds) *Language, Image, Media*. Oxford: Blackwell.

Lemann, N. (2006) Amateur hour, *The New Yorker*, 7 August.

Len-Ríos, M.E., Rodgers, S., Thorson, E. and Yoon, D. (2005) Representation of women in news and photos: comparing content to perceptions, *Journal of Communication*, 55(1): 152–68.

Leonard, T.C. (1995) *News for All*. New York: Oxford University Press.

Levy, S. (2003) Bloggers delight, *Newsweek Web Exclusive*, MSNBC.com, 28 March.

Lewis, J. (1991) *The Ideological Octopus: An Exploration of Television and its Audience*. London: Routledge.

Lewis, J. (2001) *Constructing Public Opinion: How Political Elites Do What They Like and Why We Seem to Go Along With It*. New York: Columbia University Press.

Lewis, J. and Wahl-Jorgensen, K. (2005) Active citizen or couch potato? Journalism and public opinion, in S. Allan (ed.) *Journalism: Critical Issues*. Maidenhead and New York: Open University Press.

Lewis, J., Inthorn, S. and Wahl-Jorgensen, K. (2005) *Citizens or Consumers: What the Media Tell Us about Political Participation*. Maidenhead and New York: Open University Press.

Lewis, J., Williams, A. and Franklin, B. (2008) A compromised Fourth Estate? UK news journalism, public relations and news sources, *Journalism Studies*, 9(1): 1–20.

Lewis, P.M. and Booth, J. (1989) *The Invisible Medium*. London: Macmillan.

Lichty, L.W. and Topping, M.C. (eds) (1975) *American Broadcasting: A Source Book*. New York: Hastings House.

Liebes, T. and Curran, J. (eds) (1998) *Media, Ritual and Identity*. London: Routledge.

Lippmann, W. (1920) *Liberty and the News*. New York: Harcourt, Brace and Howe.

Lippmann, W. (1922) *Public Opinion*. New York: Free Press.

Lloyd, J. (2004) *What the Media are Doing to Our Politics*. London: Constable.

Löffelholz, M. and Weaver, D. (eds) (2008) *Global Journalism Research: Theories, Methods, Findings, Future*. Oxford: Blackwell.

Lont, C.M. (ed.) (1995) *Women and Media: Content, Careers, Criticism*. Belmont, CA: Wadsworth.

Love, A. and Morrison, A. (1989) Readers' obligations: an examination of some features of Zimbabwean newspaper editorials, *English Language Research Journal*, 3: 139–74.

Lule, J. (1995) The rape of Mike Tyson: race, the press and symbolic types, *Critical Studies in Mass Communication*, 12(2): 176–95.

Lull, J. and Hinerman, S. (eds) (1997) *Media Scandals*. Cambridge: Polity.

Lupton, D. (1994) *Moral Threats and Dangerous Desires: AIDS in the News Media*. London: Taylor and Francis.

Lynch, J. (2009) Peace journalism, in S. Allan (ed.) *The Routledge Companion to News and Journalism*. London and New York: Routledge.

McCarthy, M. (2003) War photo doctored in field shows ease of technology, *Wall Street Journal*, 2 April.

McChesney, R.W. (2004) *The Problem of the Media: US Communication Politics in the 21st Century*. New York: Monthly Review Press.

MacDonald, J.F. (1979) *Don't Touch That Dial! Radio Programming in American Life, 1920–1960*. Chicago, IL: Nelson-Hall.

Macdonald, M. (1998) Politicizing the personal: women's voices in British television documentaries, in C. Carter, G. Branston and S. Allan (eds) *News, Gender and Power*. London: Routledge.

MacGregor, B. (1997) *Live, Direct and Biased? Making Television News in the Satellite Age*. London: Arnold.

McGregor, J. (2006) The pervasive power of man-made news, *Pacific Journalism Review*, 12(1): 21–34.

McGuigan, J. (1992) *Cultural Populism*. London: Routledge.

McGuigan, J. (1999) *Modernity and Postmodern Culture*. Buckingham: Open University Press.

McGuigan, J. (2004) *Rethinking Cultural Policy*. Maidenhead and New York: Open University Press.

Machin, D. and Papatheoderou, F. (2002) Commercialization and tabloid television in Southern Europe, *Journal of European Area Studies*, 10(1): 31–48.

McKay, J. and Smith, P. (1995) Exonerating the hero: frames and narratives in media coverage of the OJ Simpson story, *Media Information Australia*, 75: 57–66.

McLauchlin, R.J. (1975) What the *Detroit News* has done in broadcasting, in L.W. Lichty and M.C. Topping (eds) *American Broadcasting: A Source Book*. New York: Hastings House.

McLaughlin, E. (2005) Recovering blackness/repudiating whiteness: the *Daily Mail*'s construction of the five white suspects accused of the racist murder of Stephen Lawrence, in K. Murji and J. Solomos (eds) *Racialization: Studies in Theory and Practice*. Oxford: Oxford University Press.

McLaughlin, G. (2002) *The War Correspondent*. London: Pluto.

McLaughlin, L. (1993) Feminism, the public sphere, media and democracy, *Media, Culture and Society*, 15(4): 599–620.

McLaughlin, L. (1998) Gender, privacy and publicity in media event space, in C. Carter, G. Branston and S. Allan (eds) *News, Gender and Power*. London: Routledge.

McLeod, D.M. and Hertog, J.K. (1992) The manufacture of 'public opinion' by reporters: informal cues for public perceptions of protest groups, *Discourse and Society*, 3(3): 259–75.

McNair, B. (1998) *The Sociology of Journalism*. London: Arnold.

McNair, B. (2000) *Journalism and Democracy: An Evaluation of the Political Public Sphere*. London: Routledge.

McNair, B. (2005) The emerging chaos of global news culture, in S. Allan (ed.) *Journalism: Critical Issues*. Maidenhead and New York: Open University Press.

McNair, B. (2009) *News and Journalism in the UK*, 5th edn. London: Routledge.

McQuail, D. (1992) *Media Performance: Mass Communication and the Public Interest*. London: Sage Publications.

Madianou, M. (2009) Living with news: ethnographies of news consumption, in S. Allan (ed.) *The Routledge Companion to News and Journalism*. London and New York: Routledge.

Mahtani, M. (2005) Gendered news practices: examining experiences of women journalists in different national contexts, in S. Allan (ed.) *Journalism: Critical Issues*. Maidenhead and New York: Open University Press.

Mandel, C. (2005) Readers become the reporters with launch of Wikinews website, *Calgary Herald*, 16 September.

Manning, P. (2001) *News and News Sources*. London: Sage Publications.

Marjoribanks, T. (2000) *News Corporation, Technology and the Workplace*. Cambridge: Cambridge University Press.

Marlière, P. (1998) The rules of the journalistic field, *European Journal of Communication*, 13(2): 219–34.

Marriott, S. (1995) Intersubjectivity and temporal reference in television commentary, *Time and Society*, 4(3): 345–64.

Marshall, P.D. (1997) *Celebrity and Power*. Minneapolis, MN: University of Minnesota Press.

Marshall, P.D. (2005) Intimately intertwined in the most public way: celebrity and journalism, in S. Allan (ed.) *Journalism: Critical Issues*. Maidenhead and New York: Open University Press.

Marx, K. and Engels, F. (1970 [1845]) *The German Ideology*. New York: International.

Mason, P. and Monckton-Smith, J. (2008) Conflation, collocation and confusion: British press coverage of the sexual murder of women, *Journalism*, 9(6): 691–701.

Matheson D. (2000) The birth of news discourse: changes in news language in British newspapers, 1980–1930, *Media, Culture and Society*, 22(8): 557–73

Matheson, D. (2003) Scowling at their notebooks: the management of writing within British journalism's reflexive identity, *Journalism*, 4(2): 165–83.

Matheson, D. (2005) *Media Discourses*. Maidenhead and New York: Open University Press.

Matheson, D. and Allan, S. (2009) *Digital War Reporting*. Cambridge: Polity Press.

Matthews, J. (2009) The morgue: a reporter's elegy for his dying paper, *The New Republic*, 4 March.

Mayes, I. (1998) Trying to get it right, *Guardian*, 25 July.

Megna, M. (2003) Embedded in technology, *Daily News*, 6 April.

Meikle, G. (2009) *Interpreting the News*. London: Palgrave Macmillan.

Meinhof, U.H. and Richardson, K. (eds) (1994) *Text, Discourse and Context: Representations of Poverty in Britain*. London: Longman.

Mendes, K., Carter, C. and Messenger Davies, M. (2009) Young citizens and the news, in S. Allan (ed.) *The Routledge Companion to News and Journalism*. London and New York: Routledge.

Mernit, S. (2003) Kevin Sites and the blogging controversy, Online Journalism Review, 3 April.

Merritt, D. (1995) *Public Journalism and Public Life*. Hillsdale, NJ: Lawrence Erlbaum.

Meyer, P. (2003) The *LA Times* fires a photographer, ZoneZero. Available at: www.zonezero.com/magazine/articles/altered/altered.html

Meyers, M. (1997) *News Coverage of Violence Against Women: Engendering Blame*. Thousand Oaks, CA and London: Sage Publications.

Miall, L. (ed.) (1966) *Richard Dimbleby: Broadcaster*. London: BBC Publications.

Miall, L. (1994) *Inside the BBC*. London: Weidenfeld and Nicolson.

Miller, D. (1993) Official sources and 'primary definition': the case of Northern Ireland, *Media, Culture and Society*, 15(3): 385–406.

Miller, D. (1994) *Don't Mention the War: Northern Ireland, Propaganda and the Media*. London: Pluto.

Miller, D. (ed.) (2004) *Tell Me Lies: Propaganda and Media Distortion in the Attack on Iraq*. London: Pluto.

Miller, D., Kitzinger, J., Williams, K. and Beharrell, P. (1998) *The Circuit of Mass Communication*. London: Sage Publications.

Mills, K. (1990) *A Place in the News: From the Women's Pages to the Front Page*. New York: Columbia University Press.

Mills, S. (1995) *Feminist Stylistics*. London: Routledge.

Moeller, S.D. (1999) *Compassion Fatigue: How the Media Sell Disease, Famine, War and Death*. New York and London: Routledge.

Moeller, S.D. (2009) *Packaging Terrorism: Co-opting the News for Politics and Profit*. Oxford: Wiley-Blackwell.

Molotch, H. and Lester, M. (1974) News as purposive behaviour: on the strategic use of routine events, accidents and scandals, *American Sociological Review*, 39(1): 101–12.

Montgomery, M. (1995) *An Introduction to Language and Society*. London: Routledge.

Montgomery, M. (2005) Talking war: how journalism responded to the events of 9/11, in S. Allan (ed.) *Journalism: Critical Issues*. Maidenhead and New York: Open University Press.

Montgomery, M. (2009) The television news interview: questions of discourse, in S. Allan (ed.) *The Routledge Companion to News and Journalism*. London and New York: Routledge.

Moores, S. (1993) *Interpreting Audiences*. London: Sage Publications.

Moritz, M. (2009) Getting it straight: gay news narratives and changing cultural values, in S. Allan (ed.) *The Routledge Companion to News and Journalism*. London and New York: Routledge.

Moritz, M.J. (1992) How US news media represent sexual minorities, in P. Dahlgren and C. Sparks (eds) *Journalism and Popular Culture*. London: Sage Publications.

Morley, D. (1986) *Family Television: Cultural Power and Domestic Leisure*. London: Comedia.

Morley, D. (1992) *Television, Audiences and Cultural Studies*. London: Routledge.

Morrison, T. and Lacour, C.B. (eds) (1997) *Birth of a Nationhood: Gaze, Script, and Spectacle in the O.J. Simpson Case*. New York: Pantheon.

Morse, M. (1986) The television news personality and credibility: reflections on the news in transition, in T. Modleski (ed.) *Studies in Entertainment*. Bloomington, IN: Indiana University Press.

Morse, M. (1998) *Virtualities*. Bloomington, IN: Indiana University Press.

Mullan, B. (1996) *Not a Pretty Picture: Ethnic Minority Views of Television*. Aldershot: Avebury.

Murdoch, R. (2005) Speech to American Society of Newspaper Editors, press release, Newscorp.com, 13 April.

NABJ (National Association of Black Journalists) (2008) Newspaper industry should not treat diversity like a passing fad, Press Release, www.nabj.org, 3 July.

Naughton, J. (1999) *A Brief History of the Future: The Origins of the Internet*. London: Phoenix.

Negrine, R. (1996) *The Communication of Politics*. London: Sage Publications.

Neil, A. (1996) *Full Disclosure*. London: Macmillan.

Neuzil, M. and Kovarik, W. (1996) *Mass Media and Environmental Conflict: America's Green Crusades*. Thousand Oaks, CA: Sage Publications.

Newkirk, P. (1998) Some are down, some are out, *The Nation*, 28 September.

Newkirk, P. (2000) *Within the Veil: Black Journalists, White Media*. New York and London: New York University Press.

Niblock, S. (1996) *Inside Journalism*. London: Blueprint.

Nicholas, S. (1996) *The Echo of War*. Manchester: Manchester University Press.

Nichols, B. (1994) *Blurred Boundaries*. Bloomington, IN: Indiana University Press.

Nielsen, T. (1975) A history of network television news, in L.W. Lichty and M.C. Topping (eds) *American Broadcasting: A Source Book*. New York: Hastings House.

Nip, N. (2009) Citizen journalism in China: the case of the Wenchuan earthquake, in S. Allan and E. Thorsen (eds) *Citizen Journalism: Global Perspectives*. New York: Peter Lang.

Nord, D.P. (2001) *Communities of Journalism: A History of American Newspapers and Their Readers*. Urbana and Chicago, IL: University of Illinois Press.

Norris, P. (ed.) (1997a) *Women, the Media and Politics*. New York: Oxford University Press.

Norris, P. (ed.) (1997b) *Politics and the Press*. Boulder, CO: Lynne Rienner.

O'Malley, T. (1986) Religion and the newspaper press, 1660–1685: a study of the *London Gazette*, in M. Harris and A. Lee (eds) *The Press in English Society from the Seventeenth to Nineteenth Centuries*. London: Associated University Presses.

O'Malley, T., Allan, S. and Thompson, A. (1997) Tokens of antiquity: the press and the shaping of national identity in Wales, 1870–1900, *Studies in Newspaper and Periodical History*, 4: 127–52.

O'Neill, J. (1992) Journalism in the market place, in A. Belsey and C. Chadwick (eds) *Ethical Issues in Journalism and the Media*. London: Routledge.

O'Neill, O. (2002) A question of trust, BBC Reith Lectures.

Örnebring, H. (2009) Reassessing journalism as a profession, in S. Allan (ed.) *The Routledge Companion to News and Journalism*. London and New York: Routledge.

Ostrom, M.A. (2003) Net plays big role in war news, Commentary, *The Mercury News*, 28 February.

Owen, J. and Purdey, H. (eds) (2009) *International News Reporting*. Oxford: Wiley-Blackwell.

Palmer, J. (2000) *Spinning into Control: News Values and Source Strategies*. Leicester: Leicester University Press.

Palmer, M. (1978) The British press and international news, 1851–99: of agencies and newspapers, in G. Boyce, J. Curran and P. Wingate (eds) *Newspaper History*. London: Constable.

Parkin, F. (1973) *Class Inequality and Political Order*. London: Paladin.

Paterson, R. (1990) A suitable schedule for the family, in A. Goodwin and G. Whannel (eds) *Understanding Television*. London: Routledge.

Paton, D. (1999) War of words: virtual media versus mainstream press, *Christian Science Monitor*, 3 December.

Patterson, C. and Domingo, D. (2008) *Making Online News: The Ethnography of New Media Production*. New York: Peter Lang.

Paulu, B. (1961) *British Broadcasting in Transition*. London: Macmillan.

Pegg, M. (1983) *Broadcasting and Society, 1918–1939*. London: Croom Helm.

Petley, J. (1997) Faces for spaces, in M. Bromley and T. O'Malley (eds) *A Journalism Reader*. London: Routledge.

Petley, J. (2009) Impartiality in television news: profitability versus public service, in S. Allan (ed.) *The Routledge Companion to News and Journalism*. London and New York: Routledge.

Pew Internet & American Life Project (2003) 'The internet and the Iraq war', Project Report, 1 April.

PEW (Project for Excellence in Journalism) (2005) The gender gap: women are still missing as sources for journlaists, 23 May, www.journalism.org/files/gender.pdf

PEW (2009) *State of the News Media Report*, www.stateofthenewsmedia.org/2009/index.htm

Phillips, A. (2007) Muslims and the media, *Guardian*, 15 November.

Philo, G. (1990) *Seeing and Believing: The Influence of Television*. London: Routledge.

Philo, G. (ed.) (1999) *Message Received: Glasgow Media Group Research 1993–1998*. Harlow: Longman.

Philo, G. (2009) News, audiences and the construction of public knowledge, in S. Allan (ed.) *The Routledge Companion to News and Journalism*. London and New York: Routledge.

Pickering, M. (2008) Sex in the sun: racial stereotypes and tabloid news, *Social Semiotica*, 18(3): 363–75.

Pilger, J. (1998) *Hidden Agendas*. London: Vintage.

Pincus, S. (1995) 'Coffee politicians does create': coffeehouses and restoration political culture, *The Journal of Modern History*, 67: 807–34.

Polgreen, L. (2006) All the news that fits: Liberia's blackboard headlines, *The New York Times*, 4 August.

Pollard, N. (2007) Why is it so difficult to bring diversity into the newsroom?, *Independent*, 12 February.

Ponce de Leon, C.L. (2002) *Self-exposure: Human Interest Journalism and the Emergence of Celebrity in America, 1890–1940*. Chapel Hill, NC: University of North Carolina Press.

Poole, E. and Richardson, J.E. (eds) (2006) *Muslims and the News Media*. London: I.B. Tauris.

Preston, P. (2009) *Making the News: Journalism and News Cultures in Europe*. London: Routledge.

Priest, S.H. (2005) Risk reporting: why can't they ever get it right?, in S. Allan (ed.) *Journalism: Critical Issues*. Maidenhead and New York: Open University Press.

Pritchard, D. and Hughes, K.D. (1997) Patterns of deviance in crime news, *Journal of Communication*, 47(3): 49–67.

Pritchard, D. and Stonbely, S. (2007) Racial profiling in the newsroom, *Journalism and Mass Communication Quarterly*, 84(2): 231–48.

Pursehouse, M. (1991) Looking at the *Sun*: into the nineties with a tabloid and its readers, *Cultural Studies at Birmingham*, 1: 88–133.

Purser, P. (1998) Newsreader's place in history, *Guardian*, 31 August.

Quiroga, J. (1997) Hispanic voices: is the press listening?, in P. Norris (ed.) *Politics and the Press*. Boulder, CO: Lynne Rienner.

Rakow, L.F. and Kranich, K. (1991) Woman as sign in television news, *Journal of Communication*, 41(1): 8–23.

Rantanen, T. (1997) The globalization of electronic news in the nineteenth century, *Media, Culture and Society*, 19(4): 605–20.

Rantanen, T. (2005) *The Media and Globalization*. London: Sage Publications.

Rantanen, T. (2009) *When the News was New*. Oxford: Wiley-Blackwell.

Raymond, J. (ed.) (2002) *News, Newspapers, and Society in Early Modern Britain*. London: Frank Cass.

Read, D. (1992) *The Power of News: The History of Reuters*. Oxford: Oxford University Press.

Reah, D. (1998) *The Language of Newspapers*. London: Routledge.

Reese, S.D. (2001) Prologue. Framing public life: a bridging model for media research, in S. Reese, O.H. Gandy and A.E. Grant (eds) *Framing Public Life*. Mahwah, NJ: Lawrence Erlbaum.

Reese, S.D. (2004) Militarized journalism: framing dissent in the Gulf Wars, in S. Allan and B. Zelizer (eds) *Reporting War: Journalism in Wartime*. London and New York: Routledge.

Reese, S.D. (2007) The Framing Project: a bridging model for media research revisited, *Journal of Communication*, 57: 148–54.

Reeves, G. (1993) *Communications and the 'Third World'*. London: Routledge.

Reeves, J.L. and Campbell, R. (1994) *Cracked Coverage: Television News, the Anti-Cocaine Crusade, and the Reagan Legacy*. Durham, NC: Duke University Press.

Reith, J. (1974) Speech in the debate on commercial television, in A. Smith (ed.) *British Broadcasting*. Newton Abbot: David and Charles.

Reynolds, G.H. (2003) Weblogs and journalism: back to the future?, *Nieman Reports*, Fall, 81–2.

Rhodes, J. (2005) Race, ideology and journalism: black power and television news, in S. Allan (ed.) *Journalism: Critical Issues*. Maidenhead and New York: Open University Press.

Richards, B. (2009) News and the emotional public sphere, in S. Allan (ed.) *The Routledge Companion to News and Journalism*. London and New York: Routledge.

Richardson, K. (1998) Signs and wonders: interpreting the economy through television, in A. Bell and P. Garrett (eds) *Approaches to Media Discourse*. Oxford: Blackwell.

Richtel, M. (2003) Visits to web sites surge as war begins, and most are up to task, *The New York Times*, 23 March.

Roberts, P. (2003) Al-Jazeera hobbled by DDOS Attack, Infoworld.com, 26 March.

Robinson, G.J. (2005) *Gender, Journalism and Equity: Canadian, US and European Perspectives*. Crestkill, NJ: Hampton Press.

Robinson, P. (2002) *The CNN Effect: The Myth of News, Foreign Policy and Intervention*. London: Routledge.

Rodriguez, A. (1999) *Making Latino News*. Thousand Oaks, CA: Sage Publications.

Rojek, C. (2001) *Celebrity*. London: Reaktion Books.

Rose, E.D. (1975) How the U.S. heard about Pearl Harbor, in L.W. Lichty and M.C. Topping (eds) *American Broadcasting: A Source Book*. New York: Hastings House.

Rosen, J. (1999) *What Are Journalists For?* New Haven, CT: Yale University Press.

Rosen, J. (2006) The people formerly known as the audience, *Pressthink*, 27 June.

Roshco, B. (1975) *Newsmaking*. Chicago, IL: University of Chicago Press.

Ross, K. (1998) Making race matter: an overview, in B. Franklin and D. Murphy (eds) *Making the Local News*. London: Routledge.

Ross, K. (2001) Women at work: journalism as an engendered practice, *Journalism Studies*, 2(4): 531–44.

Ross, K. (2005) Women in the boyzone: gender, news and herstory, in S. Allan (ed.) *Journalism: Critical Issues*. Maidenhead and New York: Open University Press.

Ross, K. and Nightingale, V. (2004) *Media and Audiences: New Perspectives*. Maidenhead and New York: Open University Press.

Roth, A.L. (1998) Who makes the news? Descriptions of television news interviewees' public personae, *Media, Culture and Society*, 20(1): 79–107.

Rowe, D. (1999) *Sport, Culture and the Media*. Buckingham: Open University Press.

Rowe, D. (2004) *Sport, Culture and the Media*, 2nd edn. Maidenhead and New York: Open University Press.

Rowe, D. (2005) Fourth Estate or fan club? Sports journalism engages the popular, in S. Allan (ed.) *Journalism: Critical Issues*. Maidenhead and New York: Open University Press.

Rowe, D. (2009) Tabloidization of news, in S. Allan (ed.) *The Routledge Companion to News and Journalism*. London and New York: Routledge.

Royle, T. (1987) *War Report: The War Correspondent's View of Battle from the Crimea to the Falklands*. London: Mainstream.

Rusbridger, A. (2008) New world order, in J. Gibson (ed.) *Media 08*. London: Guardian Books.

Rutenberg, J. (2003) A nation at war: the news media, *The New York Times*, 16 April.

Rutenberg, J. and Carter, B. (2002) Letterman offer was news to chief of ABC News, *The New York Times*, 2 March.

Rutenberg, J. and Schiesel, S. (2002) Doubted as business, network news is still hanging on, *The New York Times*, 18 March.

Rutten, T. (2003) Response to scandals validates credibility, *Los Angeles Times*, 7 May.

Salcetti, M. (1995) The emergence of the reporter: mechanization and the devaluation of editorial workers, in H. Hardt and B. Brennen (eds) *Newsworkers: Toward a History of the Rank and File*. Minneapolis, MN: University of Minnesota Press.

Salter, L. (2009) Indymedia and the law: issues for citizen journalism, in S. Allan and E. Thorsen (eds) *Citizen Journalism: Global Perspectives*. New York: Peter Lang.

Sambrook, R. (2006) How the net is transforming news, *BBC News Online*, 20 January.

Santos, J.P. (1997) (Re)imagining America, in E.E. Dennis and E.C. Pease (eds) *The Media in Black and White*. New Brunswick, NJ and London: Transaction.

Scannell, P. (ed.) (1991) *Broadcast Talk*. London: Sage Publications.

Scannell, P. (1996) *Radio, Television and Modern Life*. Oxford: Blackwell.

Scannell, P. (1998) Media – language – world, in A. Bell and P. Garrett (eds) *Approaches to Media Discourse*. Oxford: Blackwell.

Scannell, P. and Cardiff, D. (1991) *A Social History of British Broadcasting, Volume One 1922–1939*. Oxford: Blackwell.

Schechter, D. (1999) *The More You Watch, The Less You Know*. New York: Seven Stories.

Schiller, D. (1981) *Objectivity and the News*. Philadelphia, PA: University of Philadelphia Press.

Schlesinger, P. (1987) *Putting 'Reality' Together: BBC News*. London: Methuen.

Schlesinger, P. (1990) Rethinking the sociology of journalism: source strategies and the limits of media-centrism, in M. Ferguson (ed.) *Public Communication: The New Imperatives*. London: Sage Publications.

Schlesinger, P. and Tumber, H. (1994) *Reporting Crime: The Media Politics of Criminal Justice*. Oxford: Clarendon.

Schofield, J. (2004) Hacks of all trades, *Guardian*, 22 July.

Schudson, M. (1978) *Discovering the News*. New York: Basic Books.

Schudson, M. (1995) *The Power of News*. Cambridge, MA: Harvard University Press.

Schudson, M. (2003) *The Sociology of News*. New York: W.H. Norton.

Schudson, M. (2008) *Why Democracies Need an Unlovable Press*. Malden, MA: Polity.

Schwartz, D. (1992) To tell the truth: codes of objectivity in photojournalism, *Communication*, 13: 95–109.

Searle, C. (1989) *Your Daily Dose: Racism and the* Sun. London: Campaign for Press and Broadcasting Freedom.

Seaton, J. (ed.) (1998) *Politics and the Media*. Oxford: Blackwell.

Sebba, A. (1994) *Battling for News: The Rise of the Woman Reporter*. London: Sceptre.

Seelye, K.Q. (2005) Snared in the web of a Wikipedia liar, *The New York Times*, 4 December.

Seib, P. (2004) *Beyond the Front Lines: How the News Media Cover a World Shaped by War*. London: Palgrave Macmillan.

Seiter, E., Borchers, H., Kreutzner, G. and Warth, E. (eds) (1989) *Remote Control: Television, Audiences and Cultural Power*. London: Routledge.

Sendall, B. (1982) *Independent Television in Britain*, Vol. 1. London: Macmillan.

Seymour-Ure, C. (1975) How special are cartoonists?, *Twentieth Century Studies*, 13/14: 6–21.

Shah, H. and Thornton, M.C. (1994) Racial ideology in U.S. mainstream news magazine coverage of Black–Latino interaction, 1980–1992, *Critical Studies in Mass Communication*, 11(2): 141–61.

Shattuc, J.M. (1997) *The Talking Cure: TV Talk Shows and Women*. New York: Routledge.

Sheldon, L. (1998) The middle years: children and television – cool or just plain boring?, in S. Howard (ed.) *Wired-Up: Young People and the Electronic Media*. London: UCL Press.

Shi, D.E. (1995) *Facing Facts: Realism in American Thought and Culture, 1850–1920*. New York: Oxford University Press.

Shingler, M. and Wieringa, C. (1998) *On Air: Methods and Meanings of Radio*. London: Arnold.

Shipler, D.K. (1998) Blacks in the newsroom: progress?, *Columbia Journalism Review*, May/June.

Shipp, E.R. (1994) OJ and the Black media, *Columbia Journalism Review*, November/December.

Sholle, D. (1993) Buy our news: tabloid television and commodification, *Journal of Communication Inquiry*, 17(1): 56–72.

Silverstone, R. (1994) *Television and Everyday Life*. London: Routledge.

Silverstone, R. (2007) *Media and Morality: On the Rise of the Mediapolis*. Cambridge: Polity.

Singer, J.B. and Ashman, I. (2009) User-generated content and journalistic values, in S. Allan and E. Thorsen (eds) *Citizen Journalism: Global Perspectives*. New York: Peter Lang.

Singh, I. (1998) *Minorities and the Media. Contemporary Issues in British Journalism*. The 1998 Vauxhall Lectures. Cardiff: Centre for Journalism Studies, Cardiff University.

Sirota, D.J. (2004) The fox of war, Salon.com, 20 March.

Skidmore, P. (1998) Gender and the agenda: news reporting of child sexual abuse, in C. Carter, G. Branston and S. Allan (eds) *News, Gender and Power*. London: Routledge.

Smith, A. (1973) *The Shadow in the Cave*. London: Allen and Unwin.

Smith, A. (1978) The long road to objectivity and back again: the kinds of truth we get in journalism, in G. Boyce, J. Curran and P. Wingate (eds) *Newspaper History*. London: Constable.

Smith, A. (1979) *The Newspaper: An International History*. London: Thames and Hudson.

Smith, L. (2007) You couldn't make it up, *Guardian*, 15 November.

Sontag, S. (2003) *Regarding the Pain of Others*. New York: Farrar, Straus and Giroux.

Sonwalkar, P. (2002) 'Murdochization' of the Indian press: from by-line to bottom-line, *Media, Culture and Society*, 24(6): 821–34.

Sonwalkar, P. (2005) Banal journalism: the centrality of the 'us–them' binary in news discourse, in S. Allan (ed.) *Journalism: Critical Issues*. Maidenhead and New York: Open University Press.

Sonwalkar, P. (2009) Citizen journalism in India: the politics of recognition, in S. Allan and E. Thorsen (eds) *Citizen Journalism: Global Perspectives*. New York: Peter Lang.

Soothill, K. and Walby, S. (1991) *Sex Crime in the News*. London: Routledge.

Sparks, C. (1992) Popular journalism: theories and practice, in P. Dahlgren and C. Sparks (eds) *Journalism and Popular Culture*. London: Sage Publications.

Sparks, C. (2000) Introduction: the panic over tabloid news, in C. Sparks, and J. Tulloch, (eds) *Tabloid Tales: Global Debates Over Media Standards*. Lanham, MD: Rowman and Littlefield.

Sparks, C. and Tulloch, J. (eds) (2000) *Tabloid Tales: Global Debates Over Media Standards*. Lanham, MD: Rowman and Littlefield.

Sreberny-Mohammadi, A. (1990) Forms of media as ways of knowing, in J. Downing, A. Sreberny-Mohammadi and S. Sreberny-Mohammadi (eds) *Questioning the Media*. London: Sage Publications.

Stam, R. (1983) Television news and its spectator, in E.A. Kaplan (ed.) *Regarding Television*. Los Angeles, CA: University Publications of America.

Starr, P. (2009) Goodbye to the age of newspapers (hello to a new era of corruption), *The New Republic*, 4 March.

Steiner, L. (1998) Newsroom accounts of power at work, in C. Carter, G. Branston and S. Allan (eds) *News, Gender and Power*. London: Routledge.

Steiner, L. (2005) The 'gender matters' debate in journalism: lessons from the front, in S. Allan (ed.) *Journalism: Critical Issues*. Maidenhead and New York: Open University Press.

Stephens, M. (1988) *A History of News: From the Drum to the Satellite*. New York: Viking.

Stephenson, H. and Bromley, M. (eds) (1998) *Sex, Lies and Democracy: The Press and the Public*. London: Longman.

Sterling, C. and Kittross, J.M. (1978) *Stay Tuned: A Concise History of American Broadcasting*. Belmont, CA: Wadsworth.

Stevenson, N. (2003) *Cultural Citizenship: Cosmopolitan Questions*. Buckingham and Philadelphia, PA: Open University Press.

Stewart, P. (1997) Women of color as newspaper executives, in P. Norris (ed.) *Politics and the Press*. Boulder, CO: Lynne Rienner.

Stratford, T. (1992) Women and the press, in A. Belsey and C. Chadwick (eds) *Ethical Issues in Journalism and the Media*. London: Routledge.

Stroud, J. (1969) *Special Correspondent*. London: Ward Lock and Company.

Sutton Trust (2006) The Educational Backgrounds of Leading Journalists, June. www.suttontrust.com/reports/Journalists-backgrounds-final-report.pdf

Swenson, J.D. (1995) Rodney King, Reginald Denny, and TV news: cultural (re) construction of racism, *Journal of Communication Inquiry*, 19(1): 75–88.

Tagg, J. (1988) *The Burden of Representation: Essays on Photographies and Histories*. London: Macmillan.

Taylor, J. (1991) *War Photography: Realism in the British Press*. London: Routledge.

Taylor, J. (1998) *Body Horror: Photojournalism, Catastrophe and War*. Manchester: Manchester University Press.

Taylor, P.M. (1992) *War and the Media: Propaganda and Persuasion in the Gulf War*. Manchester: Manchester University Press.

Tester, K. (1994) *Media, Culture and Morality*. London: Routledge.

Tester, K. (2001) *Compassion, Morality and the Media*. Buckingham and Philadelphia, PA: Open University Press.

Thompson, E.P. (1980) Protest and survive, in E.P. Thompson and D. Smith (eds) *Protest and Survive*. Harmondsworth: Penguin.

Thompson, J.B. (1995) *Media and Modernity*. Cambridge: Polity.

Thompson, J.B. (2000) *Political Scandal: Power and Visibility in the Media Age*. Cambridge: Polity.

Thompson, K. (1998) *Moral Panics*. London: Routledge.

Thorsen, E. (2008) Journalistic objectivity redefined? Wikinews and the neutral point of view, *New Media & Society*, 10(6): 935–54.

Thumim, J. (1998) 'Mrs Knight *must* be balanced': methodological problems in researching early British television, in C. Carter, G. Branston and S. Allan (eds) *News, Gender and Power*. London: Routledge.

Thussu, D.K. (2009) Television news in the era of global infotainment, in S. Allan (ed.) *The Routledge Companion to News and Journalism*. London and New York: Routledge.

Thussu, D.K. and Freedman, D. (eds) (2003) *War and the Media*. London: Sage Publications.

Tiffen, R. (1989) *News and Power*. Sydney, NSW: Allen and Unwin.

Timms, D. (2003) News websites see traffic soar, *Guardian*, 20 March.

Tolson, A. (1996) *Mediations: Text and Discourse in Media Studies*. London: Arnold.

Toynbee, P. (2009) This is an emergency. Act now, or local news will die, *Guardian*, 24 March.

Trew, T. (1979) 'What the papers say': linguistic variation and ideological difference, in R. Fowler, B. Hodge, G. Kress and T. Trew, *Language and Control*. London: Routledge and Kegan Paul.

Tuchman, G. (1978) *Making News: A Study in the Construction of Reality*. New York: The Free Press.

Tulloch, J. and Blood, R.W. (2009) Iconic photojournalism and absent images: democratization and memories of terror, in S. Allan (ed.) *The Routledge Companion to News and Journalism*. London and New York: Routledge.

Tumber, H. (2005) Journalism and the war in Iraq, in S. Allan (ed.) *Journalism: Critical Issues*. Maidenhead and New York: Open University Press.

Tumber, H. (2009) Journalists and war crimes, in S. Allan (ed.) *The Routledge Companion to News and Journalism*. London and New York: Routledge.

Tumber, H. and Webster, F. (2006) *Journalists under Fire: Information, War and Journalistic Practices*. London: Sage Publications.

Tunstall, J. (1996) *Newspaper Power: The New National Press in Britain*. Oxford: Clarendon.

Turner, G. (1999) Tabloidization, journalism and the possibility of critique, *International Journal of Culture Studies*, 2(1): 59–76.

Turner, G., Bonner, F. and Marshall, P.D. (eds) (2000) *Fame Games: The Production of Celebrity in Australia*. Cambridge: Cambridge University Press.

Ulmanu, A. (2005) Collective power: 'Smart mobs' connect, share information on net, *Online Journalism Review*, 10 June.

Underwood, C. (1992) Institute of Journalists, in D. Griffiths (ed.) *The Encyclopedia of the British Press*. London: Macmillan.

Van Dijk, T.A. (1991) *Racism and the Press*. London: Routledge.

Van Dijk, T.A. (1998) Opinions and ideologies in the press, in A. Bell and P. Garrett (eds) *Approaches to Media Discourse*. Oxford: Blackwell.

Van Ginneken, J. (1998) *Understanding Global News*. London: Sage Publications.

Van Loon, J. (1997) Chronotopes: of/in the televisualization of the 1992 Los Angeles riots, *Theory, Culture and Society*, 14(2): 89–104.

Van Riper, F. (2003) Manipulating truth, losing credibility, *Camera Works*, 9 April.

Van Zoonen, L. (1994) *Feminist Media Studies*. London: Sage Publications.

Van Zoonen, L. (1998) One of the girls? The changing gender of journalism, in C. Carter, G. Branston and S. Allan (eds) *News, Gender and Power*. London: Routledge.

Varley, C. and Tapsall, S. (eds) (2001) *Journalism: Theory in Practice*. Oxford: Oxford University Press.

Viner, K. (1998) Women and children last, *Guardian*, 6 July, S2: 6.

Vis, F. (2009) Wikinews reporting of Hurricane Katrina, in S. Allan and E. Thorsen (eds) *Citizen Journalism: Global Perspectives*. New York: Peter Lang.

Volkmer, I. (2005) News in the global public space, in S. Allan (ed.) *Journalism: Critical Issues*. Maidenhead and New York: Open University Press.

Wahl-Jorgensen, K. (2007) *Journalists and the Public: Newsroom Culture, Letters to the Editor, and Democracy*. Creskill, NJ: Hampton Press.

Wahl-Jorgensen, K. and Hanitzsch, T. (2009) *The Handbook of Journalism Studies*. London: Routledge.

Waisbord, S. (2009) Rethinking 'development' journalism, in S. Allan (ed.) *The Routledge Companion to News and Journalism*. London and New York: Routledge.

Walker, L. (2003) Web use spikes on news of war, *Washington Post*, 22 March.

Walker, T. (2008) Paxo must be undergoing a mid-life crisis, *Telegraph*, 26 August.

Wall, M. (2009) The taming of the warblogs: citizen journalism and the war in Iraq, in S. Allan and E. Thorsen (eds) *Citizen Journalism: Global Perspectives*. New York: Peter Lang.

Wallis, R. and Baran, S. (1990) *The Known World of Broadcast News*. London: Routledge.

Walski, B. (2003) Brian Walski discusses his doctored photo: interview with David Walker, *Photo District News*, 7 May.

Warner, B. (2003) War bloggers get reality check, MSNBC.com, 9 April.

Wasserman, E. (2001) The videophone war, *American Journalism Review*, 1 November: 22.

Watney, S. (1987) *Policing Desire*. London: Comedia.

Weaver, C.K. (1998) *Crimewatch UK*: keeping women off the streets, in C. Carter, G. Branston and S. Allan (eds) *News, Gender and Power*. London: Routledge.

Weaver, J. (2003) Iraq war a milestone for web news, MSNBC.com, 1 April.

Welch, M. (2003) Blogworld: the new amateur journalists weigh in, Columbia Journalism Review, www.cjr.org, 5 September/October.

Wells, M. (2001) How smart was this bomb?, *Guardian*, 19 November.

Wheeler, M. (1997) *Politics and the Mass Media*. Oxford: Blackwell.

Whitaker, B. (2003) Al-Jazeera cause outcry with broadcast of battle causalities, *Guardian*, 24 March.

Whitney, J. (2005) What's the matter with IndyMedia?, *LiP Magazine*, 31 July.

Wiener, J.H. (1996) The Americanisation of the British press, 1830–1914, *Studies in Newspaper and Periodical History*, 3: 61–74.

Wilby, P. (2008) Georgia has won the PR war, *MediaGuardian*, 18 August: 7.

Williams, G. (1996) *Britain's Media: How They Are Related*. London: Campaign for Press and Broadcasting Freedom.

Williams, K. (1998) *Get Me a Murder a Day! A History of Mass Communication in Britain*. London: Arnold.

Williams, R. (1958) Culture is ordinary, in R. Gable (ed.) (1989) *Resources of Hope*. London: Verso.

Williams, R. (1974) *Television: Technology and Cultural Form*. London: Fontana.

Williams, R. (1978) The press and popular culture: an historical perspective, in G. Boyce, J. Curran and P. Wingate (eds) *Newspaper History*. London: Constable.

Williams, R. (1982) Distance, in A. O'Connor (ed.) *Raymond Williams on Television*. London: Routledge.

Williams, R. (1986 [1984]) An interview with Raymond Williams, with S. Heath and G. Skirrow, in T. Modleski (ed.) *Studies in Entertainment: Critical Approaches to Mass Culture*. Bloomington, IN: Indiana University Press.

Williams, R. (1989a [1958]) Culture is ordinary, in R. Gable (ed.) *Resources of Hope*. London: Verso.

Williams, R. (1989b) Hegemony and the selective tradition, in S. de Castell, A. Luke and C. Luke (eds) *Language, Authority and Criticism*. London: Falmer.

Willis, J. (1991) *The Shadow World: Life between the News Media and Reality*. New York: Praeger.

Wilson, C.C. and Gutiérrez, F. (1995) *Race, Multiculturalism, and the Media*, 2nd edn. Thousand Oaks, CA: Sage Publications.

Wilson, J. (1996) *Understanding Journalism*. London: Routledge.

Wilson, T. (1993) *Watching Television: Hermeneutics, Reception and Popular Culture*. Cambridge: Polity.

Winston, B. (1993) The CBS Evening News, 7 April 1949: creating an ineffable television form, in J. Eldridge (ed.) *Getting the Message: News, Truth and Power*. London: Routledge.

Winston, B. (2002) Towards tabloidization? Glasgow revisited, 1975–2001, *Journalism Studies*, 3(1): 5–20.

Wolff, M. (2008) *The Man Who Owns the News*. London: Bodley Head.

Wolfsfeld, G. (1997) *Media and Political Conflict: News from the Middle East*. Cambridge: Cambridge University Press.

Women in Journalism (1998) *The Cheaper Sex: How Women Lose Out in Journalism*. London: WIJ Secretariat.

Wong, W. (1997) Covering the invisible 'model minority', in E.E. Dennis and E.C. Pease (eds) *The Media in Black and White*. New Brunswick, NJ and London: Transaction.

Woo Young, C. (2009) OhmyNews: citizen journalism in South Korea, in S. Allan and E. Thorsen (eds) *Citizen Journalism: Global Perspectives*. New York: Peter Lang.

Wren-Lewis, J. (1983) The encoding/decoding model: criticisms and redevelopments for research on decoding, *Media, Culture and Society*, 5(2): 179–97.

Wykes, M. (1998) A family affair: the British press, sex and the Wests, in C. Carter, G. Branston and S. Allan (eds) *News, Gender and Power*. London: Routledge.

Wykes, M. (2001) *News, Crime and Culture*. London: Pluto.

Young, A. (1991) *Femininity in Dissent*. London: Routledge.

Young, P. and Jesser, P. (1997) *The Media and the Military*. London: Macmillan.

Zelizer, B. (1992) *Covering the Body: The Kennedy Assassination, the Media, and the Shaping of Collective Memory*. Chicago, IL: University of Chicago Press.

Zelizer, B. (2004) *Taking Journalism Seriously*. Thousand Oaks, CA: Sage Publications.

Zelizer, B. (2005) Journalism through the camera's eye, in S. Allan (ed.) *Journalism: Critical Issues*. Maidenhead and New York: Open University Press.

Zelizer, B. (2009) Journalists as interpretive communities, revisited, in S. Allan (ed.) *The Routledge Companion to News and Journalism*. London and New York: Routledge.

Zelizer, B. and Allan, S. (eds) (2002) *Journalism After September 11*. London and New York: Routledge.

INDEX

Related books from Open University Press

Purchase from www.openup.co.uk or order through your local bookseller

JOURNALISM

Critical Issues

Stuart Allan (ed)

This new book explores essential themes in news and journalism studies. It brings together an exciting selection of original essays which engage with the most significant topics, debates and controversies in this fast-growing field. Topics include:

- Journalism's role in a democracy
- Source dynamics in news production
- Journalism ethics
- Sexism and racism in the news
- Tabloidization, scandals and celebrity
- Reporting conflict, terrorism and war
- The future of investigative journalism

The book is written in a lively manner designed to invite discussion by identifying key questions around a critical issue. Each chapter assesses where journalism is today, its strengths and its challenges, and highlights ways to improve upon it for tomorrow.

Essential reading for students and researchers in the fields of news and journalism, media studies, cultural studies, sociology and communication studies.

Includes essays by

Stuart Allan, Alison Anderson, Olga Guedes Bailey, Steven Barnett, Oliver Boyd-Barrett, Michael Bromley, Cynthia Carter, Simon Cottle, Chas Critcher, Matthew David, Máire Messenger Davies, Bob Franklin, Robert A. Hackett, Ramaswami Harindranath, Ian Hutchby, Richard Keeble, Justin Lewis, Minelle Mahtani, P. David Marshall, Brian McNair, Martin Montgomery, Alan Petersen, Susanna Hornig Priest, Jane Rhodes, Karen Ross, David Rowe, Prasun Sonwalkar, Linda Steiner, Howard Tumber, Ingrid Volkmer, Karin Wahl-Jorgensen, Barbie Zelizer.

Contents

408pp 0 335 21475 4 (Paperback) 0 335 21484 3 (Hardback)

ONLINE NEWS
JOURNALISM AND THE INTERNET

Stuart Allan

> If the promises of online news are to be fulfilled, books like this deserve the widest possible readership
>
> Paul Bradshaw, University of Central England, UK

In this exciting and timely book Stuart Allan provides a wide-ranging analysis of online news. He offers important insights into key debates concerning the ways in which journalism is evolving on the internet, devoting particular attention to the factors influencing its development. Using a diverse range of examples, he shows how the forms, practices and epistemologies of online news are gradually becoming conventionalized, and assesses the implications for journalism's future.

The rise of online news is examined with regard to the reporting of a series of major news events. Topics include coverage of the Oklahoma City bombing, the Clinton-Lewinsky affair, the September 11 attacks, election campaigns, and the war in Iraq. The emergence of blogging is traced with an eye to its impact on journalism as a profession. The participatory journalism of news sites such as Indymedia, OhmyNews, and Wikinews is explored, as is the citizen journalist reporting of the South Asian tsunami, London bombings and Hurricane Katrina. In each instance, the uses of new technologies – from digital cameras to mobile telephones and beyond – are shown to shape journalistic innovation, often in surprising ways.

This book is essential reading for students, researchers and journalists.

Contents

2006 216pp
978-0-335-22121-9 (Paperback) 978-0-335-22122–6 (Hardback)

THE BRITISH PRESS

Mick Temple

> Mick Temple's book makes an important contribution to the debate on the critical historical role and uncertain future of newspapers and the key place of quality journalism within that debate.
>
> Jeremy Dear, General Secretary of the National Union of Journalists, UK

> A thorough and thoughtful investigation into the British press and its contribution to our social and political culture.
>
> Simon Kelner, Editor-in-Chief, *The Independent*

This exciting book offers a practical introduction to the history, theory, politics and potential future of British newspapers. Focussing on the relationship between the press and political history, it examines their social and political impact, assessing the press's contribution to enlarging and informing the public sphere.

The author provides a theoretical critique of press developments. The first part of the text leads you through key historical moments from the English Civil War to Wapping and beyond, while the second half takes an in-depth look at current empirical and theoretical concerns. Scholarly yet accessible, Mick Temple is not afraid to take a position on today's contentious issues.

The book takes a more positive perspective on the British press than has often been the case, highlighting the online strength of great brand names like the Telegraph, Guardian, Sun and Mail. Temple argues that throughout their history, our newspapers have been vital conduits for public opinion and, on occasion, catalysts for social change.

The British Press is key reading for journalism, media and social science students.

Contents

2008 272pp
978-0-335-22297-1 (Paperback) 978-0-335-22298-8 (Hardback)